UNDER THE EDITORSHIP OF

LUCIUS GARVIN

University of Maryland

INTRODUCTION TO RELIGIOUS PHILOSOPHY

GEDDES MacGREGOR

BRYN MAWR COLLEGE

Houghton Mifflin Company · Boston

The Riverside Press Cambridge

BOOKS BY GEDDES MacGREGOR

Introduction to Religious Philosophy

Corpus Christi

The Bible in the Making

The Thundering Scot

The Tichborne Impostor

The Vatican Revolution

From a Christian Ghetto

Frontières de la Morale et de la Religion

Christian Doubt

Aesthetic Experience in Religion

The Riverside Press
Cambridge, Massachusetts
Printed in the U. S. A.

To my students at Edinburgh,

at Southern California,

and at Bryn Mawr,

who helped me to write this book

FOREWORD

This book is designed for the use of college or university under-graduates and others who are making their first prolonged approach to the intellectual problems of religion with little or no philosophical training behind them. While it contains some basic materials for an understanding of central questions in religious philosophy, it is intended to provoke thought and stimulate discussion (for example, under the leadership of a college instructor), rather than to provide even the outline of a comprehensive philosophical or theological system. Nor does it purport to be a rigorous exposition of all aspects of the many difficult problems it raises, such as would do the student's thinking for him in advance. Its intention is, rather, to avoid this, without, however, leaving his presuppositions carelessly undisturbed, or unprofitably indulging any incipient delusion that his views are novel discoveries when in fact they are as likely as not to have been exploded by the writers of the Vedas or smiled upon as outmoded by the ancestors of Confucius.

The author's purpose will be partially fulfilled if his work helps students either to develop a more critical attitude toward the philosophical problems that religion raises, or to appreciate more keenly the nature of religion itself and so approach it with a more lively reverence. It will be completely fulfilled if it should succeed in doing both.

I wish to express my thanks to Drs. C. M. Nielsen and J. W. Robb for their help in reading the proofs.

Grateful acknowledgement is made to the Oxford University Press, and to Harper and Brothers, New York, for permission to quote copyright material. Permission to quote the late Dorothy Sayers' letter was kindly granted by her before her death.

GEDDES MacGREGOR

The Athenaeum,
Pall Mall,
London S.W.1.

CONTENTS

PART FOUR: HUMAN KNOWLEDGE
                           OF GOD

Difficulties · Theological Language and Historical Context

EPILOGUE: PERSONAL REFLECTIONS   315

Intellectual Integrity of the Religious Philosopher · The Religious Philosopher and the Theologian · How the Religious Philosopher May Profit From Personal Commitment · The Relevance of Personal Commitment to Religious Philosophy · Autobiographical Background · I Become an Atheist · "But With Unhurrying Chase" · The Edge Over Doubt · Psychological Truisms · The Mystery of Evil at Close Quarters · Moral Evolution · Science and Religion · Am I a Better Man? · Religion and Art · Which is Me?

PART ONE

Introduction

1

What is Religion?

Tentative Definition

Religion is commitment to a kind or quality of life that purports to recognize a source beyond itself (usually but not necessarily called God), and that issues in recognizable fruits in human conduct (e.g., law, morality), culture (e.g., art, poetry), and thought (e.g., philosophy).

This is a convenient, tentative definition of religion for working purposes. The stricter definition must come as a result of our study rather than at the beginning of it, for it requires the more technical vocabulary that we shall only gradually acquire, as our study proceeds. But already we can deduce certain consequences. For instance, religion is not necessarily good or bad; it may be either. The worship of a dictator (such as Hitler) in a totalitarian state (such as the Germany of the late thirties) is thoroughly religious in character; but most readers will very readily agree that it is an undesirable religion. Nevertheless, no one who is familiar with the outlook and setup of such movements can fail to recognize that they are exceedingly lively, that they recognize a source beyond themselves (e.g., the Soul of the Master Race), and that they issue in recognizable fruits in human conduct (e.g., anti-Semitic laws), culture (e.g., movies glorifying the dictator and his achievements), and even thought (e.g., the intellectual defense or systematization of the principles of the movement by a philosopher such as Rosenberg in Hitler's Germany). On the other hand, while a few persons would seek to argue that *all* religion is undesirable, most people would wish to maintain that, in contrast to the sort of religion we have been considering, the religion of, say, Amos or Francis of Assisi or Abraham Lincoln or John Wesley is, to say the very least, preferable. Many, of course, would wish to say far more than this, and would affirm with the greatest conviction that one or other of the religions expressed in the lives of men such as Wesley and Lincoln was the most valuable treasure known to humanity. The point is that, while there might be all kinds of judgments on the value of religions in general, or of this or that religion in particular, we are not now concerning ourselves with any of these judgments, but only with establishing at the outset the finding that religions, as we encounter them in actual experience (i.e., empirically), need not be good or bad, and may be either the one or the other.

Religion Healthy or Cancerous

So when we speak of the religious life of a man or of a society, we are speaking of something that, like animal tissue, may be healthy or cancerous. In a physiological organism such as the human body cancer cells often arrange themselves in a way that seems to simulate the arrangement of cells in healthy tissue; they look as though they are trying to arrange themselves according to the pattern of the body in which they are multiplying, and not succeeding in their mimicry. What they achieve, however, appears to be a sort of parody or carica-ture of that which they are imitating, and ends, unless checked by medical treatment, in strangling the life whose pattern they imitate. Something like this appears to happen also in the life of religion, for there have certainly been, and there are now, some very extraordinary religions that seem to be parodies of another religion alongside which they have grown up. In many cases these curious religions seem to show an immense vitality that is soon spent. If this be so, it would seem to be possible to distinguish, in some cases at any rate, between religions that might be conveniently called bogus or unhealthy, and those that would then appear to be the reverse. For instance, a certain sect that appeared in early Christian times taught that all sexual intercourse, either in marriage or outside of it, is essentially evil, and that the proper course for all mankind to take is to abstain from it entirely and so bring about the end of the human race. It might be that such a religion was a parody or caricature of Christianity, which, in common with many other religions, was teaching that moderation of one sort or another is desirable in such matters. If all this be so, it should be possible to find some criterion for distinguishing between "healthy" and "unhealthy" religions.

But this consideration raises another question. What is healthy for the bacillus that attacks my body is unhealthy for me. It may even bring about my death, while I, with the aid of doctors and penicillin and the like, may bring about its death in my natural effort to avoid my own. Might it not therefore be, likewise, that your religion is the death of me, while mine may be the death of you? As a matter of historical fact, this is exactly the kind of situation that is envisaged in most religions at the level that we commonly call "primitive." For example, in very early times the Hebrews did not regard their religion or the god whom they took to be its source (the god Yahweh) as the only religion or the only god. On the contrary, he was recognized to be *their* god, and good for them, while being, for this very reason, also very bad for their enemies. Likewise, it seemed to them, other tribes had their own respective gods too, who were just as "real." These gods were powerful; the primitive Hebrews no more underestimated the power of the gods of their enemies than the United States Army underestimated the fighting capacity of the Japanese. But Yahweh was their own god, the god of their tribe, and good for them; they trusted (not without some misgivings, for they always needed the encouragement of their leaders) that in the end Yahweh would destroy the gods of their enemies. Yahweh required obedience to certain laws, and the tribe as a whole, which was supposed to have a sort of contract or agreement with Yahweh, naturally expressed its life (i.e., its religious life) in certain plainly observable cultural ways. Certain foods, for example, were taboo; that is, strictly forbidden by the custom of the tribe. Such attitudes are very general among primitive peoples. But they do not necessarily mean that these peoples have a theory that their way, their religion, or their life is the only one that ought to be followed by all peoples. Quite the reverse. They commonly expect strange tribes to have strange customs because they have strange gods, and strange gods because they have strange customs. It is only very gradually that such peoples come to consider the view that the source of the life they prize may be common to mankind. We are not nearly ready yet to consider what is to be said in favor of the latter view, or to take account of the numerous forms in which the source of life may appear. For the present it is important to note only that this course of religious development is fairly "standard" in human history. It is not our concern, for the moment, to consider whether it is to be accounted "progress" or not.

Has Religion a Common Source?

If we confine ourselves, however, to the modern world and to what we commonly account civilized society, we shall find agreement among a great many people that the life prized in religion has a common source. But on the other hand, we shall find no clear consensus when it comes to determining the nature of this source. Many (humanists of various kinds) would say that it lies somewhere in mankind itself. Some modern nihilists would assert that there is nothing so sacrosanct about humanity as to warrant any such opinion. Others, again, the successors of the old-fashioned "materialists," might affirm that the source of religion can be no more than the source of the universe (i.e., "all there is"), and that this is, say, energy — the measurable energy of physics. There are many others who would call the source "God"; but as we shall see when we come to examine this exceedingly ambiguous term with greater care and precision than we can allow ourselves in this preliminary chapter, the fact that they call the source "God" does not in the least help us to ascertain, without further inquiry, what kind of view they are taking. They might mean, for instance, by "God," simply the sum total of all that exists, has existed, and shall exist; they might mean, rather, The Good (in Plato's sense); they might very well mean (for it is remarkable how many unreflective people in civilized societies do mean it) an elderly gentleman with an ample white beard sitting permanently on a golden throne at an indeterminable point in space and presumably at a very high altitude, dispensing justice with a strong right arm and mercy with a benevolent heart. They might also have, as we shall furthermore see, many other (perhaps less incredible) views about the nature of the God whom they have in mind as the source of the life they prize.

A Fundamental Ambiguity

We need not now concern ourselves with such ambiguities. But we must take some account, even at this stage, of an ambiguity in the word "life" itself. We English-speaking people commonly use one word, "life," where the Greeks, for instance, used several. They used the word *bios* (from which we get "biography") when they wanted to convey the notion of life as a span or continuum (e.g., a *bios* of seventy years). On the other hand, when they wished to express the idea of the strength and vital principle of the body, they used the word *psyche* (hence "psychology"). But for the notion of life itself, considered independently of a number of years or days and apart from its animating presence in this or that individual, they had the word *zoë* (hence "zoology"), perhaps the most fundamental term of all. It is certainly the one always used in the New Testament in the phrase "eternal life," where it signifies a kind of life that is fuller, richer, better, than the ordinary life we share with other animals. That is to say, it is the kind envisaged in our tentative definition of religion. The life to which religion purports to be committed is always considered a specially valuable or "deep" kind of life. It may include or take under its wing, so to speak, ordinary "animal" life: but it is always supposed to encompass much more than just this. Hence the hymn of George Matheson, a famous blind preacher in Scotland in the latter half of the last century, contains the words:

> I give Thee back the life I owe,
> That in Thine ocean depths its flow
> May richer, fuller be.

Parallels could easily be found among the poets of various religions. There would be, of course, a very great difference in the way in which this special kind of life is conceived of in Buddhism and in Christianity respectively; but the notion of a life that is intrinsically far richer or better than the kind to which we refer when we say that there is a lot of life at a party would be found central in all religions.

Religion or Religions?

There is a further point to be made at this stage. We have been talking sometimes of "religion" and sometimes of "religions." Strictly speaking, since we are attending particularly at present to the facts that we encounter, rather than to any theorizing about these facts, we should be talking first about "religions." For there is no empirical evidence for the existence of "religion" at all, but only for the existence of "religions." The notion that all religions (e.g., Roman Catholicism, Zen Buddhism, Orthodox Judaism, the Salvation Army) are all aspects of the same "thing" is a possible theory *about* religions, suggesting the further notion that there is something that can be called "religion," which is "behind" all these manifestations of it. But there is no empirical evidence for this whatsoever. It would appear, indeed, to be a difficult theory to hold, in view of the point we have already made that religions may be good or bad; but since it is a theory that has been and is held by some, it must be taken into account, later on. It is a fact that there *are* religions. That these exercise an immense influence over human activity is demonstrable in the same way that it is demonstrable that there is an oak in my garden and that some of its leaves have been attacked by the inch-worm. But a theory about religions such as the one just mentioned is one that cannot conceivably be proved or disproved in any such way. Much stress must be laid on the distinction between what can be shown by the empirical methods of the sciences and what cannot so be shown, because in the study of our subject this distinction is all too frequently forgotten. Nothing is more important, moreover, for anyone beginning the study than to look at religions as they really are, as they present themselves to us in the world of experience, and to distinguish this kind of finding from any that may come as the result of theorizing about religion. For if we come to our study with preconceived ideas about what religion ought or ought not to be, our work will be vitiated from the start, and our conclusions thoroughly wrong, however carefully and skillfully we may argue. Only by taking religions as they are to be found in fact, and setting aside any prejudices we may have about what religion is or is not, can we have a sufficiently secure foundation upon which to work.

Better to Know One Religion Well

But what kind of religion shall we then keep in mind in trying to understand and interpret our subject? Ought we not first of all to make an exhaustive study of all the religions of the world, or at least the ones that are most widespread, before trying to understand the nature of the life of religion itself? While it is true that a person who has a great deal of knowledge of this kind has obvious advantages, these advantages are not nearly so great as they tend to seem at first. It is much more advantageous to have an intimate familiarity with one religion than to have a general acquaintance (much of it necessarily "from the outside") with a great many. The reason for this is simple. One is in a much better position for understanding the meaning of, say, history, if one knows very fully and intimately the history either of France or of England or of the United States, than if one has a general smattering of the history of the whole world. Not that the history of China is in the least like the history of England; yet one is more likely to understand history itself if one knows either China's story or England's very intimately than if one has read a bit about the history of a dozen peoples. So the best possible preparation for understanding the nature of religion is not necessarily a complete survey of all the religions of the world, interesting and important though this would be. A student who comes to this subject with a thorough knowledge of the "feel" of any particular religion may be as well equipped as anybody can be. The first apostles of Christianity, for instance, knew nothing about Christianity's long history, for in their time Christianity had only a very short history. But they were quick to understand Christianity because, being thoroughly familiar with Judaism, they easily learned what the new religion was about. This does not mean that Judaism and Christianity are alike in all respects: plainly the Christian and Jewish ways were different in a fundamental respect, else the Christians would not have distinguished themselves, or been distinguishable, from other persons of Jewish background and belief. What it means is, rather, that understanding the life of one religion by having been in the stream of it, they could more readily understand the nature of another, and accept or reject this as the case might be. In other words, the best way of really understanding what it feels like to be an ardent French patriot is not to lose your affection for your own country; the best way for an American to understand the feel of such French patriotism is first to deepen his own feeling for America. If he were to empty himself of all patriotism he would never understand anybody else's. So in trying to understand the nature of religion the equipment that is most likely to serve you best is a thorough appreciation of your own, whatever it may be.

Nevertheless, some people have to come to our subject with a less intimate acquaintance of their religion than do others, and many come to it with little or no religious background of their own. Such students are at the same kind of disadvantage as is a student of the philosophy of art who has little or no previous understanding of art itself, from the point of view of the artist or the appreciator. It is a disadvantage, but not an insuperable obstacle. Such a student should, however, make a point of trying to acquaint himself, as far as possible, with one religion or another as it is actually lived. He may not, of course, wish to identify himself with any such religion, and he may not find himself able to do so; but he should try to understand it as best he can, since it is obvious that in order to understand and interpret a subject you must first know what it is you are trying to understand. This is something that no book and no instructor can teach; you might learn it, however, from the life of someone who has never thought about our subject as we are going to think about it, or from the life of some group that hardly ever talks about this but simply lives it.

Qualifications for Being a Skeptic

If we bear all this in mind, the case of the person who comes in a skeptical frame of mind to the study of religion will not be for us the problem that it is sometimes believed to be. Every thinking person is skeptical in one way or another. Your possession of a skeptical frame of mind does not in itself show anything more or anything less than that your mind is working, which is not only desirable but plainly indispensable for any study. It is as necessary, however, to know what you are skeptical about as it is to know what you are prepared to affirm, for you can no more disbelieve in or repudiate a religion without knowing what this religion is than you can believe in or accept it without this knowledge. In other words, it is necessary to know what a religion is in its living reality before you can pretend to begin being skeptical about it.

Worship

Though there are great differences among religions, and though these differences consequently issue in widely varied kinds of conduct and customs, there is much that is common to the religious *attitude*. Worship, for example, in one form or another, is generally characteristic of most religions, and in many it plays a central part. Worship itself may be of several different kinds even within the same religion, including, for instance, both corporate worship and private prayer, and varying from elaborate and complicated ritual to the ejaculations of spontaneous private devotion. In trying to understand corporate worship it is necessary to bear in mind the purpose it is partly intended to serve: it is not (or at any rate should not be) geared to the specific needs or tastes of the most artistic or intellectual members of the group; it is the expression, rather, of the devotion of the common man. At the same time, it may, when it is rich enough, contain beauty and reveal ideas far beyond what is ordinarily perceived by the common man; that is to say, it can be capable of educating the worshipers as well as of being a vehicle of their devotion. It is therefore possible to learn a great deal about the thought and feeling of a religion by actually participating in its corporate worship, so long as it is borne in mind that it is an activity that one is participating in. The traditional term used by Christians for public worship is "liturgy," which comes from two Greek words, *laos* (the people), and *ergon* (the work, activity). It is "the people's work," and so ought not to be approached as if it were a concert to be listened to.

Perversion of Religion

Of course, just because religion is what it is (a life rather than an achievement) it inevitably reveals shortcomings as soon as it is looked at as an ideal activity rather than an actual one. Moreover, as there is always a lot of dead wood wherever there are living trees, much that is encountered in a religion is dead. The French philosopher Bergson says of religious conventions that they are the derivative perversions of a once living reality. Wherever religious activities degenerate into merely conventional activities, they are to that extent dead; but what is now mere convention was once full of life, so that even the more conservative elements in religion can be instructive to the thoughtful participant. As in ordinary life itself only some of our activity is creative and the rest of it humdrum, resulting merely from habit, so religion, which can be one of the most revolutionary forces in the world, can also be exceedingly conservative and dull. If we would understand any religion, it is of first-rate importance to be ready to accept the dead wood with the living tree, and not to let the former prevent us from seeing the latter.

DISCUSSION ON CHAPTER 1

1. Suppose that, being asked to make a survey of campus opinion, you draw up a questionnaire to include the following: "*Are you in favor of religion?* YES . . . NO . . . (*Check*)." Consider (a) why anyone replying to this question is bound to utter nonsense, and (b) in what terms you might more profitably pursue your inquiry.

2. Religion is notoriously the most conservative force in society; yet it has often been behind the most radical social revolutions. Consider historical examples and discuss possible reasons for the paradox.

3. In the name of religion, children have been sacrificed; yet the impetus for the realization of the loftiest human aspiration has been also of a religious character. Can there be a criterion for evaluating religions? If so, in what might it consist? Discuss objections to various possible criteria.

2

What is Religious Philosophy?

Why Think About Religion?

In our study we are to be concerned with thought *about* religion. We are to consider, for example, the different ways in which it is possible to conceive of God, and the arguments that may be adduced for this or that way of doing so. We must be quite clear about the difference between engaging in religion and thinking about it. Thinking about art is very interesting and important to people who like to think; thinking about science is likewise interesting and important. But you might be an excellent artist without giving much thought to it, and you might be a good physicist without reflecting very deeply about what, precisely, a physicist does. The most deeply religious people are often people who do not think about theology or religious philosophy very much. Indeed, thinking about anything is always attended by certain dangers. There is said to have been a centipede who was quite happy

> Until the toad, in fun,
> Said, "Pray, which leg goes after which?"
> Which worked his mind to such a pitch,
> He lay distracted in the ditch,
> Considering how to run.

Why, indeed, should we think about religion? The answer is that if you are the sort of person who does not think much about anything, you will not want, and you probably will not much need, to think about religion either; but if you are given to thinking about other things, you will not be satisfied to encounter religion, either in your own experience or as a fact to be reckoned with in other people, without trying to understand it from an intellectual point of view. The intellectual point of view is not the only one that helps us to understand living realities. We understand our lungs and our stomach by using them as well as by reading textbooks on anatomy and pathology. The intellectual approach to religion will not satisfy your heart; but only the intellectual approach will satisfy your mind, and

10

this is surely important, not least for those of us whose minds are trained or are being trained to think about many other things.

It is true that we must always keep at the back of our minds the fact that what we are thinking about in religious philosophy is really, in a sense, beyond our thought: our thinking separates us from it as soon as we begin. Analyzing a prayer is like analyzing a poem: it must be done with delicacy and skill if you are not to kill it. Even the point of a joke is lost if you try in a clumsy way to find out what you are laughing at. A surgeon who is opening up a living human body has to remember that it is a living body that can die under his hand if he is not careful; so a religious faith may wither under your touch if you do not handle it skillfully. But when all that is said, it is surely evident that it is by intellectual inquiry that we make the greatest advances in every field of human knowledge, and that so important a field as religion needs to be thought about with at least as much skill and care as any other. Confused or naïve thinking about religion leads to just as unfortunate results, to say the least, as does such inadequate thinking in other fields.

Challenge to the Average Modern Student

Dorothy Sayers, perhaps most widely known for her detective fiction, was also a gifted religious thinker and a deeply convinced Christian. She was asked, therefore, on one occasion, to write a letter to "average people" about Christianity. This was her reply:

The only letter I ever want to address to average people is one that says: Why don't you take the trouble to find out what is Christianity and what isn't? Why, when you can bestir yourself to learn technical terms about electricity, won't you do as much for theology before you begin to argue?

Why do you never read either the ancient or the modern authorities in the subject, but take your information for the most part from biologists and physicists who have picked it up as inaccurately as yourselves? Why do you accept mildewed old heresies as bold and constructive contributions to modern thought when any handbook on Church History would tell you where they came from?

Why do you complain that the proposition that God is three-in-one is obscure and mystical and yet acquiesce meekly in the physicist's fundamental formula, "2P − PQ equals IH over 2 Pi where I equals the square root of minus 1," when you know quite well that the square root of minus 1 is paradoxical and Pi is incalculable?

What makes you suppose that the expression "God ordains"

is narrow and bigoted whereas the expressions "nature provides" or "science demands" are objective statements of fact?

You would be ashamed to know as little about internal combustion as you do about beliefs. I admit that you can practise Christianity without knowing much about theology, just as you can drive a car without understanding internal combustion. But if something breaks down in the car, you humbly go to the man who understands the works, whereas if something goes wrong with religion you merely throw the creed away and tell the theologian he is a liar.

Why do you want a letter from me telling you about God? You will never bother to check up on it and find out whether I am giving you a personal opinion or the Church's doctrine. Go away and do some work.

Yours very sincerely,
DOROTHY L. SAYERS

This is excellent advice, and no student can honestly ignore it who is hoping to approach the study of religion in the spirit of fair and free inquiry. It is impossible to understand Christian thought without doing at least what Dorothy Sayers prescribed. Indeed, even more is needed for real thinking about religion, as she would have been among the first to insist, for not only do we have to empty our minds of prejudice and fill them with information; we have to use the minds that have been so transformed. If it needs clear thinking — as it does — to make progress in understanding even the working of an automobile, let alone the psychology of a crowd, it is certainly unreasonable to expect to understand religion without a great deal of mental effort. It is hardly profitable, for instance, to compare science and religion, if what you are doing is comparing post-doctoral physics with Sunday school kindergarten.

Why Erudition About Religion?

Most students will readily see that clear thinking should be just as important in religion as it is in any other field. But what about the vast and extremely learned literature that has been written on the subject of religion? Looking at the great stacks of weighty volumes in the theological library of any good university, containing more material than even the ablest scholar could assimilate in a lifetime, a student approaching religion intellectually for the first time might well ask himself: "Is all this erudition really necessary? Should not religion be essentially simple?" Such a student would be feeling something of what the eighteenth-century thinker Berkeley felt as a young man when he wrote that philosophers of the past had first raised a dust and then complained they could not see. But while it is beyond question that much that has been written about religion is now anti-quated, the view that religion is essentially simple is based on a con-fusion that should be examined now, so that we may not be tempted to lose patience with our subject later as soon as complications arise.

According to a traditional view among religious thinkers, God, the object of religion, is perfectly simple — perhaps we might even say the personification of simplicity. But human beings are far from simple, and the process of understanding God's simplicity, or even our possible relation to it, must be, for us, anything but a simple process. The unraveling of the simple is, for us human beings, a very difficult business indeed. The great discoveries of modern physicists are often very simple, once they are discovered. Einstein's epoch-making discovery, for example, has been expressed in a formula that looks like the answer to a high school algebra question; but the process by which Einstein arrived at his answer was much less simple. The fact is, of course, that everything is simple when you know the answer. A Christian, for example, may claim that he "knows" the answer through faith in Christ, but no Christian would mean by this that he "knows" the answer to all religious problems *intellectually* by such means. Moreover, even if one could be said to "know" the "essence" of Christian behavior by reading the Sermon on the Mount, it would not follow that Christian practice is simple. The Sermon on the Mount sounds simple enough — till you try to practice it. In any case, by the way, what is specifically Christian in Christianity is not to be found in any such collection of ethical precepts.

As soon as any religious thinker tries to express his ideas he is already putting them into human language, and in the very act of doing so he raises innumerable problems. For example, in the pre-ceding paragraph we have referred to the possibility of "knowing in faith." But what precisely do we mean by such "knowledge"? What do we mean, indeed, by *any* claim to "knowledge"? What, again, do we mean by "faith"? According to the famous English schoolboy defi-nition, faith is "believing steadfastly wot you know ain't true." Some-times, indeed, this is all that is meant by "faith." But it is not what is meant when, for example, a teacher says he has faith in a student, or when a citizen says he has faith in the platform of a certain politi-cal party. When I say, "I believe there was an accident in Park Avenue yesterday," I do not mean at all the same kind of belief as I do when I say, "I believe in fair play," or "I believe in cold baths." So when someone says, "I believe in God," or "I do not believe in God," he is really telling us practically nothing. We need to know what he means by "believe," and we certainly need very much to know what he means by "God," before we can understand what his position is and what he is trying to say. Statistical affirmations such as "40 per cent of biochemists believe in God, 35 per cent do not, and 25 per cent are undecided" are meaningless except in the sense that they express theological ignorance.

Recognition of Our Involvement

Furthermore, as soon as we think seriously about religion we are standing within the field of our investigation. We cannot usefully stand outside it as does an astronomer when he examines the stars. In the field of religion, therefore, our thinking is peculiarly liable to be vitiated by irrelevancies and psychological factors. We are also inclined to think that all points of view are prejudiced and dogmatic, except our own. The writer once had a student who said, "I know nothing about religious philosophy, but at any rate I have come to the subject free of prejudice: I am an atheist." Another student who professed belief in an impersonal God objected that the pronoun "he" should not be used of God, because its use implies a prejudice in favor of belief in a personal God, the existence of whom had not been so far established. Before explaining that the use of the pronoun "he" is a mere grammatical convention, just as we conventionally use the pronoun "she" for a ship, I asked what alternative we might use that would eliminate the danger of the alleged prejudice. Unsmilingly the student proposed the use of the pronoun "it." Perhaps these are extreme cases, but they illustrate the tendency to which we are all predisposed in coming to religious philosophy. Even mature scholars are not immune from it. But one of the great advantages of a training in religious philosophy is that it makes one more aware of such pitfalls, and consequently very much more cautious than the beginner who walks straight into them.

Sociological Point of View

It is beyond dispute that religion is a fact of experience; indeed, it is many kinds of fact. It is, for instance, a sociological fact, and as such it presents problems for the sociologist. A sociologist may happen to be a devout Christian or an earnest Moslem or a militant atheist; but as a sociologist he ought to shelve such convictions, and he can shelve them because as a sociologist he is concerned only with one very limited aspect of religion. We must be very clear about this. A sociologist is concerned about the effects of religious groupings in a society, for instance, in the same way in which he is concerned about the effects of racial groupings. In a society of white and colored people his interest lies in what happens when, for example, the colored race is a strong minority with little education, and how this situation is distinguished from one in which it is a weak minority with relatively high education. He is concerned with showing what tends to happen to the death rate or the birth rate of Negroes in a given situation. But as a sociologist it is not, strictly speaking, his business to consider what *ought* to happen. He may have a personal conviction that Negroes ought to have better opportunities than they do, or that they ought to have worse; that there ought to be more segregation or less; but his business is to report on sociological events and tendencies. A sociologist may, of course, obtrude his personal views in the course of his work, but he is no more entitled to do so than an accountant called in to audit the books of a business corporation is entitled to make comments on the ethics of the directors or the value to society of the corporation whose books he is auditing. Likewise, the sociologist is not concerned with whether it would be better if Jews in the United States discarded their religion entirely or went more often to temple; their tendencies in one direction or the other in a particular community, however, and the effects of this tendency, if any, on the social habits of the Gentile population, might well be a proper question for him to investigate.

Psychological Point of View

The psychologist is in a similar situation. It is a psychological fact that people do have religious convictions and that, rightly or wrongly, these convictions have an immense effect on the psychological structure of their personalities. It is the psychologist's business to consider such effects, as it is his business to examine the religious direction in which, say, introverts, extroverts and ambiverts, respectively, tend to go. Is it possible to say that people who are attracted to the kind of worship that is traditional in religion x generally conform to a psychological type that may be distinguished from those who seem to be attracted to the kind of worship that is traditional in religion y? This would be a very proper question for the psychologist. The answer might be of great psychological interest, but it would be at most of only incidental interest to us as religious philosophers. Indeed, unless we happened to be endowed with a very saintly kind of patience, it would probably bore us very much. For although religious practices obviously must and do have a psychological aspect, as they have a sociological aspect (just because they are the practices of human beings), it does not follow that these aspects are as important as they may look to the person whose interest for the moment happens to be predominantly a psychological or sociological interest. Religions purport to be of far greater significance than anything that could come within the psychologist's scope. Psychology is an important and peculiarly fascinating subject, but for this very reason the pursuit of it often tends to obscure and distort man's full vision of himself and his world by obscuring and distorting, as it can, man's relation to his total environment. In other words, it tends to produce a one-sided view, which we may call *psychologism*, just as an excessive preoccupation with and esteem for art may be called *aestheticism*, and too exclusive a concern with morality may be termed *moralism*. Any such narrow-mindedness always blinds us in some measure to the total situation with which life confronts us whether we face it or not.

The Commitment of the Religious Philosopher

The pursuit of religious philosophy precludes, above all, any such one-sided attitude. We shall encounter, in the course of our study, many religious attitudes towards which we are not immediately sympathetic, and likewise many antireligious attitudes with which we feel no natural affinity. Perhaps we are unlikely to be in the extreme position of Mr. Thwackum, a character in Fielding's *Tom Jones*, who is reported as saying, "When I mention religion, I mean the Christian religion; and not only the Christian religion, but the Protestant religion; and not only the Protestant religion, but the Church of England." But we might, without knowing it, be approaching our subject with no less narrow a point of view, such as taking it for granted that one religion is as good as another, or that religions are useful means for educating their adherents out of them — in the direction, of course, of our own prejudices. Not only must we take seriously every religious attitude, however primitive, however stupid, however decadent it may seem to us to be; we must try to take religions seriously in the way in which their adherents take them seriously. We must expect to find much that is bogus, and we may find that the bogus and the genuine are inseparably mixed together. It would not be surprising if this were so. It has been said that Paris probably contains the most beautiful and also the most hideous works of art in the world. This is, indeed, a likely consequence of the fact that Paris is the artistic cosmopolis.

What is Existential Thinking?

It may even be that no religion has any value such as it claims for itself. We must be sufficiently open-minded to consider seriously this possibility too. But before anyone could presume to come to any such conclusion he would have to be certain that he had fully understood what the exponents of religious faiths were really saying. This is by no means always done. And if it is not done, then no thinking, however acute, however able, will give you genuine insight into the nature of religions. A religious philosopher must be able to think not only scientifically but *existentially*. What is existential thinking? It is thinking not in detachment from a situation but in involvement with it. The following story will give a hint of what existential thinking is.

A heavy cigarette smoker wanted to give up his habit. After several unsuccessful attempts he got a friend to lock him in his apartment for a week end without cigarettes. But after only a few hours he became desperate for a smoke and, hunting around the apartment, he was able to collect thirty-six butts. Laying these out on a table, he found he could make a regular-size cigarette out of every six butts. How many cigarettes did he smoke?

I once put this little conundrum to a friend of mine, a heavy smoker. He correctly answered "seven." For of course the man in the story had six butts left over after he had smoked his six home-made cigarettes and so was able to make a seventh. It is on the whole likely that a heavy smoker will not detach himself from the situation and think "mathematically," but will enter into it sympathetically. In so doing he is thinking "existentially," as one who is involved in the situation, and so he goes beyond what one is likely to be able to do when thinking in detachment from it. My then nine-year-old son, for example, when he heard the answer "seven," sighed, "That's not how we do these problems in the arithmetic class." But much older persons with a good scientific training behind them have often answered "six," for lack of entering fully into the "inner" nature of the problem as it confronted the man himself in his struggle.

Wishful Thinking

It is part of the business of the religious philosopher to be more than ordinarily aware of the psychological tendency of us human beings to restrict our thinking in one way or another according to our own predilections. There are many reasons for this tendency. It may be due not only to that lack of sympathy for and interest in anything that lies beyond our own accustomed field of exploration. Discoveries of a religious character can be so uncongenial to us, disturbing our wills as well as our minds, that we are capable of building up a tremendous resistance to them. For although some aspects of religious practice may in certain circumstances be a kind of escape from the moral struggle of life, religious teachings (and the moral example these inspire in men of faith) are much more generally a challenge to us — sometimes an unbearable challenge that we instinctively seek to escape at all costs. We contrive to avoid the challenge by insisting on a restriction of our field of vision. This can be "wishful thinking" of a negative sort; "wishful thinking" against the possibilities that we encounter in religion. It is an old saying that "there is none so deaf as he who does not wish to hear." Probably most of us have known an elderly person so extremely conservative and reluctant to admit that times have changed, let alone to change with them, as to develop a habit of pretending not to hear anything pertaining to such changed conditions. Such a person, having succeeded so well with the pretense, then often actually suffers a kind of psychological deafness, a mental block against all statements that imply any recognition of changed conditions, till eventually the deafness appears to pass from a psychological to a physiological state. Such resistance to evidence we dislike to recognize is not, however, confined to conservative old people. It is a psychological device whose use is widespread, not least against religious ideas. It is to the breaking down of the barriers we erect against religion that much of our thought must be devoted; hence the importance of an open mind.

Our Capacity for Value-Resistance

It would be quite possible, for instance, for me to deny — if only I had a sufficiently good reason for doing so — that I actually perceive any distinction between beauty and ugliness. You might show me all sorts of things that are commonly accounted ugly and lay them beside other things that would usually be called beautiful for one reason or another, and I might adamantly deny that I saw any distinction between the alleged two classes of objects. You would soon discover that it was not a question of my having an unusual sort of artistic taste, different from that of others of my upbringing and race. You would see very quickly that I was refusing to *admit* that anything appeared to me either ugly or beautiful. I would describe to you quite fairly, in answer to your questions, the appearance of both a rosebush and a nest of cockroaches; but if you then tried to get me to admit a preference for one over the other, I might very well refuse to acknowledge that I even knew what you were talking about. You might then perhaps play me *Clementine* and Beethoven's *Fourth Symphony*, only to find that while I could analyze them both with some knowledge of the grammar of music, pointing out this interval and that tempo, I was stubbornly unwilling to show any sign that I understood what it could mean to suggest that one might be more beautiful than the other. "But which, then, do you *like* better?" you might ask, in desperation. To which I might perhaps reply, quite truthfully, that sometimes I prefer Beethoven, while on other more hilarious occasions I should have no hesitation in declaring a preference for *Clementine*. Try as you might, you could not get me to admit that I knew anything about a distinction between beauty and ugliness. I would say that I had heard people make the distinction, yet I never could understand what they meant. So far, all this might be only a sort of bravado on my part. But it might well become a kind of pose, till I felt I had a reputation to keep up; a reputation for total immunity from artistic experience. I should no doubt begin to suffer a sense of uneasiness within me, feeling I was injuring myself in some way; nevertheless, my perverse vanity might cause me to repress that sense of uneasiness. In time the pretend-barrier would become a real one, till at length my artistic sense was actually quite dulled. The same might just as easily happen in the realm of morals.

Of course, if you were to watch me very closely you might be able to detect what I had been doing. It would come out in various ways. Galsworthy gives us, in one of his plays, an example of this that is sufficiently naïve to be amusing. Two young men are discussing the future of a girl whom one of them has seduced. As they have a sort of mutual undertaking to recognize no moral obligations of any kind, they cannot admit that these play any part in their thoughts:

BILL: *If you think I care two straws about the morality of the thing—*
HAROLD: *Oh! my dear old man! Of course not!*
BILL: *It's simply that I shall feel such a damned skunk, if I leave her in the lurch.*

But Galsworthy is deliberately taking for his example two young men whose minds are really quite unsophisticated. A person with a lively intellect can set up an iron curtain against inconvenient data of experience, if only he allows himself the luxury of doing so, and by exhibiting the vivacity of his mind within his deliberately restricted field he can often very successfully disguise the fact that the restriction has in fact taken place.

Empiricism Ancient and Modern

Probably ever since men began to think with any kind of philosophical rigor, there have been some who insisted that only the senses can yield knowledge properly so called. This view is known in the history of philosophy as *empiricism*. The adherents of this doctrine in its most radical or extreme form say, in effect: nothing may usefully be talked about unless it can be seen, heard, smelled, tasted or touched. From the time of the eighteenth-century Scottish philosopher David Hume, empiricism has played an increasingly important role in the thought of the English-speaking world, despite reactions against it. In our own century, so-called logical empiricism, or logical positivism, has become a very influential philosophical school. The views of its earlier exponents have been considerably modified, but its central doctrine on the empiricist side remains essentially the traditional one: no statement may be said to be meaningful unless it is of a kind that can be verified by an empirical test. For instance, if you tell me there is a dog in the next room, I can test this statement of yours by going to see. If you say there is a dog with two heads and six feet, I may look at you very skeptically; nevertheless your statement is quite meaningful, because I can ascertain whether or not it is true by going next door to find out. On the other hand, if you say there is a moral principle in the universe that makes it wrong to kill people, the logical empiricist may object that such a statement is meaningless, because there is no means of finding out whether or not it is true — that is, no possibility of empirical verification. He would likewise object that no statement about God could have any meaning, since it would be plainly impossible to make any empirical test. So it would be as meaningless to say there is no God as to say there is a God. To argue about the existence of God is, on this view, absurd. It is like arguing about whether there is a King of Ruritania, a country that is not on the map. To argue about the attributes of God is therefore somewhat like arguing about whether the King of Ruritania is a constitutional monarch or an absolute one. How could one possibly say either "yes" or "no" to any such question?

Religious Philosophy and Empiricist Presuppositions

To restrict ourselves to experience is certainly plausible. No religious philosopher need raise any objections to that. It is no less plausible to insist that all our experience is rooted in the senses. Many of the religious philosophers of the past as well as the present would agree. But those who take a standpoint such as that of the modern logical empiricists do much more. They do not only restrict themselves to sense-experience; they insist on a very special view of what constitutes sense-experience. It is because their presuppositions about this have involved them in difficulties that they have had to modify some of their earlier tenets. But they still represent a fundamentally antireligious way of thinking. Their attitude is not difficult to understand. It is indeed, fundamentally, a very commonplace one. But it is an attitude that can fetter even the most lively intellect against discovering the nature of experience itself. It can become narrow-mindedness of the worst sort, a blindness which, by confining the intellect within an artificially circumscribed area, condemns it to sterility.

In view of this tendency in certain kinds of contemporary thought, and in view also of modern preoccupation with the natural sciences, a religious philosophy should begin with an inquiry into the nature of experience itself, and in particular with an investigation to determine whether it has that cut-and-dried sort of character that modern logical empiricism and similar doctrines suggest. Our next chapter will begin here, therefore, rather than with an account of the various conceptions of God, a discussion which, just because of its interest and importance, must be deferred.

DISCUSSION ON CHAPTER 2

1. "To reflect upon religion is to obscure the fundamental religious issue." Discuss.

2. "The nonreligious person is in the best position to be a religious philosopher, since only he can have the necessary detachment from the object of his study." Discuss.

3. Consider the role of "wishful thinking" in attitudes toward religion.

3

How Can Experience Reveal What is Beyond Experience?

What is Religious Experience?

It can be irritating to listen to religious people talking about their experience of God. They sometimes seem to be talking very glibly, as if they had seen what nobody could ever see as one sees a jack rabbit; about what nobody could ever touch as one touches the kitchen table or a friend's hand. The question posed in this chapter is therefore of special importance to the religious philosopher, whose business it is to find out intellectually what is meant by such "religious talk." The Hebrew prophet Isaiah, for instance, who was a poet and a mystic, a man whose thinking was certainly far above the crude, primitive level of those who have actually thought of God as an old man sitting on a throne in the "middle of the sky," described a vision he had, saying that he "saw also the Lord sitting upon a throne, high and lifted up, and his train filled the temple." He goes on to describe the seraphim, even enumerating the number of their wings: six wings for each seraph — two for covering the seraph's face, two for covering his feet, and two for the purpose of flying. One of the seraphim flew toward Isaiah bearing a live coal in his hand. With this he touched Isaiah's lips, saying, "Thine iniquity is taken away and thy sin purged." So Isaiah got his commission as a prophet.

Isaiah was describing what we might call an inward experience of what is beyond "ordinary" experience. The Hebrews were not allowed pictures or other such representations of God, so that Isaiah could not have been referring his hearers to any religious picture or other such object that they might be supposed to have seen, as a Spanish priest, for example, might refer his people to the crucifix on the altar of the village church. But he nevertheless used verbal imagery to communicate to his hearers a notion of an experience that he evidently expected them, in some measure, to grasp. This experience purported to be no mere by-product of "ordinary" sense-experience, such as one has in idle dreams of flying through windows or swimming in champagne or beating an Olympic champion at a game one has never even played. It purported to be the experience of what is

22

beyond "ordinary" experience, so that in having it one's "range" of experience is somehow or other increased, extended or enriched. Such an experience, a religious person would insist, is "more valuable" than ordinary experience. It has a "deeper reality." What can all this mean?

Of course there are many experiences I might claim to have, which could not be called simply experiences of seeing, touching, and the like, but which you and I and everyone else would unhesitatingly accept as "normal." It would not even occur to you or me to be skeptical if a friend told us that he was feeling "inwardly depressed" this evening. We should probably tell him, in a friendly way, that we often felt "in the blues" ourselves, and that we could therefore readily understand his feeling, and that it was due perhaps to overwork or indigestion, and so on. Notice that the experience is described by metaphors. He called it an "inward depression." We called it, more colloquially, "the blues." There was, however, nothing spatial about it that could be depressed as a key on the piano or the lever on a machine can be depressed, and there was certainly nothing in it that could have a color as does a tree or a coffee cup. We should have no means of knowing precisely how our friend was feeling. Nevertheless, the experience is so familiar in a general sort of way that we should think it a very reasonable assumption that his "blues" were not radically different from yours or mine, and were due to causes which, however complex, "belong" to human beings. No doubt no two such feelings are identical, any more than any two fingerprints are ever found to be identical. But (this is the important point) they do not reveal anything beyond "ordinary" experience. The configuration of every new fingerprint filed by the F.B.I. is different from every other one already on the files; but there is nothing surprising about that. What would be very surprising indeed would be a fingerprint whose configuration expressed an intelligible idea. This is, however, the *kind* of newness that is claimed in religious experience.

The claim of religions is that their object (God) is beyond experience, so that when religious people talk about God it would seem that they are, by their own admission, talking about something of which they have no experience. They are talking of what "transcends" experience, and of its very existence, therefore, they can no more meaningfully talk than I can pretend to tell you whether the King of Ruritania takes sugar in his tea. Certain religions, notably Judaism, Christianity and Islam, lay special stress on the "transcendence" of God. God, they say, is so completely other than the world of ordinary experience that it is only in a very special sense, and due, for example, to God's own act, that I am able to "know" anything about him at all. Nevertheless, if I am to try to practice any of these religions with earnestness, I shall be expected to meditate daily to some extent on God and God's works. How can I meditate on that which "transcends" my experience?

How Can I Know What I Do Not Know?

This raises, in a special context, a very general philosophical question. How can I be said to know what I do not know? Either I know something, in which case I may talk about it; or else I do not know, in which case, it would seem, I cannot talk — except by talking gibberish, mere monkey-chatter. But I can know in one sense that which in another sense I do not know. In scientific inquiry this is a common occurrence. A dramatic example is the discovery of the planet Neptune. The planet Uranus had been discovered by Sir William Herschel in 1781. When astronomers studied its orbit, however, they found that this did not behave exactly as they expected. The deviations of the orbit of Uranus were, moreover, too considerable to be accounted for by the ordinary errors that creep into calculations of this sort. Various theories were advanced: for instance, that the mass of Saturn (a planet also already discovered by that time) was greater than had been supposed. But there was no evidence for this. The only theory that seemed to hold water was that there was yet another, so far unknown, planet, whose presence would account for the deviations in the orbit of Uranus. Uranus, it was suggested, was being disturbed by this other unknown planet. A young mathematician at Cambridge, John Couch Adams, worked out the orbit of the unknown planet that would account for the deviations of Uranus. Eventually, and largely through the more thorough investigations of the French astronomer Leverrier, the search conducted at the Berlin observatory in September 1846 was successful, and the existence of the planet, later named Neptune, was established. For about a quarter of a century before then, however, it had been "known," to those who had faith in the theory, that the planet existed. One astronomer, the month before its existence was established, had actually seen the planet through a telescope, without recognizing that the object he perceived was the sought-for planet.

In much more everyday experience we may likewise be said to "know" what we do not know. For instance, suppose that I had been carefully preserved from infancy from ever seeing the color red, while being freely permitted to see purple objects. Then, if I were suddenly confronted with a red object, I might say I had never before seen such a color; yet in fact I had been seeing it all the time, for red is a component (with blue) of the color purple. What I really ought to have said, therefore, on first encountering the red object, was that I had never before seen the color red "separated" from the color blue.

We are in fact constantly seeing what we call "things"; but what we call a thing is several things grouped together. An automobile, for example, is a great many things; but so also is the simplest thing you can name — a pencil or even a pin. I might conceivably drive an automobile for twenty years without even "knowing" that there was a gear box; yet I "know" the gears every time I shift the lever. Monsieur Jourdain in Molière's play was very surprised to learn that he had been talking prose all his life; he had not *distinguished* it as prose, but of course he knew what he was talking as well as you or I do.

From my smiles and frowns and the like, you form an impression of the kind of person I am within a few minutes of meeting me. If you were then asked whether you knew me, you would probably reply that you did not know me at all well, having only just met me. How could you be expected to form any judgment upon the sort of person I am without having had an opportunity to observe, for instance, my habits of life and the manner in which I conducted myself in certain situations? Nevertheless, even on first meeting you "knew" me in some sense, and your knowledge increased, not by a series of well-defined steps, as in a theorem in Euclid, but by a process of unfolding or growth.

Indeed, to ask the question, "How can I know what I don't know?" is a little like asking the question, "How can I see a tree growing?" or "How can I see a still picture in a movie?" Of course I cannot see a tree grow as I can see a man take off his hat, but in watching a healthy young tree in my garden for a few minutes, I have surely been watching it grow. The process is too slow to enable me to perceive expansion as I perceive it in the inflation of a toy balloon. It was, however, going on, and if I had had a more sensitive apparatus I suppose I could have perceived it.

The Effect of Degrees of Sensitivity

The effect of even a very slight difference in sensitivity is often very striking. The difference between the act of seeing in a man and the act of seeing in a worm is tremendous. A worm has no eyes, but if you approach him he will try to wriggle away. He can even dodge you after dark; if you shine a flashlight on him as he is coming up from his burrow, he will retire into it again. He has nerve endings under his skin all over his body, and some of these are sensitive to light, so that he can tell when a shadow crosses his path or a light strikes it. A man's sight is much more highly developed. Compared to the worm he is far more discriminating. But at the human level of development even the slightest improvement in the power of discrimination reveals to the possessor a whole new realm of experience;

for example, the experience of color. The difference between a color-blind person and a person with "normal" color-vision is extremely slight. The "waves" that cause me to see the color red are longer than those that cause me to see green; but they are longer only by about 1/120,000 of an inch. The retina of my eye reacts to the longer waves in a way different from that in which it reacts to the shorter ones. Hence I am able to have the experience of seeing the color red, and also the experience of seeing the color green. My color-blind friend, who lacks only the power of making this very fine distinction, is denied this experience in the world of color. On the other hand, animals less highly developed than man retain certain sensory powers man has lost. It is well known that dogs, for instance, can hear sounds not audible to the human ear. Human beings do not ordinarily hear sound waves longer than thirty-five feet or shorter than seven-eighths of an inch. Dogs, however, can hear waves shorter than this. That is why poachers use a dog whistle, which produces waves just long enough to be heard by a dog but not long enough to be heard by even the most vigilant gamekeeper. With only a very slightly greater power of discrimination or range of sensitivity, therefore, whole worlds of experience would be opened up to us.

These reflections bring us to a crucial point. The color-vision of many people is neither perfect nor is it totally absent. Many of us whose color-vision would pass for normal in many of the standard tests still do not discriminate as well as do the most color-sensitive persons. Perhaps we see reds pretty much alike, or else we cannot distinguish the delicate shades of bluish-green. Perhaps, again, we may be able to distinguish certain shades in one kind of light but not in another. Bees are especially interesting in this connection: their retinas change with the seasons, so that in early spring they react to a range of electro-magnetic vibrations measurably different from the range to which they react in the late fall, and at one period of the year there is a gap in their reaction; that is, they do not at this time react to a part of their total annual range. From all this it becomes clear that there must be many occasions on which it will not do to make sharp distinction between knowing and not-knowing that some of us nearly always expect to be able to make. If we consider the nature of knowledge in the light of the elementary examples we have just been inspecting, we shall see that, to say the least, we often have neither complete knowledge nor complete ignorance, but, rather, a glimmer, a hint, an intimation.

Fragmentariness and Interpretation

It should also be clear that there would appear to be far more "in" the world around us than any of us is capable of grasping with the equipment we have. Our experience of the external world is limited to a fraction of what it might be, the fraction that is discernible by means of the tools we have or are likely to have. Of course we do much more than just make isolated acts of apprehension such as we have been considering. We arrange what so comes to us; we integrate it into the complex experience that we have of the world around us. We build systems and propound theories, using our brains to assimilate and "understand" the various bits of knowledge by piecing them together. So we *interpret* our fragmentary experience. We are nevertheless dependent on what our senses "tell" us, for a person *entirely* devoid of all senses could not know anything at all. It is not that we are "told" everything either clearly or not at all; much that we are "told" is, so to speak, "whispered." We are given slight clues rather than clear information. What makes a good scientist or a good detective is not so much what he does with the clear information; it is what he does with the clues. The legendary Sherlock Holmes does not only use his powers of observation to a greater extent than do most other men; he has a "scent" for following up the most promising clue. It is this that makes it possible for him in some sense to "know" the murderer before he has sufficient data to convince officialdom. As St. Paul puts it in a very different context, he "sees through a glass darkly"; still, he sees. Before he is able to have his culprit arrested his knowledge is dim; nevertheless it is knowledge. He is already dimly experiencing that which is beyond his more vivid experience.

The Idea of Revelation

This chapter has done nothing to demonstrate either the existence or the nonexistence of God; nor has it refuted or established any other religious tenet. All we have tried to do has been to clear some ground. But if knowledge comes to us in the way suggested by the examples we have considered, if we can sometimes see dimly beyond what we can see clearly, then the hypothesis that we can know a divine Being who exists beyond the "ordinary" world around us becomes more intelligible and worthy of the closest scrutiny. What we have been considering suggests that, even at such an elementary level of knowing, knowledge *might* be, at any rate in some cases, of the nature of hints or intimations *to us* rather than mere discoveries *by us*. So we may at least entertain the notion that these intimations may be the intimations of a divine Being inviting us to understand Him. This would mean that He was revealing Himself to us in or through the world of our "ordinary" experience.

It should be noted — since later on we shall be making some use of the term "revelation," which is a term of great importance in religious thought — that a divine revelation need not take the dramatic, spectacular forms that some beginners suppose it has to take. It need not consist of the heavens rolling back while an oracular voice makes pithy pronouncements amid flashes of lightning in a cloud-filled sky streaked with blood and smoke. "To reveal" is "to unfold" or "to unveil" or even "to unwrap." The unfolding of the petals of a rosebud — or perhaps the drawing aside of a series of fine veils — might be in some cases, therefore, a more apposite metaphor. But the idea of divine revelation does imply that "the Other" is unfolding to us that which otherwise would be hidden. It implies some sort of breaking through barriers.

This raises the question of the nature of the barriers, a question we shall consider in our next chapter.

DISCUSSION ON CHAPTER 3

1. Discuss the question, "How can I know what I don't know?"

2. Consider examples other than the ones in the text to illustrate how scientific knowledge is extended.

3. In what way, if any, do you think scientific discovery and religious revelation may be said to resemble each other, and in what way do they differ?

4

Can We Escape Experience?

Religion as Escape

It is a commonplace that much that passes for religion is a mere psychological escape from the realities of life. Charles Kingsley (1819–1875), an English clergyman who, besides writing stories for children, was a great social reformer in his day, suggested that religion could be so "other-worldly," so irrelevant to the realities of life, as to be an opiate for the people. It was this phrase of Kingsley's, which he coined in criticism of certain tendencies that he felt were prevalent in his day and that he wanted to eradicate from the Church of England to which he belonged, that was later adapted by the Marxists and written on the Kremlin walls. Kingsley had used the phrase as a warning against what he believed to be a dangerous escapism in the life of the Church; the Marxists used it as a slogan against godliness in general. But no intelligent person would deny that any religious practice can degenerate into something that may well be described as a psychological equivalent of drug addiction. People who shut out the unpleasant realities of the life around them and find their refuge in religious paraphernalia carefully devised to secure their escape from these realities, are abusing religion so that it does become very much like a drug. Moreover, since their religion is not "grounded" it can accomplish little or nothing either for their own health or for the welfare of others.

A Unitarian speaker, Dr. Davies, has more recently put this another way. He said of contemporary American experiments in "religious" enterprise: "What we are seeing is not spiritual regeneration but mass hypnotism. It recalls the techniques of advertising. Like the radio or television announcer: 'Try God, folks. He will clear away your troubles in a twinkling. Works for you while you sleep . . . Try God! This program is brought to you by Self-Interest and Vulgarity, Incorporated.'" And again: "Most of those who think themselves religious are really atheists . . . They *think* they believe in God. But what they truly believe in is their own prosperity, deified; their own happiness, their own advantage . . . As soon as their prosperity is shrunken . . . they feel that God is doing them an injustice."

How the Escape-Mechanism Works

It is not in the least surprising that religions should be susceptible to this abuse. Practically everything is. People are constantly seeking means of escape from life's challenges. Movies and television are notorious examples, though their possibilities as media of reporting, instruction, and healthful recreation are almost unlimited. Professional football, used as an idle spectacle to the neglect of work or other responsibilities, can be an escapism. Study and research, useful in themselves, can become for some a means of escape from life's demands. Others, who cannot run their own homes or offices satisfactorily, find escape from their sense of failure by excelling in endless arguments about politics and the running of national and international affairs.

All such forms of escape represent attempts to oversimplify realities. Instead of kicking a ball myself, I may watch professional football players as I watch circus acrobats. Instead of engaging in some useful political activity in my local community, for example, I may argue in a bar about the foreign policy of the United States government, from a mere reading of the local newspaper. So the religious votaries who turn their religion into a convenient escape from life generally do so by ignoring or turning away from all aspects of life that are unsuitable for their specialized purpose. Their religion may teach them that God expects them to feed the hungry, but while the hungry starve outside their doors they are to be found arguing about the correct percentage of beeswax for the altar candles. By such means they acquire the art of constructing a fanciful picture of God, an oversimplification of the relation between God and man, which, though it could hardly satisfy their intellect for five minutes, can often provide for them a lifetime of cozy relief from their own sense of inadequacy and guilt.

It is necessary to be something of an ostrich, in one way or another, in order to perform the more elaborate escapist feats of this kind. Not all persons are equally endowed with such ostrich-like qualities. Most people, instead of actually trying to pretend that the unpleasant, challenging things of life are really pleasant and unchallenging, try to avoid them in an even easier and less obviously ridiculous way. They simply try not to think about them, a policy which can hardly call for much effort. Then when the unpleasant features of life do thrust themselves upon their minds, they resort to various well-known devices to avoid facing the issue. They try to refuse to believe anything that would require them to re-think their position or change their mode of life. They pin their hopes to everything that seems to fit in with the situation as they would like the situation to be. The political party they oppose wins at the polls and is eminently successful in the saddle; well, they say, this success is due to exceptionally favorable conditions prevailing at the time. Their own party wins and has a record of abysmal failure; well, they explain, that is because their party does not go in for short-range policies or the game of vote-catching. Such wishful thinking is notoriously widespread and affects almost every aspect of life. How should we expect it to affect religion?

Escape From God

In our last chapter we considered the plausibility of the suggestion that God might be "breaking through" our "ordinary" experience. But among possible objections to this there is one particularly obvious and important one that we must now consider. It would seem that, on such a view, God must be said to be singularly unsuccessful in His attempt to break through, for there is no doubt that many people deny that they have any experience of God whatsoever. If there were a God in the least like the Biblical God, making Himself known to us by this "breaking through" our "ordinary" experience, why should He ever fail? Why should He have the slightest difficulty? We seem to have no difficulty in knowing the world around us well enough to adapt it to our use. Nobody with normal or near-normal sense-perception has any difficulty in seeing tables and chairs, and nobody of average intelligence should have much trouble understanding elementary physics. Claim to a knowledge of God seems to have nothing to do with sensitivity or intelligence. Many distinguished artists and scholars disclaim having encountered God, while other persons, whose endowments are quite mediocre, will tell you they know Him as surely as they know their own brother or sister. So it is evident that a specially sensitive apparatus or an unusually high I.Q. does not help one to "get through" to God. On the face of it, it would seem that God should be obvious to everybody — not obvious in the way a table is obvious; but no less obvious in a different way.

We are here reminded, however, of the old proverb that there is none so blind as he who will not see. Man may be said to have an infinite capacity for pulling his own leg. It is quite possible that all men encounter God in their experience, though not all are willing to face the fact of the encounter. In view of our extraordinary skill and ingenuity as human beings in inventing means of escape from what we wish to avoid seeing or meeting, it would not be in the least difficult to suppose that we are capable of blinding ourselves to God as efficiently as we blind ourselves to various other elements in experience. But why should we wish to put on such blinders? What vested interest might we have in resisting God?

As we shall abundantly see later on, when we come to examine the various conceptions of God that men have actually held and do hold, God is generally believed to demand sacrifices as well as give benefactions. This is true not only at the primitive level, where the votary brings precious, hard-won gifts to the idol he worships, but also at the loftier stage in religious development, where, as the psalmist puts it, "the sacrifices of God are a broken spirit." For it is certainly no less unpleasant to offer a humble apology than it is to offer a pound of honey. To admit failure, to confess sin, to acknowledge that one is in the wrong — all this is very disagreeable and a hard sacrifice. Moreover, all religions teach, in some measure, that God makes great moral demands on men. Some religions present these demands of God as very great indeed, so great that they are beyond human capacity in practice. So God is very inconvenient. To say the least, there are many occasions on which it would be much more comfortable to be able to disbelieve in His existence, even if one were unable to do so. For there are many things the believer would often feel free to do were it not for the remembrance that God's "eye" is ever upon him. Apart from the question of whether God does exist, it would plainly be more comfortable in some circumstances and from certain points of view if He did not.

It is also a widespread tenet that God punishes the wicked. Sometimes hell, a place of everlasting torment, is crudely depicted as a place of boiling and roasting. But the state of spiritual anguish of which hell is said, by more intellectual, less lurid, writers, to consist, is by no means a less horrifying prospect. Nobody would like to believe in the possibility of his having such a destiny. Even purgatory, the state of trial and cleansing that is, according to certain religious teaching, a necessary prelude to final happiness, can present itself in terrifying forms. Is it not reasonable to suppose that there would be a great temptation on the part of anyone who believed in God and God's justice, to try to obliterate or escape from his own belief if he possibly could?

Why Should We Seek Escape From a Benevolent Deity?

But there is something much more terrifying than even the idea of the justice of God. It is the idea of God's forgiveness. It may sound all right to say that nothing could be easier than accepting forgiveness. In fact, however, in the existential situation, forgiveness is really very hard to accept. We do not like to be humbled, and it is less humbling to meet an angry father than a father who puts you to shame by the generosity of his forgiveness. The elder brother in Christ's parable had really no idea how difficult it is to be a returning prodigal son when you have such a thoroughly benevolent father. That it is God's infinite benevolence and compassion that make men flee from Him is the theme of Francis Thompson's great poem, *The Hound of Heaven*. In this incomparably delicate and beautiful work of Christian art, the poet expresses how his fear of Christ's love led him to flee Christ, only to be overtaken and overpowered by the relentless love in the heart of his divine pursuer:

> I fled Him down the nights and down the days;
> I fled Him, down the arches of the years;
> I fled Him, down the labyrinthine ways
> Of my own mind; and in the midst of tears
> I hid from Him, and under running laughter.
> Up vistaed hopes I sped;
> And shot, precipitated,
> Adown Titanic glooms of chasmèd fears,
> From those strong Feet that followed, followed after.
> But with unhurrying chase,
> And unperturbèd pace,
> Deliberate speed, majestic instancy,
> They beat—and a Voice beat
> More instant than the Feet—
> "All things betray thee, who betrayest Me."
>
> I pleaded, outlaw-wise,
> By many a hearted casement, curtained red,
> Trellised with intertwining charities;
> (For, though I knew His love Who followèd,
> Yet was I sore adread
> Lest, having Him, I must have naught beside)
> But, if one little casement parted wide,
> The gust of His approach would clash it to:
> Fear wist not to evade, as Love wist to pursue.

The poem is too long to quote in full. It would be very profitable for the student to consult it for himself, however, at this stage: it is written with an extraordinarily deep insight into the nature of skepticism as seen in retrospect from the standpoint of subsequent Christian experience.[1] In such retrospect, the former skepticism is recognized as an attempt to escape from God. Francis Thompson describes how astonishingly subtle a man can be in devising ruses to accomplish this end. In his own case all the ruses were ultimately unsuccessful, for in a sense God had beaten him even before the skeptical flight had begun. But if man has any moral freedom there is no reason, it would seem, why he should not stubbornly blind himself to God all his life.

---

[1] The full text of the poem may be found in *The Oxford Book of Christian Verse* and will be included in *Readings in Religious Philosophy*, now in preparation as a companion to the present volume.

In such a case a man could very well go on indefinitely seeing and understanding all that is given in "ordinary" experience, while at the same time shutting his mind to God. To Augustine God seemed "nearer, more related to us, and therefore more easily known to us, than sensible, corporeal things." [2] But our persistent skeptic would have so excluded God from his field of attention that he could say as La Place said to Napoleon when the latter pointed out there was no mention of God in his *Traité de mécanique céleste:* "Sire, I had no need of that hypothesis."

It would certainly be quite possible to restrict our vision and understanding in such a way, excluding all data that might suggest the plausibility of belief in the existence of God; for example, indications of purpose in the universe or in individual lives might be disregarded completely. For it is beyond dispute that we habitually and necessarily select the experiences we have out of a wider range of possible experiences. Philosophically, this is an elementary point. It is, however, of such great importance to grasp its full import at this stage that we shall spend some time in expounding it.

Selectivity and Interpretation

If you were writing the biography of a great man — let us say a contemporary on whom abundant information was available — you would plainly have to restrict yourself in some way in assembling your basic information about him. If, in the course of his life, he was elected to the United States Senate, or became a skating champion, or invented an important machine, you could not possibly omit any of these facts from your biography of the man. You would certainly discover many things about him, however, that you would not put in your book, even if this were an enormous volume; you would omit them for lack of space, but also because you accounted them of little or no interest. It is not likely, for instance, that you would record the way he liked his eggs boiled unless this had some relevance, by a curious chance, to something important in his life. It is exceedingly unlikely that you would mention, even if you happened to discover the fact, that on a certain morning he forgot to tie his shoelaces till he reached his car. You would not mention these things because you would be obliged to confine yourself to what was somehow or other important in his life, for otherwise your book would go on practically forever. You would not even be interested in finding out such trifles, except to the extent that they threw light on the more important elements in your subject's life.

But what would be your criterion of importance? There would be many possible criteria. You might make your selection in order to

[2] *De Genesi ad litteram,* V, 16.

show the influence of the man on the thought or life of his country; or your aim might be, rather, to exhibit the curious complexity of his character. Probably your aim would include these and others too. But you would select your facts and events according to the criteria of importance that you had predetermined. If your subject, besides being a great statesman or politician, also happened to be an enthusiastic bird-watcher in his spare time, you probably would not say very much about this, but only mention it here and there. If, however, you were writing a special biography of him for bird-watchers, you would give the fullest details of his bird-watching expeditions and include all his notes on them that you could find, while making only brief mention of the circumstances in which he became a senator.

We have been assuming, of course, that your literary integrity was beyond question. But suppose you had an ax to grind. You wanted to paint your subject blacker or whiter than he was, making him a superman or a super-scoundrel. Then you would deliberately shut your mind against anything you discovered that did not help your purpose, and you would sit up and take notice only when you came across some fact that did. You would then be perversely selective, eliminating truth and fairness from your aim.

Even as you walk down a city street you are constantly selecting the objects that you allow to command your attention. You pass a great many things without even noticing them, because you account them of no importance. For instance, you do not notice the color of the doors of the various stores unless you have some particular reason for doing so. If one of the stores you have passed every day for years changed the shade of its paintwork, you might very well not notice the fact. The door would not be one of the objects you would select for attention out of the innumerable possibilities. It is said that an old-fashioned sidewalk evangelist, having stood for weeks at a street corner offering religious tracts free, got so tired of being ignored that he substituted dollar bills for the tracts. The passers-by had by this time so much acquired the habit of shutting him out of their view that he stood for hours offering dollars without a single taker, and eventually went home with the wad of bills still in his pocket. Once people have put an object out of the field of their selection, it is difficult to regain their attention so long as there remain as many other things to look at as before; frequently, however, their attention is arrested by sheer force. This situation could very well exist in the relation between man and God.

All my ordinary observation is done by a process of selecting and grouping, mostly according to a conventional pattern — society's convention or my own. I flick a switch and on goes my radio. I do not usually think of the many events that take place in bringing the music into my room: I attend only to the flick of the switch and the music that it "causes." Only if something goes wrong am I disposed to consider the other factors. Perhaps a radio engineer tends to think of the other factors all the time; if so, in this respect his grouping is different from mine. But take an even simpler case. We habitually think of mountains sticking up in the air. Why? Because, you may say, they *do* stick up in the air. But we do not usually think of air sticking down into valleys. Perhaps a meteorologist or other specialist sometimes thinks in this way, in which case, once again, the selection and grouping of experience would be, *to me*, abnormal.

This power of selection that we constantly and necessarily exercise has immense consequences for the kind of experience we actually have. We tend to limit our experience according to our predetermined scale of values. People make widely varied choices, for instance, in reporting what they have seen in the same newspaper. It is this moral power of selection that makes it possible that

> Two men looked out from prison bars:
> One saw mud; the other, stars.

A professor once received postcards from each of five of his undergraduate students who were touring Italy together. All the cards bore the Venice postmark and had been mailed the same day. They read:

(1) *The Pala d'Oro is just oozing with jewels. Having a wonderful time.*

(2) *Venice is a dream: this is where I'd like to spend my honeymoon.*

(3) *The smell of the canals is terrible. We go on to Ravenna tomorrow.*

(4) *We went to Torcello yesterday. The peace of that island is indescribable.*

(5) *I stood for an hour last night on the Ponte Rialto trying to figure out what is so haunting in Venice. Do you think I'd find out if I stayed long enough, or would I only kill it?*

Without knowing any of his five correspondents, you can already tell a great deal about them just from their comments on what we might call their "common experience." Actually, you will see, they did not have much common experience at all. They each chose their experiences, out of a vast number of possibilities.

The prisoner who looked at the stars escaped from seeing the mud; but the prisoner who looked at the mud escaped from seeing the stars. The five correspondents all escaped from experiences they might have had. The experiences they might have had and did not have were all "real"; that is to say, they may all be presumed to belong to the external world, not to their own wild fancy. The Pala d'Oro *is* richly jeweled; Venice *does* notoriously stimulate the romantic passions in many people; the canals *are not* pre-chlorophyllated; Torcello *is* peace-inspiring; Venice *does* present aesthetic problems. The five young people neither manufactured their experiences, weaving them out of their fancy, nor did they simply find them as if the experiences rolled into their minds indiscriminately, meeting no resistance, no barrier, no check. Surely they *chose* their experiences. The field within which they had to make their choices was not, of course, unlimited. From their seat in a gondola they could not have decided to see, instead, Florence or Reykjavik. They had to take Venice; but within this their range of possible choices was enormous — everything from Istrian stone, bleached in the light and blackened in the shade, to the stucco-peeled rose-brick wall of the salt warehouse on the Zattere; perhaps everything from the grace of God to the stench of the Grand Canal.

They could, and no doubt they did, choose many experiences. But in doing so they not only excluded many others; they arranged into some sort of hierarchy the experiences they selected. That is to say, they accounted certain experiences of greater value, interest, importance or significance than others, and they arranged all their experiences according to some kind of scale.

Subjective Values and the Theocentric Attitude

This raises a question: are such evaluations entirely subjective, being relative to the feelings, interests and preoccupations of the individual experiments? In this case how could it be said that one was to be preferred to the other? It would be impossible to discuss meaningfully whether it might be "intrinsically" better to look at mud or at stars from a prison window. It would not be a question of whether there was a God or not, or whether beauty was in the mind of the artist or the stones of Venice or elsewhere; it would simply be a fact that you chose A while I chose B, since you liked to choose A while I liked to choose B. On such a view we could not be seeking, and either discovering or failing to discover, what was "intrinsically" valuable, for nothing would be intrinsically valuable. The examiner who read your term paper and gave it an A or a C, as the case might be, would not even be trying to be "fair" or "correct" in his judgment according to the intrinsic merit of the paper. He would simply be recording his own feelings.

It is, however, implicitly or explicitly, the standpoint of all the great religions of the world, Judaism as much as Christianity, Hinduism no less than Islam, that there is one "intrinsic" value, one "source of all good," which may be called God. On such a view, other values or goods may be arranged hierarchically in relation to this Absolute. This is not to say that the arrangements of values people do make are necessarily right; nevertheless people may be right in trying to make them. To make such arrangements of values with reference to one intrinsic, absolute value is to take what religious philosophers call the theocentric view; that is, a view that is focused on God as the "center" whence all other values are derived and to which they are relative. On this view, it is not a matter of indifference which experience we select and which we choose to escape. Escape from God is always an evil; full and final escape from God is hell.

DISCUSSION ON CHAPTER 4

1. Discuss the difference between the idea of religion as escape and the idea of religion as encounter.

2. Consider, in the light of Francis Thompson's poem, the idea of man's quest for God.

3. Consider what would seem to you to be implied in the concept of an intrinsic or absolute value.

PART TWO

Basic Conceptions of God

5

Dynamism and Animism

The Need for Historical Knowledge

We have now taken our bearings, and we have aired some general notions about our subject and about the plausibility of the existence of a Being or Realm beyond our "ordinary" experience. Can we go on to consider what might be said for and against "belief in God" in a more detailed and critical fashion? Not yet; for we must first make certain distinctions. It is absurd to label anyone a "believer" or an "unbeliever" without specifying in some way the kind of God he believes or does not believe in. I might be a firm believer in one kind of God while rejecting another conception of God as ridiculous. You might look askance at the idea of a personal God while eagerly considering the idea of an impersonal one; or, of course, it might be the other way around. Some who would be ill-disposed toward the notion of a Supreme Mind directing the universe would be quite prepared for the idea of some principle of eternal cosmic energy "behind" it.

It is now time to learn something of the history of the various ways in which people have actually conceived of God, and as we do so we shall make some critical comments on the philosophical implications of these various conceptions. In this way we shall acquire, as we proceed, a vocabulary for further discussion, besides getting some factual knowledge upon which to base our thinking.

Primitive and Nonprimitive Religion

At the outset we may consider whether it is legitimate to distinguish a type of religion called "primitive" from other types. It may seem to some unfair and arbitrary to make any such distinction at all. Is it not arbitrary to denigrate the conceptions of God that are associated with peoples we account "uncivilized" and to praise those associated with the cultures we choose to think more advanced? What right have we to do this? There is, indeed, no good reason to suppose that the notions of our contemporaries are *all* better than those of their forefathers. Moreover, it would seem that all human conceptions of God and formulations of these in human language are primitive, in the sense that they are susceptible to development and growth. In any human understanding we may claim to have of the divine, there must surely always be room for improvement.

In making a distinction between "primitive" and "nonprimitive" ideas about God, we refer only to the historical fact that certain conceptions do tend to die out, and that they die out because they are intellectually so unsatisfactory that they are bound to be superseded by more comprehensive notions. The discarded notions are called primitive because they are appropriate to an earlier stage in the intellectual development of a people. The notions of our own childhood, for instance, might be called primitive in contrast to our present ideas of God. Our religious faith may remain essentially the same from childhood to old age; but, though there are some people who seem to rise to an advanced level in chemistry or economics while keeping their religious concepts at a Sunday school level, it is to be hoped that most people's notions about God do mature on the intellectual side. In the religious thinking of all of us there are no doubt remnants of the primitive level just as there are remnants of superstition among people who might be expected to have left this behind them. But this is only because neither nations nor individuals are generally as mature as they fancy themselves to be. Many individuals are, in some respects, still adolescent at sixty.

The Beginnings of Religion

The idea that the universe is created and governed by one Supreme Being is one that has appeared in only comparatively recent times in the life of the human race. Comparatively recent, we may say, because apart from some anticipations of it on the part of certain remarkable individuals, it is not found to have occurred much before 800 B.C., and it was many centuries after that before it became a widespread belief. For example, the case of the famous Egyptian king known as Ikhnaten, fourteen centuries before Christ, is exceptional. In comparison with some institutions, that would make it seem a very ancient idea; but to archaeologists and others who have made discoveries about the habits of mankind fifty or even a hundred thousand years ago the idea does not seem venerable on account of its antiquity. Something may be guessed even about the religion of these extremely remote ancestors of ours. It has been found, for example, that some of them smeared the bodies of their dead with red iron oxide. This may well have been a religious ceremony intended to express hope of immortality. Human blood is red, and since without blood man dies it was also a symbol of life; so to smear a corpse with red dye could very well symbolize hope of immortality or belief in some realm beyond "ordinary" existence. At a much less remote period, but still before the discovery of the art of writing (very roughly, about six thousand years ago), there was certainly a definite hope of immortality shown by the manner in which people buried their dead by placing the corpse in Mother Earth bent up like a fetus in the womb and surrounded by various objects such as jars of food, weapons, tools, and personal ornaments.

Why Primitive Religion is Difficult to Understand

Our chief danger in trying to understand primitive religion lies in the temptation to make it more logical and coherent than it could possibly be. Primitive religion springs from no preconceived theory or doctrine, for the mentality of primitive man is neither as reflective nor as sentimental as that of civilized peoples. Uninhibited by sentimentality and intellectual reflection, he is, however, haunted by fears and other emotions, and in the context of his frankly sensationist attitude to the world around him, such emotions lead him to laws and customs to which he adheres with rigid tenacity. All human beings tend to be conservative in religious matters; but in primitive peoples this conservatism is extreme and usually unmitigated by individualistic questionings. So while the details of the religious practice of primitive peoples, both past and present, may vary as much as their sexual codes or property laws — which vary enormously from tribe to tribe — primitive religion does have certain characteristic tendencies and common features.

Dynamism: Mana and Taboo

Perhaps the most fundamental of these features is the recognition of a certain quality in particular places, persons, things and events — a quality that may, for the sake of convenience, be called "the sacred." This belief is called *dynamism*, from the Greek *dynamis*, a power. The sacred is neither good nor bad in itself; potentially it is both. It is exceedingly dangerous to touch or to have anything to do with anything possessing this quality unless one knows how to handle it. It is a mysterious power, often conceived of almost after the fashion of radioactivity or electricity, except that of course it is "wild," not being man-produced and man-organized as is the electricity supply in our houses. The Melanesian islanders call this force *mana*. Other primitive peoples such as the American Indians and the African Bantus have much the same notion, clothed in other terms. *Mana* is a hidden force, and whatever is supposed to possess it is of course a focus of attention in the community. The mysterious energy radiated from an object possessing *mana* may be transmitted to persons; persons may also transmit it to objects and to other persons. It is valuable, for it may be put to a very good use in the service of the community; but it is also dangerous and may bring the tribe incalculable injury. Primitive peoples look on it in some ways as we look on atomic power: it has great possibilities for our welfare and yet it is terrifying. It is from this negative side of *mana* that we get the well-known idea of *taboo*. It is forbidden to touch certain objects possessing *mana*: to touch them is *taboo*, because of the terrible evils that might be unleashed. Only those experienced in handling them dare do so. Magicians, whose business or calling it is to control such powers by the utterance of certain ritual words or the performance of certain ritual acts, may be entrusted with the task. They are really the primitive counterparts of modern scientific technicians.

Mana also resides in individuals, notably the chief of the tribe, and in particular the chief's head, which is therefore highly *taboo*. It is exceedingly dangerous to touch a piece of the chief's clothing, or even the carpet on which he walks: the intruder may expect dire consequences unless he takes the proper steps to counteract, by purification, these ill effects caused by the radiation of *mana* from the chief's sacred body.

The Role of the Magician

Magicians are supposed to know not only how to control *mana* and so prevent it from hurting the tribe, but also how to collect it in a *fetish*. A fetish is an object such as, say, an animal's horn that has been packed with *mana* almost as we might think of the charging of a car battery or the magnetizing of a piece of metal. A fetish can be a very useful thing to have: it is a weapon against your foes and also a powerful bargaining instrument, for if, in certain circumstances, you were to take an apparently innocent-looking wisp of hair out of your pocket and dangle it nonchalantly from your hand while a man was trying to strike a hard bargain with you, you might find he would quickly reconsider the matter and give you better terms on condition that you put the fearsome thing out of sight. Such fetishes may be almost personal; indeed *mana* itself, vague and impersonal though it would seem to be, can assume forms that look to us personal rather than impersonal. Primitive peoples do not make the distinction that has become familiar to us between "the spiritual" and "the material"; hence it is notoriously difficult to say whether a belief at the primitive level is a belief in dynamic powers or personal agencies, a belief in forces or in spirits. Hence also the easy transition between the kind of religion we are considering in this chapter and the belief in gods we shall be considering in our next. The term used for *god* in the old Japanese religion is *kami*, and *kami* means anything that inspires awe or possesses a peculiar potency — human, animal, vegetable or mineral.

Animism

To primitive peoples, all nature is pervaded by innumerable spirits, for it is not only persons or animals but also the objects that we commonly call "inanimate" that have souls or spirits in them. This view is called *animism* (from the Latin, *anima*, soul) and is very widespread among primitive peoples today. But again we must be on our guard against misinterpreting a primitive viewpoint in terms of our own. As we have just seen, primitive man does not distinguish sharply between the spiritual and the material. Therefore, not only can an impersonal force like *mana* be almost a spirit; a spirit can be almost a visible, tangible object. Certainly souls and spirits are conceived to be very much like living persons or animals: they have a shape; they may be rational or irrational according to their mood; they are often highly susceptible to flattery, and they are as likely to sulk and be spiteful when slighted or ignored as they are to be pleased and helpful when loaded with pretty gifts or otherwise pleased. They are, however, quite capricious, so that their moods have to be studied with the utmost care. Having wills of their own, and no definite moral principles, yet considerable power, they have to be coaxed like spoiled children. The attitude adopted toward them is, indeed, sometimes very like the attitude of servile cunning that might be adopted toward the spoiled child of a grandee of the latter's servant.

Souls for Sale

The souls or spirits that animate all nature wander about occasionally, behaving almost as aimlessly as *mana*. The early Arabs believed that the *nefs*, or soul, of a man slipped away through the nostrils in the case of a man who died in his bed, while in that of a man violently killed, as on the battlefield, it flowed away on the point of the spear that slew him. The early Hebrews thought that the *nephesh*, or soul, which was made of a very fine, delicate substance, could slip out of the body at will. Evidently there was an unpleasant class of witches who made a profitable business out of hunting for such unwary human souls. They caught them in handkerchiefs and elbow-pockets and sold them to families who, having a sick person in the house, believed that the soul had left him and that the person might recover if he could be furnished with another. There is an echo of this very primitive belief in the Old Testament,[1] and belief in such witchcraft is said to persist in various parts of the world today. Sorcerers among certain of the Pacific islanders, for instance, are said to set up traps suitable for all sizes of souls (for

[1] E.g., Ezek. 13·17 f

souls vary in size according to the bodies they inhabit, being miniatures, of those bodies though of a finer substance), and these traps the witches place near the houses of the sick, so that when the souls are wandering from their bodies the sorcerers can snap them up and make off with them. There are, however, also more ethical witches who do not use the souls for gain, selling them to the sick, but administer them gratis, using their stock of them as a modern hospital uses a blood bank.

Idols Must Work to Live

Idols made of, say, stone or wood, may be charged with energy in dynamistic fashion, or inhabited by a spirit, after the animistic manner. The relation between a savage and his idol has a curious side. Primitive man, though accustomed to cajoling and coaxing the spirits he believes in, and therefore prepared to try to wheedle favors out of his idol, is too practical, hardheaded and sensationist in his general outlook, to put up with an idol that does not seem to work. In fashioning and setting up an idol, he enters into a sort of business contract with it. Suppose the idol represents the rain-power, the rain-spirit. The worshiper expects to get rain by praying to it and offering certain sacrifices. This is part of his undertaking to the idol, and the idol is considered as undertaking to provide rain. If the worshiper forgets or neglects to make the agreed sacrifices, of course he cannot complain of the idol; he has only himself to blame. But if he has kept his part of the bargain, he feels aggrieved if the idol neglects to keep his. For a time he will regard the neglect as due to the general capriciousness of spirits. He will try coaxing. But if the drought continues he will begin to doubt the idol's power. At first he may try bullying and threatening him. Sometimes he will give the idol a sound beating in the hope of keeping him up to scratch: the spirit is evidently lazy, perhaps literally good for nothing. Still, the supplicant beats him by way of trying to shake the rain out of him, as perhaps you or I might shake a sluggish gadget whose workings we very imperfectly understand — sometimes with good results, at any rate for the time. But eventually, despairing of the power of a particular idol, the savage simply fires him, throws him away as powerless and therefore useless. A worshiper cannot go on indefinitely employing and offering sacrifices to an idol that does no work. He must look for a more efficient one and get rid of the slacker.

Separation of Religion From Magic

We have seen how closely animism and dynamism may be bound together. So also are magic and religion at this stage of development. The magician professes to control the mysterious forces; the priest propitiates and worships them on behalf of the community. The two functions are not always separated; nor is there necessarily a professional priesthood. At the earlier stages of development the priestly office may be undertaken by the heads of families or by the chief of the tribe. But with the development of worship there usually arises sooner or later a class of functionaries whose duty and privilege it is to offer the prescribed sacrifices and make the official supplications on behalf of the community they serve. The sacrifice may at first be a crude ritual, but it may develop into a magnificently elaborate one. A Chinese ceremony dating from the Bronze Age was so elaborated that by the beginning of this century, when it was still being performed, it had become as spectacular as a Papal High Mass. The Chinese Emperor, as the "Son of Heaven," offered Kiao (the great sacrifice) to Shang-ti at the "Altar of Heaven" near Peking. This altar consisted of three concentric circles of marble with a central platform, all in the open air. The sacrifice, conducted with immense splendor, included silk, incense, inscribed paper and bullock's blood. There was a dignified liturgy and fine music.[2]

Values Beyond Human Control

Even at the dynamistic and animistic stage, religion already expresses the recognition of values beyond man's control. Presumably food, shelter and other obvious values are recognized by primitive man. The hunter of food must soon become aware, however, of the fact that he cannot rely wholly on his own exertions to get it, for even the provision of food is seen to depend in part on something lying outside the powers of man. So it becomes evident that neither the individual nor the community can be completely self-sufficient. Even if man could live by bread alone, he could not get it alone. Fire, flood, tempest, drought and other forces might deprive him of it, however diligent and resourceful he might be. Such powers must be coaxed to cooperate with man instead of hindering him in his work. As the menace of starvation loses its urgency and terror, other values are gradually recognized. As soon as man can eke out a regular living, however precarious, it becomes apparent that food and the like are by no means the only values. On the contrary, it is seen that they are worth acquiring chiefly because they enable man to enjoy other values besides — values without which, it now appears, life would hardly be worth living. Thus duty to the tribe, filial piety, honor in battle, are gradually recognized to be contributory to the richness of life, and they become intimately associated with religion.

[2] The altar, according to fairly recent reports, has been preserved.

The Relativistic Presuppositions of Primitive Man

But in dynamism and animism the values are almost always frankly regarded as correlative to human interests and needs. There is no systematization of values and no conscious recognition of an Absolute, a Being deserving of worship for its own sake. The powers and spirits that fill the universe seem to be arbitrary and subject to no law. Primitive man does not think like a theologian or a metaphysician. He is on the whole relativist in his outlook, which is therefore, despite his pre-scientific type of thinking, in many respects fundamentally akin to that of modern positivistic secularism. That is to say, the typical modern sociologist or anthropologist has little need to orient himself to the point of view of the savage who is the subject of his study. His point of view is usually quite similar. His sympathies with the savage are easily engaged. He differs from the latter chiefly in his greater ability to defend and express the point of view they share in common. This ability is, of course, the fruit of the vastly superior mental training he has enjoyed.

DISCUSSION ON CHAPTER 5

1. Distinguish dynamism from animism.

2. Consider examples in modern civilization of dynamistic and/or animistic attitudes of mind.

3. "It was fear that first made gods in the world." (Statius) Discuss.

6

Polytheism

The Rise of Polytheism

We have already seen in the last chapter how easy the transition is from a dynamistic and animistic type of religion to the kind of religion we are now about to consider. Polytheism, the worship of many gods and goddesses, seems to be generally concomitant with certain cultural developments. By the time the urban communities developed in the great river valleys of the ancient world, polytheism was already an established view. The Sumerians, who were probably the founders of the city-state, entered the Mesopotamian valley more than seven thousand years ago. They worshiped innumerable deities, including, for example, on the one hand, the stars and planets, and on the other, personifications of the various cities they created. The importance of a city affected the status of the god who was believed to preside over it, much as the prestige of the Mayor of New York or Philadelphia is obviously greater than that of his counterpart in a small town.

The great Babylonian civilization that grew up in that region is of special interest to historians of religion, because the forms of worship used by the Babylonians may have determined in considerable measure the forms with which we are familiar in Christianity and other such religions today. For instance, in the worship of their gods the Babylonians used as their early temples artificial, man-made mountains with external stairways. This idea would come naturally to the first settlers, who were mountain-dwellers. But these artificial mountains, or ziggurats, as they were called, were among the religious paraphernalia that probably exercised a great influence on the constructions of later civilizations. The temples were essentially the palaces of the gods, who were abundantly fed with sacrifices. The priests went "up" to the temples because the gods lived "up" there; hence, for instance, the notion taken so much for granted in later ages that divinity is "up" rather than "down." The Babylonian cult of the stars persisted in medieval Christendom in which princes often employed a court astrologer, and astrology, though now in disrepute, has its devotees even to this day in civilized countries. The Babylonians also used a form of prayer from which the modern litany, common to several religions, may be ultimately derived.

For several thousand years before the great prophets of the Old Testament were born, polytheism in one form or another was the type of religion that flourished most generally throughout the most advanced civilizations in the world. It was still the pattern of religion in the Gentile world in the time of Christ, and it was long after then that it finally fell into disrepute and decay. Indeed, it has never entirely disappeared, retaining a prominent place in the folklore of most European countries. Santa Claus is an example of surviving polytheism within Christian civilization. In the polytheistic system of the ancient Teutons, Wodan, the god of war, was the protector of military heroes. He was attended by sprightly maidens, little goddesses called Valkyries, who conducted dead warriors to his domain, Valhalla. There was an echo of this at Hindenburg's funeral in Germany in 1934, when Hitler, then recently come to power and eager to make use of the old polytheistic ideas and revive certain features of the old Teutonic pantheon in the interest of his own nationalistic cult, said at the funeral oration: "Go then, dead field marshal, to Valhalla!" Such echoes of polytheism continued long after they had ceased to be the ordinary, conventional outlook of the peoples of Europe. The Scandinavian and some other northern countries were very late in being christianized — the christianization of Sweden, for instance, took place as recently as about the twelfth century A.D. — and there are many tales of the survival of the old gods. One of the most picturesque of these stories recounts how Neptune, god of the sea, appeared to some mariners aboard their vessel and, after bitterly lamenting the death of the old deities, uttered a sorrowful cry and threw himself overboard, passing into oblivion. The old tale expresses the popular regret at the decay of cherished institutions. It says in effect, "People are losing their old sense of wonder; they are becoming prosy and dull; yet there is nothing that can be done about it, for the old gods seem to have no strength left." The old mythologies are properly called wonder-tales, for they are about the way in which people expressed their sense of wonder.

The Polytheistic Attitude

This brings us to a vital clue to the understanding of the polytheistic attitude. We are naturally inclined to suppose that as we believe in or reject belief in one god, so polytheists believe in or reject belief in several gods. In other words, we are apt to imagine that the essential difference between monotheism (belief in one god, from the Greek *monos*, single, and *theos*, a god) and polytheism lies simply in the number of gods believed in. This is not so. The nature of the belief is itself different. To the polytheist, anything wonderful or mysterious is hailed as "godlike." When we encounter anything remarkable or exciting or strange, from Niagara to a new gadget for the kitchen or the car, we tend to exclaim, "Oh, it's wonderful!" The polytheist, in such circumstances, is likely to say, rather, "Aha, a god!" The fertility of nature, for instance, can hardly fail to excite wonder in anyone who is not just an unreflective animal. So in every pantheon (that is, list or collection of gods) a fertility god or goddess has an important place. The polytheist does not first believe in a fertility goddess and then attribute to her the growth of the crops. He looks first, rather, at the gleaming fields and then says, "Blessed and bountiful goddess who did this, I give you praise and thanks." The gods and goddesses always correspond to wonders already experienced in nature or life. They are personifications of these wonders. In personifying them the polytheist may give them human or animal forms, or else a stylized symbolic form such as a circle or a solar disk. But what is worshiped is really the wonderful thing itself; that is, the focus of value that seems to confront us in this or that wonderful experience. Of course, sometimes the symbolic form is worshiped through a confusion: there is no limit to human stupidity. But intelligent people, even at the most primitive level, have no doubt always seen beyond the symbol to what is symbolized. Symbolic forms are for the interpretation of what is valued. Even war is accounted a value: so long as Mars is on your side he brings you, it is believed, the blessings of victory.

Many of us are most familiar with polytheism in the form it took in ancient civilizations such as Greece and Rome. In any museum of classical antiquities we find statues of gods: Mercury, for instance, a young man with winged feet, who is the god of speed; and Venus, a beautiful woman, who is the goddess of love. In popular Hinduism we may find to this day, in India, devotion to similar gods. Some of these are venerable in tradition, such as Vishnu and Krishna. In every polytheistic civilization there is a more or less official list of a definite number of gods, all well known and generally venerated. Prominent among these may be the state deities; that is, those whom we might call government-sponsored. Suppose polytheism were officially recognized as the worship form of the United States. In the American pantheon there would be a very important deity, having a temple, presumably at Washington, who would perhaps be named simply America. There could be no doubt of this deity's official status. Some fifty other gods and goddesses, each presiding over one of the various individual states would also be on the official list, which would include also, it might be hoped, the goddess of Liberty. Other deities might, for a variety of reasons, be placed on the official list; but there would be a great many who, though their cults were almost universally popular, could hardly have that status, and there would be still more who, though much worshiped among special groups or classes of people such as press reporters and truck drivers and stockbrokers, would have little general appeal. So it is in every polytheistic society: besides the deities officially or universally recognized, there is a host of others. For besides the generally recognized wonders in human experience and public or national life, there are many other wonders, some of which are quite transitory happenings. A god may be immediately invented, named for the wonderful event, and then, should the wonder pass quickly away, so also does the god. A god may become fashionable over the course of the week end and vanish from the minds of men by the following Tuesday. Likewise, the days connected with the worship of the various gods differ in status. In a polytheistic America the days officially and universally recognized throughout the United States, such as Thanksgiving, Independence Day and Labor Day, would have a different kind of prestige from that of more restricted festivals, such as Discovery Day in Puerto Rico or Pioneer Day in Idaho, which would be associated with lesser deities in the pantheon. There would also be more private religious festivals connected with social clubs, trade unions, and the like.

A Place in the Pantheon for Chevrolet and Plymouth

Westerners have been sometimes startled to find Hindus in a modern factory worshiping their plant, and even more shocked when university-trained young Hindus are discovered to be paying religious devotion to laboratory apparatus. But against a polytheistic background all this is perfectly natural. Tools of trade are important deities to those engaged in the trade, and to the polytheist it seems as natural for the truck driver to worship his truck as it is for the medical practitioner to pay homage to the goddess of healing. There is something in the doctor's art that cannot be compassed by mere technical skill, and the behavior of machinery, even, may sometimes puzzle not only those unskilled in mechanics but trained engineers as well. Lacking mechanical skill, you will not only coax but actually talk about coaxing the engine of your automobile to start on a cold morning. If you were a polytheist you might do much the same, but you would say, rather, something such as, "O beloved goddess Chevrolet, who seest me to be in a great hurry this morning, be merciful unto me and let me hear the purr of thy pleasure and not the noise of thy wrath." Perhaps you might even say at times, "O blessed Plymouth, most patient goddess, I confess that I have lately neglected to bring thee the sacrifice of oil that is pleasing unto thee; wherefore I

beseech thee to bear with thy supplicant and conduct me safely to
the next filling station, whither I will go to make thee an abundant
sacrifice."

A Polytheist and His Favorites

A polytheist always has favorites among the gods, determined by
his own temperament, age and condition, as well as his own interest,
temporary or permanent. If it is true that everybody loves a lover,
then Venus will be a popular deity with all. But from lovers she will
elicit special devotion. In ancient Rome, when a young couple went
out together to see a procession or other show, they would of course
pay great respect to Venus, when her image appeared on the scene.
Instead of saying, "Isn't love wonderful?" they would say, "Great art
thou, O Venus." In a polytheistic society you could tell a good deal
about a person's frame of mind by the gods he favored, so that to
tell a girl you were trying to woo that you thought Venus overrated
was hardly the way to win her heart. But in any case, a lovesick
youth or maiden would be spontaneously supplicating Venus.

Anthropomorphism

The Greeks liked to present their deities in human form; it was
natural to them to symbolize the gods as human beings glorified,
idealized. But this fact is also capable of misleading us. We might
suppose that the ancients were really worshiping only themselves; that
they were, like Narcissus, beholding their own image in a pool, so
that their worship was *anthropocentric* (man-centered) rather than
theocentric (god-centered). We are in danger of assuming that they
were simply constructing the god in their own image. This is not
necessarily so. The gods must always be symbolized in one form or
another. To give them a human form is one way of doing this, technically called *anthropomorphism* (from the Greek *anthropos*, a man,
and *morphē*, form). People of certain temperaments and within certain types of culture seem to be more inclined to it than are others.
It is, however, more noticeable in others than in oneself, and those
who affect to despise it are sometimes conspicuous for their addiction
to it. A German once said an Englishman's idea of God is an Englishman twelve feet tall. Such disparagement of anthropomorphism occurred in the ancient world, too. The Celts, for instance, despised
Greek practice in this matter, preferring to use animals and other such
symbols. The Egyptians favored more abstract and stylized symbols,
among which a well-known example is the solar disk, a symbol of Rā,
the sun-god.

Professor C. S. Lewis tells of an Oxford undergraduate he knew
who, priggishly despising the conventional images of God, thought he

was overcoming anthropomorphism by thinking of the Deity as infinite vapor or smoke. Of course even the bearded-old-man image can be a better symbol of Deity than ever could be the image, even if this were psychologically possible, of an unlimited smog.

The Incoherence of Polytheism

What is really characteristic of all polytheism, however, is not the worship of idols or humanity or forests or stars; it is, rather, the worship of innumerable *powers* that confront and affect us. The powers are held to be valuable in themselves; that is why they are to be worshiped. But the values conflict. The gods do not cooperate, so you have to play them off against each other. Suppose you want rain. You know of two gods, the dry-god who sends drought and the wet-god who sends rain. You do not suppose that you can just pray to the wet-god to get busy, and simply ignore the dry-god. If you do so, the latter may be offended, so that no matter how hard the wet-god tries to oblige you, the dry-god will do his best to wither everything. Because both gods are powerful you must take both into consideration, begging the wet-god to be generous and beseeching the dry-god to stay his hand.

From all this it becomes obvious that polytheism entails a good deal of incoherence. How are the gods related to each other? The universe, it would seem, is created and sustained by a conglomeration of deities whose interests do not always coincide and whose respective powers may therefore war against each other; whose wills are, moreover, capricious and whose actions are therefore unpredictable. Polytheism is indeed so unsatisfactory that intellectuals in polytheistic societies tend to reach a point at which they express themselves in a way that suggests *monotheism* (belief in one god). Cicero speaks of nature, for instance, as a divinity that appears under many guises; as the earth she is called Ceres; as the sea her name is Neptune; and so forth. In Babylonia, the god Marduk was a high god who for long had great prestige; so we read that Ninib is the Marduk of might, Zamama the Marduk of battle, Adad the Marduk of rain. An ancient Hindu poet wrote perhaps the most striking of all lines upon this theme:

> They call him Indra, Mitra, Varuna, Agni,
> And he is heavenly noble-winged Garutman.
> To what is One, sages give many a title.
> They call it Agni, Varuna, Matarisvan.

These are the reflections of thinkers seeing beyond the popular religion of their day. Their notion is really quite an abstract, theoretical one, having little to do with living religion in a polytheistic society. But it is not only the intellectuals who feel dissatisfied with polytheism: its incoherence troubles all who think at all. It would appear that one of the most important reasons for this is its failure to answer certain fundamental questions. For instance, suppose that I, seeing terrible wrongs done all around me, cry out indignantly to heaven, "Is there no justice in the universe?" It could hardly seem very satisfactory to me to be told there was indeed a most splendid goddess of that name, a really very fine deity, and if only she hadn't been sick of late, or been bullied into silence by her husband or some other overbearing divinity, she would have had quite a lot to say. I should be inclined to complain, "Such a goddess is of no use unless she is there all the time. The rain-god may get lazy and the wind-god may get a little too lively from time to time; but if the goddess Justice ever takes a vacation or even goes to sleep for half an hour, she might as well not be there at all. Either you have a universe that is fundamentally controlled according to just principles, or else it is not so controlled, and so long as you have this goddess Justice behaving as she is, it certainly cannot be said that the universe is controlled by her." In other words, it becomes clear that certain deities, in order to be what they claim to be, must have a degree of power and authority and control such as is not customary in a pantheon. You can feel satisfied with a little rain or a little wind or even a little good fortune; but you cannot really ever feel satisfied with a little justice or a little accuracy or a little goodness. If the universe is partly or occasionally controlled by Justice and partly or occasionally runs wild, then it is in principle uncontrolled; it is *not* subject to Justice. It will not do to have parts of the universe just and other parts unjust. To suggest this is to be reminded of the story of the excessively polite English curate who, breakfasting with his bishop, was observed by the latter to be eating his egg with evident reluctance; upon which the bishop inquired if the egg were all right, only to receive the timid curate's reply, "Oh yes, my Lord, parts of it are excellent." Of course parts of an egg cannot be good while others are bad — if any of the egg is bad it is a bad egg. So if the universe is only partly or occasionally orderly and just, then it must be called a disorderly and unjust universe. A polytheistic universe is in fact chaotic.

Henotheism

Because of the intellectual unsatisfactoriness of polytheism, certain tendencies arise that are to be noted. There is a strong tendency in all polytheistic societies to recognize and exalt one of the gods above the others, a high god, a chief deity, a father of the gods. Such, for instance, was Father Zeus of the Greeks — Zeus Pater, whose name has affinities with that of the Hindu sky-god, Dyaush Pitar.

Such a high god does not absolutely control or rule the other gods: a pantheon is too anarchical for that. The high god may be, rather, a sort of president, having a certain pre-eminence over the other gods, for some reason that is often fairly vague — he is older, perhaps, or stronger. Being somehow or other just a little more powerful than the other gods, he naturally merits an extra large share of the respect that it is wise to give all deities, whether you happen to like them or not. But sometimes this exaltation of one deity over the others goes further. The highest national aspirations of a people may be objectified in one god, and where national consciousness is very strong and vigorous the national god may acquire a prestige so great that all the rest of the pantheon is overshadowed. This god becomes the personification of the national spirit of a nationalistic people. When this happens, the people have reached what may be called *henotheism* (from the Greek *henos*, one, and *theos*, a god), which means that they worship one god, while also recognizing the existence of other deities, possibly enemies or rivals. The Hebrews passed through such a stage in their religious development. The first of the traditional ten commandments does not say, "thou shalt have no other gods," but "thou shalt have no other gods before (i.e., above) me." A henotheist does not deny the reality of foreign deities, but he believes or hopes his own will triumph over all others.

Kathenotheism

Sometimes there is a different tendency. As the polytheist goes around the pantheon, flitting from one god to another, he may worship each god in turn as if, at any rate for the duration of the worship, there were no other god in the universe. This may be called *kathenotheism*, that is, the worship of one god *at a time*. This proceeding is not so absurd as it may sound. Despairing of making sense of the pantheon, the devotee takes each god singly and treats him *as if* he were the only god in the universe. Examples of this are to be found in the Vedic literature of ancient India, and no doubt it is a common attitude among the *bhaktas* of India, whose worship (*bhakti*) is a warm, personal devotion to various gods and may range from a morally lofty relationship to a very degraded sort of cult. The god Krishna, for instance, as he appears in the *Bhagavad-gita*, is an edifying deity in many ways, while his namesake in the *Puranas* is a lascivious rogue who wanders around the countryside having affairs with dairymaids. Polytheism is at every stage capable of exhibiting itself in every conceivable guise, because every notion conceivable to the human mind is capable of being deified.

DISCUSSION ON CHAPTER 6

1. "Polytheists do not take their gods seriously." Explain and discuss this judgment.

2. If you were a polytheist, on what principles would you select the gods you would worship?

3. Distinguish polytheism, kathenotheism, and henotheism.

7

Pantheism

Distinction Between the Natural and the Supernatural

We have seen that there is a strong tendency for polytheism to develop into henotheism; thence it develops into monotheism. Throughout this line of development there is usually an implied distinction between the natural and the supernatural. The natural world is invaded by supernatural powers, but these are never naturalized. They pertain to The Beyond; they are The Other. God (or a particular god in a pantheon) is the Creator and Preserver of the Universe. Whatever may be attributed to Him in power or goodness or glory, He is other than the universe we call "natural." He belongs to, or is, another realm. The natural universe is in itself prosy, dull and lifeless; it has no value in itself. It acquires value, however, by deriving it from the gods who infuse life and beauty and goodness into it. The universe more or less successfully holds what is infused into it by the gods, as my car battery more or less successfully holds a charge. But without this charge, this infusion from a supernatural powerhouse, the universe has no value. On one view it has not even any existence, apart from what is bestowed on it. In other words, it is dependent on God's (or the gods') creating and sustaining it, and giving it those qualities that we account, or recognize to be, intrinsically valuable. Such is one view.

The Ground of Pantheism

But there is another possibility. We only know fragments of the universe, and we are ourselves, each of us, a very small fragment of it. The whole universe, greater than any part of it, *is* God. This is *pantheism* (from the Greek *pantos*, all, and *theos*, a god), the doctrine that God is the totality of all existent things, and that these in their totality are God. Physical nature is therefore part of this God that is the whole universe; so also, on the pantheistic view, I am part of God. (Those who affirm that I am a spark of the divine fire or ray of the divine light are pantheists.) If you were to be unpleasant enough to point out that it is surely odd for even a part of God to have as

much trouble as I have in giving up smoking, I might reply panthe-
istically that it is not odd at all, because the partial view of the whole
is bound to be confused and deceptive; to the extent that it falls
short of the whole, it falls short of having meaning. You might play
me three notes from Beethoven's *Fifth*, knowing that I considered this
symphony the most beautiful on earth. But you would not find that
I was enraptured by your three notes. I might very well shrug my
shoulders at them, because, though part of the most perfect symphony,
they would mean nothing to me in themselves. So in order to understand the nature and beauty and goodness of the universe, and especially its orderliness and perfection, I must try to consider the
universe in its totality. This is our task as human beings, as worshipers of the universe: to attune ourselves to the nature of the whole.
A man is both wise and good to the extent that he succeeds in this
enterprise.

The Appeal of Pantheism

Pantheism has appealed to both mystics and thinkers of various
kinds. It tends to appeal to certain mystics, because these claim to
experience a oneness with God. They have less sense of a need for
reconciliation to God than of the importance of the realization that
they are part of God. A Japanese poet expresses the pantheistic outlook in Shinto (the Japanese national religion) when he writes that
Japan is not a land where men need pray: it is itself divine. The intellectual appeal of pantheism lies chiefly in its apparent "neatness" and
simplicity. It disposes of the notion of a supernatural realm while
seeming at the same time to account for the religious impulse. It accounts for evil by explaining it as a mere appearance; it is a shortcom-
ing, an inadequacy. Nothing is evil except in the sense that it is
incomplete, and in this sense everything is evil except the whole universe, which is God. Likewise, nobody can have an evil motive, except
in the sense that all motives are more or less evil because they are more
or less ignorant, and ignorance is lack of complete knowledge. Crimes
are committed because of the criminal's insufficient grasp of reality.
There is no need to look beyond the universe for the source of the
values we worship: the universe *is* this.

Much primitive thought is pantheistic in tendency. Perhaps pantheism was the earliest philosophical expression of religion. Many of
the Greek thinkers before Socrates, for instance, were pantheistic in
their outlook. They regarded the universe as a living and breathing
whole of which we are parts. The Stoics were also pantheists: they
regarded God as the universal fire, warm fluid, or ether, which is also
universal mind or reason. It is not easy to make sense of Stoic teaching
on this point, because it is very ambiguous: the "universal fire" pene-
trates all things and at certain cosmic epochs reabsorbs them all into

itself. If it be asked whether the "universal fire" (God?) is unchangeable, again the answer is difficult, because in a sense there is no change
in the universe, for everything is determined; yet in another sense
it is just the lack of immutability that makes "universal fire" a good
metaphor for the Stoic God. This vagueness in Stoic pantheism may
be seen in the famous *Meditations* of Marcus Aurelius.

Classic Expression of Pantheism in India

Pantheism received classic expression in India, particularly in the
Upanishads, which made possible its popularization by later generations of Hindus and Buddhists. According to the Indian sages, the
world of ordinary experience is an illusion, because it is full of novelty
and spatial diversity, while in the "whole" there can be neither of
these. At the most, therefore, what we ordinarily see is a sort of
attenuated reality: the Hindus call it *maya*, a term used in contrast
to *Brahman*, which is supposed to signify reality or, it might be said,
God. Neither of these terms can be satisfactorily defined. But it
should be noted that when God is accounted the whole of reality,
changeless and undiversified, and the whole of reality is identified with
God, certain consequences follow; for instance, that anything which
changes or is diversified is to this extent unreal. The moral law of
karma, which may be conveniently expressed in the phrase "you reap
what you sow," also springs from a pantheistic interpretation of the
universe. By reason of this inexorable law or principle, I am subject
to rebirth in a chain of incarnations (*samsara*) before being liberated
from the miserable effects of *maya*, and from my point of view within
maya this process may take billions of years. *Brahman* may also be
realized by techniques such as the five methods of *yoga*. The Yoga
Sutras of the Hindu mystic Patanjali are ancient, dating from at least
300 B.C., possibly very much earlier. In such techniques, fasting and
sexual abstinence play an important part, as well as certain prescribed
bodily postures and breath-control (*pranayama*). Perhaps the greatest
classical exponent of the pantheistic element in Hinduism is Sankara,
a Hindu mystic who flourished about 800 A.D. His pantheism is
thoroughly monistic; that is, it entirely excludes from reality all
beings other than *Brahman*. Sankara perfected the Vedanta philosophy.

Pantheism in the Western Tradition

In spite of the spread of Christianity in Europe, pantheistic thinking manifested itself in various ways. The medieval philosopher John
Scotus Erigena, for instance, a contemporary or near-contemporary
of Sankara, outlined a system that is, in terms of the intellectual
climate of Europe at any rate, unmistakably pantheistic. In later
medieval European thought this was, for various historical reasons,

rare, though some of the mystics use language that suggests pantheism. It should be noted that the word *mystic* is derived from the Greek verb *muein,* "to be silent" — the root *mu* is in our modern slang "mum" used to denote secrecy or silence. The experience of the mystic is supposed to be such that it is incommunicable — beyond words. Mystics are exceptional people, akin to poets rather than thinkers, so that it is one thing for a mystic to talk *as if* he were a pantheist, and another thing for a thinker to propound a pantheistic view.

Spinozism

Spinoza (1632–1677) produced probably the most complete pantheistic system. Consciously critical of the classical doctrine of God with which he was familiar (he was a Jew by birth), Spinoza devised a system that would not make God and the world external to each other. Extension in space — the physical aspect of reality — is a dimension of God. The universe is a "necessary whole." It must be what it is. Its parts, therefore, are also necessary; they are modifications of the whole, as the properties of a triangle (e.g., the property that the sum of its angles must always be 180 degrees) are "contained" in the "essence" of the triangle.

Spinoza's system, for all its subtlety, exhibits characteristic difficulties of pantheism. There is no place for any genuine freedom of choice. Even God has no choice: everything that happens happens because of the nature of God, which is as it is of necessity, so that nothing could happen otherwise than as it does happen. Though pantheists in the West have usually tried to avoid the conclusions drawn and stressed by their oriental counterparts about the unreality of the seeming contrasts within the whole (i.e., within God), there can really be no place in any pantheism for a distinction between what is or pertains to God and what is not or does not pertain to God. If we asked, "But surely there must be more of God in the prophet Amos than in a stick of candy?" the pantheist would have difficulty in agreeing. From his point of view it would be a little like saying there is more of me in my spine than there is in my thighs, or more of me in my nerves than in my blood. He would point out that my body must be considered as a whole. All its parts belong to it — my fingernails as well as my stomach; my lungs as much as my brain. So it is always difficult for the pantheist to make judgments about the relative value of the various parts of the whole.

The Importance of Pantheism in the History of Thought

Lucan (39–65 A.D.) succinctly expresses the essence of all pantheism when he asks, "Has God any dwelling-place save earth and sea, the air of heaven and virtuous hearts? Why seek Deity any further?" He answers himself in the words, "Whatever we see is God and wherever we go." In a thoroughgoing pantheism it is impossible to sing "Nearer, my God, to Thee," because you are already as near as you can get, being inside. Whether a pantheist's God (the totality of things) bears any relation at all to what is meant by God in, say, the Bible, is a question that may be deferred. The two conceptions of God would appear to be entirely different and radically incompatible.

Pantheistic systems, dull as they appear to those whose convictions exclude them, are attractive to many who for one reason or another are disinclined to embrace atheism, yet have no genuine faith in a transcendent God, and especially no sense of the need for reconciliation to The Other. Pantheism is of the greatest importance in the history of religious philosophy. Unlike polytheism, which is of historical rather than philosophical interest, pantheism is a philosophical theory about God rather than a living religion. Nevertheless, it is a theory that has exercised a profound influence on certain important religions, notably Hinduism and Buddhism. The latter, cradled in India, spread to the Far East, where it became very influential as an internationalist rival to the old national faiths such as Confucianism and Shinto. Many Hindu and Buddhist ideas are to be found in a westernized form in various American sects, some of which are pantheistic in principle. Pantheistic notions have also gained some access to American thought about God in other ways. Only brief indications have been given in this chapter of the general nature and tendencies of pantheism. We shall see later how it is related to deism and theism.

DISCUSSION ON CHAPTER 7

1. Consider examples of pantheistic attitudes that you can detect in poetry and other general literature.

2. Consider whether it is impossible to deny that a pantheistic God exists.

3. Discuss what seem to you to be the merits and demerits of pantheism as an explanation of the universe and as a solution to what you take to be the most important religious problems.

8

Humanism

Is Man Lord of All?

It would not be difficult to make a case for the superiority of mankind over all the rest of the universe. Man's character and intelligence
have enabled him to bring great areas of nature under his control.
Among other animals, his only possible rivals are so far behind him
in the qualities needed for the leadership he enjoys that it is not
usually very difficult for man to outwit them, even in circumstances
unfavorable to him; and it is easy for him, in other circumstances, to
gain almost complete dominion over them. In certain fields, say,
chemistry and engineering, man's accomplishments in the past century have been staggering. Much remains for him to do; but in
principle it would appear that he should be able to bring more and
more of nature under his subjection.

Comte

Considerations such as these have led many to the view that attained one of its classic expressions in Auguste Comte (1798–1857),
that humanity is *le grand être,* that is, the Supreme Being, God. This
French thinker, the founder of modern sociology, felt that all speculation about the nature of "ultimate reality" was futile. Our knowledge
is confined to the knowledge we obtain through the "positive" sciences (hence his view was called positivism); nevertheless, we recognize that it is humanity that attains this knowledge, and reverence is
therefore due to humanity. Altruistic endeavors to better man's lot
are always good; so also is all cultivation of reverence for human
personality. Only in humanity is there to be found the aspiration to
a finer and loftier way of life and a more perfect society. There is
something sacrosanct about man, separating him from all other
beings, animate and inanimate.

Feuerbach

Ludwig Feuerbach (1804–1872) said of his own philosophy that
it "has for its principle, not the Substance of Spinoza, not the *ego*

62

of Kant and Fichte, not the Absolute Identity of Schelling, not the Absolute Mind of Hegel, in short, no abstract, merely conceptional being, but a *real* being, the true *Ens realissimum* [1] — man." Feuerbach is often accounted an atheist; but it is only the attributes of a God such as the Biblical God that he denies. He repudiates the notion of a divine transcendence. But he reveres a principle in man — reveres it so much that it must surely be regarded as his God. Men have worshiped almost everything imaginable, and that they should worship a principle in their own nature is not remarkable. Feuerbach may be accounted, like Comte, a classical exponent of humanism as a religious philosophy. "Man," he says, "has his highest being, his God, in himself; not in himself as an individual, but in his essential nature, his species." This is the basic humanistic position.

The Ground of Humanism

There is really nothing very novel in the humanist's notion. Its ancestry is a long one in the history of thought; but it was after Comte that it came to be accepted by large numbers of people. In America, humanism as a religious philosophy has been exceedingly influential: God is to be found, not in any reality beyond man, but in man's highest social experiences. John Dewey, who has defined God as "the unity of all ideal ends arousing us to desire and actions," is perhaps the best-known exponent of religious humanism in this country. But there are many others, and in general they regard God as an active relation between the ideal and the actual; that is, religion is concerned with the actual, the existent, on the one hand, and also, on the other hand, with the ideal: it is a kind of bridge between the two.

All groups who very highly exalt humanity as such, or human potentialities, are likely to be sympathetic to humanism as a religious philosophy. Most Christians would be sympathetic to it in the sense that they would agree that human values are important: the First Epistle of St. John reminds us that since nobody has seen God with physical eyes, it would be a good idea, if we wanted to love God, to begin with the man next door whom we *have* seen. But Christians and others who believe in a God such as the Biblical one would entirely repudiate the presuppositions of humanism as a religious philosophy, together with the notion that humanity can save itself. This, which is the essence of all forms of humanism strictly so called, would be accounted by all Christians "godlessness." The Marxists banished the Biblical God, putting in His place an idealistic conception of human society to be realized by a human "proletariat." With Marxism have been associated certain special economic and political theories at variance with those of most American humanists;

[1] "most real being."

but Marxism, as a religion, is founded on notions very similar, in principle, to the presuppositions of American humanism. It is a notion peculiar to humanism, taken seriously as a religion or a religious philosophy, that human experience can be understood without going beyond it. It is this that would be questioned by pantheists as well as by theists. Theists are certainly not alone in taking the view that the confidence in humanity felt by many humanists in the nineteenth century has been shown to be unwarranted by more recent events. Even after the First World War there were still many who thought humanity was now on its way to discovering a man-made Utopia. Human progress, they felt, was assured, now that the "war to end all war" was over. They tended to look upon war as though it were a sort of sociological ailment that humanity would learn to cure as it had learned to cure certain physiological diseases and was learning to cure others. Christians who understood the evil power and terrible consequences of sin, as a wrong relationship of humanity to God its Creator, never could and never did share that sort of optimism about humanity's ability to save itself. On their view, real progress toward the essential betterment of humanity could be attained only by reconciliation to The Other that is beyond humanity and the Source of whatever good humanity can ever hope to achieve.

The Place of Man in the Universe

It is true that man's superiority to the lower animals in intelligence and skill is in some ways very striking. Not even our nearest simian relatives, the higher apes, have the power of speech. They communicate their emotions, of course, but none of the noises they make have been shown to be denotative; that is, they are not even the most rudimentary words. The best they can do is to utter sounds equivalent to our "yum, yum" at the sight of food. They cannot even say anything as reflective as "peanuts today, huh?" Compared with the extremely complicated symbolism of civilized human language, or even with what the lowest human savage can. do, the "language" of the highest apes is far nearer the growl of a dog than human language even at its most primitive, emotive level. But does man's high development in itself ensure his unaided control of the universe? No less impressive than man's intellectual and linguistic superiority over his simian ancestors is his puniness in the universe. The diminutiveness of his size is unimportant in itself. But it does lead us to reflect upon certain facts. Man is the inhabitant of one of the planets that makes its orbit around one of the innumerable stars in an unthinkably vast universe. One small mishap (small, that is, in terms of the universe) could scatter our little *parvenu* planet to pieces and obliterate our whole civilization. We are also increasingly afraid that our own technological progress with bombs and the like, coupled with our relatively retarded moral and social development, may cause us to obliterate ourselves by an explosion of our own making. Our lives are short, too. The expectation of life of a newborn baby is between sixty and seventy — greater than it was a century ago, and probably less than it will be a century hence. It is possible that, if humanity survives its own follies long enough, medical advances, especially in the elimination of the causes of death, may double or treble the present longevity. But even so it would still be a mere butterfly existence — here today and gone tomorrow. Even if we could live a thousand years it would still be a butterfly existence in terms of the universe. The human race itself is a comparative newcomer to that universe. Above all, our moral and even our emotional growth are by no means commensurate with our technical achievements. Our cities are larger and our transportation faster than they were a hundred years ago; but our prisons and our mental hospitals and our wars have all "progressed" proportionately.

Contemporary achievements in the exploration of space look impressive beside those of Columbus. It may not be long before a trip to Venus becomes almost as unremarkable as a trip to Venice. Technological progress may make even the colonization of other planets no more formidable a challenge than was, to the first settlers in this country, the development of America. What tends to be forgotten is that even interstellar travel would not make man one whit less abjectly dependent on the bounty of nature than were those no less enterprising individuals who made possible the modern development of Los Angeles abjectly dependent on the Colorado River, whose bounty they harnessed that millions of people might live in comfort in a desert. What man can now do with nuclear energy is alarming; more awesome still is his helplessness in face of even an unsplit atom.

In short, if we look at the whole picture of man instead of only one side of it, we shall find that Pascal was right when he spoke of man's "greatness and wretchedness." Man is magnificent, but pathetic; wonderful, but ridiculous; great, but miserable. There would seem to be almost no limit to either his grandeur or his folly. If this is true, it would seem that the humanist, though in a sense on the right track, has not found the right object. Human values are indeed great, but their greatness is precarious and anything other than independent. Man appears to be the bearer of values which he, far from creating, is not even very good at sustaining.

The Mystery of Human Personality

Idealized human values can be an incentive to great moral effort, and humanism as a religious philosophy can evoke genuine devotion.

But in view of what we have already considered in the first part of this book, it is questionable whether humanism really accounts for even what we find in humanity. It inspires the worship of human personality for its own sake, and the paradox about human personality is that the more self-consciously you try to cultivate it, the less personality you have; the people who have the strongest and most interesting personalities are those who seldom if ever think about the question. When you try to "develop" personality, you usually become an insufferable bore. You end up with an empty shell, a glossy lifelessness, while others, who have not given the matter a moment's reflection, are mysteriously "on fire." It may be that the source of their power is not in themselves, nor in humanity. Those who lastingly magnetize their fellow men do so because they have drawn something into themselves from beyond humanity; something that humanity sorely needs and cannot produce by itself.

DISCUSSION ON CHAPTER 8

1. "Face to face with the universe, man will be the sole evidence of his audacious dreams of divinity, since the God he vainly sought was himself." (Georges Clemenceau) Discuss.

2. Consider the affirmation of Confucius that true goodness springs from a man's own heart.

3. Consider the significance of Pascal's phrase, "the greatness and the wretchedness of man."

9

Impersonal Idealism

The Idea of the Good

"I do not believe in God; but I believe in The Good." This view has a noble lineage in the history of thought: it goes back to Plato. Plato's view of the nature of God is ambiguous; but it is characteristic of some of his thought on the subject and of that of others who have done their thinking on similar lines, that is, that the highest values must be impersonal. Personality, individuality, subjectivity, have no value of the same rank as have objective ideas. God must be, therefore, on this view, not a personal consciousness or mind or life, but, rather, an impersonal idea or law or order or principle that permeates and vivifies the whole universe, being to this as the sun is to the earth. Those who hold this view, whether among the ancients or in more recent times, deify a system or hierarchy of moral values (for instance, justice) which are, they claim, eternal principles. The universe depends on and "hangs together" by the moral order that is its very essence. All my strivings after righteousness, all the noble ideals you cherish, spring from this fundamental moral principle.

Impersonal idealism has always been a philosopher's religion rather than anyone else's. It is an intellectualistic view. Moreover, it is open to some very serious criticism even within its own limits. The impersonal idealist believes in the objectivity of a certain moral order. What is the relation between this moral order and the world of fact, the empirical world? An impersonal idealism has always some difficulty in explaining why there should be such a world of fact at all. It tends to keep the two worlds, the world of values and the world of facts, in two separate compartments because it finds such difficulty in reconciling them. To the extent that it does fail in this, its metaphysical postulates cannot be regarded as satisfactory.

Teleology

In common with those who believe in the Biblical God, the impersonal idealist is confident that the universe is essentially teleological. He believes there is *telos* (purpose) "at its core." This raises at once

67

the problem of evil, which may be crudely put in questions such as: "Then why should there be earthquakes?" A child is born without legs or arms, totally blind yet with an apparent determination to live. Its parents are normal people. They have previous children who are in all respects normal. Why, they ask, should such a child be born to them? What purpose can it possibly serve? The answer to such questions is difficult, indeed, for the believer in the Biblical God; for the impersonal idealist it is really impossible, except by somehow explaining away the evil. For if the source of the universe is a moral principle, an impersonal moral order, it is surely to be expected to work "automatically." What is there to stop it? So you must invent some other principle to stop it, to resist it, in order that you may account for evil.

It should be noted at this point that to deny there is any such "essential order" or "essential purpose" in the universe eliminates the problem of evil, but confronts one instead with the reverse problem, the problem of the good. For then one has to explain why anything should ever exhibit order or purpose. It is certainly as puzzling, to say the least, to find order and purpose in a universe that is supposed to be purposeless as it is to find lack of purpose in one that is supposed to be purposeful. On this much more will be said later.

Objection to Impersonal Idealism

Perhaps the most obvious objection to impersonal idealism is that it is very difficult to see how any abstract principle could generate the values we encounter in personal experience. Among the values we most highly prize, for instance, are love, friendship and courage. But is it conceivable that the unique love that a particular individual has for another particular individual has an abstract principle as its source? Whatever else it is I feel toward my wife, my mother or my son, it surely is not something whose source could be an impersonal principle. One person's brave action on the battlefield and another's brave rescue work in a burning building — these are not just two instances of courage, imperfectly copied from a perfect pattern of courage which, unlike them, is free of all contaminations with the personal. No, surely they are, rather, nothing if not personal acts: take away the personal quality from the acts and the acts have no longer their character. I value Tom's kindness and I value Bob's kindness; but the idea of kindness itself has no value for me to compare with anybody's kindness. So if such values as I find in Tom and Bob and others have any common source, it would seem that this source would have to be personal.

Can the Impersonal Be the Ground of Personal Values?

The reason why impersonal idealists de-personalize Deity is that they think personality is too low a quality to be attributed to the Absolute. Personality seems to imply shortcomings, defects, angularities. My personality may perhaps endear me to some people; but it is what makes me different, and therefore odd. Can God be odd? Impersonal idealists tend to look upon personality as one looks upon birthmarks or other peculiarities. They regard God as the Universal which is particularized in this or that case, and plainly you cannot have a Universal Peculiarity, so you must try to eliminate all the peculiarities in your quest for a common source. A de-personalized Deity, however, lacks just that quality that gives life to every action. The idea of Perfect Fatherhood never helped any orphan; in some cases perhaps even a drunken oaf of a father might be better. Best of all, of course, would be a Perfect Father, and this is just what an impersonal idealism cannot offer.

DISCUSSION ON CHAPTER 9

1. Consider the distinction between "value" and "fact."

2. Discuss the idea of personality with reference to God.

3. Consider the presuppositions of impersonal idealism.

10

Dualism

Zoroastrianism

In the Zoroastrian religion the Good God, Ahura Mazda, is opposed by the Evil Spirit, Angra Mainyu, who in later times came to be called Shaitin (Satan). Zoroaster's life is obscure. According to Iranian tradition he was born in 660 B.C. The beliefs he held are likewise not clear, but he was probably a monotheist. His strong emphasis on the fundamental cleavage, in nature and man, between good and evil, right and wrong, is not unfamiliar to Jews or Christians, who have a similar theme running through their sacred literature. It seems that Zoroaster believed that Ahura Mazda could not but triumph in the end. There was war between him and his enemy, and this war is carried into the heart of every man, so that every man must decide who is to be the victor on his own terrain; but in the end there is to be a reckoning. For the first time in the known history of the religions of the world we find the idea of a general resurrection, at which time the present world order will come to a close. The good, who have been industrious, thrifty, kindly and honest, and the evil, who have been the reverse, will be subjected to the Ordeal of Fire and Molten Metal. But the good will pass unharmed through the fire and to them the molten metal will be as gentle as milk, while the evil, having no such natural resistance, will reveal their unrighteousness by the terrible burns they sustain.

In later developments of this religion, however, the Evil Spirit is represented as much more on an equal footing with the Good God. Angra Mainyu coexisted with Ahura Mazda from the beginning. Indeed, according to some of the later portions of the Avesta (the Zoroastrian Bible), the world was jointly created by the Good God and the Bad God. That is why it is as it is. Ahura Mazda is responsible for creating all the good things to be found in Iran. Beautiful are all his works. But alas, for every good thing he created, his evil counterpart created a bad thing. Snakes, locusts, ants and the like — these are the work of Angra Mainyu; so also, of course, are all vices. This Evil God created no fewer than 99,999 diseases, and, to crown his wicked enterprise, he created death itself. This is a classic expression of the view known to historians of religion as dualism.

Other Forms of Dualism

Dualism may, of course, take other forms. Another Iranian, called Mani (215–276 A.D.) evolved a philosophical system whose elements were drawn from Buddhism, Christianity, and Gnosticism, as well as from Zoroaster, and which taught a dualism of spirit and matter. The soul of man is good, but it is in bondage to the vile matter that is his body. Only by denying the lusts of the flesh can men overcome evil and regain the good. The Manichaeans were for a time very numerous and, being organized like a religion, rivaled Christianity. Such dualism has reappeared later alongside of Christianity — in the Paulicians and the Bogomils in the East, for instance, and in the Cathari (or Albigenses) in the West who, in the twelfth century, were so active and successful that in Southern France it looked as though they might overthrow the Christian Church. In modern times an ancient form of dualism has reappeared in the philosophical presuppositions of Mary Morse Baker Eddy's "Christian Science." We shall see presently how the dualism breaks down.

The Plausibility of Dualism

Whatever may be said against dualistic systems, they often seem to give a very plausible account of what is so obvious in the world around us, the presence of both good and evil, purpose and lack of purpose, order and disorder. Dualism requires one to shut one's eyes to neither side of the picture. We have seen in the last chapter how difficult it is for an impersonal idealism to deal with the problem of evil. A thoroughgoing dualism, with two Gods, one the creator of good things and the other the creator of evil ones, provides a simple solution to both the problem of evil and the problem of the good. Its wide appeal is understandable.

The Breakdown of Dualism

A full-blown dualism must, however, give the Good God and the Bad God mutual independence, so that neither may in any sense be said to have created the other. It must also accept the prospect of eternal warfare between the two Gods, or else leave it an open question which is to be the victor. Probably few Zoroastrians were prepared to draw any such consequences. While it was believed that the war between Ahura Mazda and his adversary was a real war, it was felt that he was nevertheless bound to win. The angels of the Good God might have to wage frightful battle against the angels of the Bad God, but the ultimate victory of the former was assured. And of course, as soon as you begin to think along such lines as these, you have forsaken your dualism. Much the same tendency for dualism to lose its fundamental character is to be seen in other dualistic systems such as we have mentioned: the status of the dark side of the picture comes to be questioned. In a spirit–matter dualism the reality of matter is eventually denied, so that belief in its existence comes to be regarded as a mistake, an "error of mortal mind" as the Christian Scientists would say. That is why what sets out as a dualism often ends up as an uncompromising monism: the universe appeared to be divided in two, and is then seen to consist of only one of the two supposed parts. For to the qualities of goodness and spirituality and beauty that may be attributed to the one side comes to be added the quality of reality, while in the other column of evil, fleshy ugliness, is gradually put the quality of unreality or appearance.

Indeed, it would seem that as soon as we so divide the universe into two parts or sides, we establish the superiority of one over the other. If one is better than the other, why have the other at all? It would seem that it *ought* to be discarded. The coexistence of two partners in an eternal St. George-and-the-Dragon sort of partnership is inherently difficult to explain. The notion may account for what you see in the world around you, but it hardly explains itself. It is an arbitrary notion, and the list of principles put in the "good" and "bad" columns of a dualistic philosophy is usually no less arbitrary. The Pythagoreans had two such columns: in the good one they listed light, harmony, unity and the male principle, while they put the female principle in the other column, with darkness, discord and plurality. If you were a dualist living in Greenland you would presumably put warmth in the good column; but if you lived in Louisiana you might very well put it in the bad.

Dualism is in fact simply a special form of polytheism. It certainly *describes* very well the universe as this presents itself in our ordinary experience. But as an *explanation* of the prevailing state of affairs it is really as unsatisfactory as any other form of polytheism.

DISCUSSION ON CHAPTER 10

1.   *Two urns by Jove's high throne have ever stood,*
        The source of evil, one, and one of good. (Homer)

    Consider dualism as a solution of the problem to which attention is called in these lines.

2. "Evil perpetually tends to disappear." (Herbert Spencer) Discuss.

3. Distinguish between the metaphysical view that good and evil are the outcome of two equally ultimate first causes, and the doctrine that mind is good and matter is bad.

11

Agnosticism

Etymology of "Agnostic"

It was T. H. Huxley (grandfather of Aldous) who coined the word "agnostic" to express his own state of mind. In his reading he had learned, he tells us, about the Gnostics, leaders of a school of philosophy or, rather, a widespread tendency in the ancient world toward a certain kind of philosophical and religious thought. The Gnostics differed much among themselves, but they had one thing in common: they claimed a special *gnosis* (that is, knowledge) of divine truth. Generally speaking, they were also, however, dualists who sharply distinguished between the spiritual (good) world and the material (bad) world. Huxley was impressed by the contrast between their attitude and the one he felt to be his own. The Gnostics claimed to know more about God than most people would care to claim. Huxley, however, claimed so much less of such knowledge that he thought the term *a–gnostic* would suit him better. He did not categorically deny the existence of God; but he denied that we have any knowledge of God, who is beyond the realm of human knowledge and definition. If we were to attempt to define God at all, it would have to be as the unknowable source of the known. Such was in fact the view developed by Herbert Spencer (1820–1903) and others.

Agnosticism Not Opposed to the Religious Temper

Now, there is no doubt that many superficially religious people speak too glibly about God. On the other hand, no deeply religious man or woman feels inclined to "pin" attributes on God, because they know that all our human concepts are too limited, too inadequate, for God. How could our puny ideas of goodness and beauty, for instance, even at their best, measure the goodness and beauty of God? Every truly religious person is too humble to pretend that he could possibly know God in the sense that he knows his office or even his town. Such a reverent agnosticism plays a far more important role in religious, especially Christian, thought than is commonly recognized among those who give little attention to such matters.

The great medieval philosophers, the Jewish Moses Maimonides, for instance, and the Christian Thomas Aquinas, were reluctant to affirm any real knowledge of God; it was only with a good deal of caution that they were prepared, as philosophers, to say anything about God's nature. So it must not be supposed that agnosticism is fundamentally opposed to the Christian temper: on the contrary, many thoughtful Christians earnestly pray that there may be more of the agnostic temper in popular religion than there is. For such Christians know the fundamental truth in Tennyson's words: "There lives more faith in honest doubt, believe me, than in half the creeds."

Difficulty of One Type of Agnosticism

Nevertheless, it is one thing to be reverently agnostic about God's nature, another to repudiate all knowledge of Him whatsoever. If we disclaim all knowledge of God, yet say we believe in Him, we are saying, in effect, that we believe in God but do not know whether the God we believe in is good or bad, wise or foolish. We claim to know there is an x but we cannot say more of Him except that He is the source of all that exists. He may be personal or impersonal; He may not care a button for us, or He may be so concerned for our welfare that, as the Bible says, He knows even the number of hairs on our head. To affirm that there is a divine x and yet that it is impossible to predicate anything of Him at all, is surely an intolerable position to hold.

Moreover, though it was fashionable in certain skeptical circles in the nineteenth century to be agnostic, agnosticism is no longer the fashion, having given place to the neo-positivistic contention that all utterances about God are meaningless. And what, indeed, can it mean to say that one believes in the existence of God, though one has no means of knowing whether this God be powerful or powerless, just or unjust, merciful or merciless, or even whether a merciful or a merciless man is the more *like* God? To say that the God one believes in is *completely* unknowable is to imply that He might be a streptococcus. To admit the absurdity of this is to claim to know something about Him — negatively, at any rate. For it is to affirm that whatever else God may be or may not be, He is not a streptococcus. To say even this much is to preclude complete agnosticism. We might go on to say that neither is God that patient, unselfish, holy man that it has been our good fortune to meet in "actual life"; but we might then say that, nevertheless, this very fine man we knew was surely in some respects a little more like God than is a streptococcus. No doubt the distance between God and the fine man is immeasurably greater than even the distance between the fine man and the streptococcus; still, it may be possible to say that the man does resemble God just a little more than does the other organism. Having thus negatively delineated God, we might perhaps go on to show how certain qualities rather than others may be attributed to Him, even though we confess there must always be far more in God that we do not and cannot know.

What is Mystery?

Agnosticism is sometimes commended for its reverence for mystery. But this raises the question of what mystery is. Suppose you were to say to me: "You must enter my room very reverently, because there is something in it and I will not tell you what it is. I trust, however, that you will show due reverence for the Unknown." I should reply that I had no intention whatsoever for showing any such reverence, because the "mystery" might turn out to be a common cat or even just an ashtray from the five-and-ten. If you were to expect me to exhibit a sense of reverence, you would have to show me some reason why I should do so. Suppose, however, that I had formed a very high opinion of your judgment in music, and that you came to me saying: "Come and hear this extraordinary boy play the piano — I have no idea who he is, but he sounds like a prodigy, a real genius." This would be enough to make me listen with respect. But notice that in the case of the boy who was possibly a genius, there was both much I knew and much I did not know. In the case of religious mystery, this principle also holds. A mystery reveals as well as conceals. When we talk about the mystery of God's love, we do not mean that we have no experience of it; we mean, rather, that the experience we have had of it *suggests* much more than has so far been given. We have already seen in an earlier chapter how this could be. The only kind of agnosticism that is to be commended for its reverence for mystery, therefore, is the kind in which mystery is actually perceived, or believed to be perceived. There is no mystery about a divine *x* of whom *nothing* is known. So a thoroughgoing agnostic cannot be reverent for there is nothing for him to be reverent about.

DISCUSSION ON CHAPTER 11

1. "Reason refuseth its homage to a God who can be fully understood." (Tupper) Consider this affirmation with reference to the skeptical element in all profound religion.

2. Consider agnosticism as "suspension of judgment." How does this differ from reverence toward mystery?

3. Discuss what it means to say that doubt is an implicate of faith.

12

Evolutionary Naturalism

Democritus and the Materialist Tradition

Materialism was well known to the ancients. Democritus, who flourished about 400 B.C., held that everything is reducible to atoms of various sizes and shapes. These atoms, he said, were the sum total of reality. The atoms out of which all things are constructed are pieces of solid matter. Ironically, it seems today, Democritus believed these atoms to be unsplittable. The more people learned of physical reality, however, the more difficult it became to uphold the materialist view. It became clear that matter is much more complicated than the earlier philosophers and scientists had thought. Matter has been described, indeed, as "that which scientists are trying to understand." Modern scientists would be much less confident about defining matter than was Democritus or any of the other older materialists.

The Idea of Emergence

For such reasons, it has become unfashionable to call oneself a materialist, as our great-grandfathers might have done. The successors of the old materialists recognize the complexity of nature and see that, far from being a mere collection of atoms, it is a creative process. In the process of creative advance that they see in nature, new properties arise. These new properties, which could hardly have been foreseen until they actually appeared, are called emergents. So those who are in the lineage of the old materialists may be called evolutionary naturalists, because they define God as the tendency that is in nature to support or produce values. For instance, out of "inanimate" nature there *emerges* life. After millions of years there emerges, out of that "mere" life, a consciousness. Whatever lies just ahead of what is actually achieved, plays the part of deity. We worship an ideal that lies ahead of us and is actually destined to become actual; that is, it is in the process of emerging.

Alexander

Such was the view of the British philosopher Samuel Alexander

76

(1859–1938). Alexander distinguished between deity and God. Deity is, on his view, the fact that just beyond any level of evolution, something new is in process of emerging. God is the universe conceived of as having such emergent deities forever "around the corner." Such an evolutionary naturalism resembles in some ways pantheism, in other ways humanism. It resembles pantheism, for God is not *merely* an ideal, but is an objective reality. It resembles humanism because it recognizes something in the human spirit as deity. But it is really different from both, conceiving of nature as ever-developing and actually deity-producing.

Wieman

The American philosopher Henry Nelson Wieman has thought along similar lines. God is, for him, "the growth of meaning and value in the world." Nature has within itself energies that make possible rational and social experience. This experience has likewise within itself the seed of something greater still, and so forth.

The Appeal of Evolutionary Naturalism

The notions of evolutionary naturalism reflect the recognition of modern thinkers that whatever nature is it is more like something living than a bunch of inert atoms; more like energy than mass. There is, however, nothing novel in the notion that nature is alive: this is, in fact, in itself a typically primitive view of the universe. What is modern in the evolutionary naturalist's view is the notion that the universe that is alive is also in process of growth or expansion. Though there is no "supernatural" deity, there is always, however you look at nature, a deity emerging from it. The deity of the little boy is the bigger boy he is to be; the deity of the bigger boy is the man he is becoming. So with nature as a whole. Nature has grown till it has produced man's highest conscious life and mind. But nature's growth is still proceeding: even now something "higher still" is emerging. Something "higher still" always shall be emerging; for such is the nature of the universe that was and is and ever shall be emergent.

It is assumed that progress is always being made by nature in the unfolding of itself so as to cause higher and higher values to emerge within it. There is no concern for values lost in the process of development. One deity dies only to be superseded by another, and the new deity is always better than all its predecessors. Nor need there ever be any regrets. The inevitability of progress in nature is a dogmatic presupposition of the theory. Wherever there appears to be decay, there is renewal, as in the cells of a healthy living body. Man as we know him must gradually become extinct; his place shall be taken by Superman.

Fundamental Objections to Evolutionary Naturalism

An obvious objection to evolutionary naturalism is that there is no explanation of why the growth should take place at all. It conforms to what the physicists say about the expansion of the universe; but it does not tell us why the universe should be an expanding one. Of course it may be pointed out that no theory can account for everything: all theories begin with axioms. Still, the evolutionary naturalist's universe does not only, like Topsy, "just grow"; it has always contained within itself the potentiality of everything that shall be evolved. God is growing, constantly improving. In the distant past He had not realized the values that He realizes now, nor does He now realize the values He shall realize in the remote future. But how can the greater value that is realized now be contained in the lesser value that was realized then? Can the lesser contain the greater?

In Alexander's form of the theory, each new emergent quality is unpredictable; that is, nature is advancing into the unknown. So he avoids the determinism of a pantheistic system such as Spinoza's, which has no place, as we have seen, for genuine freedom. Bertrand Russell has neatly expressed the difficulty this view involves, however, by pointing out that in order to escape from determinism the theory makes the prediction of the next stage of evolution impossible; nevertheless we are assured that, though we cannot tell what it is, it must be deity. This requires a blind faith. The difficulty is akin to the one we noticed in dealing with agnosticism. How can we tell that the next stage in evolution is to be better if we have no means of knowing anything about it? A very arbitrary sort of faith is necessary in order to make the view work.

DISCUSSION ON CHAPTER 12

1. Discuss the concept of a "growing" God.

2. Compare and contrast the following: (a) evolutionary naturalism, (b) pantheism, (c) humanism.

3. Consider Russell's criticism of evolutionary naturalism.

13

Deism

An Alternative to Pantheism

When we were discussing polytheism, we noted the lines of the ancient Hindu poet who saw in the various deities of his religion the manifold expressions of the One: "To what is One, sages give many a title." Long before this notion dawns upon people generally in polytheistic societies, it is recognized by many of their thinkers. But to the question, "What is the One?" there are many possible answers. One of these, pantheism, we have already considered at some length. According to this view, the many gods are to be regarded as but fumbling attempts to express the unity that is the universe. The One is the All, often conceived as impersonal. Since I am a part of the All, I am a part of God, who is therefore indeed near to me.

A very different road, however, may be taken by those who discover that the many gods are but names for the One. They may see the deities as the imperfectly conceived aspects of a divinity which is personal and completely transcendent. On this view, God is not the All. He is the Source of all that is not He. Reigning over the universe which He has created and which He sustains, He takes no interest in it and has no care for it, in the sense in which we generally speak of having a care for something. He is so aloof from the universe that it is impossible for us to form any conception of Him by analogy with any human qualities or values, though because deists believe God to be conscious mind, he may perhaps be said to be in some sense personal. But far from being even like the highest value we know, He is quite unlike any human value whatsoever. Beyond good and evil, He is beyond the categories of human thought. Our goodness is no more like Him than is our badness. But for the fact that deists generally think of God as personal, they regard Him as like the Brahman of Upanishadic Hinduism, the Great Self who is beyond both existence and nonexistence. He is wholly other than His creation, and we cannot by any means communicate with Him, not merely because of the gulf between God and man, which is indeed insuperable, but also because of the radical opposition between God and man. Some deists allow for a kind of supernaturalistic revelation by God to man. Should God choose to reveal Himself, it will be to show that He is quite unlike anything that we might expect. Not only are His ways not our ways; not only are His ways past finding out; they are opposed to our ways. Man has lofty aspirations, and these help him to build gigantic systems; but in the sight of God man's highest aspirations are but vanity. The gulf between God and man is so great that we are fortunate if we even get so far as to discover the immense disparity between Him and us. As for His nature, we cannot hope to get the faintest insight, for God is hidden from us in every way.

Islam

The Moslem conception of Allah has deistic traits. According to Islamic theology, there is nothing at all rational in Allah's enactments, which are quite abitrary. Mohammed was by no means always consistent in his teaching; but in his later days, at any rate, when he had become the militant leader of a new religion, he depicted Allah as a hidden Majesty who acts according to divine ends that are entirely beyond man's understanding. Allah is a pure will, and all that He wills is right because He wills it. So there is really no problem of evil, for what we call evil is not evil in Allah's sight; else He would not will it. Human beings have no freedom of will, and goodness consists in resignation to the will of Allah who has predestined some to love Him and some to hate Him. The latter he rejects; to the former He is compassionate and merciful. Allah has plans of His own, but He does not let men in on them at all. He does not stand at the door of men's hearts, knocking for entrance. Moslems would think it beneath the dignity of Allah to stoop to win man and so pass under what Evelyn Underhill has called "the low lintel of the human heart." Allah is absolute Will. He does not plead or struggle or strive with his creatures. If He breaks in upon them at all, it is with despotic might and power. Allah does not parley or negotiate or woo: He ordains. All this springs from a deistic conception of God.

Forms of Deism

Deism, like pantheism, takes many forms. What is probably best known to historians as deism is a view that became fashionable in the eighteenth century. The men of that age, seeing the universe through the eyes of Galileo and Newton, thought of it as a beautiful, smooth-running machine. But Christianity spoke of "miracles" and of God caring for each one of His children. Many who wished still to believe in God thought they could not accept the notion of a God who *interfered* with His universe. Conceiving of the universe as a perfectly running clock, and God as the perfect clock maker, they thought the notion of God touching His creation was like the notion of the clock maker tinkering with his finished clock. It made God seem trivial, anxious, ridiculous. So the eighteenth-century deists, among whom were many of the English clergy, are said to have politely bowed God out of the universe. They professed to revere Him as the Great Architect, the Supreme Being, the Ancient of Days; but with such a remote deity the religion taught by preachers who had come under this influence was so chilly that an innkeeper is said to have observed that if he served food as cold as Parson served religion he would soon have no customers.

Deism Yesterday and Today

Because of the changed attitude toward the relation between science and religion, deism is now very much less prevalent than it was in the eighteenth century. Nowadays people are disinclined toward the sort of deism that was then so fashionable, and to uphold it now would be fighting the science of your grandfather with the religion of your grandmother. People are now usually disposed either to accept a God who cares for His creation, or else to repudiate the notion of God altogether. Echoes of eighteenth-century deism may still be heard occasionally, however, in those traditions in the religious life of the English-speaking world that escaped the strong reaction against deism that eventually was manifested. Notable among these, perhaps, is Unitarianism, a religious view that is to be found not only among those labeled Unitarians, but also among many others; some Quakers, for example. Because deism happened to be at the peak of its influence at the time of the War of Independence, the deistic tradition has perhaps retained a greater historical interest in America than it has in England or elsewhere; but it is none the less irrelevant to modern thought about both science and religion.

On the other hand, for the religious philosopher, deism is important as the formal "opposite" of pantheism. The challenge of theism, to which we are about to address ourselves, cannot be fully understood without some understanding of both pantheism and deism.

DISCUSSION ON CHAPTER 13

1. Compare and contrast deism and pantheism.

2. "Are not two sparrows sold for a farthing? and not one of them shall fall on the ground without your Father." (Matthew 10:29) Consider this with reference to deism.

3. Consider historical examples of deism and its relevance (if any) to contemporary thought.

14

Theism and Atheism

Pantheism, Deism, and Theism

Theism recognizes, against pantheism, that God transcends the universe, while at the same time, against deism, it recognizes His immanence in the universe. It is not, however, a compromise between pantheism and deism, or a way of moderation between the two extremes these represent. It is, rather, a highly developed and complex view that claims to do justice to both the truth of deism and the truth of pantheism, presenting us with the paradox that God who is, as the deist says, beyond and remote from the universe He has created, is *also*, as pantheism witnesses, nearer to us than life itself. He who transcends the universe is also immanent in it. A hidden God, He reveals Himself to us. So we may know Him though we certainly can never comprehend Him.

The Theistic Position

Theists generally take the view that God expresses Himself in values that are discoverable by man in experience. They differ about many questions, including the extent, if any, to which God may be known apart from His "breaking in" upon us, and the measure in which pure intellectual inquiry may enrich our knowledge of God. But they all agree (a) that God is *at least* personal and *at least* conscious mind, and (b) that He is both beyond the universe and immanent in it.

Christianity Presupposes Theism

Christianity is a religion whose doctrine, in its historic, orthodox form, is a special form of theism, extremely rich and complex. For Christians hold that God penetrated His own creation in a unique way, by taking human flesh in the Person of Jesus Christ, in whom, therefore, God may be seen perfectly revealed to us in terms of our own human nature. Nevertheless, although Christ makes human salvation possible, the gulf between God and man is preserved: even in heaven, where man's individuality is perfectly and fully developed, man never becomes God. That man should become "as God" was Satan's deceitful promise, a means of tempting man to indulge in delusions of self-grandeur that would be his undoing, leading him to misery and ruin. So Christian doctrine, by its elaborate provisions, expresses to the fullest extent both the remoteness and inaccessibility of God, on the one hand, and, on the other, His intimate nearness and abiding presence. In Christianity, theism is presented in its most startling, provocative and dramatic form.

The Relevance of Theism

The appeal of theism cannot be fully appreciated till you have faced the dilemma of having either a God who is so transcendent that He is beyond all human "realities," or else a God who is so near that He is commonplace and even ridiculous. The choice, to the theist, is somewhat like the choice between freezing to death in the open air or suffocating to death in a sealed room. Theism, considered as an alternative to both deism and pantheism, might be said to claim to provide both shelter and ventilation.

The Choice Between Theism and Atheism

It will be convenient for us to take theism as the norm of "belief"; atheism will therefore be the norm of "unbelief." It is not only the historical importance of theism that justifies this procedure. A genuine choice between theism and atheism, which has immense moral implications affecting the whole personality, has intellectual consequences of the greatest importance, affecting at a radical point the whole thinking of the person who has made the choice. This is by no means to say that the other conceptions of God that we have considered are all to be set aside as not to be taken seriously. On the contrary, we must be prepared, in our thinking, to reckon with them all the time. But it is in the choice between theism and atheism that we can best see what is, existentially, a religious choice.

The choice between theism and atheism is serious, for there is apparently conclusive evidence for both sides. Wherever you find evidence of order and purpose in the universe, as you certainly do, there you find evidence that is, *prima facie*, evidence for God. That is, in face of such evidence it is easier to reach an honest conclusion that a supreme Mind is in benevolent control of the universe than to conclude there is no God. On the other hand, wherever you find evidence of disorder and lack of purpose, you find evidence that is, *prima facie*, evidence against God. In face of *this* evidence it is more difficult to conclude that there is a God than to conclude there is not. In all this we are assuming moral sincerity and the absence of intellectual cheating. We must not forget, however, how deeply ingrained are our habits of self-deception, especially in matters that involve important choices.

Careful observation of the universe, as this confronts us in our ordinary, everyday experience, presents us with a choice that is apparently baffling. It is not that we find inadequate proof or indecisive evidence for the existence of God. If that were all we found, the only choice we could possibly make without cheating would be for that kind of agnosticism that involves suspension of judgment. For to say, "I think there is rather more evidence for theism than for atheism, so I will be a theist," would make no more sense than to say, "It seems to me the evidence for the existence of God is slighter than the evidence against it, poor though this is, so I will be an atheist and think no more of the matter." This would be like saying, "It might rain and it might not, so I believe it will." All you are entitled to say would be, "The evidence is insufficient on either side, so there is no conclusion to be reached." Your verdict would be like the one allowed in the Scottish criminal courts when there is some evidence of guilt but not sufficient for a verdict of "guilty," though, on the other hand, enough to make a "not-guilty" verdict seem wrong: in such circumstances, the Scottish courts allow the jury to give a verdict of "not proven." On giving such a verdict the jury are usually saying, in effect, something like this: "Probably everybody in this courtroom believes this man to be the murderer. But our personal feelings about his innocence or guilt, however strong, have nothing to do with the case. This is a court of law in which conclusive evidence is necessary to establish a man's guilt, and the evidence that has been produced is, though noteworthy, insufficient." Likewise, the most you could say if the evidence for the existence of God were noteworthy but insufficient would be: "You and I and many others have strong personal convictions in the matter, but we are forced to admit that there just isn't enough evidence. Of course we will go on having our personal feelings, but being honest men we will not pretend that these feelings are intellectual conclusions: we will not say we know when in fact we do not have evidence."

Abundant Evidence on Both Sides

In the choice between theism and atheism, the situation is, however, really quite different. We are not presented with inadequate proof or indecisive evidence for the existence of God. We are presented with apparently irrefutable evidence for the existence of God and at the same time apparently irrefutable evidence against it! It is not as if we were listening to a trial in which neither the prosecution nor the defense was very convincing. It is, rather, as if we were listening to a trial in which the prosecution established its case beyond question and the defense then came up with no less abundant and irrefutable evidence for the other side. As the jury, you cannot properly give a verdict for either side, and the Scottish "not-proven" verdict would be even more inappropriate. Strictly speaking, you would need a fourth verdict, demanding that the case be reopened for re-examination of the evidence. In face of the abundance of evidence for and against the existence of God, this is precisely the demand that a religious philosopher should make.

Evidence for Theism

The evidence for theism includes, first of all, the fact that the universe does seem to make sense. That is to say, even we, whose powers at best are limited, cannot avoid making sense of it. Wherever we turn there is a vivid impression of purpose. The seasons succeed each other as if they were carrying out a plan. The planets keep whirling as if they were taking part in a carefully organized military exercise. There is a systematic order in heredity. Particularly striking is the case of biological evolution. A process went on for millions of years, in the course of which man was at length evolved. Reconstructing this process in our minds as best we can, we find that it incontestably bears a marked resemblance to everything we should call the working out of a plan, while it is quite unlike anything that we could call the workings of chance. A monkey trained to the use of a typewriter would, according to the laws of probability, produce a fine English sonnet if only he could sit for a million years or so, hammering away at an indestructible and self-inking machine. But the rest of the monkey's literary output would be merely monkey chatter in typescript. There would be no steady development of purpose, no gradual unfolding of plan. It is just such unfolding that we discover in biological evolution and other such processes of nature. The processes are difficult to explain except on the hypothesis that they are organized by an intelligent agent. It certainly cannot be we who have organized them, for they were going on before we human beings came on the scene at all, and there is no reason to doubt that they would continue to go on even if we blasted ourselves out of existence.

The notion of the survival of the fittest points to creative purpose, because, as Borden Parker Bowne used to put it, the survival of the fit presupposes the arrival of the fit. The fit organisms do not arise occasionally, like the hypothetical monkey's literary triumphs; they are produced regularly and in great number. Values are being steadily created. In the earlier stages of the evolutionary process organisms are produced that are fit to survive for a short time in a restricted environment. In the later stages, organisms such as the human are able to survive for a longer time in a much more varied environment. There is also a tremendous increase in the power of the organism to alter the environment to suit its needs. Consider, for instance, our human control over forces such as electricity. It is indeed an intelligent dog that can be trained to use an electric switch. Man has much more control of his environment. He has been able to harness the immense power of electricity so skillfully that he has invented a device simple enough for even a dog to use.

Man's conquest of nature is achieved, not by the use of superior force, but by a wise submission, as a clever wrestler uses jujitsu. It is only the survivors in the evolutionary process that display such abilities. The chameleon changes color, and all animals that have been successful in the struggle for survival have learned one sort of instinctive cunning or another. Man, however, is in every way conspicuously advanced in such matters. Yet the abilities he possesses cannot be said to have just grown. On the contrary, they have been created in a process in which only those in whom such abilities were developed could survive. All this suggests a creative Mind vast enough to undertake and accomplish such purposes.

Evidence for Atheism

On the other side, there is the evidence for atheism. This includes the fact that, viewed in another way, the universe does not seem to make sense at all. Even we who are, after all, disposed to try to find order whether it is there or not, and endowed with remarkable abilities for doing so, cannot but admit that on all sides there is ample testimony to aimlessness, futility, waste and chance. The conclusion to which this seems to lead is that the universe is purposeless and therefore in itself meaningless. The estimated human population of the world at present is between two and three billions. But one single protozoon can have such a number of offspring in the course of one year. We lament the high death rate among humans in certain countries of the world: that thousands of babies should be brought into existence to die of neglect, disease or malnutrition within a few years of birth may seem pointless indeed. But it is not to be compared with the futility and waste in the death rate among protozoa. There is also in nature a vast amount of evidently unsuccessful experimentation: whole species, such as the dinosaur, after taking countless ages to evolve, simply perished. There seems to be some wisdom in the question raised in the limerick about one of his extinct cousins:

> There once was an ichthyosaurus
> Who lived when the earth was quite porous.
> He fainted for shame
> (Ah, who was to blame?)
> And expired many ages before us.

Such apparent aimlessness is certainly evidence for atheism.

It is true that much of what we call evil really ministers to and makes possible what we call good. Sickness, for example: we never fully appreciate the blessing of health till we have been deprived of it. But being bedridden for forty years is another matter: what purpose does this serve? Living on the edge of a desert may make you more appreciative of the blessings of rain and a fertile land; but you do not need the whole Sahara for the purpose.

But there is another difficulty. Is there anything that can be called good or evil without qualification? A streptococcal infection is an evil for me; but presumably it is a good for the streptococci that succeed in infecting me. Unarmed in the jungle, a man looks upon the tiger as a terrible evil; yet the same man, in other circumstances, may look upon the tiger as a good. The theist's answer to this difficulty is that nothing is good without qualification, except God. Man, made in the image of God, is made in the image of that which is good without qualification; but the image may be and is sadly distorted. No action is good in itself, however. That is to say, there is, strictly speaking, nothing I can *do* that is necessarily good in itself; yet I can *be* what is intrinsically good, namely, what God intended me to be.

Still, this does not answer the question about the origin of evil or explain the lack of purpose that is discoverable in the universe. Is God eternally working on an eternal chaos and so eternally creating order out of disorder and exhibiting purpose in a purposeless universe? If so, the chaos is co-eternal with God, and God is eternally struggling against it as a sculptor struggles with his clay and marble. Though some hold this view and call themselves theists, the view would appear to have dualistic elements in it that are hardly compatible with classical theism, which looks upon God as the Creator and Source of all Being other than God. On the classical theistic view, God creates *ex nihilo*, that is, out of nothing. Therefore, if there is chaos or disorder or confusion or evil, God must be in some sense or other its Source. The notion that God is eternally working on an eternal chaos, creating order out of disorder, is an attempt to mitigate some of the difficulties of theism without falling into the certainly no less serious difficulties of atheism. But it is a position that perhaps presents as many problems as it solves. It is at any rate better at this stage to face theism and atheism as opposite conclusions, both reasonable in their way, from seemingly contradictory evidence. Choose theism and you are left with the problem of evil. Choose atheism and you are left with the problem of the Good. What is involved in the choice will be the next subject for our consideration.

The Modern Positivist's Claim to Escape the Choice

Before passing, however, to the next subject, a word should be said on the difference of intellectual motivation for the atheistic position that was claimed at, say, the beginning of this century and that is claimed today. At the beginning of the century, atheists usually claimed that their choice was made on grounds similar to those on which the theist made his choice. That is to say, atheists of that generation frequently claimed that, as theists were convinced that the preponderance of the evidence was in favor of the existence of God, they found the contrary. This would not be the ground on which a modern atheist (in intellectual circles, at any rate) would base his claim. The modern atheist would say, rather, that he was an atheist because he was first a positivist, and his positivism would prevent him from taking seriously any inquiry into the existence of God. The philosophical position held by positivists who adhere to the extreme form of positivism likely to issue in such a view about the question of the existence of God is typical of much modern thought, being rightly associated with the characteristic preoccupations of an age that is so much engaged in scientific and technological pursuits. It is a position characterized by unwillingness to consider a hypothesis of any kind that appears to be insusceptible to verification by the empirical methods of science. On such a view, not only questions about God but also all other questions of a metaphysical nature appear to be meaningless, and it therefore appears to such a positivist that it is a waste of time even to raise them at all. It is not necessary, on such a view, to be able immediately to conduct the test. For instance, it would be perfectly legitimate to speculate about the structure of the other side of the moon, or of some other part of the solar system beyond our present means of detailed investigation. For though we could not investigate the situation at the moment in order to come to a conclusion that would verify the hypothesis one way or another, the future may bring such means within our reach. In other words, such a hypothesis is not intrinsically unverifiable; it only happens to be beyond the reach of our present means of verification. It is essentially in the same case as would be your affirming that there is a black cat in the room next door but that as the door is locked you have no present means of finding out. The case of a proposition such as "God exists" is not the same, for there is no conceivable means by which such a proposition could ever be verified on such lines. Argument by a modern theist against a modern atheist would therefore generally proceed along lines calculated to bring in question the positivistic presuppositions behind the atheist's position. The modern theist might well question, for instance, the

[margin handwriting: belief based solely on scientific observable facts, it rejects speculation on ultimate origins.]

legitimacy of restricting philosophic inquiry in the manner insisted upon by contemporary positivists. These have, in fact, greatly modified the position held by positivists a generation ago; nevertheless their resistance to religious discourse is basically unmitigated by the technical modifications they have come to recognize.

DISCUSSION ON CHAPTER 14

1. Critically consider the notion that there is not enough evidence for either theism or atheism to enable one to choose between them.

2. Consider the consequences for thought and action of theism and atheism respectively.

3. "I see little evidence in this world of the so-called goodness of God. On the contrary, it seems to me that, on the strength of His daily acts, He must be set down as a most stupid, cruel and villainous fellow." (H. L. Mencken) Discuss.

PART THREE

The Traditional Case for Theism

15

The Problem of the Existence of God

The Nature of the Problem

Probably few people, if any, have ever become theists because of any argument they have heard for the existence of God. They have, rather, first of all believed and then sought an argument to justify their belief. This is not necessarily what psychologists call "rationalization." Many, probably most, of the people holding the view we have described as theistic go through life without ever feeling any urgent need to justify their belief; indeed, such people might well be surprised to learn they were theists. But when we do seek to justify a belief such as theism, we are trying to do something that we often do in other matters. The quest for an argument to prove the existence of God is natural enough. It is only a particular case of what we are doing all the time. Whether it is successful in this particular case is what we are going to consider.

The Role of Theistic Argument

Since many modern thinkers would question, however, even the legitimacy of the quest for an argument for the existence of God, it is important to understand what we mean by saying that the quest is *natural* for believers. There are many things in ordinary life that I have to accept because they seem to be "real" or "true" though I have no means, or time, or opportunity to investigate whether I am right or wrong; that is to say, whether I can *justify* my acceptance of them. For instance, I occasionally travel by air, though, being extremely ignorant of even the most elementary principles of aeronautics, I could not give any satisfactory account of how the flight was accomplished. Fortunately people do not usually ask me. So I go on accepting what engineers and others tell me about such matters, being unable to check what they say, and very often, indeed, I just do not think about the question. Nor could I do so effectively without a great deal of training in highly specialized fields. I suppose I could not, strictly speaking, claim to understand what happens when I fly from New York to Montreal unless I were not only to follow all these specialized courses but actually help to build an aircraft engine. Though I cannot say that this question bothers me very much, my position is, on reflection, unsatisfactory. I talk glibly about being delayed because "they" had "engine trouble," though to be quite honest I should have to confess that I could not give anything like an accurate description of even what such trouble might have been, let alone what it actually was. Nobody seems to mind my ignorance of these matters, so I go on accepting. I can afford to do so, because flying actually plays a comparatively small part in my life. But suppose that somehow it were suddenly going to play a very important, perhaps a vital, part in my life. Suppose, for example, that I were going to be flown on a secret mission across Russia by a pilot of dubious integrity — one who might tell me there was engine trouble when there wasn't. It would become much more important for me to get at least enough understanding to be able to make some sort of judgment about whether I was being hoodwinked, and enough knowledge to deal with the situation in case he tried any unpleasant tricks. Or of course it might be just the itch of intellectual curiosity that impelled me to discover reasons for the many things I am in the habit of accepting when I make a flight.

What Kind of Evidence is Required?

But now suppose a different sort of case: one in which there is an obvious obstacle to your investigating the situation as you would an aircraft engine. Imagine that you somehow find yourself enlisted in the service of a very curious organization. People tell you it is headed by an extraordinarily able administrator, whom you are, however, never able to see. At first, perhaps, you are content not to see him, for there appears to be no particular reason why you should. The organization seems to be remarkably well run, on the whole, and it is natural to assume that it is run by the great administrator whom you never see but whose existence and attributes other people seem to take for granted. The highest officials of the organization, let us suppose, speak with special reverence for this curiously invisible and inaccessible president. You get to know some of these officials, and you ask them if they have ever seen the Great Man. In answer, they hedge. They have not really seen him, they tell you; yet they are as certain of his existence as if they had seen him — *more* certain, some of them say. And then they go on extolling his virtues and the magnificent job he is doing. At first you say, "Yes, of course he must exist, and of course he must be a splendid person"; but then you begin to wonder. What if it were all a hoax? Is this possible? Or a delusion? Perhaps you do not really wonder very hard until one day things seem to go wrong. The people around you mostly try to explain away what has gone wrong: they say, "Ah, I bet the Great Man has something very clever up his sleeve." The men at the top shout more vigorously than ever what a great man the Great Man is. Then, as things seem to go from bad to worse you feel it is time you looked into the whole matter for yourself. The question is, "How exactly would you go about it?"

You say you would first of all look for his office. A president, however elusive, must be administering his organization from some desk, or office, or other such place. He cannot be always absent, if he is really administering the organization in any genuine sense. At last one of your friends among the high officials explains to you that not only does the Great Man not have an office or even a desk; he does not even have a pencil; in short, he is only called "the Great Man," and actually he is not a man at all.

"In other words," you say, "there just isn't any such person. You've been talking about Santa Claus all this time and calling him the president of our company?"

"On the contrary," your friend asserts; "the reason you can't see him is that he is *more* than a man. And he exists more really than any man. You can tell that from what he does — look at this organization, for instance — it's all his work. You can see his brain in it though you can't see *him*."

"Now I can't even imagine what he's like," you say, disguising your suspicions. "Before, I had a pretty definite picture in my mind of a very thoughtful and industrious man working away in a hidden room; now I just can't think of anything but a blur."

"Think of the greatest perfection you can conceive," comes the reply, "and you will be getting close."

For a moment this sounds an interesting idea. Then you say:

"All right, I'm thinking of the greatest perfection I can conceive. . . . There now, it's right in my mind. I think I've got the idea. The trouble is, however, it's only an idea I've got. How do I know the idea has any counterpart in reality?"

You might go on talking like this indefinitely without getting any further forward. The question is: what *kind* of evidence, if any, might convince you, in such a case, of the existence of the invisible, inaccessible president, the mysterious master-mind behind your organization?

How Should the Question be Formulated?

The problem of God's existence has traditionally been presented in just such a guise. The traditional question is: "Does God exist?" It seems a natural way to put the question. That is not to say, however, that it is necessarily the best or even a profitable way to put it, and it may be very unfortunate for the history of thought that it was so presented. But the fact remains that this is the classic way of presenting it, and this presentation has affected the whole course of western thought on the subject. Whatever we are to say of traditional answers to the traditional question, we cannot ignore them. Later on, we may be able to find a way of dealing with the problem that is more suited to our modern requirements. In the first instance we shall simply take the classical arguments, set them forth, and indicate their shortcomings.

The Traditional Arguments

There are four principal traditional arguments for the existence of God, all of which purport to answer affirmatively the question, "Does God exist?" The first three form a group by themselves, a trilogy purporting to answer the question inferentially, by rational demonstration. For various reasons that will become apparent under discussion, the fourth stands by itself. The arguments are:

(1) The Ontological Argument (the argument from the idea of perfection);

(2) The Cosmological Argument (the argument from "logical necessity");

(3) The Teleological Argument (the argument from apparent design or purpose); and

(4) The Moral Argument (the argument from the experience of values, notably, but not exclusively, ethical or moral values).

We shall consider these traditional arguments in turn.

DISCUSSION ON CHAPTER 15

1. Consider various types of objection to the question: "Does God exist?"

2. Discuss the meaning of "proof" in relation to arguments for or against the existence of God.

3. What kind of argument, if any, do you think would be sufficient to establish the existence of God?

16

The Ontological Argument

Historical Background

The ontological argument for the existence of God is the one already hinted at in the previous chapter in the phrase, "Think of the greatest perfection you can conceive." It has been propounded by many thinkers, including Anselm (1033–1109), Bonaventure (1221–1274), Descartes (1596–1650), Leibnitz (1646–1716), and Hegel (1770–1831). Its most notable proponents are Anselm and Descartes. The former, a canonized saint of the Roman Church, was a Benedictine monk who became Archbishop of Canterbury. The latter, some of whose principal works are still on the Roman Index of Prohibited Books, was a French philosopher and mathematician, and one of the most revolutionary thinkers in the history of western thought. The argument was sharply criticized, as we shall see, in Anselm's own time, and also centuries later, notably by Thomas Aquinas (1225–1274) and Immanuel Kant (1724–1804), both figures of the greatest importance in the history of philosophy. It is an argument congenial to that important strand in Christian tradition that has its roots in the thought of Augustine (354–430) and, more remotely, in the heritage of Plato.

Anselm

Anselm begins by asking whether there might be found one single argument that would be entirely sufficient to demonstrate that God exists, that He is the Supreme Good, and that while He depends on nothing outside Himself for His existence, all other beings in the universe depend on Him "for their existence and well-being." He tells us that for long it seemed to him that the answer must be just around the corner. Yet it kept evading him. In despair he was about to give up the quest as hopeless. He found, however, that this was not so easy as he had imagined: the problem kept forcing itself importunately on his attention. Then one day, when he was feeling fatigued by the very effort of trying not to bother with the problem any more, there came to him "in the very conflict of my thoughts," the proof he had been seeking. (These steps in the history of the process of Anselm's discovery are noteworthy, apart from the conclusion at which he arrived.) In a prayer he humbly acknowledges before God that he does not seek to *comprehend* God, for in the nature of the case God must be beyond human understanding, but only "to understand in some degree Thy Truth, which my heart believes and loves." In a famous sentence he says: "For I do not seek to understand that I may believe, but I believe in order that I may understand." [1] He acknowledges that "unless I believed, I should not understand."

This is fair enough: Anselm does not profess to be able to demonstrate the existence of God to someone who did not already believe in God, but only to show that he can justify to his intellect the faith that he enjoys.

Anselm says, in effect, that the existence of God is self-evident. Everyone really believes in God though not everyone admits it even to himself. Everyone believes in God, thinks Anselm, because it is impossible to do otherwise. For God is simply "*a being than which nothing greater can be conceived.*" The psalmist spoke of the fool who "saith in his heart there is no God." But such a fool, when he hears of a being such as Anselm refers to, the being than which nothing greater can be conceived, does in fact conceive of such a being. He cannot help it. However, Anselm recognizes that this is not enough. "For it is one thing for an object to be in the understanding, and another to understand that the object exists." It is true, as Anselm says, that I actually have in my mind the *notion* of the x than which nothing greater can be conceived. But does this x exist outside my mind? Does it exist "in reality"? Anselm points out that a painter may very well have an idea of a painting in his mind; but it doesn't exist till he has transferred his idea to his canvas.

To settle this difficulty, Anselm argues that if the x exists only in my understanding, then it is still not the x than which nothing greater can be conceived. For I *can* think of something greater than that x that is only in my understanding — I can think of an x that is not only in my understanding but actually exists in itself, independently of me. "So truly, therefore, dost Thou exist, O Lord, my God, that Thou canst not be conceived not to exist."

Gaunilo Attacks Anselm

This exceedingly simple way of proving the existence of God was discussed by some of Anselm's contemporaries, and a French monk, Gaunilo, undertook to write an answer to Anselm in a work which he

[1] *Credo ut intelligam.*

entitled *A Book on behalf of the Fool*. Gaunilo admits that the idea of God is inevitably in his understanding, as Anselm showed; but he denied that it was possible to conclude from this that God exists in fact. If someone told him of a wonderful island, a most glorious earthly paradise, it would be easy enough for him to form the idea and hold this idea in his mind. But from the idea in his mind he would never deduce that the island necessarily existed in fact.

Anselm Replies to Gaunilo

Anselm replied to Gaunilo. He admitted that Gaunilo's reasoning was correct in regard to the island; indeed it would be correct in all cases but one. The case of God, Anselm argues, is a special one. In all other cases, such as the island, it is just as possible to conceive of nonexistence as of existence. In the case of God, thinks Anselm, this is not so: it is not possible to conceive of God's nonexistence. For in this case we are not thinking of an island or a horse or a school that is the greatest and most perfect of its kind; we are thinking of whatever it is that is the greatest and most perfect of all kinds of being. To pass from existence-in-thought to existence-in-reality is possible in this one case only. If it is admitted that existents differ in value or greatness or perfection, then one may go on to consider *x*, the highest that one can conceive; but for being to qualify as this *x* it must exist independently of my thought.

Descartes Reformulates the Argument

It is to be expected that Descartes, in formulating a similar type of argument more than five hundred years afterwards in a very different climate of thought, should present his argument in another guise. Descartes was a mathematician and was fascinated by what he thought mathematics could do. Drawing an example from this field, he considers a triangle that never existed in fact. I can imagine such a triangle: one that is dependent on my imagination, having no "real" existence. But, Descartes points out, we must notice a curious fact about this imaginary triangle. While it depends on my imagination, there are certain qualities in it that do not depend on my imagination at all, but are entirely independent of me; for instance, the property of having the sum of its angles equal to two right angles; also the fact that its greatest side is subtended by its greatest angle; and so forth. Then Descartes goes on to suggest that just as having the sum of its angles equal to 180 degrees is an implicate of the very idea of a triangle, so existence is involved in the very idea of an infinitely perfect being. Therefore, it would entail just as much of a contradiction to say that an infinitely perfect being does not exist as to say that the sum of the angles of a triangle is not 180 degrees. A triangle is a figure whose very nature it is to have angles amounting to

180 degrees; so an infinitely perfect being is one whose nature it is to exist. Such a perfect being exists by necessity, just as the angles necessarily add up to two right angles.

It will be noticed that Descartes is treating existence as if it were a property or quality. But is it? To say that a table has the quality of being square or brown or wooden is not at all the same as to say that it has the quality of existing. When I say that a table is square or brown or wooden I am amplifying the concept of a table by delineating to you certain properties of the particular table in question. But it is not the same to say that a table exists. This does not in any such way amplify a concept or delineate properties. If I say that some Americans have legs and others do not, you can understand me. But if I were to say that some Americans exist and others do not, you would very rightly accuse me of talking nonsense. Thomas Aquinas saw that the Ontological Argument for the existence of God treats existence as though it were a quality. But existence is not a quality; certainly it is not a quality as is squareness or brownness. It is just because of this that it *is* possible, logically, to affirm the existence of God, as it is also logically possible to deny it. If Anselm had been right, it would have been logically impossible to deny the existence of God, for the existence of God would have been a truism, so that to say "I believe God exists" would have been somewhat like saying, "I believe the events of tomorrow are in the future." Thomas Aquinas saw the reason why it is not a truism to say "I believe God exists."

Kant's Criticism

To Kant, the Ontological Argument seemed to be at the very heart of the whole traditional theology he sought to criticize. So he took it very seriously, since it appeared to him to be of the very essence of the "dogmatic" position against which he was struggling. In a famous passage, Kant attacks the ground of the Ontological Argument as follows. It is possible to talk about real dollars and it is possible to talk about imaginary dollars. But you cannot add the one to the other. A hundred dollars in my mind are not at all the same as a hundred dollars in my pocket. (This is, of course, really Gaunilo's objection in another form. But Kant goes further.) Kant goes on to show that the *conception* of a thing *as existing* adds nothing fresh to the *bare* conception of it. That is to say, there is really no difference between the conception of a table and the conception of a table as existing, so that while it is informative to say that a table is square or brown, it is not informative at all to say that it exists, since it could not but exist and "be" a table. There is therefore no force, Kant points out, in the argument that the *conception* of a Perfect Being *implies* the existence of such a Being.

In the Ontological Argument it is affirmed that the highest perfection in my mind is not the highest perfection in my mind unless it *includes* real existence. For, it is suggested, such a "highest perfection" would lack something, namely existence. But this reasoning, Kant shows, will not do. For the *concept* of the highest perfection lacks nothing *as a concept* when it lacks real existence in the "outside" world. You cannot "improve upon" such a concept by adding "reality" to it. To attempt so to add "reality" to it would be like trying to "improve" the value of the hundred imaginary dollars by adding a real one from my pocket. It is an impossible feat. The hundred imaginary dollars remain just what they were before. You can no more add a real dollar to an imaginary hundred than you can add an imaginary dollar to a real hundred. Moreover, the question whether dollars exist in my mind or in my pocket is a very important question.

The Ontological Argument and the Modern Mind

Anselm seemed to be saying that it just happens that the case of God is unique, so that Gaunilo's objection does not apply to it. He appeared to be asserting that among all the notions in my mind there is one particular notion (Perfect Being) that has the power of assuring me about itself. But Anselm's argument really implies more than that. It is based on a special conception of the relation between thought and reality. The view underlying Anselm's argument is one deeply rooted in ancient thought and not always readily understandable to the modern mind when this becomes, by philosophical and scientific training, accustomed to entirely different presuppositions. According to an ancient view, *all* thought must be in some sense thought of reality. On such a basic presupposition it is not difficult to go on to what is implied in Anselm's view, namely, that it is a truism that the Perfect Being I conceive must exist in reality. For, it would be natural to Anselm to ask, if such a Perfect Being did not exist in reality, how could I, who am at every turn conscious of my own imperfection, form the thought of it? How could a D-quality being conceive of an A-quality being, if an A-quality being did not exist? A man cannot think a thought higher than himself, unless there is some higher being to provoke that thought. A low-grade being must be incapable of conjuring up to himself any being entirely superior to himself; therefore the occurrence in his mind of the concept of a Being who is totally perfect can be due only to the fact that such a Being really does exist. There could be no other explanation.

This kind of thinking is not always so far from that of the plain man today as some people in academic circles are inclined to suppose. The ordinary man who happens to be disposed to take a theistic attitude often thinks along such lines. It is true that the *language* of Anselm may indeed sound to him an antiquated form of word-juggling dependent on an outmoded kind of intellectual sleight of hand, and he may even applaud as the voice of common sense what Kant says about the real and the imaginary dollars. But he misses the point of Kant's criticism. For an appreciation of this some acquaintance with the history of philosophy is required. It is necessary to understand how revolutionary in the history of human thought was the critical method used by Kant in treating this subject. It is still natural for the ordinary man, untrained in philosophy, to assume, as many philosophers in the past tended to take for granted, that the fact that we *must conceive* something to be so is the best possible reason for concluding that it *is* so. Kant repudiates this. He sees that, on the contrary, the very fact that we are psychologically obliged to think in certain terms points to a dichotomy between reality and thought. Between the two there is a gulf that must not be bridged in any facile manner.

So the Ontological Argument does not carry conviction. Of course, if you are untroubled by the Kantian type of criticism you may accept its conclusions; but you will accept them only because you are already disposed to believe in the existence of God — only because your own underlying presuppositions are already favorable to theism.[2]

DISCUSSION ON CHAPTER 16

1. Consider the presuppositions of Anselm's argument.

2. Compare the Anselmic and the Cartesian [3] forms of the Ontological Argument.

3. Wherein precisely lies the force of Kant's criticism of the Ontological Argument? Discuss.

[2] Some students may find it useful to consult, at this stage, the following passage on the Ontological Argument: Paul Tillich, *Systematic Theology*, I (Chicago: University of Chicago Press, 1951), pp. 204–208.
[3] "Cartesian" is the adjectival form of "Descartes."

17

The Cosmological Argument

Historical Background

The Cosmological Argument is very ancient. Its classic presentation is to be found in Aristotle (384–322 B.C.). Since the Aristotelian tradition plays a dominant role in the development of thirteenth-century thought, it reappears in medieval philosophy, sometimes in a Christian, sometimes in a Moslem or other guise. The famous "five proofs" of Thomas Aquinas are largely variations of this argument.

The Presuppositions of the Argument

It is an argument that looks at first sight more promising than the Ontological Argument, for it takes its starting-point in the everyday world. It is commonly presented as follows: Everything that exists in the world of ordinary experience, such as the table, or my secretary, or your sweater, might very well not exist. That is to say, though such entities certainly do exist, they do not exist of necessity. The table might very well never have been constructed; my secretary might never have been born; your sweater might never have been manu-factured. The existence of all such entities is what the exponents of the argument call *contingent* existence. Is there any other kind of existence? Does everything that actually exists have an existence of this kind, or is there some more "solid" kind of existence? That is to say, we are all agreed that in the case of the examples cited the ex-istence is not a "necessary" existence, since the entities "need" not exist; but is there any entity that would be in a different case?

We might look at the question in this way. But for my parents, I should have no existence: my existence depends upon them, and it is obviously possible that they might never have brought about my existence. Likewise, they depend for their existence upon their parents, and so on. But, it is argued, there must be some "ultimate" cause for the process. To explain the process that is manifested in these "contingent" entities such as myself, these entities that exist but need not exist, there must be some "ultimate" or "first" cause that does *necessarily* exist.

Contingent Existence Demands Explanation

Why? Let us put the question in yet another way. Existence as we know it, that is, "contingent" existence, seems to demand an explanation. There must be a reason why anything or any aggregate of things does in fact exist; yet there certainly appears to be no reason contained, so to speak, within the things themselves. Nothing in the world of ordinary experience is self-caused. Nothing sets itself in motion. If we look for an explanation of what makes something "tick," we must always look beyond the thing itself. Smog does not just happen: there is a scientific explanation for it. This scientific explanation lies, however, beyond the phenomenon we call "smog." Every effect has a cause, and that cause is the effect of something else which is its cause, and so on. But must there not then be some "ultimate" cause to bring the concatenation of causes and effects into existence? Must not there be a Being that necessarily exists and that is therefore the cause of all else, the very ground, indeed, of causation itself? The argument then proceeds as follows: Let us suppose that there is such a "first" cause, a Being existing of necessity, a Being independent of all else and not to be found in anything but itself. Everything else is growing, changing, moving. But this Being, this "ultimate" or "first" cause is the *source* of growth, the *source* of change, the *source* of movement. Everything, it is suggested, must have an "ultimate" source. Let that source be called X. If, then, it be asked whether X may be said to be "living," the reply is: not only must it be living; it must be *more than* living as we commonly understand life, for it is the source of the life we know. If it be asked whether X may be said to be "mind," it is replied likewise that it must be not only mind but more than mind, super-mind, since it is the source of all we call mind. If it be asked whether X may be said to be "good," the reply, once again, is that it must be more than any "good" we know, since it is the spring of all goodness.

Thomas Aquinas Christianizes the Formulation

In Aristotle's presentation of the argument, X seems remote from the world, a self-contemplating Deity the sole object of whose attention can be only the Divine Being itself. For God, if He applied Himself to the contemplation of the world of change, which is the world as we know it, could not Himself be changeless. Thomas Aquinas reinterprets this view in such a way as to give Aristotle's highly abstract conception of God a great vitality and beauty. Thomas argues that God's knowledge of Himself must *include* his knowledge of all else. So Thomas endeavors to express the Christian conception of God in Aristotelian terms. God attends to everything, numbering even the hairs on our head, caring for every sparrow that falls to the ground. He is Love *personified*, that Love which, in the concluding phrase of Dante's *Paradiso*, "moves the sun in heaven and all the stars," yet is Himself the unchanging source of all.

Modern Objections

The Cosmological Argument has been subjected to several different sorts of criticism. A typical modern objection to it would run as follows. The X of the Cosmological Argument is supposed to be a Being whose existence is "necessary" in the sense that His non-existence is really inconceivable. That is to say, to conceive of His non-existence would be like conceiving of a circular square. A circular square is inconceivable because it is the very nature of a square *not* to be circular: if anything is circular it cannot be a square. You do not have to examine different circles to see whether, by chance, one of them may not happen to be a square: you know that no circle can be a square and no square a circle. Such a question as, "Might not one of these circles be a square?" is not worth asking. So, it is argued, since the Cosmological Argument really affirms that God *must* exist, the question "Does God exist?" is not worth asking. Yet this is precisely the question the argument is designed to answer. To say that God must exist is to say that the existence of God is as self-evident as the circularity of a circle or the squareness of a square. It is a truism. For the question, "Does God exist?" to be worth asking, it must be possible that God exists and possible that He does not exist, for otherwise there is no question to answer.

Another way to put the objection is to ask whether the notion of a "necessary" Being, a Being whose existence is self-evident, is not radically mistaken. How could the existence of any being ever be self-evident? Is it not the very nature of every being that it might and yet might not exist? The circularity of a circle is self-evident; it is a tautology to talk of a circular circle. But the *existence* of this or that circle can never be self-evident.

The modern objection to the Cosmological Argument in its traditional Aristotelian form is really an objection to the Aristotelian system itself. The modern critic of the argument repudiates, of course, the whole Aristotelian system that culminates in or implies Aristotle's conception of God. It is true that in a sense God *is* self-evident in Aristotle's system. If we were told nothing about it, presumably we might be able to deduce it from the rest. The self-evident character of the existence of Aristotle's God may be disguised. But it is plain that He is self-evident in the sense that He is the logical implicate of all that we see in the "ordinary" world. That is to say, when we look at the world as Aristotle does, we do not discover God directly, and we certainly do not have any mystical intuition of Him. Nevertheless, His existence is the logical implicate of all that we do see. In other words, there is no way in which, in the last resort, we can make sense of what we do see, except by positing the existence of God. In this sense, God "belongs" in the Aristotelian system. But it may then be objected that an argument for theism should not have to depend on one particular philosophical system, especially on an ancient system that is widely discarded by thinkers today.

A Kantian Objection

Yet another objection is offered by Kant. If the X, which exists "of necessity," produces the world, which exists "contingently," it would seem that the world itself must have in it some kind of "necessity." For it would seem that the "necessary" Being must "necessarily" produce the world. Or else we may say, on the other hand, that if the production of the world is *not* "necessary," we are left with the question: "Why did the 'necessary' Being produce it?"

A Medieval Explanation

The medieval Christian philosophers who adapted Aristotle have an ingenious explanation to account for all this. God is indeed perfectly happy and sufficient without the world. He has no need of it whatsoever. He was in no way bound to produce it; he might very well have refrained from producing it had he so chosen. The creation of the world is due, not to any "necessity," but to the superabundance of the divine Love. Such is the immensity of that Love that God freely chose to create the world, though He would have been just as complete and sufficient and happy without it.

Further Philosophical Objections

This does not, however, answer the philosophical difficulty. For apart from the very special system provided by Aristotle, there seems no philosophical reason why the "necessary" Being should be other than the totality of the world we know. In other words, it might well be that the X is "necessary" in the sense in which Spinoza's God is "necessary"; that is, if there are parts, there must be a whole.

The Cosmological Argument always purports, however, to provide for the existence of the X as a "necessary" Being *beyond and above* the world. But a "necessary" Being that was so beyond and above the world would appear to have nothing to do with the world. How, then, could He be an explanation of it? It could hardly be contended that the "necessary" whole is made up of parts that are "contingent." The whole must be "necessary" throughout, in the parts as well as in itself. The "contingent" parts would be "necessarily" dependent on each other and on the whole. So the whole itself would be "contingent" in the sense that it would be dependent upon the parts. In any case, however, it is not a Spinozistic God whose existence the Cosmological Argument purports to prove, but an Aristotelian one, if not a Biblical one.

A final point must be noted. It may not be entirely fatal to the Cosmological Argument to point out that it depends upon the now widely discarded philosophical system of Aristotle. But it purports to provide an affirmative answer to a question Aristotle never asked — "Does God exist?" As an answer in Aristotelian terms to a non-Aristotelian question, it is a singular failure, being of no greater weight than the Ontological Argument.

DISCUSSION ON CHAPTER 17

1. Consider the notion that everything must have an "ultimate source" or "first cause." Might there be other ways, more congenial to modern scientific thinking, of accounting for the universe we know?

2. Compare and contrast the Ontological and the Cosmological Arguments.

3. Discuss the distinction between "necessary" existence and "contingent" existence. Is it a legitimate distinction? Or can you detect a fallacy in the underlying presuppositions?

18

The Teleological Argument

Traditional Importance of the Argument

Probably the most popular of all arguments for the existence of God has been the very ancient one commonly called the Argument from (better, *to*) Design. This is the Teleological Argument. The word "teleological" is from the Greek *telos*, an end. So a teleological universe is one that is ordered for the sake of an end; a dysteleological one would not be so ordered. You might consider the human eye, as did the English theologian William Paley (1743–1805), as an instrument perfectly adapted to a purpose, namely the act of seeing. The whole universe might be so considered. Suppose you had never seen a watch and that you were to find one lying on the sands. All you could see in it would be a mechanical structure exhibiting an intricate adaptation of parts to one another. You would naturally infer from this, however, that it was constructed by an intelligent being who designed this mutual adaptation in order to accomplish a certain end. But this (so runs the argument) is just what we encounter in the universe:

> The spacious firmament on high,
> With all the blue ethereal sky,
> And spangled heav'ns, a shining frame,
> Their great Original proclaim.
> Th' unweary'd sun, from day to day,
> Does his Creator's pow'r display;
> And publishes to ev'ry land
> The work of an Almighty hand.[1]

Another English writer, Henry More (1614–1687) of the Cambridge Platonist school, puts the argument pointedly: "For why have we three joints in our legs and arms, as also in our fingers, but that it was much better than having two or four? And why are our fore-teeth sharp like chisels to cut, but our inward teeth broad to

---

[1] Hymn by Joseph Addison (1672–1719), based on Psalm 19: "The heavens declare the glory of God; and the firmament showeth his handywork."

107

grind . . . ? . . . But the reason is, nothing is done foolishly or in vain; that is, there is a divine Providence that orders all things."

Darwin and the Evidence for Lack of Purpose

In such forms, the Teleological Argument was bound to seem to lose much of its force in the nineteenth century, after the publication of *The Origin of Species* in 1859. For as Darwin's theory came to be widely accepted it became plain to a larger number of people than ever before that the analogy between watch–watchmaker and man–Creator was not at all a satisfactory analogy. If man evolved from lower forms of life, he could hardly have been designed as a watch is designed by a watchmaker. Darwin was not by any means the first to suggest man's evolution from lower forms of life: Empedocles (c. 494–434 b.c.) had suggested a similar view before Plato was born. Empedocles thought that man had survived because he was best fitted to survive. To anyone, either in the ancient or in the modern world, who is thinking in terms of any such evolutionary theory, there is another, more obvious, explanation of why our teeth are so well placed and why the number of joints in our fingers is the most convenient number. The reason is plain: those species that did not possess the most convenient features perished in the struggle for survival, so that *of course* the survivor has the most convenient features. (Why is it that all Olympic winners are such good athletes?) Even quite simple people, however, who had never heard of either Darwin or Empedocles, must have felt uneasy about arguments such as Paley's and More's. Anybody who lives close to nature, as country people do, must see on all sides evidence of seemingly purposeless waste as well as seeming purpose.

"It is wonderful what God can do in a garden," said the clergyman to one of the villagers in his parish as he stood admiring the latter's holding.

"I guess so," drawled the old man. Then he added: "But, Pastor, you shudda seen this un when God had it all to hisself."

Other Formulations of the Argument

The Teleological Argument need not, however, be presented in the form in which it comes to us in Paley or More. Plato, in the *Philebus*, argued that the origin of man's living body from the great mass of like elements in the universe suggests by analogy that the mind of man has likewise its source in "a royal soul and mind in the nature of Zeus." Francis Bacon (1561–1626) says: "I had rather beleave all the Fables in the Legend and the Talmud and the Alcoran than that this Universal Frame is without a Minde." It may be pointed out that such thinkers were in one way or another *disposed* to believe as they did on such matters. But such a disposition in favor of theism can hardly be attributed to, say, David Hume (1711–1776), who after lengthily attacking the Teleological Argument goes on to admit: "A purpose, an intention, a design strikes everywhere the most careless, the most stupid thinker; and no man can be so hardened in absurd systems as at all times to reject it . . . all the sciences almost lead us insensibly to acknowledge a first Author." It is a natural, and also an impressive argument.

Kant's Attitude Toward the Teleological Argument

Kant, though he repudiates the Teleological Argument, pays it the following tribute: "This proof always deserves to be mentioned with respect. It is the oldest, the clearest and the most accordant with the common reason of mankind. It enlivens the study of nature, just as it itself derives its existence and gains ever new vigour from that source. It suggests ends and purposes, where our observation would not have detected them by itself, and extends our knowledge of nature by means of the guiding-concept of a special unity, the principle of which is outside nature. This knowledge . . . so strengthens the belief in a supreme Author of nature that the belief acquires the force of an irresistible conviction."

Surely no argument ever got higher praise from an opponent. What Kant is recognizing is the fact to which we have already alluded in an earlier chapter: it is not that there is too little evidence for theism, or atheism, but rather that there is abundant evidence for both. So long as we are trying to find rational arguments, we have plenty of data that can be used in evidence. But when we have listened to both sides of a rationalist case for and against theism, it is impossible to say that either has been conclusively proved.

Evolution and Purpose

All evidence for purpose and order in the universe is *prima facie* evidence for a Supreme Mind. To those who are deeply impressed by the presence of order and purpose in the universe, there is no need to produce evidence of special wonders or miracles. To such people, the whole universe appears wonderful: the order is more wonderful than any miraculous deviation from it would seem likely to be. The miraculous could only bring to one's notice the presence and activity of a divine Mind that is already superabundantly manifested in nature.

Evolutionary theories do not in themselves explode the notion of purpose in the universe. We recall what has already been noticed: granted the fact that it is the fit that *survive*; there is still the mysterious fact that they *arrive*. The whole process of evolution suggests two apparently conflicting notions: (1) out of a vast number of fail-

ures there is one success that survives, and (2) it is difficult to believe
that the successes could be accidental. The countryman in our story
who was a little peeved by the suggestion that the flourishing condition of his holding was to be attributed solely to the beneficence of
the divine Majesty would certainly have been no less outraged, to say
the least, by the suggestion that it was due to an accident, such as the
fortuitous concurrence of atoms. That the whole universe should by
accident exhibit what tidiness it does exhibit would be even more
incredible.

Kant's objection to the Teleological Argument was chiefly on the
ground that it does not prove the *kind* of God it is presumably expected to prove — a Creator who not only orders and designs but also
calls into being that which is ordered and designed. After all, even
if we were to accept Paley's watchmaker analogy, we should still be
entitled to ask: where did the watchmaker get the metal and other
materials for making the watch? The Teleological Argument, even
if it persuaded us of the activity of a Great Designer, could not very
well explain where he obtained his supplies. This is why the Teleological Argument has traditionally been eked out with the Cosmological Argument. But no matter how we may try to supplement
or combine one of the traditional arguments with the others, we do
not really succeed in demonstrating the existence of God as God is
portrayed to us in, say, the Scriptures of either the Old or the New
Testament. The Teleological Argument is probably the least incon-
clusive, however, and the conclusion to which it points, far though
it may be from the goal we may have hoped for, is by no means negli-
gible. On the contrary, it commands our special attention.

The Value of the Argument

The presence of order and purpose that confronts us, then, is intolerably difficult to explain without some hypothesis *such as* the
existence of a Great Designer. It must be admitted that it only points
to the existence of such a Being; it does not prove this, in any
ordinary sense of the word "prove." It does not enable the theist
to compel the assent of anyone to his view by means of a rational
"Argument to Design"; but perhaps the contemplation of the evidence
of order and purpose does make the atheist look inexcusably smug.[2]

DISCUSSION ON CHAPTER 18

1. "Suppose I had found a watch upon the ground. . . . The mechanism being observed, . . . the inference we think is inevitable that
   the watch must have a maker; that there must have existed, at some

---

[2] Some students may find it useful to consult, at this stage, the following
passage: Paul Tillich, *op. cit.*, pp. 208–210.

time, and at some place or other, an artificer or artificers, who formed it for the purpose which we find it actually to answer; who comprehended its construction and designed its use." (William Paley) Consider the force of this argument for the existence of God and the objections that might be raised against it.

2. "Men are not flattered by being shown that there has been a difference of purpose between the Almighty and them." (Abraham Lincoln) Consider this observation with reference to the Teleological Argument.

3. "O God, I am thinking Thy thoughts after Thee." (John Kepler, referring to his discoveries in astronomy) Discuss.

19

The Moral Argument

Review of the First Three Arguments

The three proofs we have just been considering are all closely related. Some historians of philosophy have indeed regarded them as variations of the Ontological, others as variations of the Cosmological Argument. The objection to which they are commonly exposed is that they are insufficient to communicate conviction to minds that are not already convinced. They lack assent-compelling force. Their weakness appears to have been recognized even by the thinkers who have favored their use in the attempt to move from the realm of faith to the domain of understanding. For it has been customary to supplement one proof by another — a procedure that plainly implies a recognition of the insufficiency of the arguments taken singly. To an argument that is sufficient in itself it is unnecessary to add further arguments: it can stand in no need of reinforcement or support. Were we confronted by arguments any one of which was conclusive, we should feel like the judge whom counsel promised to offer a dozen reasons why his client could not appear in court, and who discovered that one of the dozen reasons was that the gentleman in question was dead. In such a case the eleven other reasons could hardly add much weight. At any rate, it is plain that the theistic proofs we have been considering are certainly not to be accounted individually conclusive. The best that might be claimed for them would be that one helps out the other, but no one of them by itself does the required job. This is not a fatal objection. But it does call attention to the precariousness of the position of him who uses them. Such arguments, it must be admitted, are not proofs at all. At most they can be only pointers. Or perhaps they might be regarded as providing a welcome boost to a commitment that has already been made on other grounds. But they certainly cannot be regarded as providing conclusive evidence for the existence of God. It would not do for the prosecution in a murder trial to ask the jury for a verdict of guilty because, though there was no proof, there were three arguments which, taken together, might lead to a somewhat less weak

112

indication of guilt than would be provided by any one of them by itself. No jury in the world would accept that as sufficient evidence to convict a man on so grave a charge.

Moral Decisions

We are now to consider the Moral Argument which, though forms of it are ancient, is generally associated with the name of Kant. We have just seen that Kant, with a slight reservation in favor of the Teleological Argument, repudiated all the three arguments we have been considering. "Two things," declared Kant in a celebrated passage, "fill the mind with ever new and increasing admiration and awe, the oftener and more steadily we reflect on them: the starry heavens above and the moral law within." Kant was among those who are deeply impressed by the presence of moral *facts*. Let us consider this notion in general. Whatever freedom or lack of freedom is to be found in the world of atoms and electrons, there is freedom in the "inner life" of a man. I choose one course of action rather than another. The choice I make is neither inevitable nor fortuitous. If you offer me two identical cookies and I select the one on the left of the plate rather than the one on the right, I am not really making a choice at all. But if you offer me the choice of a ticket for *King Lear* or a ticket for *War and Peace* this is a real choice, and I am making a moral decision when I choose one or the other. We are making such moral decisions every hour of our lives. In choosing *King Lear* (let us say) I am choosing what, for one reason or another, I think I *ought* to choose. I may think I ought to choose it for some reason you might think of little account, such as that the parking arrangements are better at the theatre that is showing it; or I may feel I ought to choose it for some "higher" reason, such as that I believe it will do my soul more good. (The probability is that in fact, in such a case, my reasons would be neither as trivial as the first nor as lofty as the second.) I choose among values. Some of these choices are extremely important in our lives: for instance, when you choose to be an engineer rather than a salesman, or to stay at home for a few years to be with your sick father rather than take a job offered you in a distant city, and so forth. In making such a decision we feel the experience of *obligation*; we believe we *ought* to do the thing. If we fail to do it we are troubled in conscience. "I ought to have been more considerate to my mother when she was ill"; or even (a more trivial case), "I ought to have written sooner."

Independence of Moral Action

This feeling or awareness that I *ought* to do this or that has nothing to do with any consequence I think may follow. It is not because your father will be angry if you waste your money at college and find you are "broke" weeks before your next allowance is due, that you say you *ought* to be reasonably thrifty. It is, rather, that to spend your allowance recklessly just "wouldn't be fair to Dad." You may happen to have a very generous father who says, "Don't scrimp yourself — I'll find you the money somehow." You might nevertheless feel that it wouldn't be fair to take advantage of his generosity, because he really can't afford it. Nor is it wrong to be a spendthrift because society says so. You might be at a college where it was the fashion to spend more money than you could afford, and still you might feel an obligation to defy custom in this matter. You may say, perhaps very rightly, that you ought to have a more adequate allowance. But you are confronted with the economic fact that you do have *this* allowance, and with the moral fact that you *ought* to spend it in such and such a way. In other words, you find yourself, as Kant suggests, the inhabitant of two worlds — the "is" world and the "ought" world. Are these two worlds quite distinct from each other, having no unity, or are they, rather, two aspects of the same world? If the world of the "moral law within" us has nothing (or nothing much) to do with the world of "brute fact," then it might well be questioned whether the world of thought (including, of course, "scientific" thought) has anything (or anything much) to do with the "real" world. Such skepticism may be theoretically possible, but it is not convincing or even very plausible. If we were to indulge in it, we might as well give up all serious attempts to understand the universe, for they would be unprofitable. If, on the other hand, we are to admit that the "two worlds" are related to each other, then it follows that moral knowledge is not essentially different, *as knowledge*, from knowledge of tables and chairs. This is not to say there is no place for skepticism about moral values, for there is certainly place for (indeed, urgent need of) skepticism about what we see and hear and smell and touch and taste. Contrary to the adage that "seeing is believing," we find that things are often not what they seem. The oar lying in the water looks bent, yet it is straight. I cry out, "There goes a pussy-cat," only to discover, to my dismay, that it was a skunk. So we may make mistakes in the moral sphere too. But that is not to say we must give up hope of discovering where our duty lies any more than it means we have to stop bothering to look at anything lest we might be mistaken.

Sovereignty of Moral Order

According to Kant, the moral order claims unlimited sovereignty. For the "ought" comes to me as a demand, an imperative. Moreover, if I ought, I can. It would be absurd for me to consider whether I ought to address Hungarian refugees in Magyar, for I do not know a word of that language. It would be ridiculous for me to wonder whether I ought to allow my blood to circulate, for I have no say in the matter. I am compelled to let my blood circulate. But I am not compelled to smoke, and if my doctor strongly advises me against it, I decide I ought to forego this pleasure. I am *free* to smoke or not, and I *choose* to abstain. Freedom is one of the three postulates of the moral life, according to Kant; the other two are God and the immortality of the soul. Let us see how he arrived at these.

The "Practical Reason"

Kant was convinced that neither God nor the immortality of the soul could be proved by pure reason. But he held that what he called the "practical reason," the will, could validate in another way what could not be demonstrated by ordinary logical reasoning. Such are the moral demands, the requirements of the moral realm that confronts us, that they establish God, freedom and the immortality of the soul, where ordinary logical reasoning fails to do so. If we recognize the existence of the moral law and of the object of our will, the *summum bonum* which is perfect happiness, it becomes necessary to conclude to the existence of God in order to maintain the necessary relation between the moral law and the *summum bonum*; likewise it becomes necessary to postulate the immortality of the soul in order to provide man with unlimited time in which to realize his end, for human life is too short for this. Considering the question of immortality, Kant says:

> The realization of the summum bonum in the world is the necessary object of a will determinable by the moral law. But in this will the perfect accordance of the mind with the moral law is the supreme condition of the summum bonum. This then must be possible, as well as its object, since it is contained in the command to promote the latter. Now, the perfect accordance of the will with the moral law is holiness, a perfection of which no rational being of the sensible world is capable at any moment of his existence. Since, nevertheless, it is required as practically necessary, it can only be found in a progress in infinitum towards that perfect accordance, and on the principles of pure practical reason it is necessary to assume such a practical progress as the real object of our will.
>
> Now, this endless progress is only possible on the supposition of an endless duration of the existence and personality of the same rational being (which is called the immortality of the soul). The summum bonum, then, practically is only possible on the supposition of the immortality of the soul; consequently this immortality,

being inseparably connected with the moral law, is a postulate of pure practical reason (by which I mean a theoretical proposition, not demonstrable as such, but which is an inseparable result of an unconditional a priori practical law).[1]

The Existence of God a Necessary Postulate

Kant goes on to exhibit the necessity for postulating the existence of God:

Happiness is the condition of a rational being in the world with whom everything goes according to his wish and will; it rests, therefore, on the harmony of physical nature with his whole end, and likewise with the essential determining principle of his will. Now the moral law as a law of freedom commands by determining principles, which ought to be quite independent of nature and of its harmony with our faculty of desire. . . . But the acting rational being in the world is not the cause of the world and of nature itself. There is not the least ground, therefore, in the moral law for a necessary connection between morality and proportionate happiness in a being that belongs to the world as part of it, and therefore dependent on it, and which for that reason cannot by his will be a cause of this nature, nor by his own power make it thoroughly harmonize, as far as his happiness is concerned, with his practical principles. Nevertheless, in the practical problem of pure reason, i.e., the necessary pursuit of the summum bonum, such a connection is postulated as necessary: we ought to endeavour to promote the summum bonum, which, therefore, must be possible. Accordingly, the existence of a cause of all nature, distinct from nature itself, and containing the principle of this connection, namely, of the exact harmony of happiness with morality, is also postulated. Now, this supreme cause must contain the principle of the harmony of nature, not merely with a law of the will of rational beings, but with the conception of this law, in so far as they make it the supreme determining principle of the will, and consequently not merely with the form of morals, but with their morality as their motive, that is, with their moral character. Therefore, the summum bonum is possible in the world only on the supposition of a Supreme Being who has a causality corresponding to moral character. Now a being that is capable of acting on the conception of laws is an intelligence (a rational being), and the causality of such a being according to this conception of laws is his will; therefore the supreme course of nature which must be presupposed as a condition of the summum bonum is a being which is the cause of nature by intelligence and will, consequently its author, that is God. It follows that the pos-

[1] Immanuel Kant, *Critique of Practical Reason*, Part I, Book II, Chapter II, iv.

tulate of the possibility of the highest derived good (the best world) is likewise the postulate of the reality of a highest original good, that is to say, of the existence of God. Now it was seen to be a duty for us to promote the summum bonum; consequently it is not merely allowable, but it is a necessity connected with duty as a requisite, that we should presuppose the possibility of this summum bonum; and as this is possible only on condition of the existence of God, it inseparably connects the supposition of this with duty; that is, it is morally necessary to assume the existence of God.[2]

Kant is aware that the moral necessity of which he speaks is subjective. Considered as a principle of explanation, it may be called a hypothesis; but as a requirement for practical purposes it is faith, and, moreover, "a pure *rational faith*, since pure reason (both in its theoretical and its practical use) is the sole source from which it springs."

Such is the character of the moral order that confronts me that it must fully permeate, so to speak, the world of "ordinary" experience. Without postulating the existence of God it would be impossible to link the moral order to the natural order: the two realms would remain separated. How could the moral laws confront me with the *kind* of demands they do, how could they come to me with the *kind* of force they do, unless they have their source in a Being who exists objectively, that is, independently, of me and is essentially good?

Objections to the Moral Argument

It is not possible in a brief summary of Kant's argument to be fair to such a great thinker, and by the same token it is not possible to criticize him adequately without devoting to the task much more space than is at our disposal. But certain objections must be stated. Kant proceeds on the theory that rational human beings are aware of an objective moral order, an order that is independent of them but reveals itself to them. This order, it turns out, is identifiable with God. This is no doubt a good description of what the believer believes is happening in his life, and he may very well rejoice at having the nature of the process so admirably expressed. But as an argument for demonstrating the existence of God to an unbeliever, it is circular. For if the unbeliever refuses to admit the objectivity of moral values, or even to concede any meaning to this notion, the proponent of the argument has reached a dead end. But suppose, even, that he is dealing with a more pliable and openminded unbeliever — one who is ready, for instance, to recognize moral imperatives presented to all men in association with the notion of, say, bravery or compassion. He may say: "The notion of courage is one that I find both intelligible and also important in my life, and it seems to be likewise important

2 *Loc. cit.*, v.

and intelligible in the lives of all men, irrespective of race, color or creed. The kind of courage admired by a Chinese may seem strange to me; nevertheless I can understand it, just as I can understand the way his mind works, though this likewise is a process not as familiar to me as the way my own brother's mind works. What I cannot understand or even conceive of is a courage apart from human situations and existing independently of them. Yet you talk as though this courage existed as a quality of God and would exist even if no human being had ever been confronted with it in day-to-day experience."

In fact, the objections to the Moral Argument are in the long run reminiscent of the objections to the Cosmological Argument. As the proponents of the latter try to find a "home" in God for causation, so the proponents of the Moral Argument try to find a "home" in God for values as these are experienced in human life. The Moral Argument, as presented by Kant, is based on the sovereignty of the moral will instead of being based, as are the other arguments, on the sovereignty of logical reasoning. Man's moral consciousness and moral dignity demand God as a postulate, according to Kant. But while *my* moral consciousness and *my* moral dignity may demand it, I have no means of compelling my atheist friend to assent to the view that *his* moral consciousness and *his* moral dignity demand it. My moral consciousness demands God because it is a moral consciousness that implies God already. It may even be true that his moral consciousness also implies God; but if he denies that he has a moral consciousness of this sort I cannot hope to persuade him that he has. As a proof of the existence of God, the Moral Argument cannot compel assent. My atheist friend may be endowed with the kind of moral consciousness that implies God; but if he chooses to suppress it or suspend it or otherwise extinguish it, he may, with no abdication of his reason, claim that he can see no justification for concluding to the existence of God.

Kant and Modern Man

In Kant's day people were commonly disposed to take for granted the moral nature of man. They might be very skeptical about the dogmas of "revealed religion"; but man's moral dignity was generally beyond question. They were often ready to acknowledge a "moral belief" in God although disinclined to allow an intellectual, doctrinal belief. Twentieth-century man has had to face the unpleasant fact that in certain circumstances men who are superficially civilized and seemingly endowed with the moral consciousness our forefathers generally thought indestructible, can degenerate with alarming speed to a subhuman level. Apparently healthy, normal, pleasant young German lads, the counterparts of those who in America would be called "fine college boys," could be and were — thousands of them — turned quickly into cruel, coarse bullies who, in the uniform of the notorious *Schutzstaffel*, flogged elderly doctors and schoolmasters into unconsciousness for the facilitating of the process of opening the jaws and purloining the gold fillings of their wretched victims before these were wheeled off to one of the crematoria. That children should learn to spy for the secret police on their own parents by casual conversation around a Christmas tree would have been unthinkable in Europe or America fifty years ago. Under Hitler, however, it became an all too familiar part of the family life of many homes. I can myself well remember dining at the home of a German professor on the eve of the Second World War, and feeling a curious abstractness in his social conversation. He later privately explained to me, however, that the reason he was unable to discuss with me any but the most abstract, academic questions at the dinner table was that he was in terror of his daughter, an attractive, slightly shy, seventeen-year-old girl sitting opposite me. He had reason to believe she was spying on her parents for the Gestapo. So long as a civilization preserves a certain moral veneer, it seems plausible enough to take man's "ethical consciousness" and "moral dignity" for granted: there is something in every man, it may then seem, that demands God as a postulate. But the argument is much less convincing when you see how people can behave in more desperate circumstances. It is then that you may best see the glorious heroism to which man can rise; but you also see the depravity to which he is equally capable of descending.

The Moral Argument had great influence in the nineteenth and early twentieth century. Rightly so, for it is powerful, impressive, and in certain circumstances it can be very convincing. Standing apart from the trilogy of "logical" arguments, it is uniquely important in the development of thought on the subject; but it is not, in the long run, any more assent-compelling than these. It does, however, draw attention, as none of the other arguments could well do, to the whole question of proving the existence of God, and indeed to the nature of proof itself. Is there any kind of argument conceivable that could prove the *existence* of anything in the mind of a person prepared to deny that existence?

DISCUSSION ON CHAPTER 19

1. Discuss Kant's view that the moral consciousness carries with it a demand that reality shall accord with it.

2. Why are freedom and immortality to be affirmed, according to Kant, as postulates of the moral life?

3. Discuss whether the Moral Argument is more convincing than the other traditional arguments for the existence of God.

20

The Problem of the
Persistence of God

Defiance of God

Erich Frank, in a passage written in the spirit of Dostoevski, exhibits the modern nihilist's defiance of God:

> If I only see what is good, I shall act accordingly, no matter what the ultimate principle of the world may be. Whether it is nothingness, or whether it is evil, whether it may crush myself and my own will and thus forever destroy my own goodness and that of everyone else—all I can say is this: so much the worse for the ultimate principle. I shall not acknowledge it, even though its power may be unlimited. I shall persist in utter metaphysical defiance, infinitely lonely, supported only by my moral insight. I shall offer absolute resistance to the ultimate principle and shall despise it.[1]

So a modern unbeliever might turn the moral independence that Kant's argument implies, against the argument itself. To a theist his attitude may seem morally irrational, as irrational as that of Lucifer himself, who according to the old story set himself up as independent of God. But the point is that though a man's attitudes and ways of conducting his life may seem unreasonable to me, this does not entitle me to say he is bereft of reason. On the contrary, a man whom you recognize to have a better brain than you (that is, say, one who is more capable than you of sustaining a long and difficult piece of reasoning) may nevertheless appear to you to be a fool when it comes to what he does with his life. You cannot, however, say that on that account he is an idiot or a lunatic. You feel you ought to be able to persuade him of the existence of God, if you believe in this, because you believe that both you and he are rational minds. But the fact that you are both rational minds and that he is, let us suppose, an exceptionally able and clear-thinking man, is of no avail to you in certain circumstances. For instance, suppose that your friend, whom

[1] Erich Frank, *Philosophical Understanding and Religious Truth* (New York: Oxford University Press, 1952), p. 38.

you know to have outstanding ability and who is at the moment in the prime of his life and at the peak of his fortunes, suddenly announces to you that he proposes to shoot himself that evening. He says he can see no particular reason for living as opposed to being dead. How would you go about proving to him that he is wrong? You could argue with him for the rest of the day without convincing him and (the important point) you could not tell yourself, after the shot from his bedroom intimated your failure, either that there was anything wrong with your arguments or that there was any lack of capacity in him to follow them.

Impossibility of Assent-Compelling Proof

Let us hear Erich Frank again on this subject:

Thus the modern philosopher can never cogently prove the existence of a God beyond this world, either through logical or through moral arguments, to him who has no faith. How should he be able to do so, since human reason, in his opinion, is only the formal faculty of clarifying a given and clearly perceptible content and of reducing it to general abstract ideas? In science, our thinking is based on sense-perception and verifies its concepts by this means. But if human reason tries to transcend the limits of the perceptible world or of mathematics—as it must do in philosophy—its thinking is bound to get entangled in contradictions. While the metaphysician, starting from certain facts, may feel sure that he can prove through logically cogent arguments the truth of certain principles which transcend the objects of sense-perception, the Positivist, starting from the same facts, will feel equally sure that with the same logical stringency he can prove just the opposite, namely that all such metaphysical concepts have no meaning whatever. Every philosophical thesis can easily be disproved by its opposite.[2] If philosophers, nevertheless, stubbornly stick to their theses and refuse to yield to logical arguments, then a pre-logical presupposition, some pre-rational belief, must unknowingly be shaping their thought. The Positivist is right in saying that it is not merely the logic of the theoretical arguments which directs the argumentation of the metaphysician, but rather a certain preconceived conviction which has been borne out throughout his life. Yet the same is true of the Positivist himself; for it cannot be merely on the strength of the logic of his argument that he offers theories far transcending the mere facts of science. Instead, it must be an irrational[3] belief, this selfsame be-

[2] Frank observes, in a note, that this has been recognized by both Plato and Kant.

[3] I would venture the suggestion that "pre-rational" would be a less misleading word here and would accord with what Frank is saying throughout this passage.

lief in the perceptible world and in natural life which, to him, is
the ultimate truth upon which he has decided to stake his whole
existence once and for all.

Human reason, then, as modern scepticism has shown, does not
rest upon itself. Rational conclusions are dependent on certain
premises which reason itself is unable to prove because they are
rooted in a deeper stratum of the human mind. They spring from
a more or less unconscious belief or instinct, the justification of
which is one of the principal tasks of the philosopher. Even in
the exact sciences, a certain belief plays its part, in so far as their
truths are based on ultimate axioms which we accept as true without being able to prove them. In practical life we can rely even
less on reason alone. Here we cannot always afford a sceptical
attitude, as we may do in questions of theoretical science, which
do not demand an immediate decision. In most practical questions
we cannot wait until our reason has clarified the theoretical aspects. Life is a constant struggle with the unknown, and even our
rational arguments are based on a vague belief, on a trust or instinct or feeling of which we can give no further account. Or, to
quote Pascal's classical formulation of this fundamental epistemological fact: "The heart has its reasons which Reason does not
know."[4]

Faith Demands Metaphysical Ground

But it would be a fatal misunderstanding of Pascal to suppose that
by saying that "the heart has its reasons" he meant that we should
follow the dictates of our emotions. Frank is well aware of this
danger and points out, in effect, that if our faith in God has no more
or better ground than a subjective feeling, then we are really reverting
to polytheism. For if your belief does not somehow transcend yourself,
and if mine does not transcend myself, then we are really only believing in constructs of our own hearts. We are each, like Narcissus,
only inspecting our own faces in a pool. Such faith is only in accordance with the English schoolboy definition: "believing steadfastly wot
you know ain't true." As Frank puts it, "A belief that believes only
in itself is no longer a belief." [5] No one who has really faced up to
the mystery of belief in God can ever rest content with the kind of
belief that implies only: "I don't care whether the object of my
belief (God) is 'true' or 'real' or 'transcendent,' so long as it expresses what is in my heart and makes me 'feel better.' " This is to
make God nothing more than a psychological drug, and to justify the
jibe that religion is the opiate of the people.

[4] Frank, op. cit., pp. 38–40.
[5] Ibid., p. 42.

Faith Implies Doubt

All genuine faith implies doubt. "At the bottom of faith, there is doubt, fear lest it be our own arbitrariness from which God ensues." [6] Even at the primitive level, in animism and dynamism, there may be a hint of this; it must enter at some point if the religion of the savage is to proceed beyond fetish-beating and tribal roaring at approaching storms. It is in the struggle between faith and doubt that a man finds out what he is "up against" when he is "up against" God. The more sincerely and desperately he struggles, the more he finds that God is inescapable.

Why God is Inescapable

We are now in a better position to reconsider the question raised in Chapter 4. There we endeavored to make the point that if there were a God it would not be surprising that men should try to escape Him; indeed, to anyone who considers the character of the demands that God is always at all stages of religious development believed to make upon us, it is inconceivable that men should not so try to escape. But we must and we do also grow to protest against our own conceptions of God. Over and over again, as we revise these, substituting a more adequate for a less adequate conception, there emerges the "fear lest it be our own arbitrariness from which God ensues." Over and over again we try to dispense with the whole notion. The more serious my attempt, however, the more I am forced to come to terms with myself. It is neither in the traditional proofs nor in any subjective feeling that the real proof of God's existence is to be found. None of the traditional proofs can in itself compel assent; no subjective feeling can by itself prove anything more than the subjective feeling. The existence of God can be proved only in the struggle with God; it is in the throes of this conflict that the reality of God confronts us, compelling our awareness of Him as The Other, the infinitely Holy One. The more our awareness of Him results in our recognition of His loving purpose for us, the more we are inclined to seek our escape, for as we all know there is nothing so powerfully demanding as love; the more unselfish it is the more it disturbs our selfish complacency. An unselfish mother is a torment to a selfish son; an unselfish husband to a selfish wife; but in the discovery of God we are confronted with the possibility of infinite torment in the awareness of our own inability to measure up to what we know we ought to be. In our struggle with God this awareness deepens and increases

---

[6] *Ibid.*, p. 43. This notion is expounded in the present writer's *Christian Doubt* (London: Longmans, Green and Co., 1951).

with the most alarming force; hence the urgent need for reconciliation with God. About this all the great theistic religions have much to say.

Why Resistance is Fierce

It is because the proof of God's existence lies in the struggle with Him that, from the standpoint of the theist, the militant atheist seems poised on the razor's edge and on the verge of a profound conversion. It is to be expected that surrender should be preceded by a violent show of resistance. St. Paul was hurrying to Damascus to persecute the Christians when he was himself apprehended by God on the road, and the conversion was so deep and powerful that it turned him into the most indefatigable apostle of the Christian way. It is beyond skepticsm that the deepest faith is to be found. That is why, as Kierkegaard has abundantly shown, deeply religious people always tend to shock superficially religious people. Kierkegaard has also said that the notion of "proving the existence of God" always seems, to anyone engaged in the struggle with God and willing to admit to himself the nature of this struggle, an exceedingly ridiculous notion, somewhat like trying to prove the existence of your own mother under her very nose. It seems, indeed, even more absurd than this, since it is like trying to prove to a man engaged in a bayonet charge that there is a war on.

The Meaning of Conversion

A dramatic, yet typical case showing how the only real proof of the existence of God lies in the struggle with Him is recounted in a remarkable book by Starr Daily,[7] a once apparently incorrigible convict undergoing a life sentence, who describes how, in the midst of the horror and depravity of life in a penitentiary, after rebellion had brought him repeated punishments, including the dreaded dungeon cell (solitary confinement on bread and water), his life was permanently transformed by a religious conversion. Starr Daily's school education stopped at the fifth grade, and by his early teens he was fraternizing with thieves and fugitives. The attitude with which he was most familiar was what he later called "the deadly convict philosophy of life." So when he afterwards wrote a description of his experience in terms of a protracted and eventually unsuccessful attempt to escape from God, he was writing, not in terms of this tradition or that, of this theological literature or that, but simply as a reporter of an episode:

> Then I began to dream in a confused and pointless way. Fragments of my life's experience, with neither beginning nor end, drifted mist-like across my mind. They seemed neither good nor

7 *Release* (New York: Harper & Bros., 1942).

bad—or at least my reactions to them were indifferent. This type
of mental activity went on for several days and nights.

Finally and quite suddenly the form and content of these
dreams changed. They now began to reveal consistency and con-
tinuity. They became rational and logical in form and sequence.
Too, they were highly sane and beautiful in form and essence,
filled with meaning and implied purpose. Then into my memory
came the fact that I had known these dreams before—when I was
a child. I became aware that I was dreaming of the man I had
been trying to avoid for many years, Jesus the Christ. . . . By
some mysterious faculty of perception which operated in the
midst of my dream, I seemed to know clearly that I was sub-
merged in Reality; that I was seeing and feeling something that
would influence my life throughout all eternity. . . .

Thus, as a recipient of love, I became a transmitter of it. It
seemed to rise from within me and flow outward, as though generated from some interior source. The joy and bliss and gratitude
I felt was past articulation, and was wholly uncontainable. In
the midst of such feeling I knew I must either be changed or I
would die.[8]

This refers to what happened to Starr Daily in the dungeon cell in
which he had been standing chained up as usual twelve hours a day,
wearing "an old pair of overalls, filled with the stench of their former
victims, and a torn and faded shirt whose last wearer must have gone
mad in a foaming fit, so stiff is the shirt's front," and piling up
bitterness and hate in response to a warder's curses. The results of
the transformation were so obvious, so spectacular, that it was as if a
leper had suddenly found himself glowing with radiant health, not
in a macabre fit of fancy but according to every known laboratory
test. To such a man, after such an encounter, both the traditional
proofs and the notion of God as a subjective feeling must inevitably
seem equally beside the point, if not equally ridiculous. No one who
has had any experience of this sort has any *need* for proof of the
existence of God, even if, like Anselm, he thinks he is able to exhibit
his experience in terms of an intellectual pattern. To those who
have been engaged in such an encounter and have emerged from it
with such an entirely new integrity and creative ability, what is of
much greater concern than "proving the existence of God" is making
further discoveries about Him.

How is Atheism Possible?

The question may now be asked: if what we have been saying gives
a substantially true account of a general human experience, how can
there be any atheists at all? For does it not appear that atheism is,

8 *Ibid.*, pp. 45–47.

at most, only an episode in the drama of man's attempt to escape God and God's inevitable cornering of man? The answer must surely be that so indeed it would appear, but so in fact it is not. It would so appear to the millions whose experience, though they have never seen the inside of a penitentiary, is essentially the same as Starr Daily's. The first impulse of all these is to suppose that God's love must in the long run conquer every human heart. This impulse is based on their own experience of the divine encounter. So they are at first inclined to affirm with Francis Bacon, in his famous essay *On Atheism*, that "atheism is rather in the lip than in the heart of man." On such a view a man may say he is an atheist, but "deep down" he knows otherwise. In other words, atheism is really, on this view, only a pose, an affectation, somewhat like that of a schoolboy who, though he is inwardly devoted to his parents, belittles them to his schoolmates because it happens to be the fashion among these to do so and he does not wish to run the risk of being ridiculed or ostracized for failure to participate in this juvenile barbarity.

Is Final Resistance to God Possible?

Such is what the man who has himself experienced the divine encounter would *expect*. A little investigation shows, however, that the facts do not seem to support it. For it soon becomes plain that, unless we humans are entirely incapable of judging the inner dispositions of our fellows, it is not only certainly possible but perhaps also exceedingly common for people to persist in the flight from God *without* being overtaken. The theist does not take this to mean that such people really *escape* God ("the devils also believe, and tremble" [9]); but he is forced to take the view that apparently God does not overtake everybody. To the theist this is a mystery. For since in the divine encounter God uniformly presents Himself as infinitely loving and superabundantly powerful, there is a paradox in the seemingly inevitable conclusion that all are not overpowered by the love of God. For those who have experienced the struggle involved in the divine encounter are aware of their resistance to God while acknowledging in their hearts that He is in the long run irresistible. The fruit of the surrender, ready or reluctant, that this attitude implies, is evident in their lives and in their personality.[10]

The Theological Problem and Its Interpretation

The following three interpretations at once suggest themselves as available to the theist: (1) God is unable to overtake everybody; that is, His power is limited so that either He is forced to restrict

[9] Jas. 2:19.
[10] The divine encounter in the moral life is to be reconsidered in more general terms in Chapter 36.

Himself to certain persons or else in certain cases He fails; (2) He does not *intend* to overtake everybody; that is, He purposely restricts the activities of His overpowering love to certain persons to the exclusion of others; (3) He makes His love available to everyone, but while overtaking some He permits others to succeed in excluding Him by their own free choice. All three interpretations present serious difficulties. The first seems inconsistent with the theist's own experience. For what is exhibited to me in my encounter with God is not only One-who-is-other-than-I; it is One-who-is-other-than-we. If God can, as He does, overcome my ferocious resistance to Him, it seems incredible that He could conceivably fail with anyone else who is of the same human nature as mine. There is nothing in me that warrants, deserves, earns, or wins the infinite love that confronts me in the encounter: it comes to me as a pure, unmerited gift. The second interpretation, that God does not intend to overtake everybody, means that He deliberately restricts His gift to an elect. This is a view that has been taken not only by Paul and Augustine and Calvin, in whose thought it is especially prominent, but also by other great Christian thinkers. According to this predestinarian view God overtakes only those whom He chooses to overtake, leaving the others to the consequences of their unresolved anguish. The third interpretation is not really very different from the second, because if God permits some to resist Him, He is still refraining from overtaking them as He might do.

Other possible interpretations, such as that associated with the name of Pelagius, an early fifth-century British monk, which seem to make more of the human will, have played a large part in popular religion, but have not generally commended themselves to those who give the most convincing reports of encounter with God. We are not presently concerned with the resolution of such problems, but rather with the reason why they arise. They arise because of the seemingly inescapable fact that an experience of God claimed by some is not enjoyed by all. To the theist this is a mystery; perhaps at the core of the problem of evil.

The situation we have to consider is: theism and atheism may be not mere views or opinions, such as are, say, conservatism and liberalism in politics, or idealism and existentialism in philosophy, or impressionism and surrealism in art. The importance of this consideration cannot be overestimated. Theism and atheism may be not merely intellectual positions or hypotheses or interpretations, though capable of being abstractly so considered. They may represent, rather (and be the intellectual formalizaton of) events, choices, decisions, at a much more radical level than that with which our intellectual theories and speculations are ordinarily concerned. This point ought to be most carefully pondered.

Why Assent-Compelling Proof is Impossible

If this way of looking at the question is, in principle, anywhere near the mark, it becomes clearer why it might be that no formal proof of theism or atheism could be offered, and why no argument of the traditional sort could ever be convincing. As was noted in the tentative definition of religion in the opening sentence of the first chapter of this book, religion is essentially commitment to a kind or quality of life. It cannot be argued about as if it were only a scientific theory or a metaphysical system. This does not mean that it cannot be argued about at all. It does mean, however, that the danger of "armchair" discussion of it is peculiarly great. An example may help to show this. The practice is still current in some circles of talking of religious "persuasions": "he is of the Roman Catholic (or Mormon, or Christian) persuasion." This usage is a relic of a polite convention of trying to soft-pedal religious differences. But to those who have come to grips with God in the encounter and struggle to which we have been referring, there is something very funny, if not macabre, about alluding to it as a persuasion. For whatever else it may be, it is certainly not this. One can no more talk of a man being of a religious persuasion than one can talk of him being of a suicidal persuasion or a self-preserving persuasion. Of a man's conduct under fire or in a bayonet charge it is proper to say that he was cowardly or brave or foolhardy or cunning; it would certainly be proper (if it happened to be true) to say that he wasn't there. It could never be anything other than absurd to say he was of this persuasion or that school of thought about bayonet charges. It is true that an experienced general might be said to favor this or that view in tactics or strategy; but these views would all certainly exclude arguments about whether bayonet charges, aerial bombardments, and the like, do in fact take place. "Armchair" discussion of the conduct of war may very well proceed, however, as though such activities were of an entirely different character from that which everybody who has experienced them knows them to possess. Such discussion is properly called "unrealistic"; so also must be any arguments about God that are not immediately referable to the existential situation of encounter with Him.

Final Review of the Thomistic Demonstrations

The traditional arguments, we have seen, are ancient. But what is widely expected of them today is to a great extent due to a modern misunderstanding of them. Thomas Aquinas, for example, in setting forth his celebrated "Five Ways" of demonstrating the existence of God did not mean by demonstration what people nowadays often suppose he meant. He never called them proofs. True, he taught that the existence of God could be "known by natural reason"; but he presupposed a certain intellectual climate, a God-centered way of thinking, within which he felt prepared to exhibit or demonstrate the existence of God. In formulating his argument he was answering a somewhat technical objection that *because* it happened to be "an article of faith" that God exists, *therefore* it was impossible to have *knowledge* of it. He held that the existence of God is not really "the article of faith," but is, rather, a preamble to this, available to what might be called "natural reason." But St. Thomas, like the ancients to whom he was much indebted, used the term "reason" in a very wide sense, so that it is misleading to us to be told, as we often are, that he and other ancient and medieval thinkers intended to "prove" the existence of God by "logical" argument. According to Thomas, faith implies the assent of the intellect to what cannot be absolutely certain on purely intellectual grounds. Confronted with a choice, the intellect "turns voluntarily to one side rather than to the other; and if this be accompanied by doubt and fear of the opposite side, there will be opinion, while, if there be certainty and no fear of the other side, there will be faith." [11] This means that it is by an act of the will that what would otherwise be uncertain knowledge *becomes* certain. By the aid of the will, the intellect can, so to speak, "get below" ordinary "logical argument" and so achieve a kind of certainty that is no less authentic than the sort available in "logical argument" which, in the circumstances, could be of no avail. Such a description of the nature of faith suited the age to which Thomas was addressing himself. Though much of what we have been saying in the present chapter is couched in an idiom that did not come into general vogue till the second quarter of the present century, the notions we have been propounding are really quite ancient ones. Unconsciously or otherwise they underlay much of the thought that went into the building of the traditional arguments. It is not that the older thinkers would have disagreed with our contentions, so much as that in the intellectual climate of their age there was not the same necessity for making explicit certain points that today force themselves upon our attention.

DISCUSSION ON CHAPTER 20

1. "The whole trouble is that we won't let God help us." (George MacDonald) Discuss.

2. Discuss Starr Daily's account of his conversion in prison, comparing it with any other conversions of which you know.

3. "The only way of proving the existence of God is by faith in God." Consider the significance of this affirmation and discuss its consequences.

[11] *Summa Theologica*, II–IIae, Q. 1, 4.

PART FOUR

Human Knowledge of God

21

What is Man?

Is There a "Human Nature"?

Many people who claim to be very skeptical about the nature of God show much less inclination to see the need for any radical skepticism about human nature. Man presents to them many problems; but they tend to take it for granted that modern psychology is answering most of these and that by means of its methods, and those of sociology, anthropology and kindred sciences, scientific solutions of all problems relating to human nature must sooner or later be provided. God may remain a mystery to be believed in by some and repudiated by others, to be assigned this nature by pantheists and that nature by those who favor an evolutionary naturalism; but in regard to human nature there should be no such difficulty. Perhaps, they think, various differences of view must always remain in regard to certain questions about human nature, just as there are different views among doctors and educationalists on certain questions in their respective fields; nevertheless, human nature itself is fundamentally *understandable*.

Such was, indeed, the hope of David Hume when he wrote his *Treatise of Human Nature* more than two hundred years ago. He thought that "the science of man is the only solid foundation for the other sciences," [1] and that any defects it might have would be only those shared by these other sciences. But the question is not so simple. Modern psychology does indeed provide an enormous amount of information. By its experimental methods it can and does tell us a great deal we could not otherwise know about ourselves, about human tendencies and behavior and needs. The theories of the psychoanalysts, too, have been fruitful. Developed in the course of clinical practice, they have often provided excellent therapeutic results, showing how much this sort of approach to psychological problems can accomplish. But all this fails to answer the most fundamental questions about human nature itself. Generally speaking, it does

[1] David Hume, *Treatise of Human Nature*, Introduction.

132

not even raise them. It certainly does not answer the question of whether there is a "human nature."

The existence of a "human nature" has often been assumed without question. That is, it has been assumed that man is distinguished by certain characteristics and propensities that are intrinsically proper to him. But when it comes to defining exactly what a human being is, there is a much greater difficulty than at first might be supposed. Is he a complicated sort of robot? How precisely does he differ from a very highly advanced simian? [2] Is he a conglomeration of conditioned reflexes, and if so, by what precisely are the reflexes conditioned?

Zeno of Citium and the Idea of Conscience

It appears that, historically, it was Zeno of Citium, founder of the Stoic school of philosophy at the close of the fourth century B.C., who first excogitated the notion of a "human nature." According to him, the human soul is a detached piece of the divine nature, a piece that is imprisoned in a particular kind of body. Therefore it contains certain innate ideas, including, for example, certain moral and religious notions. This philosopher also invented the Greek term *syneidesis*, which came to be translated "conscience," by which he meant the sum of our innate moral ideas. Such a view of the question was part of the heritage that Greek philosophy bequeathed to the western tradition of thought. After the more theological elements in it had been discarded, however, belief in an essential "human nature" persisted, and it persists today in much ordinary thinking. People tend to talk of human nature as though it were something quite clearly definable; certainly as something intrinsic and unalterable that people "have." From the same source we preserve the notion that there are inalienable human rights, associated with what we call the dignity of man.

Why be "Decent"?

The careful and thoughtful reader will notice that the conception of "human nature" that has so been transmitted to us is a peculiar one. Not only is it vague; it has a special history. Originally a theological notion, it has become secularized; yet not entirely, for it bears upon itself the telltale marks of its ancestry. What has really happened in the process, only in part successful, of its secularization? Unwittingly, it may be, and unintentionally, no doubt, the content of the theological notion has been kept after the basis has

---

[2] This question has been raised in fiction in a profound French novel translated into English under the title *You shall know Them*, by Vercors [Jean Vercors Bruller] (Boston: Little, Brown and Co., 1953).

been discarded. The position of a person who has so thrown off the theological basis for, but has nevertheless tried to preserve the idea of, the sacrosanct character of human nature, is similar to that of one who, having repudiated the moral sanction against sexual promiscuity, invokes what he perhaps calls "decency" in order to restrain the practice of that which the overthrow of the moral code might seem to legitimize. His reason for seeking to impose the restraint may be a recognition of certain factors which he might call "sociological" or "psychological" — factors which seem to him to make sexual promiscuity, at any rate in the prevailing situation, undesirable. He knows, however, that the consideration of such factors would be quite insufficient to have any appreciable effect in restraining so immensely powerful an instinct as the urge for sexual expression. Something much more powerful is plainly required for that purpose. Looking about him after he has announced his rejection of the moral basis of the traditional sanction against certain kinds of sexual behavior, he finds that the only tool available for his practical purpose — the purpose of restraining men and women from an expression of their impulses in a manner that might have alarming sociological and psychological results — is what might be called the Ghost of the Seventh Commandment. He appeals to *Decency*. There is no moral reason, he says, why you should not adopt the sexual habits of the farmyard; nevertheless it would be *indecent* to do so. To say that it is "indecent" to do so is to say no more than that it is "unsuitable" or "not fitting"; it is, indeed, to say nothing in particular at all. But that does not matter, because the word "indecent" carries within it a special echo — just the echo required for the purpose in view. It does not really say anything; yet its overtones from the past do the required work. They refer the hearer back to the old moral sanction that has been repudiated, so that (it is hoped) the old "power" of that sanction will take effect after the sanction itself is dead. Having killed the tyrant, you wave his helmet in the air in the hope that you may exert his magic power without the inconvenience of keeping him alive. So you say: "There are no *moral* reasons why you should not fornicate entirely at your pleasure, as opportunity may arise and inclination dictate; but it would not be decent to do so."

Whence the Dignity of Man?

So it may be asked with good reason how those who talk of the dignity of man are to justify their profession of belief in it when they have already, sometimes with a considerable flourish of trumpets, repudiated their belief in God. For the idea of the dignity of man is derived from and dependent upon belief in God. Those humanists who are sometimes heard to complain that certain kinds of art or moral conduct or political behavior insult man's dignity are seeking to uphold a notion whose very basis they have destroyed. They are claiming that the *kind* of dignity, the *kind* of intrinsic worth, that a man claims to have when he believes in God, can be violated when such belief in God is overthrown. But what worth or dignity does man have in himself? What doctrine of human dignity can there be that is not a corollary of a belief in God? The humanist is upholding the ghost of the dogma he has sought to kill. What he is saying is no less absurd than it would be for me to say I do not believe in space and then claim my traveling expenses from Washington to New York. How could I have any traveling expenses in such circumstances? We might even liken the humanist's claim to that of a man who, having betrayed his loyalty to the United States and renounced his allegiance, insisted upon his rights as an American citizen.

The Implicates of Humanism

The humanist, once he has repudiated the transcendental values associated with theism on which his belief in the intrinsic worth of mankind depends, forfeits his title to make his claims for mankind. But the fact that he makes them may also raise the question: has he really repudiated belief in the transcendental values, or is he only pretending to himself and others that he has done so? It is a commonplace of everyday experience that people reveal, by their claims, that their beliefs are not always what they say they are. The fact that a woman of low character openly scorns the social presuppositions upon which the ideal of "ladylike behavior" depends does not mean that she does not expect to be treated as a lady. Indeed, the most vulgar sort of woman, whose tastes and moral reputation are of the lowest order, is likely to be more insistent than a duchess in her claim to be treated as a lady. She is also generally more ready than the duchess to complain of the ungentlemanly behavior of men, although according to the social doctrine she professes she has no right to expect men to be any less rude than she is. Her expectations may very well indicate, however, that she has not in fact repudiated the ideal of gentlemanly and ladylike conduct, but is only pretending to do so as a means of taking the sting out of her own remorseful dissatisfaction with herself. In so indulging herself she is only revealing her tacit acknowledgment of her own shortcomings. Theists commonly observe that the humanist's claims for mankind, together with his repudiation of God, betoken a similar attempt at self-deception.

If No God, Then No Man

Man, in his relation with God, is invested with a certain unique dignity. But in himself he is far too puny to claim to be other than ridiculous to anybody who reflects for a moment on even the physical universe. "Where there is no God there is no man," writes Berdyaev,[3] meaning that the values traditionally associated with man are lost when he is taken out of relation with God, as surely as the 100-watt lamp burning in my room will go out as soon as somebody, by detaching a fuse, breaks the electric circuit. Instead of pretending to all sorts of rights and glories and dignities as a human being, it would be more realistic for me to face the fact that apart from a relationship to God I am only a mass of protoplasm interacting in various ways with other protoplasmic masses and exhibiting a variety of needs. According to one writer, that "is what a person is." [4]

The Puniness of Man

Though I should live three or four hundred years instead of three or four score, and in that time be a Leonardo, a Shakespeare and a Beethoven, all rolled into one, besides giving the world scientific discoveries to make modern physics look like primitive superstition, I must still face two elementary biological phenomena: the fact that I was born a miserable little milk-drinking machine on inefficient legs, and the fact that I shall die and so turn into something even more insignificant, a few grains of dust in a cemetery or ash in a crematorium. Console myself as I will, there is no escaping these facts. The values I have sought seemed eternal; but in spite of all the lofty phrases that are uttered at my funeral, there is something exceedingly ridiculous about the thought of them to those who relate them to my coffin. Perhaps I have chosen death for the sake of some moral ideal. I have laid down my life for my countrymen, or given it to save that of a drowning child. There is a great flourish of trumpets at my funeral; I am called all sorts of a hero. But the stir of it all is soon forgotten; it is not long till those who have been acclaiming me are themselves turning to dust, and even if my name goes down in the history books as that of a hero, the occasional remembrance of it does not mean what the moral act of laying down my life meant to me. The child I saved may become the greatest figure in American history; but not all his deeds together can make me see a glimpse of their splendor. Where is my human dignity? Scattered, you tell me, over the most glorious pages of the annals of the human race. But this is really mere humbug. If only I could be there to complain to you, I would tell you that it was as if I had asked my wife "Where is my breakfast?" and received from her the reply that it was scattered over the garden where it would eventually bring forth beautiful fruit, being in fact a finer breakfast than I had ever eaten.

[3] Nicholas Berdyaev, *The End of Our Time*, trans. Donald Atwater (New York: Sheed & Ward, 1933), p. 80.

[4] Edwin G. Boring and others, *Introduction to Psychology* (New York: John Wiley & Sons, Inc., 1939), p. 7.

Jeté là, comme ça

So much for the future — death. But what of the past? I am told to be grateful for my heritage and reminded of my responsibilities to my parents and others. But, self-centered wretch that I am, I reply that I did not ask them to procreate me; yet I certainly cannot pretend to have created myself. I find myself dumped here in the world. As the French nihilist Jean-Paul Sartre puts it, I am *"jeté là, comme ça."* No matter how grand my accomplishments may turn out to be, how glorious my visions, the fact remains that I was born in a place, at an hour, in a society, of a mother, and was not even perfunctorily consulted about any of them. Suppose I have become a Man of Destiny in the world, a great ruler or statesman in whose hands lies the fate of millions of men. I may change the course of history; I may precipitate the Third World War or avert it. What I cannot do (since I am excluding God from the picture) is to mitigate the grimness of the unalterable fact that the most realistic account I can give of my debut on life's stage is to say I was dumped on it, without anyone's having even the decency to inquire whether I wanted to be dumped or not. If I am a humanist, pretending to human dignity and the like, it is ignominious enough to be carted off life's stage in a box after I have played my glorious part in the play. Even more ridiculous, however, is my entrance upon the stage of life, attached to a placenta.

Irrevocability of the Past

So there is a grim finality about death and a mocking absurdity about birth. But there is also another reflection the humanist would do well to make. Every deed I have ever done, every thought I have ever had, is irrevocable. For in our godless scheme there is no forgiveness, no resurrection. It is not only death that grins at us mockingly; it is our past.

> What have you done, O you there
> Incessantly weeping.
> Say, what have you done, you there,
> With your youth?[5]

Whatever it is I did, good or bad, I can no more change it than I can turn in my grave. For my deeds are dead and frozen in the past; let my friends romanticize the remembrance of them as they will, nothing can ever really bring one of them to life. We begin to die the instant we are born. I only delude myself if I claim to be the

[5] Paul Verlaine, *Le ciel est, par-dessus le toit* . . . , in *Oxford Book of French Verse*, Second Edition (1957), pp. 479–480. (English translation is the present writer's.)

creator of values without also recognizing that they drop dead the moment I create them, leaving only, at the most, a vague and evanescent fragrance.

No Satisfaction in Humanism

Such an optimistic and godless humanism is an impossible resting-place. If I am to repudiate all belief in God as creator and conserver of values, I must certainly also disclaim such a role for myself and for other human beings. To face the consequences of this choice is of the utmost importance, for it is by neglecting or refusing to face it that we humans, with our boundless capacity for self-delusion, succeed in deceiving ourselves that the life we prize and the values we cherish can be somehow immortalized in an aggregate of mortal beings. But of course such an aggregate of humanity is just as mortal as I am. If I am to repudiate all belief in God, I must therefore (since an optimistic and godless humanism of the sort we have just been considering is quite ill founded) be prepared to acknowledge that the heroism I admire, the poetry in which I delight, and the scientific achievements I applaud, are all as subject to death as I am. The Empire State Building and the Taj Mahal are just as susceptible to annihilation as the architects who designed them. Surely we need not be reminded that a few well-placed modern bombs could eliminate not only the human race but practically all evidence that it had ever existed.

Human life is neither a hymn nor a ribald song; it is a struggle. It is in our striving rather than in any external manifestation of success that we find our real satisfaction. It is not necessary to be a theist to admit this; an atheist, so long as he is a hard-working atheist, may be equally ready to recognize it. But in what consists the struggle? And what is the nature of the satisfaction? To you they may appear under one guise; to me under another. I may see them differently according to my varying moods: now as the winning of a woman I love, now as the mastery of my chosen craft or profession, now as the exhilaration of climbing a dangerous precipice with my heart pounding inside me, now as the dogged pursuit of a problem in historical research for months on end among the musty old manuscripts of some great library. But as I try to look at myself and my life from a less restricted viewpoint I find that the real struggle and the real satisfaction (or dissatisfaction, as the case may be) lie beyond all these interests and pursuits. It is well known that an acute sense of emptiness, far deeper than my satisfaction, may overtake me just as I have made the exciting discovery in my historical or scientific research. Having reached the professional status to the attainment of which I have devoted more than half a lifetime, I find that my satisfaction in the attainment quickly gives place to a feeling of the relative unimportance of professional recognition. At the summit of the mountain the thrill of the ascent begins to fade. In the pursuit of sexual love it is a commonplace that when intense desire is followed by what the little books for newlyweds call "complete fulfillment," the sense of satisfaction quickly palls, being superseded by a malaise, a longing for a something-I-know-not-what.

All our desires, longings, anxieties and ambitions are very much deeper than we know, extending far beyond the limited guise under which we see them. Indeed, man himself is far more complex than he can know, having roots that lie infinitely beyond what he can understand of himself either with or without a study of modern psychology. Modern psychology, scratching only a little below the surface of our nature, provides a pointer to, but not an explanation of, the paradoxical character of man's struggle.

The Greatness and Wretchedness of Man

There is nothing in all this to provide any intrinsically convincing demonstration of the existence or nonexistence of God. But a profound appreciation of the immense complexity of human nature does raise the question of God's existence in a peculiarly forceful way. Two interpretations are possible. On the one hand, it may be suggested that man will gradually probe the depths of his own nature till he understands it as well as he has already learned to understand, say, the chemistry of plants — a subject which, till comparatively recent times, was little understood and seemed infinitely mysterious. Or, on the other hand, it may be held that the fundamental nature of man can no more be understood without relating it to a Being beyond man than the motion of the earth can be understood without relating it to the solar system, the Milky Way, and the rest of the physical universe.

We have spoken of the paradoxical character of man's struggle. The paradox in human nature arises from the fact that while man is on the one hand as puny as we have depicted him, he is also greater than his most extravagant praise of himself can even hint. While I revolt against the smug humanism of those who would seek to exalt man into the immortal god that he certainly is not, I rebel no less against the attitude that belittles me as less than a worm. Such are the reflections behind Pascal's famous phrase, *la grandeur et la misère de l'homme*, man's greatness and wretchedness. It is not a question of whether man is great or small; the paradox is that he is both. Writing from a scientific standpoint, Alexis Carrel discusses, in a most provocative book, *Man, the Unknown*, the nature of man's place in the universe:

The human body is placed, on the scale of magnitudes, half-way between the atom and the star. According to the size of the objects selected for comparison, it appears either large or small. Its length is equivalent to that of two hundred thousand tissue cells, or of two millions of ordinary microbes, or of two billions of albumin molecules, placed end to end. Man is gigantic in comparison with an electron, an atom, a molecule, a microbe. But, when compared with a mountain, or with the earth, he is tiny. More than four thousand individuals would have to stand one upon the other in order to equal the height of Mount Everest. A terrestrial meridian is approximately equivalent to twenty millions of them placed end to end. Light, as is well known, travels about one hundred and fifty million times the length of our body in one second. The interstellar distances are such that they have to be measured in light years. Our stature, in relation to such a system of reference, becomes inconceivably small. For this reason . . . books of popular astronomy . . . succeed in impressing their readers with the complete insignificance of man in the universe. In reality, our spatial greatness or smallness is without importance. For what is specific of man has no physical dimensions. The meaning of our presence in this world assuredly does not depend upon our size.[6]

Man is not only both great and small; he is also both good and wicked. This fact is obvious. A novel would hardly be readable, let alone convincing, if the hero had no shortcomings at all, or the villain no redeeming qualities. It would not be convincing, because everyone knows that there are no such persons. But the significance of this is liable to be overlooked or misunderstood. It is not that we humans are a pedestrian lot, the best of us not much better than average and the worst of us not much below it. It is, rather, that we are all extremely susceptible to the influences of both good and evil. It is as though we were all half-demonic and half-divine. It is this fact of ordinary experience that finds expression in the ancient Orphic myth about the origin of humanity. According to one form of this myth, evil demons, jealous of the son of Zeus, the high god, killed him and ate him up. Father Zeus, in anger, sent a thunderbolt to destroy the wicked demons, and it was from their ashes (with which had been mingled the son of good Zeus) that men sprang. The myth would account for the fact that we human beings have such an extraordinary capacity for *both* good and evil. In the moral as well as in other aspects of our nature we are a puzzle — such a puzzle that it is exceedingly difficult to imagine how we might ever hope really to understand

[6] Alexis Carrel, *Man, the Unknown* (New York: Harper & Bros., 1935), pp. 60–61.

our own nature as we have learned to understand certain other components of the universe that confronts us. Our nature is such as to *suggest*, at any rate, that the key to an understanding of it lies not in ourselves but beyond ourselves. A theistic interpretation of our human nature is offered by Reinhold Niebuhr in these words:

> Man is an individual, but he is not self-sufficing. The law of his nature is love, a harmonious relation of life to life in obedience to the divine centre and source of his life. This law is violated when man seeks to make himself the centre and source of his own life. His sin is therefore spiritual and not carnal, though the infection of rebellion spreads from the spirit to the body and disturbs its harmonies also. Man, in other words, is a sinner not because he is one limited individual within a whole but rather because he is betrayed, by his very ability to survey the whole, to imagine himself the whole.[7]

The Paradox of Freedom Through Obedience

But this is not to say that man's roots in a Being beyond him restrict his freedom: on the contrary, they engender it. Once again we find a paradox in our human nature — one that presents a perennial puzzle to the theistic philosopher. For according to the traditional interpretations of theism, the more I bend myself to the will of God, the greater is my liberty. How can conformity to the will of another Being establish or enhance the freedom of my will? At first sight it would seem that any such yielding of my will to the will of another, even the will of a divine Being, must restrict my freedom. But there are analogies of this mystery in physical nature. The Zen Buddhists of Japan have for long recognized the principle and widely applied it. They call it *wu wei*. To illustrate it they remind us that a tree whose branches are laden with heavy snow "knows" not to resist the snow. If it resisted, holding its branches taut against the weight, these would break under the burden. By gently bending, the tree lets the snow slide softly off them. This is also the principle that lies behind the Japanese wrestling technique, jujitsu. Again, it is not the strong or healthy person who resists the efforts of doctor or psychiatrist; it is the distraught or neurotic person who is the difficult patient, being unduly suspicious and resentful. The stronger, healthier one has more buoyancy, more trust, more pliability. In yielding without fear to the will beyond me I find that, far from losing my will, I realize and develop it.

It is not always, however, a question of yielding my will. Some-

[7] *The Nature and Destiny of Man* (New York: Charles Scribner's Sons, 1945), I, pp. 16–17.

times it is rather by an effort to assert it that I succeed in maintaining and developing a relationship. If you have ever had to shake hands with hundreds of people in one evening, you will have felt ready to quit with fatigue after the first fifty unless you had already learned the technique of coping with such ordeals. If you extend a limp hand to each of your benevolent tormentors to squeeze and pump-handle at his will, you will soon quail. Experience teaches the handshaker that it is less fatiguing to grip the other's hand than let his be gripped by the other. But it is neither a question of yielding your will nor a question of asserting it; it is a question of entering usefully and creatively into a relationship. Timidity is as unprofitable as arrogance.

> Tender-hearted stroke a nettle
>   And it stings you for your pains;
> Grasp it like a man of mettle
>   And it soft as silk remains.

So, the theist maintains, the only way in which we can fully realize ourselves as human beings is to put ourselves into relationship with God.

The Mystery of Man

Our acceptance of the view just described must depend, of course, on our belief in theism. But the foregoing considerations do indicate that whatever human nature may or may not be, it is more complex than any humanism, however sophisticated, can account for; more complex than we commonly imagine; probably more complex than we can ever know. The theist maintains that man's incapacity for self-knowledge is itself a pointer to the existence of God. He holds that man is incomprehensible in himself for the excellent reason that it is his relationship to God that is the key to an understanding of the mystery of man. If our present civilization were largely destroyed, leaving only fragmentary evidence of what it is like, a future archaeologist who chanced to find a solitary surviving phonograph record would find it exceedingly difficult to explain what it was for. Despite the ingenious conjectures that no doubt he would make, it would be practically impossible to give a satisfactory explanation of the nature and purpose of the surviving phonograph record without reference to a surviving phonograph. If a few bits of this were available, even in the most distorted form, they might at least put a diligent archaeologist on the right track. This, the theist would suggest, is the only way in which the mystery of man can begin to be unraveled: he must find the relationship of which he is a part. Human nature, whatever it is, is much too complex to be accounted for or even discussed in terms only of itself. The honest man must be agnostic not only about God; his own human nature demands of him no less profound an agnosticism.

DISCUSSION ON CHAPTER 21

> Know then thyself, presume not God to scan;
> The proper study of mankind is Man.   (Pope)

Critically consider this injunction.

2. "Man is the only animal that laughs and weeps; for he is the only animal that is struck with the difference between what things are, and what they ought to be." (Hazlitt) Discuss.

3. "What a chimera, then, is man! What a novelty! What a monster, what a chaos, what a contradiction, what a prodigy! Judge of all things, feeble worm of the earth, depository of truth, a sink of uncertainty and error, the glory and the shame of the universe." (Pascal) Discuss.

22

The Place of Agnosticism
in Religion

Agnosticism and Humility

Far from being essentially opposed to religion, the agnostic spirit plays an important part in all profoundly religious experience. It has a peculiarly important role in Christianity, inasmuch as it is an expression of the virtue of humility, which is a highly prized Christian virtue, being the opposite of pride which, according to the Christian theologians, is the root of all sin. Because humility may therefore be accounted the root of all the Christian virtues, all arrogant dogmatism is fundamentally contrary to the disposition that deeply Christian experience engenders.

We have already seen that all genuine faith implies profound doubt; but the quality of that doubt must be further exhibited. What commonly passes for doubt is not really doubt at all, but only a perverted, negative sort of dogmatism. The same is true of humility itself. It is an elusive virtue. To illustrate its elusiveness, the story is told that a novice of the Trappist Order, which stresses the practice of humility, was asked by his novice-master to distinguish the spirit of their order from that of other religious orders in the Roman Church. He replied: "For learning, the Benedictines are unequalled; the Jesuits beat all others in their missionary skill; for the virtue of Holy Poverty, the Franciscans remain unchallenged; but for Humility we Trappists beat them all!" It is, of course, the special nature of humility that makes the novice's reply so absurd. A learned man may boast of his learning; a punctual man may boast of his punctuality; but as soon as a man boasts of his humility you know he is boasting of that which he does not have. So with agnosticism. The reason why the profession of agnosticism appears ridiculous to the Christian is that the profession of it belies the claim to its possession. The truly agnostic spirit is much more delicate than is commonly imagined.

Faith a Descant Upon Doubt

Christian humility is intimately associated with love. It is symbolically expressed in the monastic ceremony on Maundy Thursday

144

in which the abbot kneels before each of the assembled monks in turn, beginning with the youngest, to wash the feet of each as a sign that he who is placed in the highest position of authority should be humbler than all the rest. So the most profound Christian thinkers have recognized that agnosticism is a mark of religious insight. But, as one writer has put it, it is "worthy of honour and respect when it takes the form of the mind's abasement before divine mysteries in the face of which all our creeds are but childish prattle and all our worship a superstitious mummery; when, that is to say, it represents the recognition by religion of its own inability to solve its own problems. But when it is flaunted by a complacent religiosity as an excuse for believing anything it likes, in defiance of the protests made by the scientific and historical consciousness, it deserves nothing but the contempt which, happily, it as a rule excites." [1] The genuine agnostic is not the man who, being indifferent to the claims of various religions, complacently asserts that he simply will not take a stand. The genuine agnostic is he who, having struggled to the breaking-point with religious difficulties, acknowledges that when his faith is most vivacious it is accompanied by the most profound awe that prevents him from ever being satisfied with any expression of it. The superficial spectator of religions is really professing uncertainty; the other is acknowledging himself to be in the presence of a mystery in which, for everything that is revealed, there is something that is concealed. His faith may rise beyond this, like a descant upon the doubt; but as a descant is not a descant apart from the rest of the music, so his faith is not faith apart from the awe that the believer feels before the divine mysteries that confront him.

It is true that such an attitude is hardly typical of, say, the majority of churchgoers in a suburban parish. But it is to be expected that people should have superficial ideas about religion, as they have superficial ideas on other subjects. People with no artistic gifts are often those who talk most loudly about art at cocktail parties, and people who would not know the difference between a beaker and a burette talk glibly about physics and chemistry as though they were unlucky to have missed the Nobel Prize. So it is hardly surprising that people are ready to be eloquently dogmatic about religion. But anyone who has scratched below the surface of things in religion knows that no arrogant dogmatism is worth a moment's attention.

Agnosticism in the Historic Creeds

But it is also to be noticed that not all seemingly bold utterances are as arrogantly dogmatic as they may sound. The Nicene Creed

[1] R. G. Collingwood, *Speculum Mentis* (New York: Oxford University Press, 1924), p. 131.

sounds the most outrageous piece of smug arrogance when you listen to it being bawled as though it were a football cheer. When you know something of the immensely complicated controversy behind it, however, you can begin to see that it is really the expression of great humility in face of divine mysteries that the limits of our human understanding as well as the poverty of our human speech prevent us from expressing adequately. Yet the believer cannot be entirely silent, for silence itself can betoken an exceedingly dogmatic attitude. The historic Christian Creeds are really attempts to *avoid* excessively dogmatic utterances. For instance, it might be held by some that since the Bible speaks of Father, Son and Holy Spirit, there are really three Gods. But, proclaims the so-called Athanasian Creed, this is not so: God is One. It might be held by others that since God is One, it is wrong to distinguish between Father, Son and Holy Spirit. No, declares the same Creed, it is not so simple as all that: though God the Father, God the Son, and God the Holy Spirit, are of one essence, yet they are distinguishable in another way. It is a warning, as it were, to both sides; a demand for the recognition of mystery rather than a mere assertion.

Agnosticism as a Philosophical Position

Such an agnostic component in all lively faith must, of course, be distinguished from agnosticism as a philosophical *position*. But even the latter, though it may appear to the superficial observer to be fundamentally alien to, if not incompatible with, the theistic position, is closer to this than is commonly supposed. Theism can give unrestricted hospitality to every form of genuine agnosticism. But the more vivid the anguish in the agnostic's position, the more eagerly is it to be welcomed by the theist. Agnosticism never really becomes alienated from theism until it loses that which is really most fully characteristic of itself, the tension in a situation of moral choice. When agnosticism becomes, however, crystallized into a dogmatic position, so that the anguish peculiar to it is not really felt any longer, it becomes a mere parody of itself. The agnostic who has lost the existential anguish that is proper to his position has not necessarily become a *poseur*. But his agnosticism has become a perversion of what it might have been. He no longer *feels* the agony of his position: he has retreated from the reality of it and is now indulging, rather, in the contemplation of a picture of himself as the agnostic that he no longer has the courage to be. Whether agnosticism as a philosophical position is to be accounted the friend of theism depends only upon this: has it retained or lost its own essence, its own characteristic vitality? Only when the agnostic has become smug has he taken up a position alien and perhaps even hostile to theism; but then he has departed from true agnosticism itself. The theist does not value agnosticism only because, as a component of theism, it may be expected to have some sort of theistic tendency that is naturally congenial to the theist. The latter ought to value agnosticism for its own sake. He ought to value it because the most characteristic mood of the agnostic — far removed though the agnostic's attitude may seem, in the eyes of the casual observer who often knows it only in its more petrified form, from the theistic commitment — is so internally akin to that which issues in the choice the theist makes as to command the unqualified sympathy and respect of the latter.

Why Genuine Agnosticism Evokes the Theist's Sympathy

If you have ever been faced with the making of a great decision in your life, all this will be easy enough to understand. If you have spent sleepless nights in considering the pros and cons of a course of action that is of the greatest importance, your eventual decision for or against will never make you unsympathetic to the attitude of the person whom you find facing a similar situation and who is still having the sleepless nights. You know that what he is suffering is part of your own experience in making the choice — the most real part of it, from one point of view. It is only toward a person who has really given up the facing of that situation and resorted to a pretense to take its place, that you would feel impatience. And your impatience with him would be due not so much to his having given up the struggle as to his continuing to pretend to be engaged in it.

Why "a God Comprehended is No God"

If my experience forces me to recognize the existence of God, I say I believe in God. The conviction I have is inescapable; it is always a step ahead of the rest of my attitudes and thoughts, in the sense that it is so strong that I find it easier to disbelieve in the universe around me than to disbelieve in God. But if my belief in God is as compelling as that, it will be full of awe about the nature of God. I must see that I am beholding God all the time through my own frail, finite eyes, attributing to Him qualities in terms of my own, though I know that the God in whom I believe must be greater than ever I can conceive. I cannot hope to comprehend Him. As Tersteegen put it, "a God comprehended is no God." Nevertheless, I am compelled to think of God somehow or other, even though I know that my thought is inadequate. I will think of God "as best I can." If I am a very simple person I may think of God as a sort of Santa Claus in the clouds. If I am a Plato or a Kant I will not think in this childish fashion, it is true; nevertheless, however subtly I think, my thought must be quite inadequate to the object of my belief. I can do no more than delineate *my* conception of God. This is the subjective element in my belief. I cannot escape this element, and because of it I am full of doubts; that is, I am forced to say "I don't know" to a great many of the questions you are likely to put to me about God, and that I am likely indeed to put to myself. The agnostic who says that such is the limitation of our faculties that in the nature of the case adequate answers to questions about God are not merely difficult or even impossible, but inconceivable, is right. But this fact does not eliminate the immense fact that God still confronts me as The Other who, to use the language of piety, "encompasses me with His love."

Pious Language Misleading

The language of piety is notoriously misleading. Here, for instance, it is apt to suggest questions such as: "Ah, but is not your whole notion that there is a God no more than a psychological projection? Is it not an expression of your own need for security, a disguised craving for return to the prenatal comfort of your mother's womb and the irresponsibility you once enjoyed there, free from the cares of an independent existence and the responsibilities involved in the struggle of life?" To this the theist replies that belief in God, when genuine, engenders no such reversion to irresponsibility but, on the contrary, manifests itself in an acutely heightened sense of responsibility.

The theist maintains, then, that his experience of God is the experience of a relationship with The Other. The relationship is at least as much a part of his everyday experience as is, say, his relationship with the physical universe. He finds himself confronted by The Other, and he finds (among other things) that The Other makes demands on him that exceed the demands he would make on himself even in his most morally vivacious moments. He finds that these demands are essentially the demands of a Being other than himself, and that this Being's part in the relationship is to be described, in terms of our inadequate human language, as one of infinite love. More simply, it may be said that this Being is "our Father."

But for all this certainty on the part of the theist about the reality and importance of his experience, he makes no claim to *understand* God. It is in this sense that he is agnostic. This element of agnosticism in religion is striking and widespread: it is to be found very vividly in the medieval Jewish philosopher Maimonides, for example, as well as in Christian thought. Nicholas of Cusa (1401–1464), Blaise Pascal (1623–1662) and John Henry Newman (1801–1890) are but a few examples of Christian thinkers who have stressed it. Such agnosticism acknowledges great limits to our knowledge of God while nevertheless fully recognizing the reality of the encounter with God that the theist insists upon as the most striking and challenging of all the experiences of his life.

The Travail of Faith

That God should be so incomprehensible is not surprising. We have seen already how mysterious I must be to myself, and though according to the theist man becomes less mysterious when God is postulated, it does not follow that God is thereby made more comprehensible. At the most we may expect only to have what might be called a faint glimpse of the divine as mediated through our relationship to God. Even the Christian, who maintains that Jesus, the Christ, is the full, final and perfect revelation of God to man, must admit that this perfect revelation does not really make God comprehensible or diminish the force of the agnostic element that must be present in all genuine religion. God may be revealed sufficiently for the moment to me when, to use the Quaker phrase, He is revealed "to my condition." But not even God could reveal Himself to humanity beyond the capacity of humanity, except to the extent that He improved that capacity, and as He never makes mankind "measure up" to God, nor diminishes the enormous gulf that lies between God and man, the agnostic element in religion remains of fundamental importance.

The fact that a great deal of popular religion falls far short of the disposition we have been considering makes it inevitable that there should be many people talking about God as glibly as a spoiled child talks about his teddy-bear. This has, however, nothing to do with the points brought forward for consideration in this chapter. It has no more to do with them than hypochondria has to do with the practice of medicine, or idle chatter about "a perfectly divine concert" has to do with the travail of musical composition.

DISCUSSION ON CHAPTER 22

1. In theological discussions about the precise nature of the presence of Christ in the Eucharist, the following rhyme, attributed to Queen Elizabeth I of England, has often been quoted:

> 'Twas God the word that spake it,
> He took the bread and brake it;
> And what the word did make it,
> That I believe and take it.

Consider this with reference to the notions discussed in the present chapter.

2.   The man that feareth, Lord, to doubt,
           In that fear doubteth thee.   (George MacDonald)

Discuss.

3. President John S. Dickey of Dartmouth, writing in the *Atlantic* (April, 1955) on the subject of religious questionings among university undergraduates, quoted President William Jewett Tucker: "The doubting mind always seemed to me a part of the believing mind." President Dickey, commenting on this, observed: "The understanding of such paradox is the fruit of full maturity, rarely, if ever, within the reach of any undergraduate." Discuss.

23

The Illative Sense

Faith Depends on What Informs It

Being in great trouble, I go to a friend and say, "What shall I do? I have come to an impasse in life. Where shall I turn? How am I to go on from here?" My friend, being unable to offer me any "rational" advice says, "You must have faith." I am annoyed and say, "But I haven't got faith, so what?" Weakly, my friend murmurs, "Ah, faith is a gift." This does not help me if I feel I have not got the gift.

"Faith" is indeed a much abused term, being applied to one of the vaguest of all feelings and so opposed to all that is precise and rigorous in thought. It would seem to be a sort of instinct. And yet it is not, even at the worst, an instinct that is entirely uninformed. The quality of the faith depends, in fact, upon how it is informed and by what it is informed.

Newman on the Ground of Conviction

A man's convictions are not merely intellectual. It is not by what a man says that we judge his convictions; nor is it even by what I think that I can judge my own. A man's convictions are to be judged in terms of what he does with his life. It is not by reason alone that we succeed in life, though reason plays an extremely important part. Describing a step in his spiritual pilgrimage, Newman wrote:

> For myself, it was not logic, then, that carried me on; as well might one say that the quicksilver in the barometer changes the weather. It is the concrete being that reasons; pass a number of years, and I find my mind in a new place; how? the whole man moves; paper logic is but the record of it.[1]

Elsewhere,[2] Newman tries to describe in detail how our religious convictions are in fact arrived at. He distinguishes between inference and

[1] J. H. Newman, *Apologia pro vita sua*, Second Edition (London, 1865), p. 188.
[2] *Essay in Aid of a Grammar of Assent.*

assent. The former does not necessarily imply the latter, for inference is hypothetical; that is, it takes the form, *if* P *then* Q. Inference is concerned with the relations between propositions: it is either valid or invalid. From the proposition, "You can go without clothes in Greenland if you are as hardy as a polar bear," I may develop an argument eventually yielding the conclusion that you could be a Greenland nudist. The conclusion is valid, but you would not assent to it. This simple example shows the basis of the difference between inference and assent.

Inference and Assent

Newman is concerned to show that assent to a reasoned conclusion is not to be identified with logical inference. He contends that assent is not a stage *within* inference and therefore inseparable from it. He thinks that inference and assent are separable, because (a) we often assent to a proposition long after we have forgotten the inferential means of arriving at it, and (b) the movement from inference to assent, from an acceptance that is conditional to an acceptance that is unconditional, is by no means as automatic as it may sometimes appear to be. It is, rather, that after the inferential process has been completed, there is a further and all-important step — one that is taken not by the intellect only, but by the entire man. The validity of an argument may be incontestable, and the premises on which it is founded may look fairly acceptable; yet the slightest doubt or misgiving, however vague, will be sufficient to prevent my assent to the conclusion.

"Real" and "Notional" Thinking

Newman makes another distinction between what he calls "real" and "notional" thinking. "Notional" propositions are such as: "all men are mortal," "some men are French," "the sum of the angles of a triangle is equal to two right angles." Examples of "real" propositions would be: "George Washington was the first President of the United States," "my mother has lumbago," and "Mr. Smith forgave the man who killed his son." This distinction between real and notional thinking is associated with his distinction between inference and assent. Though Newman falls into a technical confusion in the course of his treatment of these distinctions, what he says is nevertheless suggestive and important. Much of our thinking is done with symbols which we never refer back to what may be called the "real currency" of experience. Such symbols are of great utility. They are easily manipulated with rapidity, reminding us of some of the advantages that bank checks have over hard-cash transactions. Mathematics is an obvious, striking example of what may be called "notionalized"

thinking; but Newman saw that even in the most com[
thought-processes we "notionalize." For instance, we label a
span of history "the eighteenth century," and go on to tall
this as a period, contrasting it with "the seventeenth centu., as
though we had a full and clear idea of the two contrasting notions.
We may likewise label and classify persons, so that, as Newman
says, a person becomes "the logarithm of his true self, and in that
shape is worked with the ease and satisfaction of logarithms." [3]

So long as such notional thinking is recognized as such and not
abused, it is of immense value, enabling us to think rapidly and without the private, emotional associations that inevitably come to be
attached to certain images. Instead of thinking of hospital patients
as "the nice old lady in the corner who is so brave in her suffering
and considerate toward everybody" and "that awful woman in the
other corner who is always grumbling," we call them simply "Case
17" and "Case 18," respectively. But the latter way of labeling
people can lead us into losing sight of the reality of their personalities,
so that we treat them as cases, not as real people. So we talk of "a
million men killed in the First World War" without the agony of
the reality behind this statement being conveyed to us at all. The
horror of a family dying of starvation during an economic depression
is heavily disguised when the fact is translated into notional thinking
and expressed statistically to the effect that the mortality rate for malnutrition was .05 per cent higher than in the previous year; that is to
say, only one more person in 2000 actually died of starvation this year.
Such procedures are nevertheless extremely useful. No less inevitable
are the propositions of theology, though of course they similarly distort
the reality of the religious experience behind them.

The Spring of Action

Newman was reacting against the rationalism and mathematicism of
Descartes. Historically, this is not difficult to understand. After his
conversion to Rome, Newman became a priest of the Congregation of
the Oratory, and the Oratorian tradition, through Malebranche (1638–
1715) and others, owed much to the Cartesian heritage. Newman's
compatriot, however, John Locke (1632–1704), though accounted
the father of modern empiricism, had been also deeply imbued with
rationalism. Kemp Smith thinks that "Locke gives more extreme
expression than even Descartes does, to the mystically conceived
mathematical method." [4] At any rate, it was Locke that Newman
used as a springboard for his own doctrine of the illative sense.

[3] *Ibid*, p. 25.
[4] N. K. Smith, *Commentary to Kant's Critique of Pure Reason* (London:
Macmillan & Co., Ltd., 1923), p. 592.

Locke had very properly insisted that no lover of truth would entertain any proposition with greater assurance than the evidence warranted.[5] As Locke put it, "the surplusage of assurance is owing to some other affection and not to the love of truth." [6] Newman points out, however, that whatever we may say in the study, we act in life with a far greater assurance than the evidence warrants. We do not, strictly speaking, *know* many of the things we assume every day for practical purposes.[7] We act on probabilities that are so strong that for practical purposes they are indistinguishable from certainties. So Newman insists that besides the formal inference of logic there is an informal inference, used in everyday life. He cites examples. The mainland of Britain is an island, and no one ever doubts it. But how many people have really investigated the truth of the statement for themselves? Generally we take such statements on the say-so of others. We trust the map. But even if I were to determine to inquire for myself, it would be a more difficult undertaking than it might at first appear to be. It would not be easy to be quite certain, in the rationalist sense, that I was not being deluded, and if a very pedantic skeptic insisted on formal proof it would be extremely difficult for me to provide it. Nevertheless, nobody ever really hesitates to act on the assumption that Britain is an island. I habitually act on much more dangerous assumptions, such as that the stair outside the classroom is still there. For instance, I open the classroom door and walk quickly downstairs without even looking to make sure that the stair has not collapsed or been removed. No one has ever stopped me to inquire, "But haven't you forgotten to make a formal inference before undertaking the descent?"

The Illative Sense

We do not make separate, formal inferences before taking action. We see, rather, a great mass of facts that seem to fit together in the framework of our general view of life. We see the evidences of our belief as a whole, some parts more clearly than others, but all clearly enough to enable us to get an adequate picture. It is this "faculty" that Newman calls "the illative sense." It is not confined to any special field, and yet it is itself a special "faculty." It is a sort of native genius that may, however, be developed by experience, on the principle suggested by another writer that genius is two per cent inspiration and ninety-eight per cent perspiration. An experienced lawyer with great natural ability will sometimes pick up the essentials of a new, complicated case that is presented to him, not by a series of

[5] *Essay concerning the Human Understanding*, Book IV, Chapter 19, Section 1.

[6] *Ibid.*

[7] This had already been shown by David Hume (1711–1776).

detached logical steps and the exercise of a great feat of memory, but almost as if he were absorbing the case as a sponge absorbs water. Newman cites the instance of Napoleon's military genius, which enabled him to sum up a military situation with such speed that it seemed that just by looking for a minute or two through a telescope he could know quite clearly not only the position of the opposing army but its strength and even its intention. It is what is sometimes called "a flair," or "a nose," akin to the uncanny sense that old farmers often have about the morrow's weather. It is a sense that is far more valuable than any other in the practice of any profession: in medicine, for instance, the good diagnostician is always a step beyond his colleagues, even when their technical knowledge is superior to his.

There is nothing magical about this illative sense. It is not, however, based on certainties, but on a "cumulation of probabilities." So it is that, as Newman puts it, "what to one intellect is a proof is not so to another." What really convinces us in the arguments that are presented to our minds is not entirely the logic, but "the intellectual and moral character of the person maintaining them, and the ultimate silent effect of his arguments or conclusions upon our minds." [8]

One must distinguish between the propositions, "It is certain that . . . ," and "I am certain that . . . ." Strictly speaking, the former opening may be used only in self-evident propositions such as, "a blank sheet of paper has no writing upon it," and "twice twenty-seven is the sum of twenty-seven plus twenty-seven." In the case of all other kinds of proposition, I can only say, "I am certain that. . . ."

It was the application of all this to religion that especially interested Newman. He did not repudiate the traditional demonstrations of the existence of God, for example; but he wished to draw attention to the fact that these demonstrations are not really assent-compelling. Once again, it is by the illative sense that we reach our conclusions about religious matters. So I may be able to offer grounds for my religious faith which are truly sufficient for me as an intellectually honest man, though they cannot enforce *your* assent. Newman thinks that the case of religion is not essentially different from any other, so far as the illative sense is concerned. In religion we are faced with a very complex subject-matter; but basically the mental process by which I come to the conclusion that Jesus Christ is my Saviour is the same as that by which I come to the conclusion that Britain is an island.

Limitations of Newman's Doctrine

Newman was less successful as a constructive than as a critical

[8] *Essay in Aid of a Grammar of Assent*, p. 230.

thinker. The same may be said of greater philosophers than he. He perceived clearly enough the limitations of human knowledge and exhibited them in an interesting and provocative way. But it was not generally seen in Newman's day that the case of religion is even more complex than he supposed it to be, or that he might be confusing different sorts of propositions. Nevertheless, although Newman's "grammar of assent" is open to a great deal of technical criticism today,[9] his theory of the illative sense draws our attention to an error about the nature of the beliefs on which we actually base our daily lives. It is an error to which, in the nature of the case, thinkers are particularly subject, and one that can vitiate and even fatally destroy thought about religion.

DISCUSSION ON CHAPTER 23

1. Consider further illustrations of the use of the illative sense.

2. "Lord, I believe; help thou mine unbelief." (Mark 9:24) Expound.

3. Consider carefully Newman's distinction between inference and assent.

[9] M. C. D'Arcy, S.J., in *The Nature of Belief* (New York: Sheed & Ward, 1945), has evaluated and criticized it from within the Roman Church.

24

The Epistemological
Implicates of Faith

What Kind of Knowledge Does the Believer Claim?

People who, on the one hand, do not claim to have any extraordinary, direct, mystical communication with God, and who, on the other, affirm that the term "God" has a very important significance for them, are making a definite knowledge-claim that must be considered seriously. In this chapter we shall discuss such a claim to knowledge of God, contradistinguished from the claims of mystics, which we shall consider later on. We are to be concerned now with the man whom we may conveniently call the "ordinary believer."

The "ordinary believer" does not claim mystical knowledge; neither does he usually claim that his conclusion that there is a God who judges him and loves him has been arrived at after a process of logical inference ending with a triumphant "Q.E.D." such as we have at the end of a theorem in geometry. In many cases he will find it difficult to say precisely why he believes in God at all, for in many cases he will not have given a great deal of thought to the question or considered it as we are trying to do now. Because of this, a superficial observer will be inclined to conclude that his inability to give a reason for his belief is due to the fact that his belief springs from an emotional inclination toward theism or a lazy acceptance of a view with which he has been indoctrinated at an early age and which he finds it psychologically convenient not to discard. "Every man, wherever he goes," writes Bertrand Russell, "is encompassed by a cloud of comforting convictions, which move with him like flies on a summer day." The superficial observer's conclusion will often be strengthened by the fact that the "ordinary believer" has indeed mixed up with his belief in God a great deal of vulgar superstition and has also idly or lazily acquiesced in all sorts of worthless conventionalities. The more careful observer will not, however, be so easily misled. The fact that an artist has short or long hair should not be allowed to prejudice us for or against his work: we ought to take care, rather, that our dislike of short or long hair does not enter into our judgment. A lecturer on economics may introduce a great number of trashy asides about politics or music or golf into what is nevertheless, fundamentally, an excellent lecture on economics. I may deplore the introduction of the trash; but I ought not to confound it with the lecture.

The Basis of the Claim

The claim of the "ordinary believer" is based, not on a logical argument from particular premises to a particular conclusion, but on a much wider and deeper foundation than could ever be the basis of such a formal argument. For the experience of God that he claims is not detached at any point from the rest of experience, but permeates this. To use the poetry of the Bible, he sees everything cradled in "the everlasting arms" of God. At first sight this may seem to be a procedure entirely peculiar to religion; but it has, on the contrary, counterparts in the attitudes we all have, whether we are religious or not. For we all find it necessary to make "tacit assumptions," as we may please to call them, to the effect that somehow or other life "makes sense." Were it not so it would be impossible to carry on in sanity at all. Somehow or other, and in some measure or other, we are able to "make sense" of life. Yet we cannot really give a logical argument to justify the interpretation by which we are so enabled to "make sense" of what confronts us. The theistic interpretation is but one interpretation among others; but it is, to say the least, as "rational" as any of its competitors. This awareness of our environment's "making sense" is the most basic awareness we have. It always "lies behind" and also permeates the rest of our experience. To have no awareness of any such kind is to go crazy, to lose our reason. Of course, as Kant has shown, it is impossible for anything to enter our experience unless it enters into a certain framework of basic relations correlated with the general structure of our consciousness. We cannot make sense of nonsense, and therefore nonsense does not really present itself to our minds except as a barrier or frontier, an impenetrable wall surrounding that which is alien to us.

It is a question, therefore, of how we are going to interpret that which, confronting us as it does, "makes sense." We have to adapt ourselves to the universe around us. Doing this involves the "recognition" of what we commonly think of as "individual objects" or "things." But as we saw much earlier in our study, these "things" are not perceived or recognized or known by us in isolation. All the time we are relating one object to another, and this in turn involves "making sense" of the whole. We do not succeed in this to such a degree that we can give by any means complete answers to all the questions that occur even to ourselves as we go along; nevertheless we do succeed sufficiently to be aware of the whole as cohering in some way or other. We may hesitate to say that this "making sense" of what confronts us is a "revelation" to us; nevertheless, it is difficult to call it anything else, unless we really take seriously the possibility that we are spinning the whole of our experience out of ourselves. Few of us would be willing to accept such an interpretation, for it does not really account for the way in which our environment presents itself to us. But the more we are forced, in coming to terms with what confronts us, to provide ourselves with this basic interpretation that seems to be the foundation of our whole response to life, the more we become aware of the need for a special hypothesis. For the universe that confronts us is not self-explanatory. We may fit ourselves into it well enough to carry on in it; but we cannot rest there. We are obliged sooner or later to posit an explanation beyond both us and what immediately confronts us. We may defer doing this, for it is quite possible for us to play a game of make-believe with ourselves; that is, we can make ourselves believe, in some circumstances, that we have found a satisfactory foundation on which to work, when we have not really found any such foundation at all. The illusion is pleasant enough: why should anyone want to indulge in an illusion if it were not pleasant? No doubt many prolong the illusion till death; others, obliged to discard it, find in the long run that the last thing they would wish would be its recovery.

Such is the situation from the theist's point of view. We are not concerned at the moment with the correctness or incorrectness of his interpretation. The point is, rather, that the theist's view implies a claim to a *kind* of knowledge of God. It is certainly not knowledge in the sense in which we use the term when we speak of knowing a house, or knowing German, or knowing astronomy, or even knowing one's father or brother. The "ordinary believer" (and even the theologian who acts as his spokesman and commentator) does not usually call it knowledge at all, preferring the term "faith." There are very good reasons for his preference. It avoids the danger of confusing this unique kind of knowledge with any other, and the term "faith" suggests many of the qualities peculiar to the ordinary believer's implicit claim to knowledge of God. Nevertheless, in the context of contemporary society, the term "faith" is perhaps even more misleading, not only because it suggests to many what we have called the "schoolboy" definition of faith, but also because it fails to draw attention to one important aspect of the ordinary believer's claim, namely, that he has really *encountered* God.

Encounter in Faith Distinguished From Mystical Experience

The encounter that is so claimed by the ordinary believer differs from mystical encounter in two important respects. In the first place, it is frequent or constant, underlying all other experience, while on the other hand the ineffable experience that the mystic claims is brief, lasting for an instant or, say, ten minutes, and not playing the same role in the general pattern of life as the kind of encounter with which we are now concerned. In the second place, it lacks the poignant intensity of mystical experience. This is not to say that it is not a "moving" experience; on the contrary, it moves the believer's whole life. But it bears a relation to the rest of his life such as space bears to the building that the architect designs. The architect does not first have a "vision of space" and then get down to the work of designing the building; the concept of space underlies all his drawings and calculations. He does not encounter it as he encounters pencil and paper, stones and cement, for these he encounters separately and successively, while he encounters space all the time, even when he is momentarily sitting back and yawning over his work. So, for the believer, God is, like space, "everywhere." The believer finds himself constantly in the presence of God in this sense. Nevertheless, as soon as the believer focuses his attention upon this presence he finds also an infinite "distance" between himself and it. To the extent that he is aware of the presence as the architect is aware of space, he leans towards pantheism. To the extent that he is impressed, rather, by the "infinite distance," he leans towards deism. To the theist, however, the essential mystery in the situation is: God who is, to say the least, as omnipresent as space, is also a "subject" standing in a personal relationship to me, a relationship that is more personal and particular than that of father and son or husband and wife. The believer is conscious of resisting God (sin) and of being reconciled to God (forgiveness), so that, although God is omnipresent, the believer can be alienated from and restored to the divine presence. The relationship between him and God may therefore be called, as it generally is, a relationship of faith on the believer's part; nevertheless my act of faith entails a claim to a unique knowledge.

Verification of Fundamental Beliefs

The claim to the knowledge of God that belief implies may vary enormously. But the same may be said of any claim to knowledge of anything. If you ask me whether I know an automobile that is parked around the corner, I may reply that I know it, meaning that I designed the engine and intimately understand how it works, all its weaknesses and all its good points. Or I may mean only that I know it in the sense that it happens to be mine and that I drive it every day. Or, again, I may mean only that I know it is there. But one cannot even know that something is there without knowing at the same time *more* than its existence. All this is perhaps even more obvious in the case of our knowledge of persons. But if, at the end of all such inquiries, you insist on demanding that I should *justify* my claim to knowledge, I cannot really do so. Of course I may give all sorts of answers in the hope that you will accept them, or that I shall persuade myself that they are good answers. My attempts may vary from a crude, "Don't be silly, of course I know," to an erudite disquisition on the verification of hypotheses. But if you care to be persistent enough you will force me to admit that my claim to knowledge turns out to be always a great deal less than it seemed at first to be. It turns out to be always what is commonly called belief. I may have a theory by which I claim to justify my preference for one sort of belief rather than another; but this does not get me any nearer to doing what people expect of me when they demand proof.

In practice, however, the "proof" of our fundamental postulates is that they appear to be corroborated in our experience as a whole. A scientific hypothesis is tested by experiment, and a scientific view of the physical universe as a whole is upheld because it "works" in the sense that all scientific findings appear to corroborate it. To the extent that they do not it has to be modified. Similarly, the "ordinary believer" whose claims we have been investigating maintains in effect that his theistic view is corroborated in his own experience and that of others. It is verified, he thinks, not only in the integration of his own personality (which would provide only a subjective type of verification) but in the working out of history, for example. It will be objected that everybody accepts the postulates of science while only a certain number of people accept theism. To this it may be replied that it is a delusion of academic people that everybody accepts the postulates of science, for many, if not most, people have a very different notion of the foundations of physics from that which is held by modern physicists. They continue to accept long-discarded views of science or content themselves with naïve inventions of their own. Might not much the same be said of the theist's claim? No, because while no one offers a serious, carefully constructed alternative to the theories accepted by modern scientists about the physical universe, there are indeed serious alternatives offered in place of theism: atheism itself for instance. Moreover, the traditional "proofs" of theism have been widely abandoned by religious philosophers. Not all of these, by any means, have fully recognized the implications of a theology without proofs. It is, however, being more and more widely admitted that a disposition toward theistic belief is a necessary antecedent to the presentation of a reasoned case for theism.

This does not mean that the intellectual respectability of theism is diminished. It might mean, however, that traditional theism requires basic modification. At the same time, we must not lose sight of the fact that in the nature of the case the religious philosopher cannot be expected to provide that *kind* of verification that is expected of the physicist or the chemist. There is no crucial observation that could be made such as would show that, if *x* occurs, theism follows, while if *y* occurs, theism must be rejected. But no intelligent theist ever really maintained this. Even at the best, with all the moral earnestness of which he is capable, he must admit, as does Paul, that "now we see through a glass darkly." We are not intended to see better, in our present human situation, and even at the best our knowledge of God could not but be limited. We have to resist the temptation — a temptation that is perhaps a professional hazard of religious philosophers — to make it seem knowledge of a sort different from that which it must be. Knowledge of God, being knowledge *ex hypothesi* of the most fundamental kind possible, not only must be limited in our present situation; it could not but be limited even were we to be much better informed than we presently are on "scientific" matters. For a claim to an unlimited knowledge of God would really be a claim to be God, and no sane person would ever pretend to identify himself with the God of theism.

The Believer's Attitude Toward Other Kinds of Knowledge

The truly religious person, far from looking with suspicion or distrust or fear at the progress of scientific inquiry and the accumulation of scientific knowledge, has reason to be much more excited about it than the atheist or positivist ever can be. For him every scientific advance is in one way or another a revelation of God. Every important step in scientific development unfolds to him a new aspect of the infinite wisdom and power of God. "Miraculous operations" — plastic surgery, eye grafts, and the like — do not cause him to ask himself whether man will one day be able to do all that was formerly attributed to God alone. Even to put the question in such a way betokens a narrow conception of God, a lack of that sense of openmindedness, of love and awe before the divine Presence. It is the expression of a faith with an insecure foundation. To the theist whose faith is securely rooted, all such questions are vaguely comical. The conviction of the theist is expressed in the words of the psalmist: "Therefore will not we fear, though the earth be removed, and though the mountains be carried into the midst of the sea. . . . The Lord of hosts is with us; the God of Jacob is our refuge."

The Certainty of Faith

The non-theist, looking on at such an expression of theistic belief, is inclined to say: "Ah, his god is an escape-mechanism. It helps the poor devil to dream himself out of his misery." To this the theist cannot possibly reply. He *knows* that the interpretation reveals a fundamental misunderstanding of the experience familiar to him. He *knows* that when the Christian martyrs sang such phrases in their human helplessness as a hungry lion approached them, they must have enjoyed in a peculiarly vivid way the peace that is the fruit of a well-grounded faith. He *knows* that such Christian martyrs were often far more lacking in "physical courage" than are many "average" men and women, and that consequently they must have felt more terror than most of us at the sight of a wild beast leaping at them with awful certainty in every step. He *knows* that their terror was such as no psychological device could ever mitigate, since it had gone far beyond the scope of even the most resourceful methods of psychological escape. As he reads their story he *knows* that they *knew*, as he *knows* that even in the moment of man's most excruciating agony, all is well because "the Lord of hosts is with us; the God of Jacob is our refuge." He has learned to distinguish between the effect of the escape-mechanism (potent in its way, yet exceedingly limited from the point of view of the circumstances that interest believers) and the effect of well-grounded faith. The former is of considerable use as a buffer against the irksomeness of coming to grips daily with the challenge of circumstance; but it is, after all, only a "tranquilizer," a "happy pill," and no one should expect more of it than it is designed to perform. The power of well-grounded faith is *known* by its fortunate possessor to play a very different role indeed. Far from providing a sedation, it has the effect — alarming at first — of making the unpleasant reality of the challenge of circumstance look much more inescapable than ever it was before — so much so that, if this were all, the possessor of such faith would cry out for a tranquilizer to suppress it, were not the increased awareness of what is really going on around him accompanied by the inward certainty that all is well, since God is at the helm.

Such certainty is called by some religious writers "subjective," as distinguished from the "objective" certainty of science. This terminology is not, however, wthout danger. For it has a tendency to suggest that the certainty associated with scientific knowledge is "more real" than the other sort, and that the "certainty of faith" is a kind of psychological assurance grounded only upon the psychological make-up of the individual who enjoys it. The case is otherwise. Scientific certainty is achieved by means of a careful detachment from the object about which the certainty is sought. Religious certainty can be achieved only by an involvement with the object. The two kinds of certainty are different — so different that there can never be any question of one having an "edge over" the other. But though they are of different kinds, not only is the one not incompatible with the other or opposed to it; they ought to be complementary to each other. Scientific certainty is not diminished by the possession of the other kind; nor is religious certainty disturbed by that knowledge which is the result of scientific inquiry and laborious experiment.

Neither Modesty Nor Arrogance

We have already noted in an earlier chapter that there would appear to be a sort of arrogance in the theist's claim; that it would seem more modest to be a skeptic. We have seen that many persons claiming to uphold religion can be exceedingly arrogant indeed. Yet the claim to the kind of knowledge of God that is designated religious faith is in itself neither arrogant nor modest. Were the theist to say, "I think there is probably a God, but I may of course be wrong," he would not be expressing his conviction at all. He would be uttering a lie. For his conviction is much more than that. In claiming to have a kind of knowledge of God, the theist affirms his inability, in the long run, to make sense of anything that confronts him, except on the theistic view. Whatever may be thought of the view, the claim, if honestly made, demands every kind of respect, for it is eminently compatible, to say the least, with the most profound humility of which any man is capable.

DISCUSSION ON CHAPTER 24

1. "As a result of lack of faith we miss much knowledge of divine things." (Heraclitus) Discuss.

2. Consider to what extent faith may be regarded as a kind of knowledge and in what way it is not knowledge at all.

3. "Faith has no merit where human reason provides the proof." (Gregory the Great) Consider.

25

Mysticism

Etymology of "Mysticism"

"Mysticism" is a notoriously difficult term to define. Dean Inge, in an appendix to one of his books, *Christian Mysticism*, quoted twenty-six definitions of it by authorities on the subject. Even that list is by no means exhaustive. The first thing to be learned about mysticism is the etymology of the word, for this shows why the term is by nature indefinable in human language. The word comes from the Greek root *mu*, in the verb *muō*, meaning "I close," or "I keep silent," or "I hold my tongue." It is an onomatopoeic root; that is, it mimics the sound made by a person who deliberately closes his lips. It has affinities with the modern word "mum" in the phrase "keeping mum," in the sense of "maintaining a discreet silence." The mystic is primarily "one who keeps silent."

Mystical Silence

The mystic's silence is due to the fact that he claims to have an experience of God that is incommunicable. It is not that he does not wish to communicate. The incommunicability is due to the unique-ness of the experience, which is unique because the relationship in which it occurs is unique. It purports to be a special relationship between *this* man, *this* individual, and God. The man cannot com-municate the experience to anyone else because in order to communi-cate an experience, there must be a common basis for the communication, and in this case there is none. There may be analo-gous experiences. The experience that the mystic claims may not be entirely without a counterpart in "ordinary" life. You cannot really communicate to me, however, the peculiar character of the bond that exists between you and someone else with whom you are very intimate, such as your mother or your close friend. You may say in a general sort of way, "Oh, it is the same relationship that exists between you and your friend." But under your breath you are also saying, "Of course I know it is quite different, really, because what I value most in the relationship between my friend and me is precisely its uniqueness, its incommunicability: no one else can really understand it or enter into it. If one could, it would not be what it is; it would not be itself." So the mystic's alleged experience of direct relationship with God is in this sense incommunicable, ineffable.

Faith and Mystical Experience

Traditionally, this mystical experience is sharply distinguished from the faith of the ordinary believer, the epistemological implications of which we have briefly considered in the last chapter. It is extremely difficult, however, to say where, in practice, faith ends and mystical experience begins. Whether, as some hold, all religion is essentially mystical, is a disputed, controversial question. What is indisputable is that mystical experience implies a special *kind* of cognition, quite different from what we ordinarily intend when we speak of knowledge of an object. John Burnaby gives a picturesque illustration that may help to indicate the difference. He writes: "I know (let us say) the face and the voice of the Archbishop of Canterbury; but I am not entitled to say that I know the Archbishop unless he knows me. This is a knowledge which by its very nature cannot belong to a single knower: it is an exchange, a sharing by which two human lives are in some measure joined together, giving and receiving. In the Bible, what is meant by the knowledge of God is always a union of this kind between God and man." [1]

Analogy of Human Love

This leads us to the classic analogy that mystical writers make. Though the experience that the mystic claims is unique, it is possible to convey in some measure its general character by the analogy of the relationship of human love and friendship. In this way I can get some notion of why the mystic's experience is ineffable, even if I have no mystical experience myself, because I know what it is to love a friend and to be loved by my friend. Anyone who has been in love with a person of the opposite sex and whose love has been reciprocated knows how different is this experience from the more immature experience of being "in love with love." Compared with such a sexual experience, all other sexual experience seems auto-erotic. The mystic is saying, in effect, that the relationship between his experience of God and what often passes for "religious belief" is analogous to the relationship between "real" human love and that more or less auto-erotic experience that often passes for it. It is above all the claim to reciprocated love in the mystical relationship that makes the mystic's alleged knowledge fundamentally incommunicable.

[1] John Burnaby, *Christian Words and Christian Meanings* (London: Hodder & Stoughton, Ltd., 1955), pp 23–24.

Mystical Experience of Augustine

The fact that the mystical encounter with God is essentially in-communicable does not, however, prevent the mystics from pouring forth a vast literature on the subject. The mystic is indeed, as a rule, as extraordinarily talkative as the lover, and for a similar reason. He knows he cannot really communicate his experience; yet he cannot help longing to do so, just because it is so incommunicable. And when the mystic talks about his experience it is in terms borrowed from the poet's language about human love. Augustine, for instance, in his *Confessions*, a work which is, after all, a love-poem addressed to God, tells the story of his quest for love, and of how in the course of it he was overtaken by God. Even as an infant at his mother's breast, he was searching (so it seemed to him in retrospect) for the heavenly nourishment, and indeed he was, he afterwards believed, already tasting God's riches there, for these reach to the very core of all things. As a young man he sought to combine the pursuit of truth with a fully sensual life. According to the fashion of the day, he took a concubine at the age of seventeen. He longed to understand the "essence" of all things. He searched deep into the corporeal. Then, as his conversion was approaching, his heart, he tells us, "cried out violently against all mental images," and as he strove to "beat off this fluttering crowd" from his mind's eye, they were gone but for an instant when again they poured in upon him, till he began to con-ceive of God as a huge corporeal substance piercing the whole world. He had tasted the joys of sexual love, and he had enjoyed also the glory of being a successful young orator. By pagan standards he was very much a "golden" young man. Still he was uneasy, dissatisfied. Then, entering, under divine guidance, into his "inmost self," the core of his being, he discovered with his mind's eye "the unchangeable light" of God. At last his mind reached, he tells, us, "that which is," God himself.

When he reflects upon the knowledge that he has thus acquired, he distinguishes it from all earthly, aesthetic experience. For, he says, it is "not the pleasant melodies of songs, nor the fragrant smell of ointment and flowers and spices." And yet, when he loves God, he does love a certain *kind* of light, a *kind* of voice, a *kind* of fragrance. Poetically, he asks the earth what it is he so loves, and the earth answers, "It is not I." He asks the same question of the heavens, and they give the same answer. But when he presses for a more satisfactory reply, they say, "He made us."

Sexual Analogy Apposite yet Misleading

The frankness of the mystical writers in using language borrowed from sexual love can be very misleading. The psychological con-

ı sex and religion is well known to us today. But it
ʌn also to the ancients. It is not only the modern
ʌas been inclined to wonder whether the outpourings of
ͻ are not attempts to express repressed or thwarted sexual
ıs not only in recent times that people have learned of the
va   ͻ of the sexual instinct! That is why Augustine and others who
write in the mystical tradition are careful to draw our attention to the
difference from, as well as the likeness to, the experience of human
love. We cannot too often remind ourselves, in trying to understand
the mystics, that the fact that there is plainly a close connection between sex and mysticism does not mean that mysticism can be explained in terms of sex any more than it means that sex can be
accounted for by mysticism.

The ancients seem to have assigned to bodily organs such as the
liver, the heart, and even the kidneys, functions which no one would
nowadays think of assigning to them. The kidneys stood for "the
passions." In the King James Version, the Hebrew word for "kidneys"
is usually rendered "reins"; but some English translations have "kidneys," as in the phrase, "Examine, O Lord, my kidneys." To a modern
reader this makes God sound like a urologist; but to an ancient Hebrew
it no more suggested anything like this than "Create in me a clean
heart, O God," suggests to us that God is a heart specialist. Such
relics of older ways of thinking survive in modern speech, as when we
say that a man "went away with a heavy heart," and that a girl's heart
has been "broken." It would indeed be very absurd to suppose that
a disappointment increases the weight of the heart or that anyone is
really walking around with a cardiac fracture. An electrocardiograph
would not directly record what the language of poetry calls "the affairs
of the heart," any more than what we call a "magnetic personality"
would constitute a "magnetic field" such as would affect, say, a clock-
work mechanism. Nevertheless, cardiologists do recognize the effects
of emotional, psychological disturbances on the heart, so that the
ancients were not entirely wrong in the association they made. This is
by no means to say, however, that primitive peoples were right in
assigning to the heart the functions they did assign to it. Nor is it
less absurd for us today to pretend to explain mystical experience by
the activity of the sexual glands.

So the mystics are unrestrained in their use of sexual analogies for
the encounter with God. Bernard of Clairvaux speaks of the mind
falling into a deep sleep "in the arms of God" and of its being em-
braced by God. Christ is depicted as the Bridegroom, while the
mystic is the Bride. Bernard prefers this figure of speech to that of
father-son or master-servant, because while a father is honored and
a master is feared, a bridegroom is loved, and love is the notion that

comes closest to what is experienced in the mystical encounter with God. To love God with one's whole being is, as it were, to be wedded to him. Gregory makes frequent use of the Latin words *rapit* and *raptim* to indicate something of the swiftness of the mystical experience: the soul is seized by God. It is "stretched out wholly" to the divine love.

The Spanish mystics describe the process of the mystical ascent to God in even more vividly amorous language. Saint Teresa speaks sometimes of a fragrance that spreads outwards till it permeates the whole soul, sometimes of a fire that ends by setting the soul aflame. She asks us to imagine a palace consisting of seven concentric rooms, and she takes us in imagination through each of them. In the fifth room the soul is "betrothed" to God. Teresa likens the mystically betrothed soul to a silkworm which, having fed upon the foliage in the Church's garden (that is, theological doctrine and the practice of the faith within a rigid ecclesiastical framework), spins with this the silken prison in which it is to die in order that it may emerge a butterfly. Then in the sixth stage of the pilgrimage comes the agony of waiting, an experience which, says Teresa, is as if a spark were entering the soul from God, causing "most welcome pain." At last, in the seventh room, comes the spiritual marriage, in which the soul (the Bride) is abandoned to God (the Bridegroom) in complete, reciprocal love.

Mysticism and Theology

All mysticism tends by its nature to express itself in pantheistic terms. Hindu and Buddhist mysticism is, of course, naturally pantheistic. But even the Christian mystics use language that suggests a pantheistic direction. Christian theologians defend such mystics from the charge of pantheism by claiming that the apparent pantheism in the case of these mystics is due to the poverty of human language, and does not mean that there is no fundamental difference between the theological or metaphysical presuppositions of Christian and other mystics. Since all mysticism is beyond, or irreducible to, the categories of theological discourse, we cannot really say anything about it in terms of theology. It is no less true, however, that all forms of mysticism have a springboard of one sort or another, and so it is certainly possible to distinguish between the theological presuppositions that the mystics of various religions and religious traditions claim to get beyond. In comparing the respective *processes* involved in these various mystical pilgrimages, differences are indeed found, and it is arguable that the authenticity of the experience claimed by a mystic may be tested with reference to the total process by which he arrives at it. If we are to make any judgment at all about the authenticity of this or that claim to mystical experience, we must

use some criterion other than the experience itself, since this is
unique and incommunicable.

Mystical Experience as Foretaste of Beatific Vision

Some types of religion seem to be of their nature mystical, in the
sense that they are directly and frankly oriented toward a mystical
goal, so that the life of a faithful adherent of such a religion is expected to be a steady progress in mystical experience, somewhat as
the life of a good student at college is expected to be a steady progress
in academic skills. In other types of religion, mysticism appears as
something which, welcome as it may be, is regarded as exceptional.
Though some Christian traditions seem more hospitable to mysticism
than do others, the emphasis of all on faith rather than direct "vision
of God" is sufficiently marked to make mysticism a phenomenon that
is out of the ordinary run of Christian experience. Nevertheless,
Christianity holds out a hope of eternal life "nearer" to God, a future
life in which the divine presence will be more fully realized and enjoyed. Whatever Christians may feel about the nature of their pilgrimage on earth, they recognize that its goal is that future enjoyment
that the medieval theologians called the Beatific Vision. The whole
direction of Christian experience on earth must therefore be regarded
as toward that goal. What the Christian mystics claim is a sort of
foretaste of the Beatific Vision; a brief anticipation of heaven, and
the Christian notion of heaven is that it essentially consists in a fuller
knowledge of God. "Blessed are the pure in heart," is Christ's promise,
"for they shall see God." To "see" God is, of course, to see him "with
the eye of the mind," that is, to know him.

Bogus Mysticism

Mysticism is indubitably a most important, perhaps the most vital
element in religion. It is also very much open to abuse by charlatans
and others whose religion is of a superficial kind. Those who,
in principle, recognize the claims of the mystics would be the first to
acknowledge that much mysticism is bogus. This is as we should
expect. People who set out to "cultivate" mystical experience are
rightly suspect. Once again the analogy of human love is illuminating,
for we do not take very seriously the affairs of those who go out in
quest of adventures, since it is well known to mature people that important, enduring love affairs are seldom sought; they come, rather, as
we say, "out of the blue." So the genuine mystic does not go forth
seeking mystical experience. On the contrary, it comes to him un-
sought, when he least expects it. It is surely this more than anything
else in the mystical experience that so fully convinces the mystic that
he has been admitted to a very special kind of knowledge of God.

DISCUSSION ON CHAPTER 25

1. "All kinds of symbolic language come naturally to the articulate
   mystic, who is usually a literary artist as well: so naturally, that he
   sometimes forgets to explain that his utterance is but symbolic;
   a desperate attempt to translate the truth of that world into the
   beauty of this. It is here that mysticism joins hands with music
   and poetry: had this fact always been recognized by its critics, they
   would have been saved from many regrettable and some ludicrous
   misconceptions. . . . Hence the persons who imagine that the
   'Spiritual Marriage' of St. Catherine or St. Teresa veils a perverted
   sexuality, that the vision of the Sacred Heart involved an incredible anatomical experience, or that the divine inebriation of the
   Sufis[2] is the apotheosis of drunkenness, do but advertise their
   ignorance of the mechanism of the arts, like the lady who thought
   that Blake *must* be mad because he said that he had touched the
   sky with his finger." (Evelyn Underhill) Discuss.

2. Consider possible criteria for distinguishing genuine mysticism
   from bogus.

3. Compare and contrast religious faith and mystical experience.

   [2] Moslem mystics.

26

Psychological Considerations

Freud's Forerunners

Since the popularization of the work of Freud and other psychologists associated with or influenced by him, all claims to knowledge of God have been very widely discussed. In both Europe and America they have been subjected to a very special kind of criticism as a result of the considerations put forward by psychologists of various schools, especially the psychoanalysts. To many this has seemed an entirely new development, a revolution in thought. There is indeed no doubt that the work of the modern psychologists has drawn attention to an intellectual problem that was often neglected before and has thrown a great deal of light on the psychology of some of the phenomena of religion. There are, however, two considerations that ought to be carefully borne in mind in all modern discussions of the psychology of religion.

First, it must not be imagined that the objections raised by modern psychologists, important as they are, were entirely unknown in the past, or that the psychological approach to religion is something novel that did not even come within the scope of our forefathers' imagination. The notion of a "region" of the mind "below" the level of consciousness, for example, was by no means unknown before Freud popularized it. Franz Delitzsch, writing on theology in 1855, a year before Freud's birth, alluded not only to the need for more attention to the subconscious realms of the soul, but to the fact that, as he alleges, the existence of such realms was by that time widely recognized. "It has been a fundamental error of most psychologists hitherto," he wrote, "to make the soul only extend so far as its consciousness extends; it embraces, as is now always acknowledged, a far greater abundance of powers and relations than can possibly appear in its consciousness." [1] Two years later, in 1857, just after Freud's birth, a great English ecclesiastic was writing to his old Oxford

[1] Franz Delitzsch, A *System of Biblical Psychology*, trans. E. Wallis (Edinburgh: T. & T. Clark, 1890), p. 330. The original German edition was published in 1855.

teacher as follows: "Our theology has been cast in a scholastic mould, i.e., all based on logic. We are in need of, and we are being gradually forced into, a theology based on psychology." [2] These writers had grown up in an intellectual environment in which the psychological approach to religious questions had been for long under suspicion as leading to the romantic, subjectivistic sort of attitude that some German theology, under the influence of Schleiermacher, had engendered. For various complex historical reasons, logic and theology had been developed in the Middle Ages together, so that it was difficult to extricate the one from the other. The Reformation produced a theology that was as closely allied in many ways with medieval logic as the pre-Reformation theology had been. But that is not to say that people a thousand or more years ago did not know anything about what has been so endlessly discussed by modern readers of books about Freud. Even ancient writers such as Demosthenes and Cicero were very well aware indeed of many of the psychological phenomena (wishful thinking, for instance) that have been in recent decades so much drawn to the attention of the public. The preoccupations of devoutly religious people — Jews, Christians, and others — is such that in no age could the psychological aspects of religion have been overlooked. So much in the history of the religions of the world is so blatantly connected with sex (one need only think of the role of temple prostitution in India, for instance, or of the fertility rites of the primitive ancestors of the early Christians, Jews and Gentiles alike) that no thinking person could conceivably have overlooked the connection. It was indeed, as a matter of history, an acute awareness of the connection that led many of the early Fathers of the Christian Church into overemphasizing sex in a way that is now widely discarded.

Relevance and Irrelevance of Sexual Basis

Second, and even more important, the undoubted connection between sex and religion, and the acute relevance of the whole psychological approach to religion, ought not to blind us to the fact that no psychological approach can ever completely solve the central problems of religious philosophy. That religion takes its *origin* in sex may be true; but it does not follow that it is simply an erotic phenomenon. The value of an activity cannot be determined in terms of its origin. Again, it has been observed that mystics, alcoholics and erotomaniacs describe their experiences in terms that suggest a common denominator. But this tells us nothing of the nature of the *object* of mysticism or religion. We have already noted that much of what passes for religion is not far removed from drug addiction. But it does not

[2] E. G. Sandford (ed.), *Memoirs of Archbishop Temple* (1906), II, p. 517.

follow that all religion is to be accounted for so simply. One of the factors in a great scientific discovery may be something as commonplace as a psychological peculiarity in the scientist who makes the discovery — fetishism, for instance; but this has nothing to do with the validity of the results of the scientist's work. Some great music has been composed by men who, being confined to ghettos in time of persecution, were forced to find some means of occupying their time. But for the filthy conditions in which they lived and the restricted environment to which they were condemned, their talents might very well never have been developed. It would, however, be absurd to evaluate their musical compositions in terms of bad living conditions. The bad conditions are of psychological interest; but they do not affect one way or another the quality of the music that was composed. Religious activities may likewise often be the outcome, in a sense, of emotional disturbances or neurotic tendencies that may be very easily explained from a psychological standpoint; but it does not at all follow that the religious activities can be explained as emotional disturbances or neurotic perversions. To suggest that such an explanation is sufficient is to beg the question whether religion is or is not something much more than such a psychological phenomenon; it is not to answer this question at all.

The external trappings of religious practice do indeed provide ample corroboration of what the psychologists have stressed, the sexual element common to religion and other human strivings and experiences. But what is characteristic of the interior of the mystical and religious quest is an extraordinary variety: in the last resort we find we are looking not at a "type" of experience, that is, a "religious type" of experience, but at a series of experiences or activities each of which is unique. This is admitted by Leuba, a skeptical psychologist whose hostility to religion was notorious in his day. "If the great Christian mystics," he says, "could by some miracle be all brought together in the same place, each in his habitual environment, there to live according to his manner, the world would soon perceive that they constitute one of the most amazing and profound variations of which the human race has yet been witness." [3] This could hardly be said of the sexual activities, as such, of individual men and women, for however numerous may be the forms of sexual perversion, the libidinal urge is tediously and monotonously the same. Relationships that have a sexual aspect are unique precisely to the extent that they depart from or transcend the sexual aspect. This is not to say that sex is uninteresting; of course it gives to human life most delicate and most thrilling joys. Yet in itself, apart from the concomitants that transcend it, it is of unparalleled dreariness.

[3] J. H. Leuba in *Revue Philosophique*, July, 1902.

Discovering the writings of St. John of the Cross, a reader once exclaimed, "Here is a monk who could give lessons to lovers!" Why not? If mysticism is anything like what it purports to be, there is no paradox in the notion that a mystic should be able to teach lovers more than Ovid ever knew. For the mystics do not deny that sex and religion are closely connected. On the contrary, they are, as we have seen, acutely conscious of the connection; hence their use of language that is sometimes startlingly erotic in tone. It is crude to say, as has been said, that the young man who knocks at the door of a brothel is unconsciously looking for God; nevertheless, this aphorism draws our attention to the fact that what the mystics claim is precisely that the finite passions of the sensuous man are only the feeble and fumbling gropings after that which the infinite passion of the mystic alone can hope to grasp, and that but fleetingly. The gratification of the senses, the mystics tell us, cannot in itself liberate us from our desires; its effect is to imprison us more securely in their grip. But erotic hunger is an image of the even more terrible hunger for God. So it may be said that sex prefigures religion but does not explain it.

Neurotic Element in Religion

Much of the psychoanalysts' criticism of religious practices and attitudes is thoroughly deserved. Freud looked upon religion as a neurosis and sometimes spoke of it as a delusion. But no serious student would deny that much religion is neurotic, and that some religions not only keep their adherents at the child-level but are at pains to impede all attempts of the more heroic of their adherents to emancipate themselves and face the world as adults. It is notoriously difficult to grow up, and there is some truth in the observation that some people prolong adolescence till they are eighty. So for many people religion consists chiefly in an attempt to prolong the conditions of their childhood days, the period which they are emotionally unable to discard. As the "father-substitute," the idea of God can become, moreover, a kind of mass-delusion: individuals, finding themselves in a society in which others indulge in the same delusion, take comfort from the discovery that their belief is shared. But the fact that much religion is of the nursery level does not justify the conclusion that all religion is. It would not be unfair to observe here that owing to the vulgarization of psychoanalysis this does not lack nursery-level counterparts of nursery-level religion. That much of the current preoccupation with modern psychological ideas is itself neurotic would be denied by no one, least of all by the psychologists. But no one would deduce from this that the pursuit of psychological studies is necessarily neurotic.

Religion as Illusion

Freud and other psychologists have spoken of religion as illusion, implying that we spin out of our heads what Feuerbach called *Wunschwesen* (wish-beings) or *personifizierte Wünsche* (personified wishes) as a means of obtaining security from fear in a world which, being tailor-cut to our own needs, is a fairyland quite apart from reality. Once again, let it be conceded that wishful thinking plays a part in religion as in other human activities. It is something to be guarded against, to be watched for, in religion as elsewhere. But if, as the psychologists urge, religious people design their beliefs as a protection from fear, is it not odd that so many should have believed, for instance, in everlasting punishment in hell? Such a belief certainly affords no protection from fear: on the contrary, it is one of the standard jibes against certain kinds of religion that these have *instilled* fear into men's minds, especially the fear of damnation. Christianity's opponents cannot have it both ways: they cannot say both that people fly to religion to escape from hard facts into a cozy world of make-believe where all is sweetness and light, and that religion invents hell and the like in order to frighten people. So while it is a good and necessary thing to consider religion from a psychological standpoint, it is important that *all* the psychological facts should be considered, not just those that happen to suit the investigator's theory. In inviting such inquiry the religious person is fully entitled to demand that no psychological facts be ignored. It will usually be found that these are much more complex than appear in psychologists' descriptions of them.

Mass-Hypnotism or Uncomfortable Words

Critics of religion rightly point to certain mass-movements, religious revivals in which all the well-known techniques of mass-hypnotism and suggestion are freely used. They point to superstitions deliberately inculcated by people who ought to know better. They note that much religion appears to consist in giving people the "kind of stuff" they like to hear. All such criticism is amply justified and deserved. But what, then, is to be said of the other side of the picture? For it cannot but be noticed that some Christian preachers, at any rate, far from preaching what people want to hear, preach the reverse. Their message is anything but comforting in the conventional sense. The Anglican priest, Father Huddleston, writing on the thorny question of the color bar in South Africa, called his book *Naught for your Comfort*. It is indeed anything but a comforting book. Christianity is not, when fearlessly preached, a religion that is at all comforting in the ordinary sense of this term. It comes as a challenge to relinquish cherished ideas and prejudices, not as a balm or a solace. Christians speak of "the offense of the Gospel," and it is well known to those who have encountered the Gospel challenge that it is anything other than an unmitigated consolation. If I want to "escape from real life," I had better go to see a Walt Disney cartoon: the last thing I should do is to go to hear a sermon by a conscientious Christian preacher, for he will confront me with certain very unpleasant realities about myself.

Facing the Fact of Death

Freud, who admits that the "riddle of death" probably admits of no scientific solution, sees nothing more in any religious solution of the problem than the provision of a dream of new adventures after death — what is vulgarly called "pie in the sky when you die." But while Christianity has a doctrine about life after death, it has also a great deal to say about the fact of death itself. It is an awareness of the nature and reality of death that inspires interest in an afterlife. Death is not a fact that we like to consider too closely: it is easier to pretend not to notice it. By soft-pedaling it or laughing it off we try to avoid recognizing the very unpleasant fact that time passes increasingly fast as life proceeds and at the end of it comes the banality of a full stop. The Trappist monks have a practice that seems macabre to the worldling, of visiting an open grave every day. The grave is used when one of the monks dies, and immediately afterwards another is dug open for the daily visit that is a reminder of the reality of death. "Remember, Man, that thou art dust and unto dust thou shalt return," says the priest to the people on Ash Wednesday as he places a smudge of ash on the forehead of each, as a reminder of the certainty of death. Surely all this is a more realistic attitude toward death than is usually encountered in secularistic circles. It is in very healthy contrast to the reluctance to face the fact of death that enables morticians and others to enjoy a flourishing trade in cosmetics for corpses to give the illusion that death has somehow or other not really occurred. The Christian attitude is the reverse of this. It drives home the stark reality of death. Yet such facts tend to be ignored in the misleading accounts of the nature of religion that are too often given by psychologists.

DISCUSSION ON CHAPTER 26

1. Discuss the limits of the psychological approach to religion.

2. Consider how "wishful thinking" may enter into (a) acceptance of, and (b) resistance to, a religious idea.

3. Consider the following judgments on a sermon: (a) "I just loved it. Best sermon I ever heard"; and (b) "I just hated it. Best sermon I ever heard."

PART FIVE

The Destiny of Man

27

Belief in Immortality

Antiquity and Prevalence of Belief in Immortality

So prevalent is belief in immortality that some writers on the history of religion have pronounced it to be almost universal. In an earlier chapter we took note of the fact that the ceremonial practices of our remotest ancestors suggest such a belief or hope: the smearing of the bodies of their dead with a red lotion probably signified blood, the symbol of life. Some modern investigators of current beliefs in America have claimed to find that in our own day there are more people who profess a "belief in immortality" of one sort or another than there are people willing to affirm a "belief in God." There are, however, some religions, notably Hinayana Buddhism, in which belief in conscious, personal immortality is not found, and others, such as Old Testament Judaism, in which it is inconspicuous. Nevertheless, it remains true that immortality beliefs are very widespread.

Idea of Immortality in Primitive Religion

How does the belief in personal survival arise? Everyone sees what appears to happen at death: where a personality formerly communicated itself to us through a body, it now no longer does so; life is extinct and the corpse quickly decomposes like any other dead matter. What is there in death to suggest survival? It seems that the belief in survival is suggested to primitive man by the dreams he has in which, very naturally, he sees the deceased father or brother or friend whom in life he had known and loved. Such dreams are recounted to other members of the tribe who remark on their having had similar experiences of encountering the deceased in dreams. So a belief in ghosts comes to be established, implying belief in survival and in the communication of the living with their departed ancestors and friends. The ground of such primitive forms of belief in personal survival is of course entirely repudiated by civilized man; nevertheless, the latter's belief in personal survival may be far more definite and vigorous than the savage's. When civilized man believes in personal survival, his belief is more likely to spring from his sense of purpose and his recognition of the fact that while we are conscious of purpose that has begun we are also conscious that the purpose cannot be completed within the span of our earthly existence. I know that though I should live to be a hundred and fifty I could not fulfill the purpose that I think I see now at work in my life. Such is the theme of Browning's poem, *Cleon.*

Death and Purpose

We are confronted with two circumstances: on the one hand, an awareness of purpose the realization of which must take a far longer time than we can expect to have on earth, and on the other hand, the certainty of death. The conjunction of these two circumstances seems, the more we think about it, extraordinarily cruel. It is not only as though a child were told he was taken to see a most exciting movie and that, while he must be right on time for the beginning, he was to be taken home and put to bed after the first half-hour. It is worse even than if an ambitious young man were told that he was going to be accepted for training in his chosen career, that the training would be very rigorous, and that he would be taken away in the middle of it. It is worse than any such case, for "while there is life there is hope." The prospect of death puts an end to all hope and confronts us with a terrible finality. Hence the conventional picture of Death as a grinning skeleton: the grin symbolizes the mockery of a life filled with purposes that cannot be fulfilled.

Irrelevance of Desire for Immortality

The hope of personal survival is therefore very understandable. It is no argument, however, to say that because the hope is so very widespread it is well founded. Perhaps life *is* the mockery we have suggested. Nor is it any evidence of survival to note that the hope of it is very inspiring and that without it men probably would not attempt many of the noble deeds they do attempt. In the case of certain "other-worldly" types of religion the belief in personal survival has the opposite effect: people may and do sometimes take up the attitude that since this life is relatively unimportant in comparison with the life that is expected after death, there is no urgent need to strive very hard in this life, for there will be plenty of time later. On the other hand, it has been said that "he sins against this life who slights the next." [1] In any case, such considerations cannot do anything to prove either that there is, or that there is not, an afterlife. Some humanists and others point out that the desire for personal immortality is selfish. This is misleading, for it might be argued

[1] Edward Young, *Night Thoughts,* Night VII.

that *all* desires are selfish from one point of view, even the highest desires we can have and those that are commonly looked upon as altruistic. At any rate, whether the desire for personal survival is selfish or unselfish is irrelevant to the question of whether there *is* personal survival. Nor are arguments by analogy from nature convincing in either direction. From one point of view, everything in nature dies, so that it might be asked: why should I be an exception? From another point of view it has been argued that caterpillars become butterflies, so why should not I rise to new and more glorious life after death? Such arguments are quite feeble, if by personal survival is meant that I am to look forward to a life in which my identity, my selfhood, is to be somehow definitely preserved.

What is Immortality?

This brings us to the crucial question. What precisely do we mean by immortality? We may mean many quite different things. In a sense we all believe that when a man dies he "lives on" — he lives on in the memory of his friends, for instance, and in what are called his "lasting achievements." It is with this in mind that I might, if I were a rich man, found a hospital and have it named after me. Or I might have a fine monument erected over my grave to tell people about me hundreds of years hence, or a tablet bearing my name on the wall of a church. Many men find solace in their old age in the thought that they are to "live on" in their children. But my children, though they bear a strong physical resemblance to me and perhaps even exhibit certain temperamental affinities, are very different persons from me, and if I am wise I shall be glad that this is so. I would not want them to be mere channels for the perpetuating of my personality, and in any case, even if I did want it, they could not be such channels. They may very well turn out to be far better persons than I am, or else they may turn out to be rogues. They can never really immortalize what I want to have immortalized, the values that have been created in the personality that is my own and that is, for good or ill, unique. And when all is said, what I really want to have immortalized is "me," not my noble thoughts or my lofty aspirations.

Immortality may mean, however, that though I lose my own personal identity, I am absorbed, with all that is valuable in me, in some greater Being. The Buddhist conception of *nirvana* implies a belief of this kind: I survive as a river survives when it flows into the ocean. None of the water is lost. But does a river really survive when it enters the sea? What does survival mean? If I lose a tooth or even a leg, I have no difficulty in claiming that I have survived the loss, and even if by reason of a severe trauma my personality is much altered or my memory seriously affected, it is possible for you to say that in spite of all I have survived. But if I were to be incorporated or fused into someone or something else, you could hardly look upon me as having survived.

Again, it might be held by some protagonists of belief in immortality that I shall survive whether I "deserve" it or not, because I have a soul and it is the nature of souls to survive — they are immortal in their own right, so that I cannot help surviving whether I like it or not. Others, however, would look upon personal survival as a gift or reward for merit. According to this doctrine of "conditional immortality," I may survive and I may not: whether I do will depend on the quality of my soul. According to an ancient and picturesque legend, some souls, being weighted down by mundanities, are too heavy to soar heavenwards; only those souls that are light enough to mount upwards without hindrance can reach the realm of everlasting life.

Moreover, there are various ways of looking at the present life. For a brief period of time, varying from perhaps only an hour or so, in the case of some who die in infancy, to a hundred years in the case of the few who reach this great age, we live our earthly lives. But is this the only life of its kind? Are we to suppose that this pilgrimage is unique and that we are then to be, let us say, labeled for evermore in terms of what we have done with this brief span of life? Or else is this earthly life of ours, as the ancient doctrine of transmigration depicts it, but one in a series of millions of such life-spans? Does immortality mean that we are to go from life to life indefinitely, or does it mean that when our life here is over we enter into a new *kind* of life?

Ambiguity of "Immortality"

The fact is that there are really several quite different types of belief in immortality, and even within the Christian religion, for instance, the concept of immortality has been sometimes very confused. Before we can hope to argue for or against any doctrine of this sort we must first know what doctrine of immortality we have before us. Otherwise we shall find ourselves working out an argument against immortality that is effective against a certain type of doctrine but ineffective against others. Or else we shall find ourselves trying to find evidence in favor of immortality, only to discover that while our evidence does support one kind of doctrine it does not even buttress another type. For example, suppose that psychical research did provide some really convincing evidence for the continuing existence of "departed spirits"; it would not by any means follow that we were justified in, say, the traditional conception of heaven. An argument that supported the latter, on the other hand, might even be evidence against the kind of spirit-world that modern spiritists claim to know.

DISCUSSION ON CHAPTER 27

1. Suppose that a friend of yours has died and that you wish to write suitable letters of sympathy to his three sisters. One of these believes in no personal survival after death; the second considers death to be a mere incident in the soul's eternal pilgrimage; the third is a Christian. What considerations would you bear in mind in composing your three letters?

2. "That the end of life should be death may sound sad: yet what other ending can anything have? . . . An invitation to the dance is not rendered ironical because the dance cannot last for ever; the youngest of us and the most vigorously wound up, after a few hours has had enough of sinuous stepping and prancing." (Santayana) Critically consider this estimate of the significance of death.

3. "I am about to take my last voyage, a great leap in the dark." (Reputed dying words of Hobbes) Discuss.

28

Two Doctrines of Survival

The Soul-Substance Theory

According to an ancient philosophic theory there is, in contrast to the material world, a spiritual substance that is indestructible. This philosophic theory of substance is now generally discarded; but since it is associated with some very important notions about immortality in the history of religions, we must consider it seriously. The soul is an "eternal" substance, while physical substances such as the human body are of a definitely lower status, being transitory in character. It is by no means always clear in the doctrines that depend on such a view, whether by the "eternity" of the spiritual realm of soul-substance is meant the notion that it is of endless duration or the notion that, being beyond time itself, it cannot be said to have any duration at all.

Transmigration

There is a classic expression of this view among the ancients in India, and it has been bequeathed to the western world through Pythagoras and Plato. According to a typical form of the doctrine of metempsychosis or transmigration, the body is but the temporary lodging of the soul in the course of the latter's pilgrimage. Or, to change the metaphor, it may be considered as a dress that the soul dons at the time of earthly birth and discards at death. After discarding a body, the soul remains "naked" for a period and then gets a new body again. It is not always clear precisely why this should happen; but another typical theory is that the soul needs a body for its progress or education. The body may also be regarded as a sort of tool or instrument of the soul which requires it as a pianist requires a piano, although he does not require it all the time, nor does it have to be always the same piano. In this form of the theory it seems that the soul is in process of development. An environment is provided suitable to the progress the soul has made. As a beginner at the piano deserves only an inferior instrument, so at the lower stages of the soul's progress only an inferior sort of environment is provided. The soul is rewarded with a better environment as a pianist might be rewarded with a better quality of instrument as his improved virtuosity makes him entitled to this and capable of making use of it. According to the Indo-Aryan form of this doctrine, there is an endless chain (*samsara*) of rebirths not only on earth but in a series of universes of which the earth is one. The incarnation of the soul may be an incarnation into human form or into some other form above or below the human. With this doctrine is associated the Hindu caste system: a man born into, say, the Vaisya caste, may be promoted in his next incarnation to a place among the Kshatriyas, or among the Brahmins, or he may be degraded to the Shudra caste. What determines his immediate destiny is his moral conduct. In the language of the Chandogya Upanishad, those whose conduct is good in their present life will enter into a good womb, such as that of a woman of high caste, while those whose conduct is bad may expect to enter into the womb of an outcaste or even, in some cases, into that of a pig or other animal. In more developed accounts, the reincarnation process is governed by the inexorable law of *karma*, the interpretation of which is that every action a man does, however trivial, and even every thought he thinks, is weighed; so it helps to determine his destiny. The law of *karma* operates automatically: as surely as an apple falls to the ground by the force of gravity, so the soul returns to the environment it has worked out for itself. What the soul sows now it must reap hereafter. The process is impersonal; it is a law of nature, not the administration of justice by a divine judge. There is no question of reward and punishment as a Christian or a Jew would understand these notions. The principle is, rather, one of cause and effect in a spiritual realm corresponding to the principle of cause and effect that is thought to be seen in "physical" processes.

This theory has had an immense influence in India, not only in Hinduism and its institutional caste system, but among the Jains and Buddhists who branched off from the main Hindu stem two thousand five hundred years ago, and also among the Sikhs, who appeared in India as recently as about the time of the Reformation in Europe. One of the moral effects of belief in reincarnation is well known: it has engendered in millions an attitude of resignation to one's lot, because this is viewed as the result of one's deeds in a previous incarnation. I am a Shudra by birth because I deserve no better, having sinned in a previous life. Or, if I am a Brahmin, my good fortune in being born into this high caste is due to my good behavior in earlier incarnations; that is, I have earned my dignity. One is not born into one's caste by chance, and there is therefore no question of an arbitrary fate, or of some people's having had the hard luck of being born poor or blind or diseased, while others are born, as we say, with a silver spoon in their mouths. But in the last resort the fact that the lot of some is cast in relatively pleasant places while that of others is miserable is seen to be of less importance than is commonly imagined. Release from the tedious cycle of rebirths may be obtained by a full knowledge of one's essential identity with *Brahman*, the spiritual reality or substance that is above or beyond all else. This entails the elimination of all desires, even good ones, and the absorption of one's selfhood into the Great Self, *Brahman*. So from a timeless point of view all strivings and desires are unimportant. Looking back on my childhood days there are many things I find that seemed all-important to me then, such as, say, competing for a class prize or being selected for an athletic team, that now seem to have been of no importance at all to justify the concern they had for me at the time. Nevertheless, I admit that at the time they really were, in a sense, important to me: they were important, not in themselves, but for the development of my personality. So, in the view of man's destiny that we are considering, nothing that occurs in this world of *maya* or illusion is really important in itself, yet it is important at the time, from a subjective point of view within the realm of *maya*.

These ideas, expounded by the writers of the Upanishadic literature several centuries B.C., play a great part in later Indian thought. The general presuppositions of the theory are to be found in Plato and their consequences are worked into his philosophy in various ways. The appeal of the transmigration theory is not difficult to understand if we consider the context in which it arose. It had an appeal both to the intellect and to the moral consciousness. Its show of "rationality" satisfied a deep longing in man beyond mere intellectual curiosity. To the Greeks, the world of flux that is familiar to us in ordinary experience seemed to demand something "behind" or "below" it to give it support. Change, motion, seemed to require a permanent, immutable "ground" to hold it, and much early Greek speculation consisted in trying to discover what that ground was. According to one of Plato's theories on this subject it was a spiritual or mental world, and to this the human soul belonged. That permanent world, more "real" than the world of flux, must be the soul's true home, while the body, a very inferior part of man, belonged, rather, to the world of flux, and should stand in relation to the soul as a slave stands in relation to his master.

This doctrine still has great influence over the thought of many people who unconsciously adopt it as the basis of their religious views about the soul and human immortality. It cannot be refuted. As a metaphysical doctrine it had, however, a much greater appeal to thinkers in the ancient world than it has today, for we do not feel the same need for it. Modern scientists do need to record and measure change in terms of an x that does not itself change to any important extent in the course of the investigation in hand. But they do not require, for their experiments, anything absolute or indestructible such as a "permanent substance" or "soul-stuff." In other words, the modern scientist is content with a background that is stable for practical purposes, and he finds he can make enormous progress in understanding the universe without positing any absolute stability such as the Greek thinkers felt to be necessary.

Presuppositions about a permanent basis or stuff are so deeply rooted in the history of human thought that their influence is enormous and their effects incalculably varied. Totemism and animal worship in primitive religion arose from a feeling of the kinship of human beings with other animals: all share a common essence, and so life passes easily from one to the other. Hence we have many tales in folklore about vampires and werewolves, about princes turned into frogs, and so forth, while certain animals acquire a sacred character: for example, the bull in Greece, the cow in India, the kangaroo in Australia. Zeus turned himself into a beautiful swan in order to seduce Leda. Man's kinship with all nature is also an ancient notion, from which arises worship of the "elements" — earth, water, air and fire. Fire is still honored by the Parsees. In Europe, even late into the Middle Ages, the Doge of Venice was ceremonially married every year to the Adriatic. So it is hardly surprising that old Buddhist and Pythagorean ideas about the soul's being of an immutable and indestructible essence should not only have lived on in religious thought in theosophical movements seeking to perpetuate the old reincarnation theories of the Upanishads, but have affected also even some Christian thought about the destiny of man.

Essence of Soul-Substance Theory

What is essential to the theory we have been considering is not personal survival, though the theory may be adapted to provide for this, but the view that to the extent that anybody or anything has a soul it is in some sense immortal. Immortality is not something that is won; it is something that is inherent in the nature of everything that has soul-stuff. You are immortal whether you like it or not, and the question is, rather, what are you to do about your destiny in view of the fact that you are immortal? The wise man, on this view, is the one who takes his immortality into account and arranges his life accordingly. He is the man who is provident and far-seeing, and so he is contrasted with the man who, being shortsighted and thoughtless, concerns himself only with what lies immediately before him in his present life. As in ordinary life the thriftless man lives from day to day seeking the pleasures of the moment with no thought of the consequences ten years hence, while the provident man looks ahead and sees his whole life in better perspective, so in the theory we have been describing, the wise man, the holy man, is the one who is far-sighted, bearing in view his immortal nature. He looks ahead, not only in terms of this one fleeting life, but in terms of a series of innumerable lives of which this life is only a tiny link in the endless chain. Once the essential immortality of soul-substance is admitted, there are many difficulties to be dealt with, such as whether there is a final destiny, and if so what it is, and why, if the *samsara* or chain of incarnations is somehow apart from my "real" and "permanent" state, it should ever have been begun. Whether the individuality of the self as we know it is to be preserved or poured back into a common soul-substance or "Great Self" is a question that evokes many variations of the theory; but the theory itself may be critically examined apart from the solution of this problem. What is really essential to the theory is that we cannot help being immortal and the important thing is that we should face the fact. To the man who holds the theory in any of its forms, a recognition of the essential immortality of the soul is the most realistic attitude that can be taken. The wise man is looked upon, not as one who flees from the hard realities of life, but as the only thoroughgoing realist.

The Personal Survival Theory

Quite different from the view we have been considering, although often mixed up with this both in thought and in practice, is an even more primitive one that we are now to examine. Belief in survival after death occurs to savages in connection with their encounters with their relatives and friends in the course of dreaming. Rivers, mountains and other natural objects are, moreover, personified, and so believed to have souls or spirits too. The eleventh book of Homer's Odyssey provides an excellent example of this view, in which the soul is not the "eternal spark of divinity," or "permanent stuff," but is, rather, a kind of shadow of the living reality we know on earth. It is the living man in an attenuated form. The world of shades is a poor substitute, according to this view, for the present, "real" world. So the shade of Achilles begs Odysseus not to attempt to console him for death, for there is no use pretending that he has not been deprived by death of something very precious. Indeed, he points out to Odysseus, he would rather be a servant in the house of a poor man among the living than a king in the land of shades.

This view was prevalent in Socrates' time, and he conceived it to be his task to combat it in favor of the soul-substance type of theory. In our western culture it has never been abandoned, however, Socrates and Plato notwithstanding. It underlies a great deal of popular thinking in our own time about life after death. According to this primitive conception of survival, the departed soul is a sort of pale copy of the living man; hence, because of the resemblance, the latter is recognizable when encountered as a ghost. But the ghost resembles the once-living man somewhat as would a walking daguerreotype: no color is to be found in his face, no pitch in his voice, no strength in his limbs — in short, no life as we know it, but only a weak, pale substitute of the man that once laughed, talked, drank wine, made love, and went forth to battle with his shield glittering in the sunlight.

Psychical Research

Though most people in our western culture would nowadays ridicule belief in ghosts, this form of immortality theory still persists in our civilization as in others. When immortality is in question it is very often this sort of notion that presents itself to people's minds. It is certainly the kind of notion that underlies modern spiritistic beliefs. The sort of spirit that modern spiritists endeavor to conjure up at séances seems to be much the kind that primitive man sees in dreams. The communications that are alleged to come from such visitants are the sort of communications that one would expect from this sort of ghost, and so without our being either skeptical or otherwise about the activities of modern spiritists, it should be noted that this is the sort of survival-belief that they imply. Likewise it should be noted that while modern psychical research has yielded many very remarkable data and presented some curious puzzles, the evidences for survival that it sometimes offers for our consideration, whatever their worth may be, are evidences only of this kind of survival. Certain psychic phenomena that have been studied in a scientific fashion, notably telepathy, must be taken very seriously indeed: it seems that there are such phenomena that are still little understood and require further investigation. Though there are some reasons from a physiological point of view for rejecting belief in survival of the sort that we are now considering, the evidence is not by any means conclusive in either direction, and it is not impossible that something survives the man after death and hovers around the place where he was, as smoke hovers around an area long after the fire has been extinguished. But then such a survival would be the survival of only a remnant of the living man — enough, perhaps, to be felt or apprehended by certain individuals sensitive to "atmosphere" or possessed of what is sometimes regarded as a gift of "second sight," but no more than an epiphenomenon, that is, a sort of by-product of the once-living man.

Triviality of Personal Survival Hope

It is important to bear all this in mind in considering the problem of immortality. Certain ideas of immortality are very attractive and it can be a question of the greatest importance in religion whether we survive death or not; but the kind of immortality that is envisaged in this type of doctrine is not attractive at all. The possibility of immortality becomes interesting only when there is a prospect of a fuller or richer life after death; at least one as exciting as the present life. If it is only a question of whether, after my death, I shall continue to live on as a puff of smoke lives on after the candle has gone out, I can hardly care very much, either from a religious point of view or any other. The whole question becomes morbid, and perhaps not radically different from the question of whether, for certain chemical or physiological reasons, it is possible for a man to turn in his grave. Suppose even that it could be scientifically established that at death I might continue for a time in a dim consciousness, and that a distant echo of my voice were to be audible to certain persons endowed with a peculiar sensitivity; the prospect could be of little interest to even the most sentimental of my friends, and it would certainly fail to exhilarate me.

DISCUSSION ON CHAPTER 28

1. Distinguish between the theory that there is a "something" that survives the body of a man, and the doctrine that the soul is in its nature eternal.

2. "The Hellenic conception of man has been described as that of an angel in a slot machine, a soul (the invisible, spiritual, essential ego) incarcerated in a frame of matter, from which it trusts eventually to be liberated. The body is non-essential to the personality: it is something which a man possesses, or, rather, is possessed by. 'The Hebrew idea of the personality,' on the other hand, wrote the late Dr. Wheeler Robinson . . . 'is an animated body, and not an incarnated soul.' " (J. A. T. Robinson) Discuss.

3.   *I do not set my life at a pin's fee;*
        And, for my soul, what can it do to that,
        Being a thing immortal as itself?
                    (Shakespeare, *Hamlet*)
  Discuss.

29

Zoë: the Concept of Eternal Life

Bios, Psychē *and* Zoë

Three words are used in Greek to express ideas connected with life. One is *bios*, which refers to the life span; another is *psychē*, which stands for the animating principle (hence "psychology"); yet another is *zoë*, with which we are to be concerned in the present chapter.

The Concept of Eternal Life

The Christian hope is certainly not to be described as the hope of survival, personal or otherwise. What is promised above all in the New Testament is, as we noted in our first chapter, always described in terms of *life*. The word used in the Greek text in regard to this promise is *zoë*. According to Matthew, for example, the result of becoming as a little child is *zoë*.[1] According to John, *zoë* is the result of "being born from above." [2] Likewise, *zoë* is the consequence of "putting on Christ," [3] of being "quickened together with Christ," [4] of being "in Christ," [5] of "putting on the new man," [6] and of being "a new creature." [7] Moreover, it is noteworthy that the word *zoë* is used in the New Testament primarily with the definite article in such a way as to indicate that it is being referred to as something already somehow understood: it is *the* life, that is, the life that Christ's hearers, for instance, are assumed to be seeking. *Zoë* is the supreme blessing mediated by Christ to men.

The idea of *zoë* came from the Old Testament writers. True, the Hebrews inherited the survival theory common to primitive peoples: the disembodied soul did not cease to exist, but it forfeited its portion in the true life and departed either to the shadowy world of Sheol or else (according to a later view expressed in Ecclesiastes), "returned to God who gave it." [8] To the Hebrew, "length of days" was the

---

[1] Matt. 18:3.   [2] John 3:3.   [3] Gal. 3:27.
[4] Eph. 2:5.   [5] II Cor. 5:17.   [6] Eph. 4:24.
[7] Gal. 6:15.   [8] Eccles. 12:7.

great promise to the good man. Latent in much Old Testament teaching, however, is the notion that life, which is essentially activity, is pre-eminently in God, the "living God" and the "God of the living." "With thee," says the psalmist, "is the fountain of life." [9] This notion is developed in New Testament teaching. To Christ, "the life" is in one sense physical existence ("Take no thought for your life. . . ." [10]), but essentially it is to be distinguished from this: "the life is more than meat." [11] Here is the paradox: "He that findeth his life shall lose it, and he that loseth his life for my sake shall find it." [12] Zoë is sometimes regarded, it seems, as a new state of being, sometimes as a prize. Though it can be spoken of in the future, it is also in the present. This appears to be implied in Christ's injunction not to delay following Him on the pretext of attending a funeral: let the dead bury their dead.[13] So also in the parable of the Prodigal who "was dead and is alive again." [14]

The essential notion underlying zoë as the term is used in the New Testament seems to be that life varies in quality, and that what is held out to those who are ingrafted into the life of Christ is the highest quality of life that one could have. By communion with Christ the disciple has not only new life now, by reason of the moral relationship in which he finds himself, but the prospect of entering completely into his inheritance of life: his heritage is "the life everlasting" or, as it is elsewhere translated, "eternal life." [15] Zoë is a favorite term in the Fourth Gospel where the idea of life as a present possession of believers is central. "He that believeth on the Son *hath* everlasting life." [16] So it is that physical death can be called a "falling asleep" [17] that cannot deprive the believer of his everlasting possession. The nature of the life that is so much the theme of this evangelist is not clearly defined, and occasionally the concept of zoë as a spiritual possession seems to give place to another view not entirely consistent with this and probably an echo of an earlier, traditional doctrine; nevertheless the predominant view in the Fourth Gospel, which seems to be developed out of a combination of Hebrew and Greek traditions of thought, is that the life of Christ is an immense energy, yet one that is abstracted from all forms of sensible manifestation. Jesus tells the woman at the well that whosoever should drink of the water that He should provide should never thirst again: this water should be "a well of water springing up into everlasting life." [18]

[9] Ps. 36:9. [10] Matt. 6:25.
[11] Luke 12:23. [12] Matt. 10:39; 16:25.
[13] Matt. 8:22; Luke 9:60. [14] Luke 15:32.
[15] In the King James Version the rendering "eternal life" is given 42 times and "everlasting life" 24 times.
[16] John 3:36. [17] John 11:11. [18] John 4:14.

The concept of eternal life is indeed quite unlike the notion of survival. What is remarkable about zoë, as we have been considering it in the present chapter, is its quality: this life is qualitatively different from any other. It is timeless, and the essence of the Christian promise is inheritance of this timeless life. The significance of this qualitative difference must not be overlooked, and to appreciate it more fully it may be useful to contrast it with another kind of vision of immortality.

Medical Science and the Indefinite Postponement of Old Age

It has been predicted by a distinguished modern scientist, a Nobel Laureate, that with the continued progress of medical science old age may be indefinitely postponed." [19] Consider the consequences of such indefinite postponement of old age. All death would be either by accident or by intent. Such conditions would revolutionize our thinking about many things. Life insurance premiums would not be calculated on the present actuarial basis: you would be insuring not merely your life but your "immortality." Our first reaction to the prospect of such an increase in the life span (not to say the prospect of immortality on earth) is that it might be all right if one's health were to be maintained. In other words, so long as senescence were eliminated or postponed as indefinitely as death itself, the prospect would seem to be bearable, even attractive. But is it really so? Would two hundred years of life, even with senility not setting in till you were one hundred ninety-nine, be essentially more desirable than eighty years of life with senility setting in at seventy-nine? You would indeed have longer to achieve what you feel you want to achieve, yet still not long enough. Moreover, you would also have a more extensive opportunity for making a mess of things. Your larger store of pleasant memories would be offset by the increased weight of your regrets.

Quality, Not Quantity of Life

The more carefully we consider such questions, the greater the wisdom we can see in Benjamin Franklin's counsel in *Poor Richard:* "Wish not so much to live long as to live well." "Life," Crabbe reminds us, "is not to be measured by the time we live." [20] As Emerson puts it, "it is the depth at which we live and not at all the surface extension that imports." [21] This idea of "depth" of life was familiar to thoughtful people in the ancient world. Half a century before

[19] George Paget Thomson, *The Foreseeable Future* (New York: Cambridge University Press, 1955).
[20] *The Village,* Book II.
[21] *Society and Solitude,* "Works and Days."

Christ, the Roman historian Sallust wrote: "No parent would wish for his children that they might live forever, but rather that their lives might be good and honorable." [22] Seneca likewise says that the wise man will live as long as he ought, not as long as he can, for "he is always thinking about the quality, not the quantity of his life." [23] Such were also no doubt the thoughts of Socrates before he drank the deadly hemlock.

The Quest for Zoë

By the time of Christ, the notion that life is to be measured by its "depth" or quality rather than by its "length" or span had already become fairly familiar. The Hebrews, for all their traditional emphasis on longevity as a blessing, were acquainted with the notion of another "dimension" of life, as well as were the Greeks and the Romans. So to those who listened to Jesus there was nothing essentially novel in the idea of such a life: only the claim that it was to be found superlatively in Him was startling. The rich young man who asked Jesus what he ought to do to inherit zoë was raising no particularly "supernatural" question in the minds of the bystanders. He was, rather, engaged in a quest familiar to all, the quest for fullness of life. He was asking, not for longevity, not for "length of days," but for "depth." He had tried obedience to the law of Moses, but apparently it had failed to give him what he sought. How could he get more "depth"? Jesus, impressed by his sincerity, prescribed a still more difficult course: the young man was to give away his rich estates and become the personal disciple of Jesus. It is said that he then "went away grieved," for he had great possessions.[24]

We might say that the young man was seeking a special kind of vivacity. What, precisely, was it? Not intellectual vivacity, surely, such as that of a mathematical prodigy, nor yet the creative vivacity of the artist. Apparently we are to understand that he already possessed moral vivacity, so it could not have been this that he sought. All these vivacities may have been subsumed under the concept zoë; but they were not the zoë he sought. Perhaps we might come nearer the mark were we to think of his quest in terms of a quest for what in modern language we might call "richer personality"; yet that is much too self-centered a notion to meet the case. We should not overlook the fact that presumably he had some experience already of what he was seeking, for it seems that he knew something about it. He appears to have felt he did have some access to what he was seeking, but that he could only get at it in an indirect and unsatisfactory way. His feeling may perhaps be compared to that of a man who is getting water in a

22 *Jurgurtha*, Chap. 85, Sec. 50.
23 *Epist. ad Lucilium*, 70, 4. 24 Mark 10:22.

chemically purified form from a faucet in a room on the eighteenth floor of a block of apartments and who has heard how ill it compares with that which others get fresh from a spring on the hillside.

The Tree of Life

It will be remembered that in the Garden of Eden stood the Tree of Life. After the fall of Adam, it was necessary that this tree should be guarded by cherubim with flaming swords in order to prevent Adam from getting at it, eating its fruit, and so coming into his immortal inheritance. Cut off from the fruit of the tree he would die and return to dust. There is an older, Babylonian version of the Garden of Eden story, according to which there was a plant whose fruit conferred on those who ate it the power of remaining forever young. Man was about to eat the fruit when the serpent grabbed it from him and devoured it, so gaining for himself the coveted prize. (Serpents, who shed their skin, are commonly credited by primitive peoples with perpetual youth, and they are also widely regarded as symbols of evil.) The implication of the Biblical story and its counterparts in other ancient literature is apparently that man *should* be immortal and has been deprived in one way or another of his inheritance. Such reflections may help us to see how various notions of immortality that people in the time of Christ had inherited from remote antiquity could be reconciled to each other. Zoë was indeed the energy in all living beings; but it is of varying degrees or quality. Christ announces that He has come that his disciples may have zoë in superabundance.[25] Indeed, He says, "I am the Zoë." [26]

Beyond Duration

The zoë that the fourth evangelist says Christ claimed to be must be considered as a kind, quality or intensity of life that can be possessed or enjoyed all at once. Duration has nothing to do with it. It is *beyond* duration. According to the orthodox Christian view, the destiny of man consists in this enjoyment. To the first question in the Scottish Catechism, "What is man's chief end?" the answer is given: "Man's chief end is to glorify God and to enjoy Him for ever." It is to enjoy "the Eternal" and you cannot enjoy the Eternal for any length of time, short or long. It is, rather, that in enjoying the Eternal you are beyond the limitations of time itself. "Eternity," says Boethius, "is the perfect possession of unending life all at once."

Though this notion finds dramatic expression and dynamic power in Christianity, it is to be met with elsewhere. In Spinoza's view, for instance, to the extent that we human beings are able to conceive all things ordered and united together we are actually partaking of eternal

[25] John 10:10.   [26] John 14:6.

life. As he puts it, "the mind is eternal in so far as it conceives things under the form of eternity." [27] Some of Plato's doctrines also imply the timelessness of truths and the timelessness of the mind or *nous* that apprehends them. The most important argument in the *Phaedo*, for example, suggests that immortality is the immortality of eternal life rather than the immortality of successive lives in a chain of re-incarnations, as another of Plato's theories has it.

Zoë and the Fact of Death

What is peculiar to the Christian conception is that over against its doctrine of "eternal life" there is a strong emphasis on the reality of *death*. Death is not for the Christian a mere "incident" of little importance. On the contrary, it is only by facing the stark reality of death that we can make any progress toward understanding our destiny. Our destiny is, in the first place, death and extinction, for as human beings we are indeed mortal: this is our inheritance. The power of death is absolute over us, and its fatal hurt is inescapable. But, according to Christian teaching, Christ is "victorious over death" and in fulfillment of Christ's promise the Christian may enter into the eternal life. So, though the Christian does not escape physical death, this has lost its sting. Death becomes, then, not the mocking visitant that puts an end to our existence, but the very portal of eternal life. Through death we are not merely granted an indefinite lease of life as we know it; we are received, rather, into a new realm in which we enjoy a new quality of life, life eternal, world without end.

Combination of Immortality Theories in the Bible

This is indeed very different from either of the conceptions we considered in the previous chapter. It has often been mixed up with one or both of these. In the thought of the Biblical writers there are traces of several theories of immortality. The Bible is not designed, of course, as a philosophical treatise but is accounted, rather, the revelation of God through the writings of men who think with all the limitations of human thought just as they write with all the limitations of human language. The early Christian Fathers likewise reflect the influence of various immortality theories. But there is a good case for contending that the view we have been considering in the present chapter expresses the specifically Christian hope. At any rate it is important to distinguish this view in our minds from the others, when we discuss what is to be said for and against the notion of immortality or affirm or deny belief in a "future" life.

[27] Spinoza, *Ethics*, V, Prop. 31, scholium.

DISCUSSION ON CHAPTER 29

1. Compare and contrast the view that immortality consists in a special quality of life, with the two theories that have been considered in a previous chapter.

2. "If some devil were to convince us that our dream of perpetual immortality is no dream but a hard fact, such a shriek of despair would go up from the human race as no other conceivable horror could provoke. . . . What man is capable of the insane self-conceit of believing that an eternity of himself would be tolerable even to himself?" (Bernard Shaw) Discuss this passage with reference to the notion of eternal life.

3. "Eternity is not an everlasting flux of time, but time is as a short parenthesis in a long period." (John Donne) Discuss.

30

Arguments For and Against Immortality

Complexity of the Problem

It is plain enough to the man in the street that there is an obvious objection at the outset to any argument for or against a "future life," namely, that in the nature of the case we could not possibly know. Still, he might admit that it would be interesting to see just what arguments could be set up on one side or the other: such arguments, though they could not be expected to "prove" anything one way or the other, might nevertheless carry some weight, inclining us to believe one way or the other. Now that we have reviewed the different types of belief in immortality, however, there is an added and very serious difficulty that the ordinary person is not likely to see. If it were simply a question of setting up arguments for and against one belief in immortality we might well do so, at least as a philosophical exercise. It would not be very difficult, even, if we were to be called upon to attempt to provide a series of arguments for a series of separate immortality beliefs. The difficulty is that the various types of immortality beliefs are so mixed up with each other that it seems hardly possible even to formulate an argument for or against, let alone to demonstrate anything that might help to convince anybody one way or another.

Plato's Arguments

Let us, however, examine the situation more closely. In western philosophy, at any rate, the classic demonstration of the immortality of the soul is to be found in the *Phaedo*. But even to his own contemporaries Plato was talking of immortality in a revolutionary way. Traditionally, the Greeks, no less than the Hebrews, looked forward to no prospect such as Plato was arguing about, because their view was that the soul of a man was an epiphenomenon, that is, a by-product of the real self. The real self died when the breath went out of the body, though the by-product continued a shadowy existence for a while. Plato is concerned to show that the situation is, rather, the other way around. He presents an argument between Socrates

199

and Simmias in which the latter looks upon the soul as being to the body what music is to the harp: the music springs from the harp and the sound of the music may survive the plucking of the harp strings till at length it fades out completely. Socrates takes up this notion and endeavors to refute it. On the other hand, the Greeks were accustomed to think of the gods as immortal in the sense in which Plato was trying to make them think the human soul was immortal. To them, the gods were by definition immortal, and man was by definition mortal, though his soul might carry on for a while in a ghostly, shadowy existence.

Plato develops his immortality theme by three different arguments; but in all of these he is concerned to uphold a particular philosophical doctrine. In the *Phaedo* he presents his contention that all learning is really a process of recollection. A teacher does not impart to his pupil something entirely new, of which the pupil knows nothing; he provokes, rather, in the student's mind, the remembrance of what is there already. So when an intelligent slave in the *Meno* is confronted for the first time with a geometrical proof, he grasps what is demonstrated to him in such a way that it is as if his teacher were drawing something out of his mind rather than putting something into it. The teacher's function, on this view, must be to help the student to find in his own mind what is there already — shelved, we might say, in a corner of his mind. There is no question of his putting something into it that was not there before. Such an educational theory does make sense; it "rings a bell." Plato's explanation of what lies behind it is this: the intelligent student seems to have learned the subject before because he *has* learned the subject before. The truth now demonstrated to him is one that has been shown to him long ago, in a previous existence. His teacher is now engaged only in the task of bringing back the memory of it. His own task is to respond to his teacher's efforts to stimulate his memory. On this view, all lessons are really revisions or reviews. Some people are able to remember more quickly than others; it may be that, being further advanced in the process of reincarnation, they have a greater store of knowledge from which to draw. But everyone has a store of some kind, and the patient teacher will try to help even the slower, the duller student, to dig into his mind's recesses and eventually come forth with the mislaid treasures.

Plato's second argument is more philosophical. There are three orders of existence: bodies, forms, and souls. Bodies, composed of matter, are changing and perishable. Forms, in Plato's system, are eternal, invisible archetypes. They belong to an order beyond the "ordinary world" which depends for its existence upon them. Souls have a peculiar status. They stand between the other two orders of existence, being connected with both. Their real affinity, however, would seem to be with the realm of forms. Like the forms themselves, souls are invisible. They are capable of contemplating the forms because the realm of forms is, so to speak, their true home; they belong there. A soul encamps in the body for a while; but it is really on a sort of pilgrimage in the body, which also it uses as a carpenter uses his tools. It is not really at home in the body: its true home is the Platonic heaven — the realm of forms.

The third argument offered in the *Phaedo* is a very simple one. It is that the soul is by definition alive. The Greek word for "soul" (*psyche*) was the word used for the principle of life. So Plato could make it seem plausible to say that it is a truism to attribute immortality to the soul. What could a soul be but immortal, since "soul" *means* the very principle of life?

In one of his later dialogues, the *Phaedrus*, Plato attempts a more comprehensive demonstration of his view. "All soul is immortal," he now says, "for that is immortal which remains forever in motion; but that which, besides moving other things is moved by them, in ceasing to move, ceases also to live. Therefore only that which is self-moving never fails itself and never ceases to move, but is the source and the beginning of the motion of all other things." He then goes on to say that "every body moved from without is soul-less, but that which is moved of itself from within has a soul, this being involved in the very nature of soul. But if we are right in saying that soul is thus self-moving, then soul must be unbegotten and immortal." [1]

Objection to Plato's Theories

Many will feel sympathetic to the view expressed by Henri Bergson that Plato's conception of the soul "has not advanced our knowledge of the soul a single step, two thousand years of meditation upon it notwithstanding." [2] Indeed, probably most intelligent students when they first encounter Plato's arguments for immortality in the *Phaedo*, the *Phaedrus* and the *Republic*, find them peculiarly unsatisfactory. On the other hand, they often find them also very provocative of serious thought, and there is no question of the enormous influence that they have had on human thought for more than twenty centuries. Philosophers have copied and restated and modified and developed Plato's arguments for immortality. Meanwhile our scientific conceptions of the nature of the *psyche* and of its relation to the body have undergone a great change, so that there have arisen philosophers who have argued, in direct contradiction to Plato, not only that it

[1] *Phaedrus,* 245–246.
[2] *Les Deux Sources de la morale et de la religion,* p. 282.

cannot be demonstrated that the soul is immortal in the sense intended by him but that it can be shown that it is mortal. In fact, however, this view is really no more than a sophisticated restatement in more modern terms of the view expounded by Simmias, that the soul, being a dependent epiphenomenon of the body, is by its nature mortal. Neither side can win in any such argument. The kind of immortality that Plato predicated of the soul and desired to establish for it, which his adversaries have sought to disprove, is not susceptible to demonstration. So far as can be seen it is unlikely that it could ever be the subject of human knowledge; at any rate it is certainly no more so now than it was in the fifth century B.C. If you say there is a soul-stuff and I deny it, I cannot prove you wrong, and if you say there is no soul-stuff you cannot prove yourself right.

Human Life as a Pilgrimage

Nevertheless, the doctrine of immortality that Plato taught has had a great fascination for thoughtful men throughout the ages. It strikes a responsive chord in us. Not only has the idea of transmigration been a most powerful force in the great civilization and ancient culture of India; not only has it been very influential elsewhere in the history of human thought; it still captivates the imagination of intelligent students today when they first encounter it. But perhaps of even more universal appeal is the idea that we are pilgrims on earth and that the present life, important sojourn though it be, is a journey away from home. And perhaps this is the essential point of Plato's doctrine on the destiny of man.

Immortality in Greek Mythology

The Greek poets had toyed with a fanciful idea that in exceptional cases mortals could escape mortal fate (that is, the shadowy survival leading to extinction) and become "as the gods." Penelope and Telemachus, it would seem, did not share the fate of ordinary mortals but were translated to the Elysian Fields or (as Hesiod has it) the Isles of the Blest, a very agreeable paradise where the climate is most equable and life is rich and good. All this was part of Greek folklore, as was also the later notion that besides the gods there were heroes, a race of exceptional men destined for immortality. Such heroes, according to the Greek poets, first went like other men to the shadowy abode of the departed, but instead of sharing the dreary afterlife fate of ordinary mortals they were miraculously revived and raised to life among the gods.[3] All this was mere poetic fancy, of course; but the notion reappears in one of the Greek mystery cults. Those who participated in the Eleusinian mysteries were promised a fate as

[3] Cf. the Teutonic Valhalla, *supra*, Chapter 6.

wonderful as that which the poets had fancifully attributed to the heroes. To those initiated into the esoteric mysteries the promise was held out that if they should fulfill certain ritual conditions in worshiping Demeter and her attendant deities, they should not suffer the fate of ordinary mortals, wearily surviving among the shades of the dead, but should somehow enter into a superior *sort* of life. Then in the Dionysian cult, especially as this developed under the influence of Orphism, a bolder conception still was proposed and a still more glorious prospect held out to the initiated. Probably not even the most skeptical of modern Americans would find it as startling as it must have appeared to many if not most Greeks of the time. Those who performed the rites prescribed might look forward to the realization in fact of what had been but a poet's dream for extraordinary heroes of a past age; they might hope to be exalted after death to a truly god-like life, a life of richer quality than any life lived on earth.

How Could We Know?

Our natural reaction to all this is likely to be: "But this is pure fantasy: how could they know? How, indeed, could they even put any content into the idea since they had no experience of such a 'super-life' and so could not even understand what they themselves were talking about?" Now comes the interesting point. The practitioners of this cult did not make the promise *in vacuo*. The rites themselves included an experience of a very dramatic kind: the method of getting this coveted experience was to go up to a mountain-top and engage in a wild, ritual dance in the course of which the soul was said to leave the body and know, though but for a fleeting instant, the joy of liberation. At any rate, so impressive was this experience, whatever it was, that the devotee of the cult felt he knew very well what was the essential nature of the "super-life" that was promised him after death, for he had, he believed, enjoyed a very real foretaste of it in the practice of his religion. In our language, he knew what heaven was like because he had been privileged to catch a fleeting glimpse of it on earth; it had been revealed to him even in his earthly experience so that he never could forget it. Henceforth nothing could be more important in his life than to ensure that he would not miss a share in such a glorious life after death as that which he had tasted on the mountain-top in the course of the practice of his cult.

Hebrew Thought on Immortality

The Hebrews were on the whole certainly no more inclined to this sort of thing than were the Greeks. One has only to read Old Testament accounts of the death of a great man to see that even their heroes are recorded as simply dying and so being "gathered" to the

people. The people might be immortal in some sense; the individual
was not. Even the great Hebrew prophets, for all that they discovered
about the importance of the individual, had nothing much to say
about the possibility of anything in the least like the conceptions we
have just been examining in the Greek mystery religions. It is not
until we come to the Jewish apocalyptic [4] literature, beginning with
the Book of Daniel, that we encounter the notion of immortality
that eventually developed into a theory that the righteous would
after death acquire a new body, one which would be superior to the
sort we now have and in which life would be fuller and better.[5] This
teaching took various forms and was by no means universally accepted
among the Jews by the time of Christ. We read in the Gospels of
the Sadducees, who repudiated it,[6] and of how Jesus on this point took
the part of the Pharisees against them.

It is important to notice what brought about this new temper in
Hebrew thinking. The older Hebrew tradition was that God rewarded
the righteous and punished the wicked in this life, and so there was
no need for a future life to fulfill the divine justice. One could not fail
to observe, however, that very often the wicked, far from being punished, seemed to get away with their wickedness and "have a good
time," while the righteous, on the other hand, met with all sorts of
misfortunes and suffered all manner of distress. "Wherefore doth the
way of the wicked prosper?" cries the anguished Jeremiah. [7] "Wherefore," asks Job, "do the wicked live, become old, yea, are mighty in
power?" [8] For while the wicked were not expected to enjoy the
blessing of "length of days," observation could not but disclose the
fact that many scoundrels lived on in health and comfort to an
advanced age while good, honest men died in their prime, and seemed
to have even in their shorter lives endured woeful trials. Where was
the justice in that? God, who was both just and mighty, could not
be content to leave matters thus. Surely, it came to be argued, there
must be a way of putting all this right after death. What we ought
to note especially here is that the belief in a glorious future life was
seen as a corollary of belief in the infinite righteousness and justice
of God, who would not in the long run allow the wicked to trample
with impunity on the just and mock them in their distress. God's
goodness seemed to demand a life beyond the grave that looked as

---

[4] There is a literature, Jewish and Christian, to which the term "apocalyptic"
is applied. It begins about 250 B.C. and continues into the first century A.D.
A Christian example is the "Apocalypse" or "Revelation of St. John the
Divine." Apocalyptic scripture aims at comforting the faithful in their suffer-
ings by prefiguring the eventual triumph of "the Kingdom of God" (Israel or
the New Jerusalem) over the world.

[5] Cf. Josephus, *The Jewish War*, Book II, Chap. 8.

[6] Matt. 22:23.   [7] Jer. 12:1.   [8] Job 21:7.

though it must be even more important than this life which to the Hebrews had always seemed very important indeed.

The Importance of the Question

Now we are in a position to consider the weight of arguments for and against immortality. We have already concluded that so far as the soul-stuff conception of immortality is concerned, there is really nothing that can be proved one way or the other. It is a speculative doctrine, interesting, fascinating and provocative; but it depends on a special metaphysical presupposition. The primitive survival theory, on the other hand, is hardly worth arguing about at all. Whether I die with or without a long echo is not the sort of question that is likely to stimulate my interest, even in my most idly argumentative moods. I could scarcely care less which of these alternatives is to be my lot, even if I were convinced that I must choose between them. The really important question is, rather, whether I may hope for a richer and fuller life after death. Even if such a life were supposed to be limited in duration, though richer in content, it would still be a matter of lively interest to an inquiring mind. But if it were envisaged as beyond duration itself and therefore infinitely rich in all respects, and if the possibility of my gaining it were in question, then nothing could be of more profound concern to me, except the danger of losing it.

What Kind of Argument Would be Relevant?

Let us put the question in the first instance, then, as follows: what *kind* of argument, if any, could be adduced for or against the inheritance of *zoë*, the eternal life that we have discussed? It could not be a logical argument based on "ordinary" experience, unless we recognized the presence of an extraordinary experience entering into this. And even at the most, any such argument would be vulnerable to all sorts of objections, not least the obvious physio-psychological objection that consciousness is known in our experience to depend upon the brain. If the brain is injured, consciousness is injured, so that it may be supposed that when the brain ceases entirely to function, consciousness ceases too. Counterobjections to positivism and materialism might of course be made; but what would then be in question would be not the possibility of my inheritance of eternal life, but postulates underlying acceptance or rejection of this. To meet opposition to the notion of eternal life by glowing accounts of the intensity of the faith of millions in it, or of the ardor of their hope for it, would of course have no assent-compelling force at all. Such considerations could succeed only in confirming each individual in his own opinion, for or against.

A Corollary of Theism

The only real argument for the possibility of inheriting eternal life is one that depends wholly on acceptance of theism. If there is a Creator God who is infinitely benevolent as well as the source of all values, then he must be committed to the conservation of values. The highest values we know are experiences of the fulfillment of ideal purposes by individual persons. The existence of these values depends upon persons. God must therefore be the conserver of persons.[9] Every argument for theism is an argument for the preservation of all persons whose extinction would seem to entail a failure on God's part in His benevolent purpose. If the saints of old have just perished, being now as dust, our sadness at the thought springs from our recognition of the consequence that theism has been emptied of meaning, for God would seem to have no purpose or to have failed in the purpose He has. *Ex hypothesi*, He would still be the source of life; but the life of which He was the source would be as fleeting as our own passing joys and pains. Indeed, He would have become only a sort of divine playboy, able to exist Himself and able to create toys for Himself while being unable to communicate to His creation the most valuable quality in Himself. He would have to be accounted a sort of would-be artist who had failed to express Himself in His creative act.

Is a Godless Heaven Conceivable?

It is noteworthy that only one important philosopher has ever both denied theism and affirmed a godless eternity, upholding the notion that the human soul is immortal in its own right. This is the British humanist philosopher, J. M. E. McTaggart. He wrote to a friend that he knew few people who believed as vividly in heaven as he did, but at the same time he repudiated theism so strongly that his biographer says he seemed to have "a positive dislike" for the very notion of God. McTaggart's heaven is, however, a very curious notion indeed, for it is not easy to see wherein consists its bliss. In some respects a western adaptation of a Jainist theory, McTaggart's pluralism makes the totality of human souls a kind of collegiate deity and it is not perhaps entirely unfair to parody McTaggart's heaven as a kind of glorified eternal faculty meeting, a prospect that does not by any means commend itself to college professors any more than it commends itself to the man in the street. Indeed, McTaggart's godless heaven is curiously reminiscent of the orthodox Christian notion of hell, which consists of eternity without God. It is an interesting metaphysical speculation; but there is nothing to warrant it.

[9] This, of course, raises the very difficult question, "What is a person?"

Only theism, accepted consciously or otherwise, can justify belief in the possibility of eternal life. It not only justifies it; it implies it.

DISCUSSION ON CHAPTER 30

1. "All men deserve to be saved, but he above all deserves immortality who desires it passionately and even in the face of reason." (Unamuno) Discuss.

2. "The origin of the absurd idea of immortal life is easy to discover; it is kept alive by hope and fear, by childish faith, and by cowardice." (Clarence Darrow) "Immortality is the bravest gesture of our humanity toward the unknown. It is always a faith, never a demonstration." (G. A. Atkins) Discuss.

3. Consider difficulties in the notion of a heaven such as that envisaged by McTaggart.

31

Conditional Immortality

Immortality as a Prize

According to the soul-stuff theory of immortality there can be no question in any individual case of survival or nonsurvival: souls are imperishable in their own right and by reason of ther own nature. Likewise, in the primitive survival theory that we also considered, such survival as there is may be considered automatic. Everybody survives in a dim, vague, and limited fashion. Perhaps one "puff of smoke" trails further than another; but this is of no importance. Nothing that I could do, on either of these theories, would really affect my immortality, for my immortality is independent of my conduct. It would no doubt be in my interest, according to some theories of this kind, to behave myself; but it would be in my interest for other reasons, for reasons not directly relevant to my immortal status. My behavior could not affect this one way or another.

Immortality, as the inheritance of *zoë* or eternal life, raises, however, another question. Suppose that I accept this theory as a corollary of theism. It at once becomes apparent that there are formally two possibilities arising out of its acceptance. Either I may be assured that all persons eventually inherit eternal life, or else I may be warned that, since only some do, I may be excluded from it. It would seem that exclusion from it would entail my extinction; but to this we shall presently return. For the moment let us confine ourselves to the question: is the soul, according to the eternal life theory, necessarily immortal?

Since *zoë* is generally represented as a gift or a prize it would seem that there is no reason why belief in this *kind of* immortality should imply that I am immortal by nature. The presumption must surely be that I may, and again that I may not, inherit the prize. Otherwise how could it be called a prize? Moreover, this theory implies that since *zoë* is a peculiarly rich *quality* of life, I must be capable of having or enjoying that quality of life. Not even God could give a man the enjoyment of a quality of life of which the man was incapable. It would be somewhat like giving a deaf man a ticket for the most

208

wonderful concert in the world: it would not enable the man to enjoy the concert even if you bought him the concert hall.

Universalism

But let us return for a moment to the source of belief in this type of immortality. Its source in theism immediately draws to our attention the fact that the answer to the question now raised must depend on the situation that theism envisages. It is arguable that there is something valuable in all persons, however wicked or sensual or thoughtless or selfish, and that, therefore, in order to conform to the requirements of the argument already developed on this subject, all persons must in some way and to some degree inherit eternal life. That is to say, even though there is no question of an imperishable soul-stuff, all men must in fact be "saved unto life eternal." In other words again, eternal life is not a necessity arising from the metaphysical nature of soul-substance; nevertheless, it is inevitable in fact because God's creatures all reflect and are derived from the eternal life that has its source in Him. This is the doctrine of universalism.

Objections to Universalism

Few theists would be willing to say, however, that such universalism applies to *all* creatures, including, say, a cabbage, which has life, or even monkeys. Some theists might keep an open mind on the subject of the possible inheritance of eternal life by some animals other than men; but universalism as it is ordinarily understood is confined to the human creation. In the Biblical and patristic view about the creation of man was included a traditional assumption that the human race is an entirely separate creation. Consequently, no difficulty was felt in the notion that eternal life was for human beings only. The scientific doctrine that man is evolved from the lower animals (a notion not unknown to the ancients and therefore not entirely novel in itself when set forth by Darwin last century) is compatible with the Biblical account of creation, symbolically interpreted. On the other hand, the implications of an evolutionary theory are not always fully taken into account. It makes it impossible to uphold any sharp dichotomy between man and other creatures, and this constitutes a general objection at the outset against universalism in its traditional form, that is, the ultimate salvation of all, but only of, human beings.

But even if he ignores this general objection that arises from acceptance of the evolutionary account of the origin of man, the universalist must face another objection from the theological side. For it is basic Christian doctrine that man is free to accept or reject God's claims of love upon him. Man must have this freedom, for otherwise the only love he could return to God would be an automatic reflex. In order for man to love God of his own accord, he must have a genuine moral freedom to love or not to love. No love, indeed, can be genuine unless there is such freedom, and God desires only genuine love from his creatures. It is therefore at least theoretically possible for man to turn his back upon God and refuse to return God's love. Moreover, so far as any human being can tell, it seems plain that some, perhaps most, men do so repudiate God. Since eternal life, zoë, depends, we have seen, on God as its source, it cannot be supposed that a creature could both be capable of inheriting eternal life and at the same time seek to defy or repudiate God. Finally, there is abundant Scriptural support for the view that eternal life is a gift or prize for those who accept God's offer, and that many do not accept it.

Incapacity for Eternal Life

It would appear plausible that since some people are, for one reason or another, capable of eternal life, while others are, for one reason or another, incapable of it, some are to inherit eternal life while others are to be extinguished. The extinction of those who do not "win" eternal life would appear to follow, for there is nothing in the zoë theory that would make immortality inherent in human nature. Either we inherit eternal life or we do not, and if we do not there is no reason why we should expect any fate other than the extinction that the materialist or positivist associates with all death.

Conditional Immortality

The doctrine that eternal life is to be received or won by some and that others are to suffer extinction is known as the doctrine of conditional immortality. Philosophically, this is what would seem to follow from the zoë doctrine in its "pure" form. The zoë doctrine does not, however, seem to be worked out in such a form in the New Testament, and certainly not in Christian tradition. On the contrary, it has been mixed with the soul-stuff doctrine. The Christian fathers appear to have taken over both doctrines as if they felt it necessary to preserve both. This circumstance has introduced a great complexity, not to say ambiguity, into the Christian doctrine of the future life. For upon the basic view that eternal life is a prize is superimposed another doctrine, namely the soul-stuff doctrine that man is in any case inherently immortal. So while the faithful win a crown of zoë-immortality, the unfaithful have in any case the soul-stuff-immortality common to all men. It is this superimposition of one doctrine of immortality upon another that allows for the development of a reward-and-punishment doctrine in the form of the terrible final alternative of an eternal zoë-heaven and an eternal soul-stuff-hell.

It is well known that the doctrine of eternal damnation has played an enormous part in Christian teaching throughout the centuries. In the popular imagination, fed by dramatic imagery from some pulpits, it has been represented as a place of unspeakable torture, a foul prison in which the damned are roasted by leering devils. Such was the conventional medieval picture and it has persisted in much popular belief down to the present day. The Founder of the Salvation Army, for instance, declared in a letter to his future wife that people "must have hell-fire flashed in their faces, or they will not move." [1] On the other hand, the doctrine of hell expounded by learned theologians such as, in the thirteenth century, Thomas Aquinas, has been very different from the vulgar conception. In our next chapter we shall revert to this. For the present, noting that a revulsion against the notion of eternal damnation has led some Christian theologians to take very seriously the doctrine of conditional immortality, let us see what is to be said for it. Philosophically, it has the advantage of simplicity, avoiding the confusion of two sorts of immortality and the difficulties this presents. But can it also be defended from a theological and Biblical standpoint in such a way as to satisfy the religious consciousness?

Paul

It has been suggested that Paul held a doctrine of conditional immortality, for he has nothing to say about hell, and he associates the ideas of sin and death. The implication, some think, is that he took the view that in the ordinary course sinful men are simply extinguished by death, which is "the wages of sin," that which is the sinner's due. Immortality, on the other hand, is the prize awarded to God's elect. Moreover, a doctrine of conditional immortality is also suggested even in some of Christ's utterances as recorded in the Gospels. In some Gospel passages, [2] the Greek word that is translated "hell" is a word elsewhere rendered in English "Gehenna." Gehenna, the Valley of Hinnom, was the traditional site of the worship paid to Moloch, and it was later made the city dump or rubbish heap. In later Jewish thought it became a symbol of the place of future punishment, so that its use in the New Testament was natural and traditional. However, the fact that it was the city dump does suggest the notion that the wicked, who are unworthy of eternal life (or incapable of it) are regarded as fit only to be "dumped"; that is, they

---

[1] H. Begbie, *The Life of William Booth* (London: Macmillan & Co., 1920), I, p. 228.

[2] Matt. 5:22, 29, 30; 10:28; 18:9; 23:15, 33; Mark 9:43, 45, 47; Luke 12:5. Cf. Jas. 3:6.

are simply thrown out with the trash to perish as trash does. So Christ urges his hearers not to fear that which kills the body, but to fear only that which is able to destroy *both soul and body* in Gehenna.[3]

Argument for Hell

The most obvious objection to all this is that there are other passages in the New Testament that plainly imply that those who fail to win eternal life do continue in existence — a very unpleasant kind of existence. The protagonists of conditional immortality point to the fact that this doctrine exhibits God in terms that seem more in accordance with His infinite love. It is very intelligible that some people should be raised to eternal life while others are simply allowed to extinguish themselves. It is also compatible with what is predicated of God's nature. God cannot force people to love Him or to live in such a way as to "qualify" for eternal life. But on the other hand, no New Testament doctrine is more fundamental than the doctrine of salvation, and if by Christ's redemptive act man is saved, it must surely be that he is saved from a terrible fate. To many earnest believers it seems unrealistic to suppose that the "perdition" from which man is saved is simply extinction. It seems to them that the immense importance of salvation consists in being saved *from* a terrible destiny and saved *to* a glorious one. Extinction does not appear to them to be a sufficiently terrible destiny to justify the enormous importance attached to salvation. Moreover, they point out, there is to be considered the wrath of God. Some may feel that the notion that God is wrathful is a primitive one that should find no place in theology; but it may be pointed out that God's wrath is the other side of God's love. We tend to think of God's love in far too sentimental a fashion, as though it were the more sugary aspect of God's nature. But no genuine love, human or divine, can be this: all real love implies sacrifice, and so makes all sorts of demands upon the lover, taking up into itself the whole moral character. So God's love, it is argued, involves His judgment against injustice and cruelty, and those who are so self-centered that they spread their poison wherever they go, and are so impenitent that they do not even want to receive eternal joy, must live forever outside God's love and know the torment of living beyond the mercy of God. It need not be that God punishes them: it may be that they punish themselves with their own poison. But they cannot cease to exist. Their own poison keeps them in existence: "their worm dieth not, and the fire is not quenched." [4] As the blessed in heaven have within them the principle of *zoë* that they receive from God, its source, so the damned in hell have within them another principle of immortality, and their anguish consists

---

[3] Matt. 10:28.   [4] Mark 9:44. Cf. Isa. 66:24.

in their having this while knowing that they have cut themselves off from the infinite joy that could have been theirs in an eternal heaven.

The fact that the doctrine of hell is horrific is not in itself an argument against it. The state of being alienated from God in our present life is, from the standpoint of those whose experience teaches them to contrast it with the joy of being reconciled to him, horrifying enough. As far as the human judgment of believers can determine, people do live in such a state of alienation from God and die in impenitent rebellion against His love. In their rejection of the source of all good there appears to be a demonic quality that seems to have within it an immortality of its own evil kind. It is therefore plausible to argue that if some win an eternal life that has God as its source, those whose adamant self-will and self-centeredness preclude them from being able to enjoy that life, inherit instead an immortality of their own — an eternal rebellion against God that sustains them forever in the poison of their own egoism. "Their worm dieth not." Each creates an inverted immortality of his own and stews forever in the juice of his own self-centered pride. Hell is the state of being shut up forever in an unexpanding self. Look at the kind of self that is likely to suffer this fate and you will conclude that fire and brimstone would be a relatively painless punishment compared with the poison they generate in themselves.

But is the doctrine of hell necessary? Is not the "everlasting destruction" that is held out in the New Testament, for example by Paul,[5] as the doom of those who "obey not the gospel of our Lord Jesus Christ," a sufficiently terrifying prospect? Or, if it does not terrify us, does this matter, except in the sense that we are fools to forego the joy of eternal life with God that we might have? Is it not more intelligible to say, as is often suggested in the New Testament itself, that those who repudiate eternal life simply do not get it, so that when they die it may be said of them that their quota of life is exhausted and they are extinct? May it not be said, in New Testament language, that they have *had* their "reward" in life as we know it on earth, and that this has been filed "paid"? The answer to all such questions must be that the doctrine of eternal life does not logically imply a doctrine of hell, but that *other* theological considerations may lead to this doctrine. Among such considerations would be the nature of evil itself. In discussing the arguments for the existence of God, especially the teleological argument, we have touched on the problem of evil already; but this problem is so difficult and yet so fundamental in theism that we must postpone its full discussion till later.

[5] II Thess. 1:9.

Death of the Soul

Meanwhile, the doctrine of conditional immortality that has been proposed by some as an attractive alternative to belief in hell should be considered on its own merits. According to a very early Christian notion that has become stylized in modern Roman theology, the innumerable offenses we all commit and the shortcomings that we all exhibit in our lives ("venial" sins) must be distinguished from sin which, alienating us from God, demands reconciliation if it is not to be fatal to our hope of inheriting eternal life. *This* kind of sin is traditionally called "mortal" (from the Latin, *mors*, "death") because, the theologians say, it *kills* the soul. A protagonist of conditional immortality might very well argue: "This is precisely what I am saying — the soul, being reconciled to God, acquires a capacity for eternal life, but alienation from God destroys this capacity, so that the soul's power to inherit eternal life is killed, as the theologians say, and that is an end of the whole matter." In interpreting the notion of "mortal" sin, an opponent of the doctrine of conditional immortality would have to reply on lines such as these: "True, the soul's capacity for eternal life with God is destroyed, but nothing can destroy the soul's existence, so that the soul that has lost eternal life with God is at death plunged into eternity no less than the soul that has won it; only, it is an eternity of the unspeakable anguish and misery of being impotently and irrevocably ranged against God."

DISCUSSION ON CHAPTER 31

1. Roaming in thought over the universe, I saw the little that is
    Good steadily hastening towards immortality,
    And the vast all that is called Evil I saw hastening to merge itself
    and become lost and dead. (Walt Whitman)

Discuss.

2. Consider arguments that might be advanced by theists in favor of the doctrine of hell.

3. The notion that the soul is "killed" by sin would seem to imply a doctrine of conditional immortality. Those among whom the doctrine is traditional (e.g., Roman Catholics) are, however, committed to a view that excludes this doctrine. Consider.

32

The Springs of Belief
in Eternal Life

Theocentricity of Belief

John Baillie relates a simple story to illustrate the nature of Christian agnosticism about the future life.[1] It was once his lot, he tells us, to visit a dying Christian who spoke freely about his thoughts concerning the pilgrimage he was about to make into the unknown. The dying man recalled a story he had heard of another man at the point of death who had asked his doctor if he had any conviction about the future life. While the doctor was fumbling for an answer, there was a scratching at the door. "Do you hear that?" the doctor asked. "That is my dog. I left him downstairs, but he grew impatient and has come up and hears my voice. He has no notion what is inside that door, but he knows I am here. Now, is it not the same with you? You do not know what lies beyond the Door, but you know your Master is there."

This story draws once again to our attention the dependence of our belief or unbelief in immortality upon our belief or unbelief in God. But let us note further the anguish of Christian belief in immortality as well as its confidence. There are many things we do not know; but our ignorance of these things does not trouble us at all. The believer, however, who is honest enough to admit that he does not know the answer to most of the questions he asks himself about the future life, must also admit that the subject is of immense interest to him. Yet his interest is not at all a mere idle curiosity. It is the interest arising from an existential situation in which he feels himself deeply involved. And yet again, just because his belief in immortality springs from his belief in God, his interest is not the self-centered interest that it appears to the outsider. In short, he is interested in the life beyond because he believes God is there and he is interested in God. Hence the anguish of his ignorance is mixed with the overwhelming confidence expressed by Whittier in lines that Baillie quotes:

[1] John Baillie, *And the Life Everlasting* (New York: Oxford University Press, 1956), pp. 198–199.

I know not where His islands lift
Their fronded palms in air;
I only know I cannot drift
Beyond His love and care.[2]

Release From Egocentricity

Nothing could be more foolish and nothing more arrogant than to pretend to know the details of the celestial geography. But it is no less arrogant and foolish to claim to know that beyond the veil of death lies only a hollow nothingness. All that we can claim to know about our destiny is what we can claim to know about God. Let us note, however, that for this very reason our belief or unbelief in immortality reflects with startling fidelity our belief or unbelief in God. It is not without significance that the thoroughgoing atheist does not *want* to believe in a life beyond death. In a letter to Henry Sidgwick, J. A. Symonds wrote: "Until that immortality of the individual is irrefragably demonstrated, the sweet, the immeasurably precious hope of ending, with this life, the ache and languor of existence, remains open to burdened human personalities." But this is not a description of this present life as the theist sees it; it is a description of this present life as the atheist sees it. The theist, for all the misery that he sees in this life and that he encounters in often bitter experiences, finds it ill described as an ache or a languor. To him it is much better described as an adventure which, however painful, is as exciting as the mystery it constantly reveals. "Human society," says Charles W. Eliot, "may most wisely seek justice and right in this world without depending on any other world to redress the wrongs of this." The theist, in agreeing with this statement, will also add that because he is in love with the source of the justice and right he seeks in this life, he has fallen in love with life itself which, he likewise believes, has the same source. It is not for the redress of wrongs that he longs for eternal life: in childlike language, he hopes for heaven because God is there. Like the dog in Baillie's story, he knows nothing about "the Room" and he is interested in "the Room" only because "the Master" is in it. He loves God in the manner described in the well-known hymn based on a sonnet ascribed to Francis Xavier:

> *Not with the hope of gaining aught,*
> *Nor seeking a reward:*
> *But as Thyself hast lovèd me,*
> *O ever-loving Lord!*

So the theist can agree fervently with even what is implied in

[2] *Loc. cit.*

Bernard Shaw's question: "What man is capable of the insane self-conceit of believing that an eternity of himself would be tolerable even to himself?" [3] For it is precisely the expectation of final release from self-centeredness and the entry into a fully theocentric relationship that makes the prospect of eternal life so attractive to the theist. The theist may certainly likewise echo the highminded disparagement of the idea of survival that poets have voiced in various ways. For if we are thinking in terms of a survival theory of immortality, then it is true that, as Longfellow has it,

> The thought of life that ne'er shall cease
> Has something in it like despair. [4]

The kind of life we now have is not in itself worth infinite extension in time, and the prospect of this is horrifying. The theist's hope is for a richer quality of life rather than for a greater quantity of it.

Immortality as New Dimension of Life

The only doubt about immortality that the theist, and more particularly the Christian, cannot share is doubt of God's power to raise us beyond the extinction that is man's natural expectation. The faith of the theist that he shall enter into eternal life springs from experience here on earth. He discovers on earth a richer quality of life than he ordinarily enjoys. He discovers in his own experience the joyful mystery of despair yielding to hope, of soul-strife being superseded by peace of soul, of a spirit being cast down by sorrow and raised "from the dead" to new life. To such as know experiences of this kind, the notion that they are but foretastes of the glorification that is to come is not in itself in the least difficult. But to those who have caught no glimpse of such inward transformations, the idea of another *dimension* of life is much less easy to grasp. We may find a hint of what the theist is talking about, however, in certain kinds of aesthetic experience, notably in music. It is said that Mozart, when he was composing, found the musical ideas somehow or other coming into his head in a stream: then if he could hold on to them they began to join themselves together till, as he put it, his soul got "heated," and at last he was apprehending the finished composition all at once in its entirety. He did not hear the piece as it is played, a succession of notes, but as an instantaneous whole which he could then sit down and write out in full score. Mozart was an extraordinary musical genius, and it is very unlikely that such a description would fit the musical experiences of most people; yet perhaps we have all had a sufficient glimmer of what Mozart describes to enable us to make sense of what he is saying. Mathematical prodigies have been like-

---

[3] *Parents and Children.*   [4] *The Golden Legend*, Part I, lines 42–43.

wise able to glance at, say, the notation 24,763 × 89,157, and read off the product that most of us could arrive at only by working out the calculation step by step. We can all, however, do much more modest feats of mental arithmetic, and so catch a glimpse of what it means to transcend temporality and succession.

The idea of "resurrection unto eternal life" becomes much more comprehensible, however, to those who are fortunate enough to have known saintly men and women who demonstrate in the quality of their lives a triumph over the narrowness and pettiness of ordinary living. It is as if they had already, in some measure, discarded the limitations of our life and actually received a token award, as it were, of the eternal life that is their final destiny. In their triumph we can see a quality that is indeed as different from the quality of ordinary life as immortality is different from mortality. No argument for immortality could ever be as convincing as an encounter with such people.

Conceptions of Heaven

On the other hand, when all that is said, it must be categorically stated that not only can the theist give no detailed account of the nature of eternal life; he cannot even profess any real knowledge of it. His poetic visions of it cannot but fall short of the reality in which he believes. Certainly no utterance he can make in an attempt to communicate his vision can be adequate, and it is likely to be often very misleading. The language of Christian theology, which, at any rate from the thirteenth century onwards, has traditionally depicted eternal life as the possession of unlimited energy, that makes it possible to enjoy endless activity, does not fully express it. Nor does the language of Christian devotion, which speaks of an eternal rest, meet the case. In Christian devotion eternal life is traditionally presented as the promised rest from the strife and turmoil of this fleeting existence. Hence the beautiful prayer: "Eternal rest give unto them, O Lord, and let light perpetual shine upon them." How misleading this can be may be illustrated from the doggerel lines attributed to the weary old Negro washerwoman, who, nearing death, told her friends:

> Don't mourn for me now, don't mourn for me never—
> Ah's gone to do nothin' for ever and ever.

The theological account of heaven is no doubt nearer the mark: as in Deutero-Isaiah's vision, "they shall run, and not be weary; and they shall walk, and not faint." [5] Endowed with superabundant energy, the blessed in heaven cannot get tired. Enjoying complete union with

[5] Isa. 40:31.

God, the source of all energy, they are able to be endlessly active in His service and praise. Yet when we translate such theological ideas into the language of the man in the street, it is not easy to avoid giving the impression of an endless church service — by no means an attractive prospect. Perhaps small children, who think in picture-language, fare better with their childish vision of the blessed in heaven, ever happy with their harps, than do we adults who go on lamenting the difficulties we keep inventing. Life eternal is of course beyond all our imaginings, and our figurative language, poetical or theological, can in the long run succeed no better than do our earliest, fumbling endeavors, in expressing the intimations of eternal life that enter into our religious experience, confirming the promises of faith.

Hope of Hereafter Rooted in Understanding of Here-and-Now

Far from being an escape from the duties of this life, belief in the life beyond springs from an awareness of what is actually going on around us and in our own lives. It is when the moral life is seen to be all-important that the goal of the life beyond acquires meaning for us. So it may be said that "he sins against this life, who slights the next." [6] Without the life beyond, the present life would be to the theist a stairway leading nowhere. Yet even for the theist life is more than a stairway to heaven. He will say, rather, that the more fully we live here on earth the more we see our life pierced by the life eternal. Von Hügel, in a profound passage, expresses the view that so great is the affinity between the life here and the life hereafter that the latter can be, for us human beings, only a fuller realization of an aspect of life as we already know it: "we are indeed actually touched," he says, "penetrated and supported by the purely Eternal; and yet . . . we ourselves shall never, either here or hereafter, be more than quasi-eternal, durational." [7] We are essentially finite and we cannot become infinite; we are essentially creatures of God, and to aspire to be in any way like God is arrogance and pride. So to inherit eternal life is not to become eternal as God is eternal: for the theist it can only mean, in the last resort, entry into a deeper relationship with God, a relationship in which the eternity of God confronts us and exalts us far more than it does on earth.

In short, the theist is on safest ground when he says quite simply that he knows nothing about heaven except that it is being nearer to God, "in knowledge of whom standeth our eternal life."

[6] Edward Young, *Night Thoughts*, Night VII.
[7] Baron Friedrich von Hügel, *Eternal Life*, Second, Revised Edition (Edinburgh: T. and T. Clark, 1913), p. 366.

DISCUSSION ON CHAPTER 32

1. Discuss the view that belief in eternal life arises from egoism or self-interest.

2. "The theist's hope is for a richer quality of life rather than a greater quantity of it." Critically consider the notion of qualitative differences and quantitative differences in this context.

3. In theological language the blessed in heaven are called "the Church Triumphant," as opposed to the faithful on earth, who are "the Church Militant." Consider the significance of this distinction.

PART SIX

Value-Experience and the Idea of God

33

The Theistic View of the Nature of Value-Experience

Value as Correlative of Interest

Ralph Barton Perry defined value as "any object of interest." This definition, famous for its neatness, is open to criticism for its exclusive emphasis on the subjective element in value-experience. There are other possible aspects. Nevertheless, let us take it for a beginning. Value, according to the view we are tentatively adopting, is to be defined as anything that is loved or desired or prized or approved by anyone anywhere any time. You are hungry; hence a bowl of soup has value for you. I like cigarettes, so when my friend gives me a present of a box of them, I am being honest when I say I "appreciate" the gift, for "to appreciate" means "to value." When I say that I love my daughter it goes without saying that I value her, for this is an implicate of my love.

For convenience (let us rate it no more highly for the present) we distinguish certain different types of value. A traditional and useful distinction, for instance, is made between aesthetic and moral values. You value a fine painting you own: you value it for its own sake, because it is beautiful, and quite apart from whether it is worth no more than a few dollars in the open market or could be sold for fifty thousand. In a very different way you value the courage that your friend displays, which you appreciate likewise for its own sake; but you could not easily compare this attitude with your appreciation of the painting. If you were asked which you would rather have, the painting or the courage of your friend, you would rightly reply that the two are so different that you would rather not compare them at all.

Values and Choice

However, we often do have to compare values and make a choice between them, and it is here, really, that our experience of values begins. As a child you were perhaps told: "you may have ice cream or apple pie but not both." You would perhaps have liked both; but you had to make up your mind which you preferred. As our range of values extends, the choice between them becomes sometimes very difficult, involving much searching of heart. It is no longer a question of deciding between ice cream and apple pie or even between going to the movies or going to a dance. It may be a question of staying at home to help a sick father or going away to an important job. It may be that both these courses of action are excellent in themselves, and that there is much to be said for both of them; but since I cannot take both I must choose between them, and the choice involves the sacrifice of something which I account good in itself for something else which I account better. In such a case as this I might very well say that, in honesty, I much prefer going away to do the job which is an interesting one and very useful to my fellow men, while staying with my father is dull, for he is difficult and ungrateful, and by staying with him I risk losing an opportunity for a career that probably will not come my way again. Nevertheless, it may be that in spite of all this I decide that it is my duty to stay at home with my sick father and sacrifice the opportunity. Such moral decisions may be extremely delicate, as when I am compelled to choose between human compassion and the singleminded pursuit of scientific truth.

Conflict in Values

Because of such conflicts in values, it is never possible for me, on any theory of value, to take up the attitude that for the broad-minded, liberal man who is full of zest for life and love of his fellow men and lively scientific curiosity, all things are good in themselves. It may be that all things are potentially good; that is, they might become good in certain circumstances. We have to deal with actual situations in which we repeatedly see that, as the proverb has it, "the good is the enemy of the better." This concept comes to have paramount importance in religion in the notion of idolatry. When a primitive society is passing from fetish-worship to a more ethical type of religion, its leaders fulminate against the idols and fetishes and enjoin the people not to bow down before what are, they say, only lumps of wood or stone. This stage is to be seen, for instance, in the early history of the Hebrews as recorded in the Old Testament. In the circumstances of modern America, on the other hand, that sort of idolatry is not felt to be a danger. One is not likely to hear a sermon against it from the pulpit of, say, a Presbyterian or Episcopal church in New York today, or in a modern Jewish synagogue. But there are other forms of idolatry that are seen by today's prophets to be just as dangerous now as the worship of stone images was long ago. From the point of view of a Christian in a modern society, not only is a man idolatrous who lives as though the pursuit of success in business were really the supreme value in life; the man who puts even a noble ideal (such as international friendship) in the place of God is certainly idolatrous. Indeed, from such a point of view it is abundantly plain that "the highest idol is the worst." That is to say, the idols of savages are no longer dangerous, since nobody among us would exalt them in the place of God, and it is not difficult to show an intelligent man of good will that a life consecrated entirely to the pursuit of wealth is an empty one; but the temptation to idolize one's pet ideal in such a way that it becomes our supreme value is much more subtle and therefore much more perilous. We are not likely to be misled into idolizing what is far "beneath" God, such as fine food or a large bank account, but we may very easily fall into the temptation of idolizing what is really "nearer" God, such as the lofty ideals of world peace, academic freedom and social justice.

God as Spring of Value-Experience

A religious attitude always implies an attitude toward value-experience as a whole. If it is a theistic attitude it also implies that all value-experience is somehow related to God and that God is the spring of values, the Supreme Value. It is the belief in or awareness of this that makes prayer and other forms of worship seem not only natural activities to the believer but the activities most proper to man, so that man is never so fully what he ought to be as when he is prostrate in prayer before his Creator. As social values organize value-experience from the standpoint of sharing, and intellectual values organize it from the standpoint of knowledge, so religious values organize it from the standpoint of worship, which, considered in its fullest form, is "man's chief end." The theist is peculiarly conscious of the dependence of all values on their source, God: no value is autonomous or sovereign, though some may be deemed more important than others.

If the theist is right, our definition of values must be revised so as not to be grossly misleading. From a theocentric standpoint it may still be true that any object of interest is valuable; but the value is proportionate to the interest, and the interest of everything is to be measured in reference to the supreme object of interest, God. Nothing else, on this view, can have autonomous value; all values are relative to and dependent upon God, their source. The theist sees all values coalescing, and yet this is not to say that they are all equally removed from the Supreme Value. On the contrary, the theist attaches a special importance, for instance, to the value of worship, an activity which positivists, for instance, would account singularly pointless and dreary in itself. Nevertheless, because theistic faith finds expression in art and above all in the development of moral character, these values are intimately associated with the values that are most highly prized in religion, so that all values, even seemingly mundane ones such as food and lodging, interpenetrate each other and form a hierarchical structure. Theists may and do dispute the relative importance of this or that value-relation in these or those circumstances; but there can be among them no radical disagreement in principle concerning either the absoluteness of God as the Supreme Value or the relativity of all other values.

So it is in relation to God that the theist evaluates everything, including, for instance, ideals. We may define ideals as general concepts of a kind of experience that is accounted valuable. We must carefully distinguish between having an ideal and having the experience to which the ideal refers. Having an ideal is having what may be called a definition of what is to be valued. For instance, we may have in mind an ideal college community. If our ideal is quite clearly in our minds, we measure all college communities in terms of it, so that we can say that this college falls short of it in such and such a respect, while that college comes nearer to it. But an ideal is an intellectual possession only; from a practical point of view it may be better to have a college community that falls far short of the ideal than to have nothing but the ideal. The theist is peculiarly aware of this: it is better to give a crust of bread, even with a grudge, to a needy man, than to have a very lofty ideal of Christian charity and never do anything about it. So ideals are really no more than a sort of abstract of value-experience, in reference to which we are able to think of and talk about value-experience more easily. From one point of view it might be said that I can no more value an ideal than I can eat a square root or fall in love with a logarithm.

From the theocentric point of view, no value is intrinsic, strictly speaking, except God; but on the other hand, no value is merely subjective. When the theist says "I believe in God," he does not mean that he thinks it is psychologically beneficial or sociologically desirable for him to believe in God, or even that it is psychologically beneficial or sociologically desirable for all human beings. He means, rather, that such is his value-orientation that God would still be, in his view, the Supreme Value *even if* belief in Him were psychologically injurious or sociologically undesirable. So even the theist's faith in God, or trust in God, is only of relative value compared with God Himself. It is not "religious experience" that is upheld as the Supreme Value; what is affirmed is that religious experience itself reveals its own relativity to the Supreme Value.

When the theist speaks, then, of a "deepening" of his understanding or an "enrichment" of his life, he is to be taken as referring to his experience of having had his understanding or his life put into a "fuller" or "closer" relationship with God. When he is presented with, say, a new scientific discovery, he does not, if his attitude is really a theocentric one, ask himself, "How much of this dare I accept, since I am a theist and this new discovery seems to conflict with my conception of God?" He rejoices, rather, that he has found a means of enlarging or enriching the conception of God that he knows must always be too narrow and too poor to be adequate to the reality that is God. So he values the scientific discovery that puts at his disposal an instrument whereby his conception of God may be improved. The whole history of the development of a religious consciousness, whether in a people or in an individual, is the history of such reinterpretations of the nature of God. At any point in the story, the truly religious man knows quite well that he still "sees through a glass darkly." Experience teaches that our apprehension of God is always growing; but for the theist this does not mean that God is growing with our apprehension of Him, or that our appreciation of the Supreme Value can make any difference to His intrinsic nature. The religious man sees an inevitable tension between values, which in an existential situation appears as a real conflict. It is, moreover, only within that existential situation that he can resolve the conflict. While there may be some useful moral guideposts in life, such as ethical codes, there are nevertheless no abstract general principles by means of which the theist can resolve the problems that confront him in an actual, existential situation. Such problems can only be resolved individually, because each existential situation stands in an individual, unique relationship to God. But everything in the universe is in the end seen to be valuable in the sense, and to the extent, that it is, as the theologians put it, "under the sovereignty of God."

Existential Basis of Theocentric Value-Theory

It must be very carefully noted that the theistic attitude toward value-experience, as we have delineated it in the present chapter, does not and cannot spring from any a priori metaphysical theory. If it purported to do so, the reasoning would plainly be circular and therefore invalid. For of course it would be objected that such a metaphysically constructed notion of God could only spring from value-experience, and therefore could not stand as a criterion for the interpretation of that experience. The theistic attitude is different from that of any such abstract metaphysic or value-theory. The theist claims encounter with God as "The Other," as we saw in an earlier chapter; hence his conviction that all values are relative to God springs from what is really one value-judgment only. This value-judgment on the supremacy of God involves an act of faith, and so cannot be assent-compelling to those who refuse to make it. It purports to spring, however, from encounter with God as a living reality, if the theist is right about the reality of the encounter, the value-judgment he makes cannot be dismissed as an arbitrary one. What is repudiated above all in any such value-judgment arising from an alleged encounter with God is the anthropocentric outlook in all its forms. Having acquired the theocentric attitude, however, the theist may find God revealing Himself through all value-experience. This value-experience is now seen as the revelation of God, not as possessing any intrinsic, autonomous quality of its own that could provide an independent criterion for the interpretation of values or their arrangment into a metaphysical system. This is not to say that religion can dispense with a metaphysic; on the contrary, it implies and demands one. But it does mean that account must be taken of the alleged meeting with God that is the inevitable pivot of any theistic philosophy.

DISCUSSION ON CHAPTER 33

1. Consider the significance for the theist of ethical codes.

2. Discuss the nature of idolatry.

3. In what way do a theist's value-judgments differ from other people's, such as pantheists, humanists and positivists?

34

Value, Nature, and God

Psychological Objection to Theocentric Value-Theory

The most commonplace objection to the theistic interpretation of value-experience that we have been considering in the preceding chapter is a psychological one. Briefly, it may be put thus: I call objects valuable when I like or desire them; you call objects valuable when you like or desire them; sometimes these objects coincide, but they need not, and so value, as the correlative of interest, has no meaning in itself and derives what meaning it has from the feelings of the person who is making the value-statement.

The Irreducible Element

In all value-experience, however, there is an element that cannot easily be reduced either to pleasure or desire. And this would seem to be the most persistent and "essential" element in value-experience as it is unfolded to us in our lives. We may perhaps agree with Hume that moral approbation is a "pleasing sentiment"; but we cannot fail to note that not every pleasing sentiment has the character of moral approbation. Nor is it just that one pleasure differs from another as an apple differs from an orange. The distinction between the value of pleasure and the value that we recognize in moral approbation is so striking that some moralists, notoriously, have felt that any course of conduct that even happens to be pleasant is on that account alone morally suspect. Aristotle advises us always to take the less agreeable of two courses, whenever we are in doubt, for then we are less likely to be deceived. We see the emergence of "higher" values in the stream of "lower" values, and we see an obligation to sacrifice the latter to the former. This certainly does not mean that the "higher" values yield a greater amount of pleasure than do the "lower" values, or that the pursuit of them is easier or more appealing.

The Element of Protest

David Livingstone, the great Christian missionary and explorer, went to a cotton factory at the age of ten and bought a Latin grammar

228

with his first week's wages. By twenty he was a cotton spinner and so was able to save enough to allow him to go, at the age of twenty-three, to take a combined course in theology and medicine at Glasgow University. When he set out on foot with his father to Glasgow, marching eight miles through the snow from his home to the city in search of lodgings cheap enough for his needs, he could hardly be said to be choosing the path that he found, psychologically or otherwise, the most agreeable. It was not that the *strength* of his desire to be a missionary was greater than the *strength* of the hundreds of natural desires that he had to sacrifice for his enterprise. The desire to pursue a calling of which, at that age, he could have had only the most vague and general notions, could hardly have been in itself more powerful than the innumerable natural cravings and desires of a lad brought up in poverty and hardship. Since it is unrealistic to imagine that his preference sprang from the strength of one desire over another, whence are we to say that it did spring?

One answer might be that the value-judgment of the young Livingstone was the result of indoctrination by his Bible-reading and churchgoing parents. For it is true that men tend to conform to the rules of their society by a kind of "second nature," even when the rules are unpleasant to obey. The beginning of the consciousness of moral obligation has been explained in such a fashion. This theory, however, is open to very grave objections. In particular, it should be noted that it is because men do look on custom as binding that they can go on to criticize it and so arrive at a different moral standard. It is, indeed, especially noteworthy that those who think value-experience can be reduced to a sociological phenomenon often combine with their observations on the subject a lively protest against the common man's apathy in so easily accepting the conventional code of his tribe instead of protesting against it. In fact, it is just such protests against mistaking "dead" value-experience for "living" value-experience that keeps our consciousness of values alive. In the example we have taken, young Livingstone was not only nurtured in a moral climate; he was protesting against that climate — so much so that the elders of the local church doubted whether he were "sound."

Moral Adventure

It is just such protest against moral climate that is generally neglected in "naturalistic" accounts of moral action. The moral adventure that the theist finds interesting does not consist merely in the choice of a supposedly "higher" course of action over a supposedly "lower" one. Its type is not to be found in a decision to go to church rather than to play golf, or to take a cold shower rather than to lie in bed. Enjoying cold showers, I may very well make a virtue out of what has become for me the psychological necessity of taking them. As for preferring church to golf, some atheists have such a distaste for the latter that they would gladly endure Evensong as the lesser evil; moreover, it is abundantly well known to spiritual directors in the Roman Catholic tradition that some people (perhaps notably nuns) delight so much in religious observances that the worst penance you could give them would be to forbid them to say their prayers for a week.

Moral Experience as Response to Unconditional Demand

The action of Livingstone and of many thousands like him is conceived, not as a choice, but as a response. They are *confronted by a demand*, the pleasantness or unpleasantness of complying with which is entirely irrelevant. The question is seen by such a man to be not whether one course is easier than another, or more agreeable, or even to be viewed as "higher" or "lower," according to this or that ethical standard or code. The question is, rather, whether, finding himself in the presence of One who alone has the right to make any such "total" demand upon him, he is to respond with obedience or disobedience. He knows obedience to be not only good, but his unique opportunity to do — for once, at least, in the course of this otherwise humdrum existence that Eliot has called "birth, copulation, death" — that which is good without qualification. Therefore, he is unmoved, not to say bored, by the psychologists who undertake to "interpret" the underlying motives of his choice. The underlying motives they discover may well be there; but from his vantage point they really do not seem to underlie very deeply. Young Livingstone trudged eight miles through the snow to find the cheap lodgings he needed: perhaps he liked snow and long walks; perhaps he liked so much, for reasons of upbringing, the vision of himself as a missionary in darkest Africa, that he could put up with the snow. But soon we find him trudging through the jungle: perhaps he likes jungles, then? Or is his fanatical obsession with the picture of himself as a missionary to the heathen so strong that it can overrule his interest in climate and geographical environment to such an extent as to make him entirely indifferent to his surroundings? Even this will hardly do, since many have reproached Livingstone for having turned out to be "great British explorer" as much as or perhaps more than "great Christian missionary."

All such explanations of such conduct leave something unexplained. The reason is that they are not really explanations at all, but highly dogmatic interpretations that fail to take into account the only element in the conduct that is more worthy of explanation than the fact that some young female criminals just love to attend Mass while others find "Positive Thinking" or the Rosary more thrilling. Every human being makes value-judgments; every human being occasionally revises them to some extent, while some unusually vivacious or restless persons are continually and drastically revising their judgments. What is the source of all this activity? The human psyche itself? To reply thus is not to answer the question but to shelve it, for such an answer does not tell us the only thing that is really important: how the idea of value, as distinguished from sensation or desire, ever enters experience at all. A man may, for very complex psychological reasons, delight in Pontifical High Mass at Seville, though as a liturgist he recognizes that it looks like an unrefereed football game. He does not, however, confuse his delight with moral response to an unconditional demand that confronts him.

If we admit that there is no explanation along such lines of awareness of the unconditional demands, we are, of course, already committed to an interpretation of value-experience as a whole. We are no longer resting content with a bare evasion of the moral problem that confronts the religious consciousness. We are saying, in one way or another, that there is a Real Presence that confronts us with such demands. We may, however, give one of many possible answers to the question of what this Real Presence is. For instance, we may say, in humanist fashion, that God is the ideal unity of our experience of values as human beings. In practice, however, many who take this position do not mean by it what they might seem to mean. They intend to affirm, not that the source of our value-experience really is humanity itself, but only that since nothing seems to be discoverable about any "deeper" source, and since we do find value-experience arising in ourselves as human beings, it is better to preserve a quiet agnosticism about a source beyond humanity and simply affirm that humanity is the deepest source *we know* of the values we prize. The humanist who looks on the problem in such a way is saying, in effect, that he is unwilling to be drawn into speculation about the source of value-experience, and finds it quite satisfactory to accept it for what it appears to be, observing a modest metaphysical agnosticism about the rest. Such an approach certainly does not give the kind of solution that many people seek. This is not to say it is wrong. But let us now see what other approach might be made.

Are Values a By-product of Nature?

We might say that value-experience, though we find ourselves the channel of it, really springs from and is conserved in the process of nature. It will be recalled that, in the thought of modern philosophers such as Alexander and Wieman,[1] nature is value-producing.

[1] *Supra*, Chapter 12.

This view, less narrow and much more plausible than the humanistic one we have just been considering, would seem to take account of the fact that our value-experience itself suggests that the values we experience come to us from outside ourselves and are apprehended by us rather than that they are our own creations. If a man looks at Niagara and says, "Not bad," or, "Quite nice," I am not content to say to myself, "Oh, he is creating values differently from the way I do." I say, rather, that there is something he is missing. People are said to have mental blocks against certain objects; but what is this but to say that they do not appreciate values that are there to be appreciated? So the hypothesis that the values we apprehend or experience are in nature is far more convincing than the assumption that they are a human creation.

What is Nature?

But what does the word "nature" mean? We have spent a good deal of time in an earlier part of this book considering different conceptions of God: if we had time to examine as carefully how many conceptions there are of nature we should find that the word "nature" is perhaps even more ambiguous than the word "God." The Greek word for "nature" is *physis*, from which we get the word "physics"; but what we understand by "physics" today is not at all what the word *physis* meant to the Greeks. Aristotle defined *physis* as "the distinctive form or quality of such things as have within themselves a principle of motion." The form or quality that Aristotle had in mind was not considered to be really separable from the things themselves: you could separate it only in thought, not as you might separate two elements in a laboratory experiment. For Aristotle, *physis* was the source of change in things, a principle that was supposed to "make the universe tick." But other thinkers have used the term "nature" in a radically different sense. For instance, Kant used it to signify the system of all the phenomena in the universe of space and time, as distinguished from the realm of mind. On a view such as Kant's one might very well speak of mind as above or beyond nature. that is to say, supernatural. So when a Christian believer spoke of a supernatural element in the Gospels, for example, he could be interpreted as meaning that certain miraculous elements in the narrative were outside the realm of nature and must be considered as belonging to the spiritual or mental realm, in which the "laws of nature" could not be expected to apply. Such a view does not necessarily eliminate mystery; but it is in itself quite intelligible. It is possible, moreover, on such a view, to say that the whole realm of values is supernatural; that is, that one should distinguish between the "brute facts" in which natural science is interested and the "values" which, not being the scientist's business, are the proper concerns of philosophers and theologians. Other thinkers, however, such as Alexander and Dewey, have abandoned Kant's usage and have gone back to one that is more like that of Spinoza. According to this other usage, "nature" is a term which by definition means everything that is, so that it becomes sheer nonsense to talk about the supernatural. In holding such a view as this you might still "believe in miracles" in the sense that you believed you found evidence of phenomena that could not be explained in terms of our present knowledge of nature; but you would then be implying that a more extensive knowledge of nature would reveal just how the "miracles" might be shown to fit into the system of nature, the system of "all there is." This would be taking a radically different attitude, however, toward the miraculous from that which, say, an Aristotelian would take who believed in the possibility of "miracles."

One is inclined to object at this point that we are concerning ourselves with a mere verbal quibble. Why not just decide one way or another what is to be meant by "nature" and proceed accordingly? Why not say "it includes God," or "it excludes God," and then get on with the argument? But unfortunately the problem is not so easy. It is not just a difference of usage, a "broad" use and a "narrow" use of the term "nature," as there is a "broad" use and a "narrow" use of the term "paper." Because of the complexity of the history of the whole subject, the modern conception of nature has become exceedingly vague, so that as soon as the term is used the vagueness of the conception is almost bound to infect thinking about related terms such as "God" and "values," no matter how the term "nature" itself be defined. No one who is familiar with modern philosophical discussions can easily rid his mind of the notions underlying the use of the term as a "blanket" one, and this is a peculiarly misleading situation to put oneself into while problems about God and values are being explored. The whole question is still further complicated by the fact that even when God is conceived of as other than nature, several views may be taken concerning the question of His relation to nature. For instance, nature might be a part of God or entirely outside Him. At any rate, if nature is to include God and all values, then the terms "God" and "values" stand for quite different notions from what is in the mind of theists when they use these terms. A God who is an unconscious energy within the system of nature is obviously a very different kind of Being from a God who creates that system.

Deistic Objection

It is plausible to suggest that if there is a God who creates the system of nature, He must be entirely beyond and "above" it. This is the view which, following a traditional usage, we have called deism.

The thoroughgoing deist thinks of God as having nothing to do with the universe that is His creation. We may well ask whether such a view of God solves any problem at all. For either the universe can be explained in terms of itself or else it must reveal in some way or other the fact that it is the handiwork of God, so that it may be said that "the hand of God" is to be seen everywhere in it, as the hand of a great painter may be seen everywhere in his work. For this reason, deism of such a thoroughgoing kind is no longer fashionable, since it can now be seen, as it could not a century or two ago, that the choice must lie between a self-explanatory universe and a universe that is "cared for" by God. But deism may take more moderate forms. It is probably not unfair to say that certain modern theologians such as Barth, whose extreme stress on the transcendence of God has an obviously reactionary quality in it, expound their theism in a curiously deistic manner.[2] According to their view, there is no conceivable way in which man could ever discover God by looking at the values he finds around him, such as, say, human courage, fraternal loyalty, maternal love, or filial devotion. Nor is there in human wisdom the slightest clue to the wisdom that is God's. Only by an entirely "supernatural" act of God, only by God's entering human experience at one point or another, can God come to be known to anyone at all, and when He is so known he is found to be entirely other than either nature or aesthetic and moral values. So He is sometimes said by such theologians to enter into human experience in a "perpendicular" way; that is to say, His entry is discontinuous with all human experience, including the experience of the highest of all values that human beings ever otherwise apprehend.

This view, which has had a considerable influence in many theological circles in recent decades, should not be lightly set aside. It has a vivid appeal to the religious instincts of many people, and it has a very great theological interest. On the other hand, it brings with it many curious theological as well as philosophical puzzles. It makes all knowledge of God so dependent upon His special revelation that it becomes difficult to see why, for instance, Christ should have used parables. For according to a familiar Sunday school definition, a parable is "an earthly story with a heavenly meaning," and how can an earthly story have a heavenly meaning if all earthly values, even the highest, are as entirely cut off from God as they are said to be? From a more philosophical side there are several other important objections, notably that it becomes exceedingly difficult to see what

---

[2] Theologians of this school, it must be noted, regard themselves as the champions of Christian orthodoxy, and their movement has been called, in certain circles, "neo-orthodoxy." The context of this usage is complex and does not concern us here.

we are to make of any meaning or purpose that may be found in the evolutionary processes discernible in the universe around us. These processes, accessible in some measure at any rate even to the human mind that is not "stayed on God," would seem to have meaning when there appears to be no reason why they should have any meaning, since they belong to a realm that is entirely divorced from God except to the extent to which He may choose to "invade" it at certain points.

Defense of the Theistic Position

Let us sum up the position as follows. We find values in human experience. It is unsatisfactory to be required to suppose that we really invent these values or that they depend on nothing but human nature itself. For the experience of these values is presented to us as the experience of something beyond ourselves that is, so to speak, addressing us. May we say that it is nature that is so addressing us? No, because the term "nature" is so ambiguous and the concept of nature in modern thinking is so confused that no useful purpose is served by trying to squeeze values under the blanket of such an extraordinarily baffling notion. The deistic hypothesis, on the other hand, is really outmoded. Either we can dispense with it altogether, as the naturalists and pantheists suppose, or else it fails to account for the estimate of values that makes us reject pantheism and naturalism. We seem to be left therefore with the notion that the values that are continually unfolded to us in life have their source in and are sustained by a Being who is beyond the universe that is known to us in ordinary experience (including humanity), and yet is in some measure present in it. So we cannot say roundly, as a pantheist might do, that the values that "speak" to us in holy men such as Vincent de Paul and David Livingstone are a part of God as a rock is a part of God; nor can we say with the deist that God is as infinitely far removed from these values as He is from a chunk of rock. We must say, rather, that it would seem that God is known to us more in the lives of such saintly men than He is in rivers and rocks, though indeed He is also independent of all these, being their Creator. And this is the theistic position.

A final observation on this theme: No one can claim to know with certainty whether another person is or is not obedient to the "voice" of God who makes the unconditional demand. In such matters a man can know only how he himself stands. Nevertheless, a difference of outlook and attitude may be detected, especially among elderly people who may be presumed to have already made the important inward decisions of their life. On the one hand, the fidgety loquaciousness of some elderly people, their inability to endure their own company, and the spate of their questions on impossibly deep subjects that appear to wait for no answer — all that suggests a personal failure far more profound than any human psychology could ever measure. On the other hand, the unshakable sense of security that is characteristic of others, their joy in silence and contentment with such solitude as the fulfillment of their human obligations may afford them, and above all their smiling awe before the wonders ever being unfolded to their consciousness — all this betokens a personal triumph, as though, having been not "disobedient to the heavenly vision," they were already beginning to reap the reward. It may be — how can we know? — that many fall into neither one category nor another, having never been vouchsafed the opportunity. So, indeed, it would often seem to the observer. But in such matters no human judgment can be final. We may like to guess; we cannot pretend to know.

DISCUSSION ON CHAPTER 34

1. In Chapter 2, a letter of Dorothy Sayers was quoted, in which the following passage occurs: "What makes you suppose that the expression 'God ordains' is narrow and bigoted, whereas the expressions 'nature provides' or 'science demands' are objective statements of fact?"

   In the light of the problem raised in Chapter 34 concerning the use of the term "nature," discuss the passage quoted.

2. Suppose that at a dinner party, at which the guests include a judge, someone broaches the subject of a reported increase in judges' salaries, and that the judge present says smilingly, "I strongly approve of that." Consider, with reference to what has been said about moral approbation, why the remark of the judge would be taken as a joke.

3. Consider whether, in the discussion of values, nature, and God, other possible solutions have been overlooked that it would be useful to inspect.

35

May Personality be Attributed to God?

Biblical Portrait of God

In the Bible and elsewhere it is taken for granted that God is personal in the sense that He behaves as if He were personal and stands in a personal relationship to His creatures. Sometimes, in those passages of the Old Testament that hand down to us traditional beliefs as these were expressed in primitive times, God is depicted in very man-like form. We find Him, for instance, walking in the Garden of Eden and addressing Adam and Eve as a squire might address his tenant. In other, less primitive, accounts of God's dealings with men, He is depicted as much less accessible, much more remote from the human gaze, but nevertheless as personal as ever. Now He rides upon the storm or sits upon clouds, carrying in His hand mighty instruments that send thunders and lightnings upon the earth. Finally, in passages of still later date, we are required to suppose that He is entirely beyond the universe we know; nevertheless He is still described in personal terms. He is still said to love the righteous and to hate the wicked, and in His ever-vigilant supervision of the world He has created, He continues to display familiar human emotions, though with the restraint and dignity that one should expect of so exalted a Being.

Depersonalization of God

All this is very repellent to some people, especially to those who are for temperamental or other reasons inclined to literalistic reading. To others it appears natural enough as the poetry of an uncivilized and culturally backward people such as the Hebrews were; at the same time it seems to such readers that if anyone today is to believe in God at all the first thing he must do is to divest his mind of the whole notion of God's having a personality and try hard to think of Him in some other way. John Macy complained that "the Old Testament is tribal in its provinciality; its god is a local god, and its village police and sanitary regulations are erected into eternal laws." In such a mood, many feel that God must be entirely depersonalized.

It is not a question of making God more "palatable" to the modern mind: modern thinking, it is suggested, demands the depersonalization of God.

Let us grant at once that there is a very reasonable and proper element in such protests. If we could be entirely satisfied with the conception of God that was current in a primitive tribe three thousand years ago, our religion would be as dead as the dodo. We can no more be satisfied with a savage's idea of God than we can be content with a child's conception of the universe. But children and savages, though they cannot think out ideas with the subtlety of a modern philosopher or express themselves with the clarity that we expect of an educated man today, have often insights greater than ours. What is so astonishing about the earlier writers of the Hebrew Scripture is that the men whose thinking was very simpleminded, by our standards, and who clothed their religious ideas in language that is often childish to us, had such important things to say. So, though we may discard the outmoded clothes in which their ideas are dressed, we ought to be very careful not to lose anything that is of permanent value in the ideas themselves. It is one thing to throw away the baby's diapers; it is another thing to throw the baby away with them.

A curious assumption underlies the notion that our conception of God must be depersonalized in order to rid it of its primitive character. The assumption is that personality is proper to limited, finite beings such as ourselves, but that it is not a fitting attribute to apply to God. Personality is, on this view, equated with limitation. You have one sort of idiosyncrasy and I another, and the sum of your idiosyncrasies makes up your personality, while the sum of my idiosyncrasies makes up mine. Of course God could not have personality in this sense, for this would mean that He differs from us only in the way in which you differ from me.

The Nature of Personality

When we talk of personality we often have in mind what may be called its negative aspect. It is as though, in speaking of a brand of cookies, we were to say, "You know the ones I mean — the ones that come in the funny red carton." So we think of people as "the man who shouts at you as if you were a public meeting," or "the girl with the piano-keys teeth," and when people talk of their personality we think of it as built up of such peculiarities. True, we are not really satisfied with this way of thinking of people, for we recognize that personality is somehow desirable in itself. It is, however, a notoriously elusive quality, not least in a civilization in which much of our energy is spent in conforming to conventional patterns, so that we often end by thinking of the process of depersonalization as the cultivation of a pleasant personality. A pleasant personality comes to be equated with one in which the corners are rubbed off; but once the corners are rubbed off there seems to be nothing much left that is of any interest.

Personality and Values

This is not surprising, because once values are really separated from personality they cease to be values. Courage is of value, but the concept of courage, courage in the abstract, has no value. It acquires value only when it is realized in the action of a brave man. Sorley states this well in a passage in which he says: "When we examine it strictly, therefore, the proposition 'moral perfection is of value' is hypothetical — moral perfection, if realised, is valuable; or it proceeds on an assumption or presumption of existence; in so far as moral perfection is realised, just so far is there value. The predication of value thus implies or assumes something existing which can be said to possess the value; the true bearer of value is an existent or something conceived as existing. Were there no existence there would be no value; value out of relation to existence has no meaning." [1] Suppose that I show you a blueprint for a house and tell you that it is the most wonderful house in the world, only for technical reasons it is unfortunately quite impossible to build it; you naturally tell me that in that case it is not even as good as the most wretched hovel in the world. Likewise, if you confide in me your dream of an ideal man whose virtues surpass those of anybody in the world, and then go on to admit that for psychological reasons he could not possibly exist, I will retort that I prefer John Smith, for all his faults. For Smith has some value, his faults notwithstanding, while your ideal man has no value, because he cannot exist.

If God is the Supreme Value, the source and sustainer of values, He cannot be an idea; He must exist. Then can He exist without personality? An impersonal God could indeed presumably generate certain kinds of value — what could be apprehended as valuable by persons such as ourselves. But the highest values we know are just those that are inseparable from persons: courage, kindness, equity and the like. Perhaps a fairly coherent account of matter could be given in terms of an impersonalism; but in such a scheme it would be impossible to account for mental and moral values, and it is just these values that most need to be accounted for.

God as Supra-personal

Of course, in attributing personality to God we do not say that God's personality is of the same order as our own, or that it is sub-

[1] W. R. Sorley, *Moral Values and the Idea of God* (Cambridge: Cambridge University Press, 1935), Chapter V ("Value and Personality"), pp. 108–109.

ject to the defects that we commonly associate with human personality. For such reasons, many theists prefer to speak of God as *supra*-personal. By this they mean to emphasize the notion that the theistic conception of God is such that God, far from His being considered as lacking personality, is accounted *more* personal than any other being in the universe. Personality is then being looked upon as the highest attribute that a being can have. On such a view it might also be said that only God is completely personal; the kind of personality that we human beings have is at the best only feeble and fragmentary. Still, a person is more valuable "in his own right" than anything else we know, and he is not valuable only for having this or that idea, or even as the bearer of this or that quality or virtue; it is, rather, that the qualities or virtues he has express the person he is. On meeting a person for the first time we do not, if we are wise, seek to ascertain the various virtues and vices he possesses, so that we may take an inventory of them in our mind and then arrive at a conclusion about the person, by giving him a final "score" of good and bad points. We try, rather, to know the person himself. If we find him to be "essentially" a "good" person, then his virtues do not surprise us and his shortcomings do not affect our general finding about him. So we are able to accept the weaknesses of our friends, not as factors diminishing the friendship, but as elements that our friends have to reckon with in the development of their personalities. The value of my friend is not lessened by his being quick-tempered, any more than the value of a growing tree is lessened by the blemishes on its bark. We hope that the tree, being a "good" tree in itself, will outgrow the blemishes, and that my friend will outgrow his hot temper or bring it more fully under his control.

Kierkegaard on God as Pure Subjectivity

In theism, God is valued not for His attributes but for Himself. It is not because He is "Eternal Justice" or "The All-knowing One" that I value God as I do. I do not worship God because He is the sum total of various qualities in their perfection; it is, rather, that these qualities are the description of the God whom I worship for Himself. Because in us subjectivity is associated with lack of detachment and maturity of judgment, we have a tendency to suppose that God must therefore be "objective" rather than "subjective." But as Kierkegaard puts it in one of his most brilliant passages: "God is pure subjectivity, sheer, pure subjectivity; it has nothing in it at all of objective being; for that which has such objectivities is subsumed under the concept of relativities." [2] Kierkegaard saw the nature of religious experience in a very different light from that in which his

---

[2] *Efterladte Papirer*, p. 247. Translated by Walter Lowrie and quoted in his *Kierkegaard* (Oxford: Oxford University Press, 1938), p. 548.

contemporaries in the early nineteenth century generally saw it. It was his awareness of the subjectivity, that is, the intense consciousness of God as personal, that inspired many of his most striking utterances. It inspired, for example, what now looks like an uncanny prediction of the global wars which we are now accustomed to regard as part of the twentieth-century scene, but which in his day must have seemed a highly fantastic notion. We quote the passage because it illustrates what it meant to this great thinker and religious genius that God is nothing if not personal:

> . . . Though there were to break out not merely a European war, but if Europe got into a war with Asia, and if Africa, America, and Australia found themselves compelled to take part in it; in and for itself alone this need never concern God at all—but that a poor man sighs to Him, that is something that concerns Him, for so it pleases His majesty, and this moves Him subjectively.
>
> But suppose now that all of Europe's emperors and kings issued a rescript commanding all the thousands of hired servants (I mean the parsons) OFFICIALLY to supplicate the aid of heaven. Suppose there was arranged a prodigious exhibition of united worship to God, with 100,000 musicians, 50,000 elected deputies, and a million of ordained hired servants, to supplicate officially the aid of heaven—that would not concern at all the heavenly majesty— but that a poor man who walked down Cheapside sighed in the sincerity of his heart unto God, that concerns Him indescribably, infinitely, for so it pleases His majesty, and it moves Him subjectively.
>
> And wherefore is it that the other did not concern Him, the prodigious official hubbub which could be heard at a distance of several miles and must have been able to penetrate to heaven— wherefore did not that concern Him in the least, wherefore? My friend, whatever conception you may have of God, you surely do not doubt that He is what one might call a "connoisseur," a fine connoisseur—He who is pure subjectivity is related to connoisseurship. Hence it is that one generally regards women (who in comparison with men are predominantly subjective) as fine connoisseurs, connoisseurs who know immediately how to distinguish between the official and the personal, know that the official is really insolence, a ceremonious fashion of making a fool of one. What an infinite distance therefore from God—an emperor who by a rescript, which a minister of state composed, commands 10,000 ordained servants to bawl officially to God, what an infinite distance compared with a poor man who sighs unto God in the sincerity of his heart.[3]

Kierkegaard, whose thought is in sharp contrast to the Hegelian thinking that was fashionable in his day, saw that, in terms of man's

[3] *Ibid*, pp. 247–248. Quoted in Lowrie, *op. cit.*, pp. 548–549.

relationship to God, the very notion of personal detachment was blasphemous. But he went further: he perceived that the religious relationship is peculiarly personal. God, if He is to be the Supreme Value that religious experience implies that He is, must be personal in a superlative degree; so much so that Kierkegaard is willing to call him "Pure Subjectivity." The fierceness of his insistence on this has an historical background that is too complex to be discussed here; but the point to be noted for our purpose at the moment is that Kierkegaard discovers the reason *why* personality is inseparable from God and how it belongs to His essential Being. According to Kierkegaard, God may graciously permit a man to enter into personal relationship with Him, but He may also withdraw Himself from a man in such a way as to make the relationship merely objective. When God so withdraws Himself it is a withdrawal of His mercy; it is a punishment. According to Kierkegaard's interpretation, those who are concerned to delineate God objectively do so because they are in fact *excluded* from knowledge of God as He really is.

Conception of God as Final Judge

For our present purpose it is not necessary that we should fully consider the philosophical difficulties in Kierkegaard's utterances on the subject under consideration. We have paused to hear him on this subject because he expresses with extraordinary vivacity a notion that is at the heart of living religion but is often forgotten or ignored in intellectual discussions about the nature of God, namely, the notion that the Supreme Value, in the nature of the case, could not be merely an object that is passively inspected and judged by us to be supreme. The Supreme Value would not be supreme if it were merely there for us to judge: the Supreme Value must be judging us.

Teleology and Divine Personality

What leads the theist to his conception of God is, from an intellectual standpoint, the discovery of purpose in the universe. Such a purpose would not be what the theist discovers it to be unless it were the expression of a conscious will; the purpose is the function of such a personal, conscious Being. All the purpose and all the energy in the universe of ordinary experience may then be shown to have its origin and source in that Being, who is prior to and independent of all life and matter, including, for instance, both the stellar system and the human race.

In one sense, we cannot "prove" the existence of any such Being; but neither can we, strictly speaking, "prove" the existence of other minds. The hypothesis of a personal God does, however, fit the facts of experience. Let us bear in mind that in physics energy and mass are known only to the extent that, in one way or another, they act upon experience and produce experience. What is presented to us in religious experience is such that the hypothesis of personal theism is, to say the least, one that fits the case peculiarly well, making the situation intelligible, which it would not otherwise be. But it is above all the theist's experience of values that makes the hypothesis of a personal God so intellectually irresistible to him. All forms of impersonalism leave unexplained that which is most strikingly characteristic of our value-experience.

Objection to Impersonalism

Finally, we should recall at this point the observations that were made in the introductory part of this book.[4] If God were impersonal (for instance, an abstract idea or other object of our attention passively receiving our judgments upon it), we should be unlikely to find the psychological resistance which we have considered at some length.[5] Very serious attention must be given to the psychological consideration that cannot be dissociated from the personalistic hypothesis of theism, namely: *if* the Supreme Value *were* the Supreme Judge, as theism very plainly implies, then there would be an overwhelmingly good reason for my psychological resistance to Him. In other words, the God of theism is exactly the inconvenient Being from whom, according to our natural impulses, we should be most disposed to flee, and against whom we should be most vigorous in erecting ingenious barriers. And when we are confronted with God as revealed in Jesus Christ to whom the New Testament bears witness, it is not surprising if we use every psychological device at our disposal to avoid having to accept His forgiveness. In brief, a genuine scholar dare not, in any serious inquiry about God, overlook the fact that there is no compelling psychological reason to resist belief in the impersonalistic hypothesis, while there are very strong psychological reasons for resisting belief in a personal God.

DISCUSSION ON CHAPTER 35

1. Is the attribution of personality to God due to anthropomorphic thinking? Discuss.

2. Consider the personal element in value-experience generally.

3. Distinguish between the religious demand for a personal God and the philosophical conclusion that the God of theism must be "at least" personal.

[4] *Supra*, Chapter 4.
[5] *Supra*, Chapters 4 and 20.

36

Moral Activity and the Will of God

Persons and Things

So far we have been considering value-experience and the idea of God in a very general fashion. Let us now approach the central problem before us in a more direct way. The religious man claims to "find" God in value-experience, particularly in the experience of moral values. What exactly does he mean by this? What is implied in the notion that he "finds" or "encounters" God?

We may begin with a well-known Kantian distinction. There is a fundamental difference in dealing with a person and in dealing with a thing. Suppose that you put yourself in the position of Pygmalion. This legendary king of Cyprus fell in love with a beautiful statue; the statue came to life and he married the lady. Imagine that you have in your room a portrait that has been in your possession for years. You sometimes look at it; more often you don't notice it. Sometimes you take it down and dust it and occasionally you change its position on the wall. Now a miracle happens: the picture suddenly comes to life! The man begins to talk to you. Your whole attitude changes fundamentally: you had been dealing with a *thing*, a thing that you could shunt around as you pleased; now you are dealing with a *person*. You had been judging a thing; now you are not only judging a person but find yourself being judged by a person.

The situation you are being asked to imagine is not quite so radically improbable as it may sound. Certainly we are not going to find a portrait coming to life and talking to us. But we often do find ourselves in the position of meeting persons whom we have for long been thinking of as things. A doctor takes up duties at a new hospital. He receives a list of the cases that are to be under his charge. Looking at the various cards and charts that are handed to him, he turns over in his mind the various cases they represent. "This is a good, standard lung cancer," he says of one. "Patient should die in a couple of months." Of another he says, "Here's rather an unusual pericarditis." So he goes through the cases in an impersonal way. The following day, however, when he meets the patients, his thinking undergoes a change. Now he is dealing with people, so he enters into an entirely different *kind* of relationship. Before he saw the patient in Room 6 he thought of him almost as an "it"; now he recognizes the patient to be a "he" or "she." The doctor has accordingly entered into an entirely new dimension, the dimension of personal relationship.

In personal relationship there is an immediacy in our awareness of "the other mind" that is not to be found in our awareness of things. This does not mean that we are aware of other people independently of our senses, for of course we are not. I watch your face, I hear your voice, as I talk with you. But as I talk with you my mind encounters your mind, and this is not the same kind of encounter as my encounter with a table or a chair or a portrait. We become friends, you and I, and this involves mutual trust. In this relationship of trust I am aware of your will meeting my will, and you are likewise aware of my will meeting yours. Because we have become friends we do not regard each other with hostility. On the contrary, I am happy to encounter your will standing, so to speak, alongside of mine, and you, too, rejoice in this. At the same time, there is no doubt that you have a will that could be opposed to mine, and I have one that could be opposed to yours. Because we are friends we respect this fact and do not seek to circumvent it. It is your will I trust: if you were a lunatic, whose emotions were quite disorderly, I could not really enter into a personal relationship with you, for I could not trust you. I trust you because I find in you, who stand "outside" me, a will that I believe to be subject, as is mine, to a standard of unconditional value. Without such belief about each other we could not enter into a real friendship. Hence Cicero's saying that "friendship is impossible except among good men." It is not that we have to be saints or even conspicuously virtuous men in order to be friends. You may be very unsatisfactory in many ways, and I may have some quite shocking failings. But we must respect a common standard of value, and unless it is an unconditional value our friendship will be radically insecure, to say the least. It is in this mutual recognition of each other as standing "along side" each other, and at the same time "under" an unconditional value, that makes it possible for us to be in the unique relation of deep and lasting friendship.

The Unconditional Element in Christian Marriage

Perhaps the most vivid illustration of this is in the relation into which people enter in Christian marriage. Here a man and a woman "plight their troth" to each other. In so pledging themselves *to* each other they imply that they are pledging themselves *under* the unconditional value that they both recognize. They take each other "for better, for worse"; that is, their pledge to each other is independent of all circumstances. This is the essence of their marriage vows. Of course a couple get married because they are in love with each other. But no man or woman can really promise he or she shall be able to feel sexual passion for the other even a year hence. So in a marriage contract in which the partners recognize only a mutual need of each other, any promise of enduring love would be plainly impossible, and to pretend to make it is idle hypocrisy. As a ground for divorce from such a marriage, even the simple consent of both parties is too much to demand; divorce should be granted, as Shaw proposed, at the will of *either* party. In Christian marriage the situation is different because both parties make their promises with reference to God, the unconditional value determining the character of their relationship and pledge. Sexual love is, of course, from one point of view, the basis of Christian marriage as of any other marriage; but it is not, for it cannot be, the basis of the marriage vows. Hence it is said that in Christian marriage it "takes three to get married"; that is, the two lovers and God, the unconditional value in whose "sight" they solemnly plight their troth. It is not, of course, that in Christian marriage one's partner must be any better a person than would be required in a marriage based on a mere recognition of mutual need; it is, rather, that both parties must see each other to be "standing under" the same unconditional value.

The moral objection to sexual prostitution consists essentially in the fact that it entails treating a person as a thing. But a marriage based *solely* on the recognition of mutual need is really a sort of two-way prostitution in which each party is treating the other as a thing, not a person. No doubt many marriages of this kind have in them a glimmer of a deeper personal relationship, perhaps often much more than a glimmer. But to the extent that any marriage falls short of the recognition by both parties of an unconditional element, its stability is imperiled. The awareness of one partner to a marriage of the personality of the other has at its heart the recognition of the other as a separate will, potentially cooperative and potentially resistant. In all personal relationships worthy to be so called there is an attitude of mutual respect. Only because of this is it "good manners" to say "please." In a truly personal relationship I do not command or cajole or coax or in any way "get at" you to take such and such a course of action; I request you. As soon as you discover that I am "trying to put something over on" you, our friendship is most seriously injured at its roots; far more so than if I had let you down by failing to measure up to your moral stature.

Encounter With God in Moral Experience

The theist, in his encounter with God, is aware of an absolute demand that is being made upon him, and of an absolute responsibility to comply with that demand. But in so describing the situation, let us be careful not to be misled. It is not that we are confronted with God and then find the moral challenge consequent upon the encounter; nor yet is it that we are confronted with the moral challenge and then discover God in it. God and the moral challenge are inseparable; it is only thus that God can enter my experience, as it is only in a personal relationship that you can enter my experience. In our friendship we make certain limited demands upon each other. God makes total, unrestricted demands on me, and gives unrestricted love to me. In submitting to God I find that I am more, not less, of a person than I was before. "He that loseth his life *for my sake*," says Christ, "shall find it."

Nature of the Encounter

But we must probe more deeply into the conditions of the divine encounter. As this is described in intellectual terms, it often gives the impression of something that "just happens," being entirely unrelated to anything else in my experience. So one is inclined to say, "Perhaps that happens to some people; but as it doesn't happen to me there isn't anything I can do about it." Religious and mystical writers also give a similar impression to many readers when they describe the divine encounter in dramatic, poetic terms, saying, for instance, that God "bursts in upon" or "breaks through" experience. The language of theology is often no less misleading to those who have no vivid awareness of what theologians are talking about. For the notions of grace and revelation suggest a similar discontinuity. All this is conducive to the spread of the idea that experience of the divine encounter must be quite sudden and entirely "out of the blue," unrelated to the main stream of a man's moral life. On the contrary, the moral life cannot but be the scene of the encounter, which takes place "right through" it. When the moral life is lived to such a degree of intensity that it is, so to speak, ready to burst its last fetters, we can become aware of its inner meaning as the scene of the encounter with God. The shock of the discovery may be so sudden that we have the impression of total collapse followed by the emergence of an entirely new life alien from all we have known. It is alien from this, however, only as the butterfly is alien from the caterpillar. We do not meet God beyond or outside the moral life; we meet Him in it, and no genuine encounter with God ever took place except when the will of the man was so active as to be stretched to breaking-point.

The notion of passively receiving God is very misleading when it suggests, as it often does, that God comes forth to meet a man who is just "sitting down doing nothing."

The Barrier of Egocentricity

In becoming aware of God we are responding, in the first place, to our environment, and our response is functioning in a synthetic and intuitive manner. We are trying desperately to fulfill ourselves — wrestling, so to speak, with every manifestation of value. It is only when we are growing, and then only when we are determined to be satisfied with nothing less than the perfect fulfillment of the aim of the moral struggle our growth involves, that we are able to apprehend what the nature of the struggle really is, and in doing so we find ourselves confronted with God. We find that He has been there all the time in the struggle in which we have been engaged; we have, indeed, been struggling against and with Him. Such is the testimony of all the Christian saints and mystics. The will is never so active as when it is making its surrender to God. "Surrender" is itself a misleading term if it suggests any lessening of the moral activity, for it is, rather, the supreme effort that the will makes in the moral struggle. As the reward of his achievement, man meets not only God but also himself, discovering that no man can know himself without knowing God, nor yet know God without knowing himself. "In all really sincere piety," a German writer has it, "in all true opening of the heart to God, the individual's interior life must be summoned to its depths in the sight of God, so that in the knowledge of self he receives knowledge of God, and in knowledge of God he receives knowledge of self." Egocentricity is not only a barrier against the divine encounter; it is a barrier against self-knowledge.

From all this it follows that there is no "human" value, not even eating or drinking, certainly not science or art, that is alien from true religion. At the same time, in all "human" values, not least in the highest of them, there is a snare. Life is short, and we are continually beset with the temptation to play with or dabble among values instead of coming to grips with the total value-situation that confronts us in life. It is in the moral life that we most fully enter upon this process, and so the moral life might be called the threshold of the divine encounter in a sense in which this could not be said of any other value. Yet for this very reason morality may be the greatest snare of all, since it can be used for the purpose of avoiding its own fulfillment in the encounter with God. So by what may be called an ethical "go-slow policy," a man may fail when he is almost in reach of life's finishing-post. It is for a similar reason that "moral" arguments for the existence of God, though nearer the heart of the matter than any other type of argument for theism, are in the long run no more satisfactory. Hence the testimony of the mystics: in the devotional and mystical life it is fatally easy to fall short of being in love with God, and to rest content instead with being in love with the love of God. To be in love with the love of God is not merely to palm off to oneself a sort of imitation encounter; it is to fail entirely, by entrenching oneself, in the deepest way and at the crucial moment, in one's egocentricity.

So it is that while all human values can be steps to the encounter with God that is the only full self-realization, they can also be, one and all, obstacles to that encounter. The love of beauty can become aestheticism; the love of truth, intellectualism or scientism; the love of right action, moralism. So also an interest in persons for their own sake, which lies very close to the heart of religion, can, and in our own time often does, degenerate into psychologism. Since this focuses attention on what is, from the point of view of the divine encounter, the most trivial aspects of personality, it can be the worst snare of all. But all that entrenches man in his self-centeredness is an obstacle to man's true growth.

Immensity of the Demand

The encounter with God makes a greater moral demand than any other challenge in life. Devotional writers sometimes give the impression that this is so only because it entails the surrender of one's self-will to the will of God. But we are misled if we suppose that we are being called upon only to empty ourselves of all will and submit instead to the will of The Other. No encounter with God could ever be just that, and anyone who tries to find God on such terms is bound to be disappointed. It is, rather, in plunging into the stream of life itself and entering into the deepest involvement with the values that confront us, exercising our wills to the utmost — to breaking-point — that we find God in the very extremity of the battle. Love is never cheaply won: the infinite generosity of God does not diminish the difficulty that we experience in bringing ourselves to receive His gift. Moral responsibility, far from being lessened by religion, is indefinitely heightened.

DISCUSSION ON CHAPTER 36

1. "A person, unlike a thing, must be treated as an end in himself." Discuss.

2. Consider why it is that the religious man accounts the noblest idol the most dangerous.

3. Discuss the moral role of generosity in the life of religion.

PART SEVEN

The Mystery of Evil

37

The Problem of Evil

Illustration of the Problem

In considering the problem of evil it is well to have a concrete example in mind at the outset. Let us take one. Suppose that it has been your ambition since your first year in high school to become a dental surgeon. There are seemingly almost insuperable financial and other difficulties. Nevertheless, by dint of your parents' self-sacrifice and your own grit and perseverance, you overcome all obstacles and eventually complete your course and are ready to practice. You are immensely happy, and eager to begin at once. You want to begin because you are at last about to realize the ambition of many years; but you also want to begin because your parents, who have done so much to help you realize it, are now urgently needing your help, which you, let us suppose, are very much looking forward to giving them. Besides all this, you have just become engaged and plan to marry in a few months' time. Your prospects are in every way rosy, and for a beginning you have found an excellent appointment to which you are to go on Monday. On Saturday afternoon, however, you are in an automobile accident, as a result of which you lose both your hands.

Everyone would agree that this is a tragic story. But in what way, exactly, does it raise the problem of evil? Suppose that you tell it to a positivist or nihilist. Such a person would be justified only in saying something such as, "That was very tough luck." He would not be justified, on his own principles, in saying something such as, "That just doesn't make sense." For there is no reason, on his principles, why it should be expected to make sense. Indeed, if such a person does say anything of this sort, you are entitled to suspect him of being at heart a theist or something rather like one. Theism is not the only view on which the existence of evil is a problem; but no one could be seriously perturbed about the existence of evil who was not in fact taking theism itself seriously.

Why Should the Good Prevail?

It is only when it is expected that good shall prevail that the presence of evil calls for explanation. If a man takes the view that there is at the core of the universe a Supreme Being who is the source of all values, he is at once confronted with the question, "Whence comes evil, which is disvalue?" Such a man may go on to try to explain that value underlies disvalue; but the problem of evil is, as we shall see, a very serious one — perhaps the most serious challenge to a theistic view of the universe. On the other hand, it ought to be noted that while theism has to explain the presence of evil, atheism has to explain the presence of the Good. The thoroughgoing atheist who is really facing the consequences of his position, ought to be as perplexed by the problem of the good as is the theist by the problem of evil. For while it is unrealistic to pretend that evil does not exist, or is an illusion, it is no less unrealistic to ignore the existence of the good — for example, that there is honesty, and heroism, and order, and beauty, and happiness, and fulfillment, as well as dishonesty, and cowardice, and anarchy, and ugliness, and misery, and failure, in our experience. So the problem of evil is really only part of a greater problem, which is the problem of good and evil.

Does the Agnostic Escape the Problem?

It may be objected that in dealing with this problem, the difficulties confronting theist and atheist alike are successfully avoided by the person who holds a position of philosophical agnosticism. The theist, committed to the view that good predominates, has to consider the problem of evil, while the atheist, committed to the view that evil predominates, has to face the problem of the good; but, it may be contended, the philosophical agnostic is committed to neither view, and so he does not have to consider either the problem of evil or the problem of the good. This is not so. On the contrary, the agnostic, in order to be honest, has to face both. For it is his profession that he does not know or cannot decide in favor of either theism or atheism, and his indecision on the question, though it means he is relieved from both the duty of explaining the presence of evil in an orderly universe and the duty of explaining the presence of the good in a disorderly one, also means he is indubitably confronted with the presence of both good and evil. Unless he is willing to deny the reality of both problems by taking up a relativistic position, saying with Protagoras that man is the measure of all things — a position that would destroy his claim to a genuine agnosticism — he is forced to acknowledge that *it seems as though* there were both good and evil forces at work. He can say he does not know why there should be; but this does not diminish his difficulties. All this does nothing *in itself* to destroy the agnostic's position. The agnostic might still maintain that it is well for him to have to face the good-and-evil question both ways. The consideration presented here is intended, rather, to show only that, in the anguish faced by both theist and atheist, the agnostic certainly does not escape.

Is Evil Part of the Good?

Of course it is not difficult to explain *some* evils as illusory in the sense that they are evil only when looked at artificially, that is, as parts of a good whole. For instance, in the process of attaining anything worth while, there is, according to the universal testimony of mankind, some discomfort or anxiety or even pain to be undergone. No cross, no crown. I cannot even enjoy my morning bath without getting up, which is, if I am feeling sleepy, by no means entirely pleasant at the time. If I am a tolerably healthy individual, I do not think anything of such evils, which I would no doubt prefer to call, rather, mere inconveniences. So it may be argued that the more fully integrated I am as a person, the more I shall be able to see that so-called evils are really trivialities when seen in their full context. Even what seems really painful at the time often turns out to be, in the long run, so incidental in an eventually happy process that I am inclined to say, now that I can look back on the process as a whole, that the pain I felt is really not worth talking about. Childbirth can cause a woman extreme pain; but apparently this is soon forgotten in the joy of the result. Moreover, I may see — and it is in keeping with a character- istically religious attitude to see it — that sorrow is sometimes very good for me. It has a disciplinary, an educational value.

Suppose that I have never had a day's illness. As a result of my excellent health I am not only inclined to be impatient or intolerant of the lugubrious tales of illness that I hear daily; I am disposed to take my own good health very much for granted, not counting it among my blessings, but just accepting it, while perhaps grumbling a great deal at other things. Then, after being visited with a serious illness, I find that I have undergone a change of outlook. I am both more sympathetically disposed toward other sufferers and more grate- ful for the good health that I enjoy. I find myself taking a kindlier and more understanding view of other people, and my changed atti- tude enriches my whole life, coloring my outlook upon everything, so that I conclude by affirming that my illness has really been "a blessing in disguise." That there are many such disguised blessings is the experience of every mature person who reflects about his life. But will this do as an "omnibus" explanation for all evil? Could it be used, for instance, to explain the evil in the tragic story with which we began this chapter? Might it be said that if only we could see everything *sub specie aeternitatis*, as God sees it, then even the young dentist's loss of his hands on the eve of his professional debut would be seen to be a triviality? Or part of an educational process? It is true that even a tragedy of that order can be productive of good. But dare we say that it always must be so?

Moral Evil and Natural Evil

A traditional distinction is made between "moral" evil and "natural" evil. Moral evil depends on the exercise of human will; natural evil is independent of this. It is easily seen, however, that any such classification is much too simple to be entirely satisfactory in itself. Many evils fall partly in one category and partly in the other. A murder is certainly to be accounted a moral evil, if human beings are at all accountable for their actions; yet it may also be in part a natural evil, since conditions over which human beings have no control may have suggested or encouraged the murderous thought. To prevent earthquakes from taking place is beyond human power in terms of the present state of scientific knowledge and achievement; nevertheless, a particular earthquake's injury to humanity might have been avoided or mitigated by the exercise of greater prudence or foresight on someone's part. In the case of more commonplace occurrences, all this is often even more obvious.

The Dysteleological Surd

As we look out on the world around us and try to "make sense of it," as our mind requires us to do, we find that while some of it does make sense there is another part of it that makes no sense at all, resisting every attempt we make to put it in any light in which it would make sense. But it is not only that much in the world is discordant or crazy; we often have the strong impression, rather, of a positive drive behind the evils we see. It is not all a mere case of disorder waiting to be put into order, or of ignorance awaiting education; sometimes it would seem as though there were a malicious purpose actually at work *against* the good purposes we also see in that which lies around us. In the case of the young dentist it might be said: "That was extraordinarily bad luck." But such a comment sounds almost macabre in its tameness. It often seems to meet the case better if we exclaim: "But this is diabolical!" What *seems* diabolical *could* have happened by chance, of course; but in a case such as we have in mind the occurrence may seem too horribly apposite to be *likely* to be the result of mere chance. We may well ask ourselves whether we are confronted in such a case by an incoherent, blind "natural force," or by a supernatural evil will. Fundamentally, however, the problem of evil for the theist remains the same, whichever interpretation is put upon such occurrences.

So long as evils are susceptible to transformation into goods the problem is perhaps soluble. But when all has been said that can be said about the disciplinary and educational value of evils in the development of goods, and when full account has been taken of the notion of evil as a "moment" in the emergence of value, we appear to be left with something that is still unexplained — that to which Edgar Brightman has given the formidable but perhaps convenient name of "dysteleological surd."

In mathematics, a surd is a quantity not expressible in rational numbers. Used in a value-theory context, the term "surd" is applied by some writers to non-value that cannot be "reduced" to good: it is basic, irreducible non-value. The term "dysteleological," used, of course, in opposition to "teleological," refers to the character of the surd, which appears to be purpose-resistant. Instead of manifesting purpose, it appears to be a manifestation of the lack of this. The theist, in facing the problem of evil, is much concerned with the question of whether any such "dysteleological surds" really exist. If they do not, the problem of evil becomes relatively trivial. If they do, the theist is faced with the difficulty expressed in the question, "If God is really in supreme control of the universe, why does He permit the existence of that which is resistant to His purpose?"

Why Does God Permit Sin?

That God permits sin and its attendant evils is explained by Christian theologians after the following manner. God, in His love, creates finite human beings so that they may enjoy Him forever. In order to enjoy Him they must love Him, for you can't enjoy what you don't love. But you can't be forced to love: if you were so to be forced, your response wouldn't be one of love. You must love spontaneously by your own free choice, which means that you must be free to love or not to love. So God, in creating you, endows you with free will. By "free will" is not meant, as some people are inclined to imagine, that you have the power to do everything. Of course your freedom is limited: you are not free, for instance, to jump over the Empire State Building, for you are not physically able to do so. But within the limits of your capacities you are free, and you have freedom of choice to accept God, which is to love Him, or to reject God, which is to decline to love Him. To be confronted by God and reject Him is to prefer something else, for example your own pleasure or glory. From a theocentric standpoint, all such selfishness is sin and produces evil. But you must be allowed to be free to sin and so produce this evil; you must be permitted the freedom to damn yourself by poisoning yourself in the juice of your own vanity. You must be granted this freedom, since without it it would not be possible for you to choose the opposite, to serve and love God and so win the priceless *zoë*. It is not difficult on those grounds to explain evil, in so far as it is the consequence of human sin. To put the matter bluntly, we may suppose that God, though He hates sin and could stop it by His fiat, permits it because of the good that is produced by the liberty that makes the evil also possible.

Why Need Sin be Possible?

It may be objected: "But why does an omnipotent God have to put up with an *arrangement* whereby sin is required in order to produce good?" To this it must be pointed out that the notion that there is any such "arrangement" is mistaken. It must also be pointed out that only by a radical misunderstanding of the nature of the good can it be supposed that even an omnipotent God could so order the universe that good could be achieved without liberty to choose sin. The good that is achieved *is* a triumph over sin: therein lies its goodness. It implies a choice, and without the possibility of such a choice there would be no possibility of such a good. No kind of "omnipotence" could so "arrange" the universe as to make it possible to produce good without introducing at the same time the possibility of not producing it. This would be akin to making it possible to succeed in an examination in which you could not fail. Such "success" would not *be* success, and whatever value there is in examination success would be unattainable under such conditions. There is no way in which even God could make it possible for you to attain whatever good there is in the triumph over ignorance and sloth that is supposed to be attested in a college diploma, if He were bound to make you succeed. That is why human life must be a struggle rather than a hymn. The notion of a God omnipotent in the sense that He could eliminate the possibility of sin in creatures endowed with the ability to achieve goodness is tantamount to the notion of a God who could create goodness without creating it. The possibility of sin is an implicate of the possibility of attaining the *kind* of goodness that theists are talking about when they talk about creaturely goodness. Theism knows nothing of a goodness that could be enjoyed without its being in some way or other achieved.

No Values "Free of Charge"

It is true that in orthodox Christianity there is a special, theological doctrine that God "imputes" merit to those who, being redeemed by Christ, are incorporated into His "Body," the Church, at baptism. This is, like most specifically Christian doctrines, an extremely subtle descant, so to speak, on a presupposed theistic melody. To consider the specifically Christian doctrine in question would take us far beyond our present subject. But it must be noted that one of the most central doctrines of Christianity, namely, that Christ shed His Blood upon the Cross in order to redeem His people, is meaningless apart from the presupposition that even God cannot bring good into exist-

ence without cost. In Christianity, the Cross of Christ is the measure
of the cost of redemption. There are no values available "free of
charge." We have to work to create them. The joyful mystery proclaimed in the Christian Gospel is that such is the astounding love of
God that He lavishes upon His children the best conditions they
need for the work they are called upon to do. So overwhelming is His
bounty in this respect that some Christians have held that it is difficult to see how anyone so surrounded by it could fail to attain his
appointed destiny. But even on this view, which recognizes in a
special way the superabundance of the divine power to aid man, man
still stands in danger of temptation. Indeed, even Christ Himself,
according to the Gospel narrative, was subject to temptation: He
differed from others in the completeness of His success in dealing with
it.

O Felix Culpa

Good, as we know it, is always in some way or other essentially a
triumph over evil. When Schopenhauer noticed that neither philosophy nor religion would ever have arisen among human beings but for
the fact of death, he was calling attention to what is really at the
heart of Christianity: it is man's need for redemption that makes
redemption possible. In the long hymn, *Exultet jam angelica turba
caelorum*, sung in the Latin Church by the deacon at the blessing of
the candles on Easter Eve, occurs the exclamatory utterance, *O felix
culpa*: "O happy guilt, which deserved to have such and so great a
Redeemer!" The same idea is to be found in the well-known fifteenth-
century English carol:

> Ne hadde the appil take ben,
> the appil take ben,
> ne hadde never our lady
> a ben Hevene qwen.
> blyssid be the tyme
> that appil take was!
> therfore we mown syngyn
> Deo gracias.

Nor is all this invalidated by the reflection that, according to orthodox
Christian doctrine, not all will profit from Christ's redemptive work.
For if the Christian conception of God be accepted, then all the evil
in the world would be "worth while" even if only two or three persons
were to gain the victory and enjoy the prize of everlasting communion
with God.

Objection to Dualistic Solution

We saw, when we considered the dualistic conception of God,

that evil is so obvious that it is natural enough to suppose there must be two gods or forces in the universe, the one good and the other evil. We saw also that there is, however, a tendency in all such dualism toward belief that in the long run the good will conquer the evil. But even the purest monotheism may allow for a diabolical agency, a demonic force, personified, for instance, as Satan or Lucifer. It is not for the moment important to decide whether such a "Satan" is to be taken seriously as a real being or is to be regarded as a figurative personification. For the moment our concern is to recognize that from a theistic standpoint the whole of human life may be seen as a struggle to outdo "Satan" and so, escaping the demonic snares, conquer evil in one's own life (with divine aid) as God conquers it in the universe. The evil that we so overcome is, however, moral evil. It may be pointed out, indeed, that moral good, at any rate so far as you and I are concerned, *consists* of conquered evil. I cannot be brave except by overcoming cowardice, or chaste except by overcoming lust. A eunuch could not properly be called chaste; nor could I be said to be brave because I do not flinch before a squirrel, for there is no reason for me to be afraid of him. So it is plausible to say that you and I need temptation in order to make it possible for us to be virtuous. But could this be said of God? To say so would imply that in some way God depends upon evil in order to be God; that is, He would not be God were there no evil for Him to conquer. How then can He be said to be the Creator of all things, since either He must be eternally wrestling with and conquering eternally coexistent evil, or else He must create evil to conquer, which is impossible since He could not create without being God, and He could not be God without already having evil to conquer.

But there is in any case another consideration. We have been talking about moral evil as perhaps a prerequisite of moral good. But what of non-value? Are earthquakes and the like really necessary? Must God have chaos and ugliness in order that He may transform them into order and beauty? Cannot He simply create an orderly and beautiful universe? And if He can, why does He not do so? In order that we may consider this aspect of the problem we must consider whether there are dysteleological surds, and if so what is their nature.

DISCUSSION ON CHAPTER 37

1. Why is the problem of the good as serious for the atheist as is the problem of evil for the theist?

2. Could a theist hold that God is beyond both good and evil as we know these? If not, why not?

3. Discuss the relation between sin and freedom.

38

The Dysteleological Surd

Interpretation of Natural Evil as Discipline

It is arguable that there are no dysteleological surds. Earthquakes, for instance, may seem bad only because we look at things too superficially. How can we tell that the agonies of those who are swallowed up and the woes of their bereaved relatives are not merely outweighed by benefits of which we know nothing, but are really blessings in disguise? War appears a great evil, yet even an ardent pacifist may admit that it does bring some good in its train, if only perhaps some courage or loyalty that might not otherwise have emerged. Might not a national disaster such as a hurricane or an earthquake be a blessing in disguise? It may be argued that a plague may be as necessary for the discipline of a nation as a taste of sickness may be for my moral education.

In order to sustain such a view, it would seem to be necessary, however, that the discipline should be applied only where needed and should also be calculated to produce the most beneficial disciplinary results. The education ought surely to fit the educational aim, if not the punishment the crime. In December, 1889, on a stormy Sunday night in Dundee, Scotland, the middle girders of the then recently built Tay Bridge, still the longest cantilever bridge in the world, were blown down, and a train was precipitated into the water. Sabbatarians accounted the disaster a divine judgment upon those who used the train, which was one of the earliest in Scotland to run on a Sunday. Such a view may seem absurd. But surely it is no less fanciful to pretend that a flood in a small country town is exactly the right kind of discipline required in the lives of all the inhabitants. How could it be claimed that an epidemic in New York of a particular kind of influenza is precisely the best discipline for the ten thousand families it affects? It is not impossible to maintain that since, according to New Testament teaching, even the hairs of our head are numbered and not even a sparrow falls to the ground without the knowledge of God, the epidemic falls within the careful workings of

260

the divine Providence. But it is not the most likely explanation, and before accepting it we naturally seek one that seems more plausible.

Are There Dysteleological Surds?

To say that such misfortunes and disasters happen by a cruel chance is not necessarily a denial of the existence of God. It may be, indeed, a way of saying that such evils happen *in spite of* God. But such a view suggests that God, though at the helm of the universe, has a limited control over it, since all does not come immediately within His divine governance and providential care. If there are any dysteleological surds in the universe, then either God puts them there or else they are there in spite of Him. Dysteleological surds need not be actively or positively malignant: the existence of the Great Sandy Desert presumably does no great harm in itself; still, it is difficult to see any purpose in it, and if indeed there is none, the absence of one calls for an explanation on the part of theists. It is not enough to say, surely, that the Great Sandy Desert reminds those who live near it, and perhaps others too, that one ought to be grateful for rain. A less extensive area of desert would fulfill this function just as well. There is no evidence of economy, but only of a seemingly infinite prodigality and waste. This is also to be noticed in the working out of the evolutionary process. In the course of expounding the traditional teleological argument for the existence of God, we remarked that besides the fact that it is the fit who survive there is also the mysterious fact that they arrive. It would seem, however, that the process is curiously wasteful. An individual protozoon can have a quarter of a billion offspring in a single month. If this process were to go on unhindered, that species of protozoa would soon take over the whole earth. If fish neglected to eat each other as they do and were allowed complete freedom to multiply and attain maturity, there would soon be no room for them to swim. The case of extinct animals is even more suggestive of a dysteleological element in the universe. It took millions of years for the saurians to develop, which means that in the evolutionary process there must have been an incalculable number of "rejects." To anyone with pre-Darwinian notions of divine creation this is puzzling enough; but it may be argued that the evolutionary process is *within* God's great creative purpose, so that in that process we see, as it were, creation actually taking place and moving according to God's plan. But if we ask what place the saurians have in this plan, the answer is difficult. After millions of years of evolution, they became extinct. There is no evidence that they produced anything of value except their own will to live, and in the end that was thwarted. They may be seen as part of a purposeful plan;

yet it would seem to be a part that is unrelated to the whole and in itself purposeless.

Evolution and Freedom

On the other hand, it might be suggested that such extinct animals failed to achieve an end that it was possible for them to have achieved. Even the most rudimentary forms of life, it may be argued, are endowed with a degree of freedom, with the consequent possibility of using it or wasting it. In other words, God gives moral freedom even to the dinosaur; but the dinosaur, wasting or otherwise abusing his freedom, perishes and is extinguished in the process, giving place to other species endowed with freedom — similarly limited, of course, as all freedom must be in finite beings — who may make better use of it. Another objection may be raised here. Does not this process involve immense cruelty? As I write, I can see from my window a cat crouching in the heavy foliage of an old tree, in a strategic position for springing at unwary birds. If the feline design is successful, a bird shall die an ugly and cruel death, while pussy, having enjoyed a delectable meal, goes home for her milk dessert at the house of the kind family that dotes upon her. Man himself, though he has achieved a considerable mastery over other animals on this planet, can still be a loser if caught unawares by a wild beast whose brother, it may be, he has watched with admiration in a zoo. Carolyn Wells writes:

> Or if some time when roaming round,
> 　A noble wild beast greets you,
> With black stripes on a yellow ground,
> 　Just notice if he eats you.
> This simple rule may help you learn
> The Bengal Tiger to discern.[1]

In jungle conditions, man becomes but a participant in the ruthless struggle to survive. It is useless for him to argue with tigers about the reverence that one should have for all forms of life, for tigers have very definite views on the subject and will express them vivaciously without even having the decency to wait for man to elucidate his metaphysical contentions. Nor was Jefferson quite right when he protested, in the course of a lamentation on the predatory habits of European nations towards each other, that "man is the only animal that devours his own kind." On the contrary, the practice is widespread among many forms of life.

Cannibalism

Cannibalism is out of fashion among humans, nowadays. However, Christian missionaries *have* been eaten in the pursuit of their vocation

[1] From *Baubles* (New York: Dodd, Mead & Co., 1917).

in the remoter parts of the world. Indeed, even within Christendom itself curious survivals of the practice have appeared from time to time. It is on record that about the year 1458 in Scotland there was a man of unsociable habits who lived with his wife and family apart from the rest of the community in the county of Angus, and that he was discovered to be killing young persons for the family meal. The sequel is even more grisly. So great was the horror at this outbreak of so savage a practice that he and his family who had shared in the proceeds were sentenced to be burned at the stake. Only the baby daughter was spared, a child of about a year old, who was then brought up in another home. At the age of twelve she was apprehended for the same offense and was sentenced to suffer death by being buried alive, presumably in the hope that the ferocity of the punishment would deter others from emulating the practice or seeking to satisfy their curiosity about it by experimentation. The record goes on to recount how, as the people followed her to the place of execution, marveling that such a horrible crime could be committed by a mere child, she turned upon them "with a countenance representing her cruel inclination," and shouted that they might spare themselves their sermons as though she had done something "contrary to the nature of man," for, she yelled after them, "I tell you, that if you knew how plesent man's flesh is in taste there would none of you all forbear to eat it." Then, concludes the record, "with an impenitent and Stubborn mind, she suffered the appointed Execution." [2] All this, it must be borne in mind, was going on in a country that had been christianized for nearly a thousand years by that time, and probably within earshot of plainsong issuing from incense-filled churches, while friars in the holy garb of the Order of Saint Francis of Assisi, who so loved all God's creatures that he insisted on calling birds and donkeys his "brethren," were passing down the streets of the town.

Ahimsa

We are shocked by an outbreak of such barbarism among human beings. But in many forms of life such savagery is taken for granted. Nature is so cruel that we hardly dare think for long about it. The total amount of suffering that has taken place in the universe in the course of the past second as a result of the cruelty of the process of self-preservation is past imagining. We are horrified when a thoughtless person says, "Why not have another war? — the human race needs weeding out every now and again." But terrible war is going on even in my own body, in which millions of germs are at this

[2] A. H. Millar (ed.), *The First History of Dundee, 1776* (Dundee: David Winter, 1923), p. 59.

moment seeking success in their attack on me: if they do not meet with resistance they will quickly overmaster me so that by tomorrow I may be dead. We have to face the fact that it is a question of my life or that of the bacilli. The Jainist monk who takes literally the Hindu doctrine of *ahimsa,* non-violence to all living beings, is to be confronted with the reminder that he would not be able to preach his favorite doctrine had he not quite recently slain millions of bacteria in his own body without even administering an anesthetic to his hapless victims.

Is Power of Self-Determination a Divine Gift?

It is not, however, merely the cruelty of the evolutionary process that seems to point to the existence of dysteleological surds. If it were plain that there were some sort of order or system in the cruelty, it might be possible to contend that the cruelty is a "necessary evil" for the production of the values that we human beings have in some measure already learned to cherish. Perhaps, it may be argued, we can arrive at these values only after a necessarily painful process slowly but surely leading up to our present stage of development. So then, when savage beasts are occupied in ripping open each other's entrails in a manner entirely out of keeping with pacifist ideals, they may be really helping to ensure the continuation of a process carefully designed by the benevolent and beneficent Creator, a process whose design is so excellent that improvement upon it is beyond the imagination of finite man. It is difficult to refute such a view because we cannot pretend to know conclusively that there *are* better ways of creating values than those which God is employing. We are entitled to say only that within the very limited range of our knowledge it would seem that there ought to be better methods. But if I talk after this fashion, you are justified in pointing out that it is hardly for me to criticize an apparent slowness or clumsiness in God's work, since I have never even tried my hand at creating a universe myself and therefore can hardly have much idea of the practical difficulties involved. But what practical difficulties can there be if God is omnipotent? The answer is that of course there can be no practical difficulties for God except that He must permit self-determination to His creatures if these are going to be capable of developing any values in themselves. For values cannot be created even by God except by the creation of some kind of self-determination. This implies the possibility of failure; at the best the process is likely to be retarded and fulfillment of the plan postponed.

Is the Divine Power Limited?

According to such a view there would be no inconsistency in denying the existence of dysteleological surds. The weight of the argument in their favor lies not so much in the clumsiness or sluggishness of the evolutionary process as in the apparent irrationality of this. If only it seemed as though it were always, or at least generally, the unpleasant, vicious animals that were attacked, overwhelmed, and destroyed by the nobler ones, then one might perhaps be able to work out a case showing how virtue triumphs over vice throughout the process, even at the lower levels of development. But of course it is far from true that the survival of predatory animals can be held to be intrinsically more desirable than the survival of their prey. We talk vaguely of "the balance of nature"; but is the balance that exists the best balance there might be? The mink is a creature whose habits seem unpleasant to man; yet man not only traps mink but deliberately breeds it, because it so happens that the fur of the unpleasant animal is exceedingly fashionable for the adornment of the female of the species that is both predatory upon it and at the same time is far from seeking its extinction. When it comes to individual cases rather than mass behavior, the apparent irrationality is even more conspicuous. Not only bad men are eaten by tigers. Wars, far from eliminating only the less desirable elements in civilization, deprive nations of the flower of their youth. Tornadoes and earthquakes are undiscriminating: they are as likely to cripple the righteous as to destroy the wicked. Is it possible to see the hand of God in such forces? What makes it so difficult is their irrationality, their "senselessness." The difference between them and the manifestations of a disciplinary Providence would seem to be analogous to the difference between the actions of a raving lunatic and those of a strict father. On the other hand, much in the universe does support the Psalmist's view that "the heavens declare the glory of God and the firmament showeth his handiwork." It looks as though there were two forces at work — one a rational, benevolent will (God) and the other an irrational, blind force (Chance). It is reported that an African tribe believes that there is a deity who is good and benevolent to men, but that he has "a half-witted brother who is always interfering with what he does." [3] This expresses in a primitive fashion exactly what has led many eminent thinkers in recent times to adopt the view that God, though infinitely good and immensely powerful, does face conditions that resist His will.

This type of theistic position, though it has come into special prominence in philosophy in the last fifty years or so, has ancient roots. It is true that certain discoveries in modern physics and other sciences appear to lend support to it. The sympathy of Einstein for

[3] W. M. Dixon, *The Human Situation* (New York: Longmans, Green & Co., Inc., 1937), p. 83.

such a view is evident.[4] But the conception itself goes back at least to Plato. According to the doctrine Plato develops in the *Timaeus* and the *Philebus*, there is indeed a creative God; but He does not create out of nothing. He is, rather, an artist, working with a "'stuff," the primordial chaos of space, and of disorderly motion. The ideas of God, the cosmic artist, are being eternally imposed upon that chaos. But the chaos is external to God, so that there is a real dualism — God and the stuff upon which God works. Whitehead's God is reminiscent of that of the *Timaeus*. Other modern thinkers, some of whom are influenced directly or indirectly by Hegel, have modified this view so as to make it seem more compatible with the now traditional theistic conception. They prefer to see the "stuff" upon which God works as an aspect of God Himself — the spatial aspect, as it were, of God's consciousness. Others again have thought of the "stuff" as a sort of "body of God" in so far as it seems to play a role analogous to that which the body plays in the life of a man. That is to say, it resists the divine will; yet, being under God's control, it is also His instrument.

DISCUSSION ON CHAPTER 38

1. Consider examples of what appear to be dysteleological surds, other than those mentioned in the text.

2. Distinguish between the view that there is a Given within God and the view that God meets and has to cope with conditions not of His own making. Assess the importance of the distinction.

3. The question of whether there are dysteleological surds is one that presupposes theism. Then are atheists confronted with the question of whether there are any *teleological* surds? If so, what would be examples of these? Discuss.

---

[4] A. Einstein, *Out of My Later Years* (New York: Philosophical Library, Inc., 1950), pp. 26–28.

39

The Concept of Omnipotence

Traditional Conception of Omnipotence

The most obvious theological objection to the notion that God faces some conditions not of His own making is to be found in the traditional concept of omnipotence. The history of this concept requires particular examination. Omnipotence is one of the traditional attributes of God: an expression of it is to be found in the historic creeds of the Christian Church. Theologians, for example Thomas Aquinas, have nevertheless recognized one limitation in the divine omnipotence. God cannot do anything contrary to His own nature. For instance, if it be asked, "Can God do a wicked act?" the answer must be that He cannot, for it would be against His own nature to do that. Nor is God able to do what is self-contradictory: He cannot, for instance, make an existent that does not exist. Likewise, to the child's question, "if I have gone upstairs can God make it that I haven't?" the answer is no, for God must respect His own decrees, and having decreed the creation of time He cannot turn past events into future events or nonexistent ones. But according to a traditional view widely accepted among orthodox Christian theologians, that is the only sort of limitation that may be placed upon the divine omnipotence: apart from this, God is able to do anything whatsoever.

Etymology of "Omnipotent"

The word "omnipotent" comes from the Latin *omnipotens*. The Latin word was used by Augustine, notably in his treatise on the Trinity, in which he refers to "Father, Son and Holy Spirit, one God, alone, great, omnipotent, good, just, merciful, creator of all things visible and invisible." [1] Augustine likewise speaks of "the omnipotent Trinity," [2] and of "one God, good, omnipotent, the Trinity itself." [3] The word used is the same as the one in the opening phrase of the Creed: *Credo in Deum, Patrem omnipotentem,* "I believe in God, the Father Almighty." It suggests at once the notion of a being who, apart from the formal limitation just indicated, is able to do any-

[1] *De Trin.*, VII, 6.   [2] *Ibid.*, VII, 4.   [3] *Ibid.*, VIII, Pref.

thing whatsoever, a God whose power is infinite. But what exactly does it mean to say that the power of God is *infinite*?

Before attempting an answer to this question we must inquire into the ancestry of the word "omnipotent." The Latin word *omnipotens* is a translation of a Greek word, *pantokratōr*. It is not an exact translation, for the Greek word means "ruler over all things" (from *kratein,* to rule), rather than "all-powerful." This Greek word is the one used in the Greek version of the Bible, the Septuagint, where it translates a Hebrew phrase that is familiar to readers of the English Bible as "the Lord of hosts," that is, "the Lord of armies." The historical background of this phrase is interesting. The early Hebrews were primitive tribesmen. It was only with difficulty that they were persuaded to accept Yahweh (Jehovah) as their tribal deity to the exclusion of other gods. That is the point of the first of the Ten Commandments: Thou shalt have no other gods *before Me*. At this stage the Hebrews were very much in danger of reverting to earlier forms of worship, as we see from the story of the Golden Calf.[4] We find that even when they accepted Yahweh as their national deity, they did not at first deny the existence of other gods, that is, the gods of other tribes: they were henotheists, affirming that Yahweh was *their* god, who would help them in their battles as the gods of their enemies would help their enemies. At this stage there was of course no question of Yahweh being "able to do anything whatsoever." It was enough that Yahweh should be powerful and be on their side. Their leaders urged them to remember this in the day of battle: they were not to fight as though trusting only to their own strength, for then they should have been quickly discouraged at the first reverse in the field. They were to fight in the knowledge that Yahweh, their heavenly ally, was fighting with them and that they were fortunate to have such a powerful deity on their side. Unfortunately, however, the enemy was also equipped with a heavenly ally whose power was not to be underestimated.

Biblical Conception of Lordship

The Hebrews gradually, through the influence of their prophets, came to recognize in Yahweh the God who is to be worshiped as Lord over all. Over all what? Still the power of the enemy deities is not overlooked; but there has come to the Hebrews the recognition that Yahweh is not merely the Hebrew deity, one among many other gods: Yahweh is now seen to be the Supreme God. There is now no need to fear hostile deities. Though the universe be filled with hosts of evil spirits, there is no ground for dismay, for Yahweh is *over* all. Therefore men should trust in Him. He will use His immense power

[4] Gen. 32.

for the triumph of righteousness, for He is the God of righteousness. The extent of His power is not specified; but He is *El-Shaddai*, the Sufficient One, that is, He whose power is sufficient.[5] In the English Bible, *El-Shaddai* is often rendered "Almighty." [6] Yahweh is all-mighty, all-powerful. That is to say, He is as powerful as He need be to ensure that in the long run all unrighteousness shall give place to righteousness, and to guarantee that good shall triumph over evil. There is no need to fear demons or any other manifestations of evil, for Yahweh is sufficiently powerful to destroy them all. "Therefore will not we fear, though the earth be removed, and though the mountains be carried into the midst of the sea . . . The Lord of hosts is with us; the God of Jacob is our refuge."[7]

By saying that Yahweh is the Lord of hosts, the Hebrews were attributing to Him lordship over all other powers, good or evil. So the Greek version sometimes rendered this phrase *kyrios tōn dynam-eōn*, that is, Lord of powers. The Greek word *dynamis* retained a good deal of its primitive force: it could be any energy or power such as the *mana* to which we referred in dealing with that primitive form of religion we called dynamism. Elsewhere, however, the Greek version translated the Hebrew phrase by *pantokratōr*, a word which, as we have just seen, connotes not the possession of power but its exercise. This is the word used in the New Testament. In the King James Version it is translated "almighty" in all cases save one: "the Lord God omnipotent reigneth." [8]

There is no suggestion anywhere in either the Old Testament or the New of the notion of omnipotence in the sense of "the ability to do anything whatsoever." Nor is there any evidence that this notion was in the minds of the Greek Fathers of the Church, or that it was implied in the use of the word *pantokratōr* in the ancient Creeds. Eventually, however, *pantokratōr* was rendered into Latin by the term *omnipotens*. This Latin term, much more than the older Greek one, carried with it the idea of "being able to do anything." For the proposition *Deus omnipotens est* ("God is omnipotent") seemed to imply *Deus omnia potest* ("God 'can' all things"). So questions such as, "Why does God allow indiscriminate suffering?" and "Why doesn't God stop the Turk?" seemed more pointed than ever. Since God is able to do all things, then He is able to do this or that or any-thing else (except for the apparent exceptions noted) that anyone cares to mention. If He does not do it, and it appears to be a good

[5] The history of the term *El-Shaddai* is complex. It may be associated with "mountain," "breast," or "power." The notion of "sufficiency" is nevertheless generally implied.

[6] E.g., Ruth 1:20, 21; Job 21:15; 31:2; Ezek. 1:24.

[7] Ps. 46.   [8] Rev. 19:6.

thing to do, an explanation is necessary. For instance, it may be that it only appears to be a good thing yet is not, or else it may be that, while it is a good, there is a higher good not presently discernible to us which God must have in mind.

Questions of this sort are of course far older than the use of the Latin term *omnipotens*. They find classic expression in the Book of Job. Job is represented as by no means underestimating the power of God [9] and therefore puzzled by the prosperity of the wicked: "Wherefore do the wicked live, become old, yea, are mighty in power? Their seed is established in their sight with them, and their offspring before their eyes. Their houses are safe from fear, neither is the rod of God upon them. Their bull gendereth, and faileth not; their cow calveth, and casteth not her calf. They send forth their little ones like a flock, and their children dance." [10] But the force of such questions is intensified in the light of the notion that divine omnipotence means that God faces no conditions not of His own making, so that, enjoying an absolute freedom such as no finite being could conceivably possess, He must be able to intervene directly in all things so that there is no room for any dysteleological element in the universe. Reflections of this sort, together with a consideration of the seemingly fortuitous development of the notion of omnipotence from a Biblical conception that seems better described as "omnigovernance," has inclined many theistic philosophers toward the view that God is somehow limited in power, in the sense that He has to face conditions not of His own making and must therefore "wrestle" with evil before He can overcome it. On this view it becomes possible to accept the dysteleological element in the universe as that which God is in process of overcoming. Evil then seems to be explained without denying the supremacy of God or His infinite benevolence.

Does Limitation of Divine Power Solve the Problem?

But while such a view does remove difficulties of one kind, it raises other problems at perhaps an even deeper level. As a matter of fact, many adherents of theistic religions have throughout the ages found the "absolutist" interpretation of divine omnipotence difficult to grasp and have tended in practice to think of God as somehow limited in power. Much petitionary prayer suggests the idea that God's power is limited, since the petitioner prays as though by pleading hard enough with God it might be possible to get Him to pay special attention to one problem rather than another and so ensure a sort of "priority" for it in the schedule of divine activities. But such an attitude has always been repudiated by deeply religious people as

9 Job 42:2.   10 Job 21:7 ff.

indicating an inadequate sense of the power and majesty of God. The notion that God could ever stand in need of a reminder, or that there could be any question of His attention to one problem diminishing His attention to another is one that would turn God into a very anthropomorphic celestial executive. The notion of God's having to wrestle with evil, even as an artist wrestles with his medium, seems no less anthropomorphic. But there is a more serious objection still. The attraction of the view that God's power is limited by conditions not of His own making is that it seems to provide a comprehensive solution to the problem of evil as this is commonly stated. But does it really solve the problem? If God, being infinitely benevolent, is limited in power, He is responsible for creating finite beings who are to be faced with the dysteleological surds that the "limited power" theory is designed to allow for. How then, it may be asked, are we to square this with His infinite benevolence?

Review of the Theory of Limitation

The view that God's power must be limited was expressed by John Stuart Mill in his *Three Essays on Religion*, published in 1874, the year after his death. It seemed to Mill that even the teleological elements in the universe, no less than the dysteleological ones, argue against the traditional conception of divine omnipotence, since they suggest that God, in using means to accomplish ends, is forced to adapt Himself to conditions, and works under this limitation. Mill thought, in nineteenth-century fashion, that the conditions eternally faced by God were "Matter and Force." Modern physicists would take a different view of the conditions; but some of them would be in principle sympathetic to Mill's general contention. Mill also maintained that because he was not "incumbered with the necessity of admitting the omnipotence of the Creator" he could believe all the more earnestly in the goodness of God. Since Mill's time many distinguished thinkers have developed the notion of a God limited in power. F. C. S. Schiller, for instance, contended, in *Riddles of the Sphinx*, that it was possible to demonstrate the existence of such a God. The great American philosopher William James looked upon God as only pre-eminent among the powers that shape the universe. Among British philosophers of the same period, McTaggart and Bradley adopted similar notions, which have been developed in various ways more recently by other thinkers, including W. K. Wright, John Bennett, Robert Calhoun, Vergilius Ferm, E. S. Brightman, Georgia Harkness, Henry Wieman, Peter Bertocci, and (perhaps most impressively) A. N. Whitehead.

The notion of a God limited in power is one that must be taken seriously, not merely because it has so many distinguished defenders, but because it results from a genuine attempt to meet difficulties inherent in the concept of divine omnipotence. But we have just seen that the difficulties reappear in another guise. Even if they did not, however, the testimony of the most profound kinds of religious insight and experience makes it an unsatisfactory solution. On the pretext of modifying one of the traditional attributes of God, without affecting the attribute of benevolence, the "limited power" theory really presents us with a fundamentally different sort of God — one who, because He is eternally at work on a "stuff," is a Super-artist, not God the Creator. It is traditionally held that God is infinite in goodness, wisdom and power. This way of expressing the nature of God may be metaphysically unclear or otherwise unsatisfactory; but the theist must note that it is an attempt to express in inadequate human language the character of the one indivisible God. The significance of this may be illustrated from the practical consequences of accepting such a view of the divine nature. It is only because God is *all* that He is thus said to be that His demands upon me come as unconditionally as they do. Suppose, for instance, that God were said to be infinitely good and powerful, yet not without certain limits in wisdom or knowledge. My trust in Him could not be the same, nor could His demands on me be unconditional, for I could argue with myself thus: God means well — infinitely well — in making this demand of me; but though He is very wise and knows a great deal more than any human being could ever hope to know, yet He is not omniscient, and so He very well may have overlooked, for instance, the circumstances of the case in which I am involved, and would not, if He did fully know them, make the demand He is making. Likewise, if God's power is limited, I may argue thus: God needs me on His side in the struggle; therefore I can enter into a sort of contract with Him, demanding, on my side, a *quid pro quo*. This is not to say that I should be putting myself on a par with God, of course; nevertheless, even the lowest servant in the household of the grandest lord in the universe has some bargaining power with his lord, so long as the latter is in any way limited by any conditions; for everyone, however great, who is so limited, can do with help, however slight, in the fulfillment of his purposes. So I can in some sense assert a measure of independence in my dealings with God. Nor would this necessarily be "cutting off my nose to spite my face." The extent of my bargaining power in such circumstances is not to be underestimated. Knowing in advance that God *needs* me for the fulfillment of His purposes, I have, so to speak, a very strong card in my hand if only I know how to play it. I can at any rate delay the fulfillment of God's purposes and so enjoy the flattery of my vanity that is implied in the knowledge that, for all my obvious puniness in the universe, I have played a notable part in it, having conspicuously resisted the divine purpose. I can play upon a weakness in the circumstances of the all-benevolent Deity.

Objection to the Theory of Limitation

Most Christians would find all this blasphemous. It is so radically opposed to what is revealed in Christian encounter with God that many Christians would account such conceptions of the nature of Deity farther removed from their own than atheism itself. For the categorical denial of the existence of God that is the expression of the atheistical position does not, they would point out, so much insult the Sovereign Majesty of the All-holy Creator as does a doctrine that enthrones in His place a Deity who is merely pre-eminent in the struggle against the eternally dysteleological elements that resist His will. Christians generally would be inclined to regard the whole attempt to solve the problem of evil by positing a Deity limited in power as an attempt springing from a fundamental failure to appreciate the implications of the nature of the divine love. Only in this light, they would say, may the problem of evil be profitably approached. In order that the problem may be presented in this light, the next chapter will be devoted to an interpretation of the creativity of divine love.

DISCUSSION ON CHAPTER 39

1. The word used in Biblical Greek (*pantokratōr*) to designate the "almightiness" of God does not necessarily imply that He can do all things. But does the conception of God as presented in the New Testament, for instance, imply this? Discuss.

2. How successful, from a metaphysical point of view, is the notion of a Deity limited in power, as a solution of the problem of evil?

3. Consider various forms that the notion of a "limited" Deity might take and discuss their merits from any point of view that might be philosophically important.

40

An Interpretation of Divine Creativity

Terrible Aspect of Love

The statement "God is Love" [1] is the most succinct definition of the Christian conception of God. It is also, for that reason, the most misleading to those who are unacquainted with the historical and theological background that gives it its content.

It is true that there is kindness in love, and therefore infinite kindness in infinite love; but there is much else besides. Even human love is, as Dante knew, "of terrible aspect." One reason — not the only one — why many people so grossly misunderstand the nature of the love of God is that they have never really known even the terrible splendor of human love. It is such people who, if they were honest with themselves, would begin the Lord's Prayer with the words, "My Rich Uncle who art in heaven." For that is how they really think of God, expecting of him what they would expect of a kindly but irresponsible old man who can afford to be generous since he has never had to work for his money. With such a conception of God they are naturally disappointed if He should ask of them even the slightest self-sacrifice, for they are expecting, rather, a large monthly allowance and payment of their bank overdrafts as well, with never a question asked.

Impotent Love

In saying that God is love, the New Testament is attributing to Him power and wisdom to match His goodness. An impotent lover may evoke a pitying smile; he can hardly be called much of a lover. Love, in order to be worthy of the name, must be potent. God, as the infinite, that is, unlimited, Source of all Goodness, must be wholly unrestricted in power to be that Source. Nor could He be this if He in any sense lacked wisdom or knowledge. For the Christian view of God is that He is Perfect Love, and even the most potent lover could not be called this if it might be justly said that he was even a little bit of a fool. It is because God's goodness, wisdom and

[1] I John 4:8.

274

power are indivisible that the Christian, seeking a single predicate to express the divine nature, affirms that God is love.

Avuncular Love

Irresponsible kindliness, such as we expect of a senile rich uncle, is perhaps endearing in its way. The man who gives every drunken tramp he meets the price of a double Scotch, in the full knowledge that it will help the wretch to drink himself to death, is an amiable sort of character — more appealing than the one who administers instead a tract entitled, "Sinner, repent." But the latter, though probably clumsy in his technique, is really much more benevolent — much more of a lover at heart. Mere kindliness does not really care for the good of the object of its attention. We are merely kind toward people that we care nothing about; toward our dearest friends and lovers and children we are much more exacting. I would rather see my son suffer than see him develop into a juvenile delinquent, and if he were a juvenile delinquent I would rather that he be punished than that he should be encouraged to become an adult criminal. But it is not only toward my children that I have such an attitude. It is toward all for whom I care deeply.

Even human love implies far more than mere kindliness giving place to thoughtful responsibility. The unremitting love of a noble and highly intelligent mother, for instance, reveals much more than this, including an ever-warm, ever-alert, ever-tender solicitude for the welfare of her child, at the cost of no matter what personal sacrifice, and in the face of even the most ludicrously inadequate gratitude. Applied to such a mother, the expression "mother-love" sounds curiously empty, betokening the relatively selfish animal instinct on which it is based but which it transcends. Nevertheless, though the highest human love does transcend the more selfish kinds, a completely altruistic love is impossible for any human being, because, as Plato says, human love is the child of poverty: it springs from a need, a lack. Human love may rise beyond its lowest forms; but this limitation persists. Even in the happiest, reciprocated sexual love in which the needs of a man and of a woman are fulfilled, the limitation is by no means eliminated: the love, though in quality it may go far beyond physical and emotional need, always remains in some measure dependent upon this. It is because God has no needs that His love is entirely untainted by self-interest. If it could be said (as in the "limited power" theory it is said) that God has need to overcome evil or to wrestle with a "stuff," His love could not be said to have that absolute perfection, that wholly unadulterated altruism that Christian doctrine predicates of Him. There would be an element of selfish concern in His love.

Does Entropy Provide a Clue to the Nature of Divine Love?

According to Christian doctrine, God's love is so pure that He can and does will the good of His creation, because He can and does care for it for its own sake. If God needed me, He might very well pamper me and so do me harm. Because He has no need of me, His love for me ensures my good *if* to His infinite love is conjoined infinite wisdom and power. But this conjunction is, we have seen, implied in the Christian conception of divine love itself The divine love expresses itself in the first place in creation. Is there anything in the realm of science that would provide us with a clue to the nature of divine creation? Let us consider the principle of entropy, expressed in the Second Law of thermodynamics. The principle of entropy is, essentially, that all chemical and physical processes must take place in such a way as either to leave unchanged or else to increase the total entropy of the bodies taking part in the process: by "entropy" is indicated the degree of change or disorder in the constituent particles of any substance, or, to put this another way, the degree to which energy becomes converted from a useful into a useless form. The amount of available energy at the end of a chemical or physical process either must be what it was at the beginning or else it must decrease, and such a decrease of available energy is an increase in entropy. Suppose that in a body having ordered motion we start with a number of molecules, which are combinations of atoms, and then bring about a rise in the temperature of the body in question. The heat represents the substitution of a disorderly motion of molecules for the original motion, which was orderly. This is easy, a transformation of order into disorder. It is less easy to do it in reverse, to transform disorder into order. It can be done, of course, but the process is always accompanied by an increase in entropy. It would seem, then, that the universe must have begun in a condition of minimum entropy, and that it will end in a condition of maximum entropy, that is, minimum available energy. This is what is meant when physicists tell us that the universe is "running down like a clock." It means that all *activity* will have ceased. The Second Law of thermodynamics is eminently compatible with the notion of a divine creation of the universe out of nothing. Dr. Pollard, expounding [2] the view that the origin of the universe about 4,000,000,000 years ago was due to the sudden appearance of a vast cloud of neutrons in a state of extremely rapid expansion, from the radioactive decay of which were produced protons and electrons to form atomic nuclei, notes how this account squares with the doctrine of creation. There are other ways of interpreting the destiny of the universe. Some, notably Fred

[2] In a pamphlet.

Hoyle, a Cambridge scientist, have suggested that the expansion of the universe that is generally recognized to be taking place is counteracted by a continuous creation of new matter so that the universe need not "run down." [3] This is a speculative theory. In any case, it is not incompatible with a doctrine of divine creation.

What is relevant to our purpose in all this is not so much its compatibility with the Christian doctrine of creation — interesting though that is — as the clue it provides to an understanding of the Christian conception of the creative love of God. We have seen that the theological conception of God's creating finite beings endowed with a certain degree of freedom (because this is necessary for their enjoyment of Himself) accounts for moral evil in the universe but does not seem to account for what has been called the dysteleological surd. But how, precisely, does the distinction between "moral" and "natural" or "surd" evil arise? It implies a special view of creation in which God is envisaged as creating free agents and "matter" — let us say "man" and "nature" — separately, as though He created the one with His right hand and the other with His left. On such a view it is indubitably very difficult to account for the dysteleological element that seems to be in nature. But such a view is arbitrary, artificial, and does not accord with anything that modern physics can tell us about the origin of the universe or that the modern biological sciences can tell us about the origin of man. What we learn from these sciences does not by any means testify against divine creation; but it does indicate a very different picture of it from the one that is implied in making the sharp, creational dichotomy between man and nature.

Two Interpretations of the Scientific Account of the Origin of the Universe

Let us now consider two possible interpretations of the scientific account of the origin of the universe to which Pollard refers. A nihilistic interpretation would be that the cloud of neutrons simply appeared out of nothing and then simply "behaved." On such a view there could not be any teleological process in the universe as a whole, though it might well be contended that, within the total process, self-conscious agents, such as we humans, emerge and, having certain ends in view, conduct themselves in a teleological manner as compared with the dysteleological way in which the rest of the universe conducts itself. In this scheme the self-conscious agents would be developing limited teleologies of their own in terms of their own aspirations and desires. With such a nihilistic interpretation we are not presently concerned, though we may note in passing that it presents

[3] See F. Hoyle, *The Nature of the Universe* (Oxford: Basil Blackwell, 1950).

very great difficulties: it is odd enough that the "cloud" should simply appear out of nothing; it would seem to be odder still that four billion years later we should find it arranging parts of itself into New York City and other parts into Albert Schweitzer. (To anyone profoundly impressed, as is the Christian, by the stupendous values realized in such developments, not the least astonishing element in the situation is that so much should have happened in a mere four billion years.) A theistic interpretation would of course begin by positing that the "cloud" was produced by God out of pure love. Having such a divine source or authorship, it was created "on purpose." That is to say, it is destined to fulfill an end that God deems "worth while." The "cloud" has therefore within itself whatever is necessary for the fulfillment of the end. God does indeed create free agents; but He does not create them ready-made, so to speak. Why not? Because moral freedom must be won: even God can no more force it to appear as by the waving of a magician's wand than He can force those who win it to use it well.

The Biological Sciences

What have the biological sciences to say about the development of life itself? As even Aristotle saw, the transition from the nonliving to the living is so gradual that it is impossible to draw a definite line between them. Modern biologists have no easy answer to a question such as, "Is that virus living or not?" What is the criterion? Certainly not growth, for inanimate matter can be said to grow. What does seem to be clear is that life emerges in the process of evolution by a novel integration of pre-existing chemical factors, so that, however the transition takes place, life cannot be said to be discontinuous with inorganic matter. Nevertheless, life is characterized by a self-renewing activity that differentiates it from that whence it immediately springs. Though it may be studied in a chemical fashion, it exhibits very distinctive features. In contrast to inorganic matter, in which the process is always from order to disorder or "randomness," entailing, we have seen, increase in entropy, the process of activity in living matter is from order to order. It is as though living cells had acquired the power to overcome entropy. According to the nihilistic interpretation, it must be said that this transition from inorganic matter to living matter simply "happens," as the "cloud" is said to have happened. The theist may contend that, on the contrary, the emergence of life from inorganic matter is possible only because the process of the universe itself has been initiated by God so as to have within it the possibility of this development. The universe has within itself, from the beginning, latent powers of this sort because it takes its origin from the creative power of God. It is beyond doubt that living matter possesses all the qualities of inanimate matter *plus* other qualities that are not manifested in this. Similarly, higher living organisms such as man have all the qualities of lower organisms, with other qualities added. The increasing complexity that characterizes certain selected stocks in the evolutionary process may be said to represent biological achievement in the sense that it represents a real cumulation of qualities.

Chance Mutations or Creative Love?

The theist is certainly justified in questioning any suggestion to the effect that the achievements discernible in the evolutionary process are the result of chance mutations only. The complexity actually attained in a comparatively short time is so astonishing that the notion that it can be accounted for by a blind, dysteleological process *alone* is one that demands greater credulity than does even the crudest religious interpretation. This is not to say that the theistic interpretation is inevitable. The theistic interpretation is certainly, however, at the lowest estimate, eminently plausible. Consider only one example of the complexity achieved. In the retina of the human eye alone there are about 137,000,000 separate "seeing" elements. How long would one expect such an achievement to take on a non-theistic interpretation? That it has in fact taken only some period within the "lifetime" of our own planet is sufficient illustration of the staggering rapidity of the achievement. The evolutionary process seems long and slow only when one neglects to consider precisely what it accomplishes. When one does, one is impressed, rather, by the speed.

The evolutionary process appears at first sight also morally meaningless because of the "tooth and claw" cruelty of it. Read a few pages of Darwin, or of a more modern account of the process, and ask, "How can this ferocious struggle, this raging conflict between species and species and between individual and individual, be in any way compatible with creation by the action of divine love?" This reflection brings us to the heart of our problem. The evolutionary process is certainly incompatible with the sentimental sort of attitude that many people choose to identify with divine love. It is incompatible with humanistic ideals of "decent conduct," as T. H. Huxley pointed out long ago when he described the conduct of animals as being "on the level of a gladiatorial show." But we are not concerned with our own limited ideals of "decent conduct" or with sugary sentimentality interpreting divine love in terms of itself. In the previous chapter we considered the notion of the dysteleological surd, and of how the apparent presence in the universe of such a surd provided, prima facie, an argument against traditional conceptions of the omnipotence of God, and of His creation of the universe out of nothing, and an argument in favor of the view that God must be eternally facing conditions not of His own choosing or making. In the present chapter, however, we have considered an alternative interpretation, according to which it is the creative process itself that entails by-products that *look* dysteleological but that are, rather, excrescences necessitated by the process of the evolution of beings who have achieved the capacity to be responsive to the divine love that is the source of all. Such an interpretation is quite possible, but it does not dispose of the problem of pain. Nor is it easy, even when we bear in mind the "terrible" character of love, to which we have referred at the beginning of the present chapter and earlier in this book, to reconcile the savage competitiveness of the evolutionary process with its creation by the outpouring of the divine love. In the next chapter we must therefore address ourselves to some difficulties involved in the interpretation of the universe as the creative process that springs exclusively from God, whose creative activity is pure love entirely unhindered by or dependent upon any factor not of His own choosing.

DISCUSSION ON CHAPTER 40

1. Consider the implications for theism of the Second Law of thermodynamics.

2. Discuss the grounds of the traditional distinction between man and nature.

3. Discuss:

> To man the earth seems altogether
> No more a mother, but a step-dame rather.
>
> (Du Bartas)

41

Is the Creative Process Cruel?

Is the Cruelty of Nature Attributable to God?

If the creative process is to be called cruel and at the same time to be taken as issuing solely from God, then cruelty is being attributed to Him. That it seems to be cruel is testified by common observation. Even apart from what we learn from the biological sciences, our imagination can fill in the rest so quickly that we can hardly bear to allow ourselves to dwell on Wordsworth's reminder:

> Ah, what a warning for a thoughtless man,
> Could field or grove, or any spot of earth,
> Show to his eye an image of the pangs
> Which it hath witnessed; render back an echo
> Of the sad steps by which it hath been trod.

It is not only the pain that we see in all this that offends even the most callous among us; it is the selfish strife that seems to be necessary as a condition of survival. For there seems to be no doubt that the animal that does not make any competitive effort to live is liquidated in the ferocious struggle for existence. We lament the ruthlessness of competition in the man-made business world, saying that it is far indeed from the kind of world that a benevolent God would wish for his creatures; but it is soft compared with the conditions that prevail in the world untouched by man. Compared with this even modern warfare is gentlemanly.

Socialization and Survival

It is true that there are some mitigating features that sometimes go unnoticed by those who call attention to the selfish savagery of the evolutionary process. Kropotkin [1] has pointed out that Darwin, Huxley and others, in stressing the selfish competition in the struggle for survival, neglected the important fact that, while no animal survives which makes no competitive effort, the animals who exhibit the greatest strength of will or the most completely selfish aggressiveness

[1] P. Kropotkin, *Mutual Aid* (London: Pelican Books).

are not necessarily those that come off best in the struggle. Animals that develop the gregarious instinct, involving the subordination of individual selfish instincts to the gregarious instinct of the community, are more likely to survive. Cooperation within a species can be more effective in the struggle for survival than is "pure" selfishness. In other words, even among the lower animals it is recognized that social-ization is good business. Nevertheless, the evolutionary process still seems to involve an enormous amount of pain.

The Problem of Pain

But what, precisely, do we mean by "an enormous amount of pain"? If you receive ten lashes with a whip you have certainly undergone a greater pain than if you had received only one; but if ten people re-ceive one lash, can it be said that a *greater* pain has been endured than if only one person had been whipped? If everybody in the world received one lash only, could it be said that there was as much pain as there would have been if one person had received two? What we find distressing is not, surely, that the number of sufferers is large. Pain cannot be so measured. What shocks us is, rather, the notion that any pain that is both intense and meaningless should be dis-coverable in a creative process directly attributable to God.

It certainly cannot be pretended that there is no pain. But it may be that, by false analogy from our own experience, we ascribe to it a character it does not possess. One writer has drawn our attention to this possibility in the following terms: "When a crab will calmly continue its meal upon a smaller crab while being itself leisurely de-voured by a larger and stronger; when a lobster will voluntarily and spontaneously divest itself of its great claws if a heavy gun be fired over the water in which it is lying; when a dragon-fly will devour fly after fly immediately after its own abdomen has been torn from the rest of its body, and a wasp sip syrup while labouring — I will not say suffering — under a similar mutilation; it is quite clear that pain must practically be almost or altogether unknown." [2] At the lower stages of evolution, pain is, at any rate, of a very different character from pain as human beings endure it. Indeed, it seems that the capacity for pain is developed by the evolutionary process in such a way that every advancement entails an increase in the capacity for pain. It is not only that there is a competitive struggle for survival. The winners of the competition are endlessly attacked by ultramicroscopic candidates far behind them. These candidates, as agents of disease, are capable of causing the most advanced candidates, and do cause these, agonizing pain. There are many types of such disease affecting both man and other higher animals, and it would be extremely difficult

[2] Theodore Wood, quoted by C. E. Raven in *The Creator Spirit* (Cambridge: Harvard University Press, 1927), p. 120.

to claim that they were all in any way really necessary for the biological process of evolution.

Moral Freedom in the Biological Process

What do we mean by "the biological process"? We mean, surely, the evolutionary process in so far as it is susceptible to study by the methods of the biological sciences. But if we are to take seriously the interpretation of the process as issuing from the creative love of God, it is a teleological process, involving *moral* evolution. The creative purpose, according to the Christian interpretation, is the evolution of beings capable of responding to the infinite love of God in such a degree as to make it possible for them to "enjoy Him forever." The process of developing the freedom this requires must begin with the evolutionary process itself. This means that there is no line to be drawn between "moral" beings (for example, humanity) and "a-moral" ones. Morality must permeate the whole evolutionary process as does, say, energy. This is not to say that ethics as we know it, textbook ethics, applies or is relevant to what goes on among wasps and lobsters. Our ethical conceptions have human action as their point of reference. It is only when we try to look beyond human action, as a theocentric attitude would compel us to do, that our moral conceptions widen, enabling us to see that in ethics as we understand it we may be looking at only a fraction of the moral universe.

The rest might, indeed, be of much greater importance as a groundwork for an adequate discussion of the ethical problems that confront human beings, and a study of it might show that the way in which we put these problems is sometimes more artificial than we suppose. This is not to deny, of course, that our ethical problems as human beings are more complex and delicate than those of robins or weasels or elephants; but there is no reason to suppose that the real situations with which these are faced do not call for some primitive kind of "decision" on their part that is just as much a moral decision in its way as is required of us when we make our more elaborate ones. Such reflections as these would lead us to take much more seriously than we commonly do the notion that many, at least, of the apparently dysteleological elements we think we see in the process that lies behind the evolution of man are the outcome of the exercise of rudimentary forms of moral freedom. This would be a means of accounting for the presence of those elements in the universe that appear to be trying to poison the rest.

Diabolical Agencies and Modern Science

There is no need, in support of such an interpretation, to bring in the notion of diabolical agencies, the legions of Satan, upon which subject there could be, of course, no empirical evidence whatsoever.

It is to be noted, however, that while nothing in the evolutionary process that is the object of modern scientific study could possibly tell us anything about such diabolical agencies, there is nothing in it that can "disprove" the existence of powerful evil beings who would correspond to the Satanic hosts about which the Bible has so much to say and who have played such a large part in Christian lore. For while there would seem to be no place for such beings in the universe that we have described as developed out of a cloud of neutrons created from nothing but the outpouring of the divine love, there can be no proof that there are not other universes besides the one that is the subject of investigation by modern physics. From a theological standpoint it is hardly likely that the universe we know should be the Creator Spirit's only work. It seems more likely that there should be innumerable other universes whose nature we are not equipped to explore. Our forefathers thought the earth was not only the center of the universe but by far the most important part of the physical creation. They would certainly have been much astonished to hear it called, as Sir Edmund Whittaker, a distinguished contemporary scientist who is also a Christian, has called it, "a little backwater in the cosmic stream." The universe that is susceptible to astronomical study is vast, staggering to our imagination. The light that travels from even the nearest of the external galaxies, moving toward us at the speed of 186,000 miles a second, takes three-quarters of a million years to traverse the distance.[3] Beyond are millions of other galaxies. If this physically gigantic universe, born of a rapidly expanding cloud of neutrons, is indeed created by God, why should it be the sole example of His handiwork? Science has limitations which nonscientists are sometimes more apt to forget than are scientists. Astronomers and physicists are entitled to point out that all talk of such other universes is but useless speculation, since there is no way of getting any empirical knowledge about them; but this should not compel us to conclude that because the Satanic legions do not fit into the scheme we know they have no "existence." Not only can the natural sciences tell us nothing of such other universes; philosophy cannot tell us enough about existence itself. All that can be concluded is: what the Bible and Christian tradition have to say about devils cannot be disproved and ought not to be set aside merely because it represents a view widely held by people in ages when less was known than is known today about physics and biology.

[3] How puny are our present space adventures may be judged in light of the reflection that even if we had colonized every planet in the solar system, and had put in solar orbit a vast artificial system of man-made asteroids, we should still be probably at least as remote from the prospect of visiting the nearest galaxy as was Aristotle from buying a round-trip ticket to the moon.

If there *were* another universe, likewise created by God but representing an evolutionary process different from the one of which we know something, it might very well be that there were powerful evil beings in it as well as good, and that their evil was the outcome of the exercise of their moral freedom. Such evil beings might very well also have the power to enter into and "poison" the universe we know, both in the earlier and in the later stages of the evolutionary process we know, endeavoring to wreck the divine purpose. Their choice of our universe for their activities rather than their own would be understandable even by us; it would be analogous to the preference that human troublemakers have for working at a level where people cannot easily see through their mischievous intent. While there can be no proof of such diabolical beings, it is noteworthy that some modern thinkers, who are by no means as credulous as were many of our forefathers in such matters, are strongly inclined toward belief in the existence of personal agencies of a demonic kind at work in the created order we know. It is a hypotheisis that would help to account for the apparently dysteleological elements in this order. It is by no means indispensable for theism; but in face of the kind of evil that Christian realism discovers it is a metaphysical possibility that should not be lightly put aside.

What is Cruelty?

The universe we know is permeated with evil as well as good, with the dysteleological as well as the teleological. One manifestation of the evil, dysteleological element is the seeming cruelty of the creative process of evolution. But "cruelty" is a conception that has as its frame of reference human ethical standards and ideals that are, so to speak, taken out of context in the moral purpose — if there is one — behind the evolutionary process. The Christian, being unfettered to merely humanitarian conceptions of ethics, can claim to see the vital clue to the demands of this larger moral purpose, for according to the central doctrine of the Christian faith, God Himself, in Christ, has entered into the created order and shared in the sacrifice which it entails, sacrificing Himself in testimony of the divine love. For Christians it is therefore not difficult to see that the creative process demands sacrifice for the achievement of its moral purpose. This is an important element in the truth that Christians try to express when they say that, so far as we human beings are concerned, the Cross of Christ is at the heart of all things.

Why Freedom is Distasteful

"You shall know the truth," says Jesus, "and the truth shall make you free." Most children at Sunday school hear these words; but their full import cannot be understood without experience of the moral fact revealed in the Christian life, that we human beings are extraordinarily reluctant to be emancipated from moral bondage. Contrary to what we generally tell ourselves, we *like* that bondage; it is less demanding, more cozy. We pretend to want to be "free"; but every Christian minister with as much as a few years' experience of counseling and guiding the souls of men knows that in fact people resist nothing so vigorously as the freedom the Christian Gospel brings them. They resist it even long after they have nominally accepted it. Sometimes their resistance is as ferocious as that of a tiger resisting captivity; always it is more subtle and cunning, for they have to try to hoodwink not only others but, even more, themselves. They do not want to be freed, because every step in freedom means an increase in moral responsibility. "Let Christ loose your bonds," says the preacher to the young converts. It would seem at first sight that nothing could be easier. Yet even the most earnest, the most determined, of his young listeners generally takes years to undo even the outer knots. If it takes a convert so long to accept and enter upon the freedom his conversion gives him, how lengthy and arduous must be the process required to bring him to the stage at which it is meaningful to talk of bond-loosing at all, let alone of loving Him "whose service is perfect freedom." On the analogy of progress in human knowledge, we should expect such moral progress to take very long indeed; for it is well known that man has learned more about the universe in the past fifty years than he did in the preceding five hundred, and more in the past five hundred years than in the preceding five thousand. The earlier steps must surely be slow and arduous beyond our imagining.

Freedom, Sacrifice and Love

If sacrifice is "cruel" then the creative process is cruel indeed, for it certainly entails this. But this is to give to the word "cruel" a significance that it was never meant to bear. That love entails sacrifice, as it certainly does, should lead us to expect sacrifice "all along the line," and this is just what we find in the evolutionary process whether we look at it through the eyes of its earlier, nineteenth-century exponents or through more modern spectacles. To this the Christian of today can add that it has for two thousand years been the faith of generations of Christians that in Christ God has assumed the heaviest share of this burden of sacrifice Himself, and that beside His sacrifice the rest is but a meager contribution to the process. On any Christian theory of the Incarnation, the sacrifice of Christ is such as to call forth our deepest awe and reverence before the infinite wonder and mystery of the divine love. Even if a man could voluntarily limit and humble himself by entering, with all his human sensitivities and all his comparatively highminded thoughts and aspirations, into the living body of a codfish or a mouse, and suffer the worst that could befall him in that extraordinary situation, he would still be unable to scratch even below the surface, so to speak, of the infinite love that lies behind the sacrifice of Christ upon the Cross.

Kierkegaard on Sacrifice

Kierkegaard, in a passage that exhibits both profoundly Christian insight and an almost unendurably intense poetic beauty, has likened God to a cook making a dish in which a great many ingredients are needed to produce the desired flavor. The cook, knowing precisely what is required, puts in a little pinch of spice. Kierkegaard's parable proceeds as follows:

A little pinch of spice! That is to say: Here a man must be sacrificed, he is needed to impart a particular taste to the rest.

These are the correctives. It is a woful error if he who is used for applying the corrective becomes impatient and would make the corrective normative for others. That is the temptation to bring everything to confusion.

A little pinch of spice! Humanly speaking, what a painful thing, thus to be sacrificed, to be the little pinch of spice! But on the other hand, God knows well him whom he elects to use in this way, and then he knows also how, in the inward understanding of it, to make it so blessed a thing for him to be sacrificed, that among the thousands of divers voices which express, each in its own way, the same thing, his also will be heard, and perhaps especially his which is truly de profundis, proclaiming: God is love. The birds on the branches, the lilies in the field, the deer in the forest, the fishes in the sea, countless hosts of happy men exultantly proclaim: God is love. But beneath all these sopranos, supporting them as it were, as the bass part does, is audible the de profundis which issues from the sacrificed one: God is love.[4]

DISCUSSION ON CHAPTER 41

1. Discuss:

For nature is one with rapine: a harm no preacher can heal;
The mayfly is torn by the swallow, the sparrow spear'd by the shrike,
And the whole little wood where I sit is a world of plunder and prey.

(Tennyson)

2. Consider the relation between pain and evil.

[4] Quoted by Walter Lowrie in *Kierkegaard* (Oxford: Oxford University Press, 1938), p. 588. The passage is from Kierkegaard's *Journal*.

3. Consider the following passages with reference to the passage from Kierkegaard quoted in the text:

  (a) "Was anything real ever gained without sacrifice of some kind?" (Arthur Helps)
  (b) "Self-sacrifice enables us to sacrifice other people without blushing." (Bernard Shaw)
  (c) "Sacrifice is the first element of religion, and resolves itself in theological language into the love of God." (J. A. Froude)

PART EIGHT

Religious Language

42

The Problem of Religious Language

Illustration of the Problem

It is easy to see that religious language is different from that of ordinary speech. Look at this typical hymn:

> Sometimes a light surprises
>   The Christian while he sings;
> It is the Lord who rises
>   With healing in his wings:
> When comforts are declining,
>   He grants the soul again
> A season of clear shining,
>   To cheer it after rain.[1]

If you forget all about religion and try to make sense of this as it stands, as if it were a "plain statement" such as, say, a newspaper report of a street accident, you might begin as follows: "It seems to be claimed that when the sort of person whose religious affiliation is 'Christian' engages in vocal musical exercises, he is liable to be taken by surprise by the appearance of a light (wattage or candle power not stated), which, however, turns out to be not a light at all, but a bird (it must be a bird, for the only other forms of winged life are bats and certain insects, and the context precludes these), which is of a species bearing a name unknown to ornithologists, and whose wings have a built-in stock of medical supplies which, nevertheless, apparently do not impede its flight." This would take you only half way; but that is as far as you would be likely to go, for by then, if not before, you would have discovered that you were talking sheer nonsense.

Are Poetry and Religion in the Same Case?

The same experiment, however, might be conducted with a "secular" poem, with the same kind of result:

[1] William Cowper.

> *She is a bird, a bird that blossoms,*
> *She is a flower, a flower that sings;*
> *And I a flower when I behold her,*
> *And when I hear her, I have wings.*[2]

Empirically, this is certainly no less nonsense than the hymn. May we say, then, that religious language and poetic language are in the same case? In answer to this question it would have to be pointed out that while they have something in common they are not at all in the same case. I may write all sorts of poems about, and paint all sorts of pictures of, elves and dragons and other such imaginary beings, and you may say they are well done or badly done, as the case may be, without either of us entertaining for a moment the notion that elves "really exist" or that there is the slightest possibility of our ever encountering a "real dragon." We have a mutual understanding before we begin that we are talking about fictitious entities. We operate accordingly. But it is a very different matter when I make affirmations about God or otherwise engage in religious discourse. However figurative the language that I have to use, it is understood from the beginning that I am *not* merely presenting you with a picturesque idea that I think you might like to share with me; I am talking about what I affirm to be *at least* as "real" as trees, tables, horses, and other objects that are susceptible to empirical study.

Aesthetic Truth

This question is complicated, however, by several very important considerations. In the first place, let us look more closely at the case of poetic, artistic language. The fact that the poet is allowed to use his imagination does not mean that he may let it run wild. Indeed, the success or failure of his work depends largely on the manner in which he controls his imagination. He may talk about fictitious entities like dragons; but he may not say anything he likes about them. If he tells me about a dragon with a soft furry coat, I will say at once: "No, no; it couldn't have been a dragon, because dragons don't have furry coats." A. E. Housman writes of a cherry tree wearing white for Eastertide, and though I know perfectly well that no cherry tree ever gives a thought to the liturgical propriety of its blossom or otherwise takes account of the Christian Year, I acclaim Housman's lines to be excellent poetry. If, however, he had said that the cherry tree sang the Easter Sequence or celebrated High Mass I should probably have thought much less of him as a poet. Yet since, from an empirical standpoint, the notion of a cherry tree deliberately donning white for a special occasion is as absurd as the notion of its saying Mass, why

2 Mary E. Coleridge.

should the one be in a different case from the other? Or again, you go to a performance of A *Midsummer Night's Dream* and come back to me with the report that the Fairy Queen was not very convincing. I ask why, and you reply, "Too tall." I know exactly what you mean: the actress who plays this part ought to be petite. I do not say to you: "But why should it matter, since there are no fairy queens anyway?" Notice, however, that the reason why an actress who takes size nine in shoes and stands six feet in them is unsuited for the part of the Fairy Queen is not the same reason why an actor of similar dimensions should not play Napoleon. The latter would make a bad Napoleon because he is intended to represent a real man who happened to be short in stature; in the case of the Fairy Queen the actress is not representing anybody to whose measurements she must conform. She is required, however, to conform to *a part in the play*. The fact is that the realm of the imagination has its own laws, its own criteria of consistency. Pascal's saying that "the heart has its reasons which reason does not know" applies to it. So the novel that conforms most closely to real life — so closely that it may be in fact a "true story" — is not necessarily the best novel. It may indeed be a particularly bad novel, while one in which the events are not really very probable in the form in which they are presented may carry aesthetic conviction, being a very good yarn, perhaps even a literary masterpiece. Probably no group of people in the world ever talked so brilliantly and fluently for hours on end as they do in a clever play; but that says nothing against the dramatist's workmanship.

The Context of Words Beyond Their Sentences

Words do not merely have to relate to other words in a sentence, as grammar teaches us they must do; they also refer to a much larger context. Each context, each situation, each occasion, has its own vocabulary, and within each system a word may acquire a meaning that it does not otherwise carry at all. In a dinghy I may shout to my companion, "Watch the boom!" He is not likely to suppose I am talking economics. On the other hand, if I use exactly the same words in the course of a speech to stockholders at a company meeting, no one is likely to imagine that I am talking about a dinghy. There are certain words which are quite inapposite to certain situations. The story is told of a government employee with a literary bent unsuited to his position who took on a bet that he could contrive to use the word "ecstatic" in official correspondence on departmental notepaper. He tried for years to find an occasion for using the word; but the first that occurred was in a letter he wrote to the department on its notepaper saying that it was with ecstatic pleasure that he resigned his position. He would not, of course, have been entitled to win his bet, for the context had changed. A more striking example still is the practice of swearing, or, as we say, "the use of bad language." What is it that makes language "bad"? The word "hell," for example, is a theological term that a bishop might very well use in a sermon on a most solemn occasion. Yet the same word may, in other circumstances, be accounted "swearing." Or suppose that I hear a man say, "My God!" No doubt I could usually tell from his tone whether he was praying or blaspheming; but it is possible that in some cases I might really be in doubt, not knowing whether to rebuke him for blasphemy or tiptoe past him so as not to disturb his devotions. As a matter of fact, it is precisely because the situations that evoke swearing are so close in nature to the situations that evoke religious devotion that the use of words proper to the latter are so distasteful to religious people. Swearing is a gesture of defiance in a situation in which a man recognizes his own finitude in face of the might of the cosmos. The swearer, by implication, resists the theocentric attitude and expresses his resistance by borrowing the language of theism for use out of context. It is in this that the blasphemy consists; hence the disapproval of this kind of "bad language" by religious people.

Verbal Propriety

But again, this situation is not without parallel in circumstances in which religion plays no direct part. Certain words and phrases are accounted impolite or improper on certain occasions and therefore to be avoided, although on other occasions their avoidance would be both improper and ridiculous. Words relating to the excretory functions, for instance, are used daily by physicians and the like and it would be ridiculous for a doctor to circumvent them in talking professionally to his patient. They would be improper at an afternoon tea party, however, not merely because an antiquated convention dictates otherwise but because they do not fit. They would be as out of place as full evening dress on the beach. Once again, there are "levels of conversation" suited to various occasions: what is brilliant conversation at a philosophers' conference would be intolerable at a cocktail party at which "small talk" is the "level." A joke that would rightly evoke a spontaneous burst of laughter at the one would fall flat at the other. The story is told of a charwoman who, on being advised to be discreet in her conversation with the new cook, since the latter was a Roman Catholic, replied that of course she understood perfectly that "in the best society religion is not even as much as mentioned." The charwoman's judgment is, of course, a caricature of what we have just been saying. But wherein, precisely, lies the caricature upon which the point of the story depends? What is it that makes the charwoman's remark mirth-provoking?

The Source of the Uniqueness of Religious Language

While it is true that there is a "religious language" and that religious terms and phrases must be related to it in order to be meaningful and tend to become meaningless as soon as they are transplanted into some other kind of discourse, such as, say, that of the economist or the mathematician, it is also true that religions claim to be relevant to *all* situations, however trivial. To confine your religion strictly to the school chapel is like confining your physical exercise strictly to the school gymnasium. Religious truths purport to be universal in their application, more so than even mathematical truths. It is not only in the mathematics classroom that the sum of the angles of a triangle are equal to two right angles: this is as true on the football field as inside the school, as true in Russia as it is in America. It is true wherever Euclidean geometry applies, wherever space is looked upon in a Euclidean way. But it need not be true in non-Euclidean geometries, in which we are not committed to Euclidean axioms. The commitment of the religious man to God is not so restricted. He is willing to die for it. But that is not all. A mother may be willing to die for her son, though she knows that the son is a rotten scoundrel unworthy of a tenth of her devotion. The religious man, in his commitment to God, claims that God is worthy of far more devotion than he could ever give Him even if he were to die a martyr's death for His sake. It is because the religious man's commitment is unique that his kind of language is unique.

The uniqueness of religious language springs from the uniqueness of what the language is "about." The words that religious people use are often quite commonplace in themselves; but this does not make what they say any more comprehensible to those who do not have the clue. The words used in a love letter may be all fairly simple, and an intelligent child of ten might very well read the love letter and understand every word of it in the sense that the child could give a fairly good dictionary definition of every word, and a fairly good grammatical analysis of every sentence. But the child could not really understand the letter because he could not understand what the letter was "about." An adult would understand at once. Yet even the adult could not understand the letter as the sender or recipient understood it; to them it would "mean more" because it would be related to their unique situation, their unique commitment. Or consider the case of "family" jokes or allusions which may be couched in quite ordinary words, but which are fraught with vivid significance for members of the family who are "in the know." The history of such a "family" phrase may be very complicated; no doubt it generally is. Suppose it were: "The green-fingered tiger wouldn't like it." The words are all perfectly intelligible; but as put together and used in family conversation the phrase would appear to an outsider to be nonsensical. To the family it would recall, however, let us suppose, a former beau of a daughter of the house, a Princeton undergraduate who happened to be so self-opinionated on the subject of gardening that he had afterwards become the symbol, within the family circle, of a very special kind of pedantry. If you didn't know the peculiar circumstances of the origin of the phrase, it might be practically impossible for a member of the family to explain it to you in such a way as to enable you to see the point of its application. You might get a vague notion of what they were talking about, but you probably would not be able to see why the family made so much of the phrase, or why they laughed so spontaneously at what seemed to you to be at the best a tame joke. Unless you are "inside" the religious situation, the language used in reference to it will be certainly no less puzzling.

Metaphor and Symbol

That a discussion of the nature of metaphor and symbol must be included in any discussion of the problem of religious language is obvious to anyone who has reflected upon religious utterances at all. But a full discussion of the problem of religious language would have to extend far beyond questions of that kind: it would have to include a prolonged examination of the notion of commitment. We shall only touch upon some of the questions that the problem of religious language raises, so as to sketch lines of inquiry rather than attempt solutions of one of the most complex and still comparatively unexplored areas in modern religious philosophy.

The figurative character of religious language is always recognized, implicitly or otherwise, by the prophets and religious thinkers who use it; nor is it overlooked by those who, though not of their prophetic stature, have had a sufficiently profound religious experience to understand what they are talking about. But there are many people whose religious experience is strong enough to make them attach an enormous importance to it, though their insight into its nature remains too feeble to permit them to wean themselves from a literalism that can pervert and distort the meaning of religion almost beyond recognition.

Misunderstanding of Religious Commitment

The misunderstandings of the irreligious are, however, more serious than the misunderstandings of the half-religious. For while the latter merely adhere to a literalistic interpretation of what is in the nature of the case figurative, the former, failing to understand the religious commitment itself, more radically misconstrue the nature of religious language. For instance, hearing religious people talk of miracles, and noticing that many of them are evidently very much interested in them, skeptical thinkers have often assumed that religious people depend to such an extent on an ample supply of miraculous or supernatural manifestations that all their religious belief would waver if only their belief in these were undermined. This is to misunderstand the role of miracle in religion. Deeply religious people, though they may evince considerable interest in what is popularly understood by "miracle" or "supernatural manifestation," do not depend upon this sort of thing at all. Indeed, to many religious people miracle stories are somewhat embarrassing just because of their susceptibility to misconstruction on all sides.

Human Parthenogenesis and the Virgin Birth

In any case, a large number of instances of a miracle may in some cases constitute a prima facie case *against* religion. For instance, it is an article of Christian orthodoxy that Christ was born of a virgin. The significance of this belief lies in its being a pointer to the uniqueness of the Incarnation, which is an essential ground of all Christian belief. Some modern apologists for Christianity who do not understand the groundwork of the Christian faith have drawn attention to instances of parthenogenesis, and have talked as though belief in the Virgin Birth would be fortified by evidence of the "possibility" of human parthenogenesis. It not infrequently happens that a woman claims she has given birth to a child under such conditions, and skeptics have sometimes talked as though every disproved instance were a nail in the coffin of this article of Christian orthodoxy. But of course, the whole point of the doctrine of the Virgin Birth depends on there being no other instances, so that it would not be entirely unplausible for a Christian to contend that every disproved instance of human parthenogenesis strengthened rather than weakened his case. In any event, the doctrine has theological importance for Christians only in the context of the Incarnation; so much so that it has even been pointed out that in view of the uniqueness of the Incarnation a birth under normal conditions would be more rather than less miraculous from a Christian point of view. Some Christians have gone so far as to reject the doctrine of the Virgin Birth on the debatable but certainly very theological ground that it fails to do justice to the humanity of Christ that is an essential part of orthodox Christian belief.

Varieties of Religious Utterance

If it is true that nothing depends upon even so traditional a miracle as the Virgin Birth, it is true, *a fortiori*, that nothing could ever depend on the liquefactions of relics and the like. In any case, the religious importance of doctrines such as the Virgin Birth is not at all what is medically important or interesting in parthenogenesis. Again, take two Christian doctrines such as these: (a) Jesus Christ was crucified for our salvation, and (b) Jesus Christ sitteth at the right hand of God. We have already seen that the language used in the latter case is highly figurative: no one really supposes that God has a right hand in the physiological sense. But suppose one were to say that the Crucifixion was likewise a figurative, poetic idea with no more historical or empirical significance than the idea that Christ sits at God's right hand: this would be a categorical denial of the essence of the Christian faith. A typical problem in religious language is: how is one to distinguish propositions of one kind from those of the other?

DISCUSSION ON CHAPTER 42

1. Consider and discuss examples, other than those in the text, illustrative of the problem of religious language.

2. "All flesh is grass." (Isaiah 40:5) Is this poetical or religious language, or both? Why?

3. "The language of religion *evokes* emotion; but it *invokes* God." Discuss this with reference to the contention that all *purely* religious language is in the second person singular, that is, addressed to God.

43

The Nature of Religious Symbolism

The Rise of Modern Linguistic Analysis

Ever since the beginning of the present century, but more especially since about 1930, the attention of philosophers has been predominantly directed to linguistic analysis and problems about the nature of language itself. It is not by any means the first time in the history of thought that philosophers have concerned themselves with problems of this sort; nevertheless, the kind of interest that has been aroused is a special one, and its intensity exceptional. It had its beginning at the turn of the century when neo-Hegelianism was in vogue and the discourse of its proponents seemed to some thinkers (for example, G. E. Moore and Bertrand Russell) to be intolerably vague and confused. The demand of such critics of the philosophy then in fashion was for greater clarity in utterance. Philosophy had acquired a widespread reputation for being obscure and difficult; people who did not profess to understand what the neo-Hegelians were talking about often assumed that they were talking about something very important in a special jargon of their own which in the nature of the case the mass of mankind could not be expected to understand. The philosophers seemed to be talking about very lofty subjects, about "reality," "the ultimate," "being," "essences," and so forth, and sometimes it almost seemed as though the greater the obscurity of the language employed, the more profound must be the thought.

A group of philosophers in Vienna who were interested in such clarification from a special point of view emphasized what came to be called the Verification Principle. Their demand upon philosophers was that no propositions were admissible unless these were susceptible to verification in terms of sense experience. With this Viennese circle are associated the names of Wittgenstein, Carnap and Schlick. It was not contended that propositions had to be verified before they could be accepted as meaningful. It is quite meaningful, on this view, to say, "there is a cat in the room next door" even though the room next door be locked so that for the time being no one is able to find out whether the statement is true or false. It is not necessary to wait to see whether it is true or false before one can decide whether it is an admissible proposition. It is admissible because it is the sort of statement that *could* be verified — for instance, as soon as someone can find the key to the room. Even a statement such as "the other side of the moon is made of rice pudding" is all right. It may seem extremely improbable that it should be true, and until space travel is more developed it is impossible to find out; nevertheless, it is theoretically possible to find out, so the proposition is a legitimate one to use. On the other hand, to say something such as "ultimate reality is coextensive with the ground of all being," or "time does not flow from eternity," is excluded because nobody could ever know one way or the other. This criticism of philosophical language ruled out most of the statements the neo-Hegelians were making; it ruled them out as illegitimate because, since nobody could ever decide whether they were true or not, they were meaningless statements, and as such they were entirely unprofitable. Apart from propositions susceptible to treatment according to the Verification Principle, these critical philosophers did allow one other sort, but the exception did not affect the basic position they maintained. The exception consisted of propositions of a logical or mathematical kind; for instance, "the sum of two right angles equals 180 degrees," and "A is-not not-A." Propositions of this kind are really tautologies: the sum of two right angles could not conceivably equal anything other than 180 degrees, because that is what the sum of two right angles is, by definition. Logic and mathematics really consist of such tautologies on a very elaborate scale, though of course they are such useful tautologies that they may be accounted indispensable for thought. The important point was that, strictly speaking, there is only one kind of proposition that may legitimately be used. People who want to be careful to avoid talking nonsense must apply the Verification Principle to all their utterances.

When is a Problem a Pseudo-problem?

It is plain that a rigorous application of this test of the meaningfulness of an utterance would exclude much of the conversation, not to say the most interesting part of the conversation, of civilized human beings. This was quickly seen; indeed some of the earlier philosophers of this school, notably Wittgenstein, saw it from the beginning. But as the influence of the movement spread — and its influence in the English-speaking world has been very notable — the questions that came to be discussed were often questions about the treatment of cases that seemed, in the light of developing techniques of linguistic analysis, to raise special problems. Those who had artistic or poetic interests, for example, would have one set of problems; those whose interests were, rather, ethical, would have another. Theological and religious concerns seemed to be the most baffling of all. We have already, in the preceding chapter, hinted at the reason why this might be expected. But of course to those who had no theological or religious concerns, the reason appeared, and still appears, to be simpler still. What appeared to be problems of this sort, they said, were not really problems at all; they should be recognized accordingly and treated as "pseudo-problems."

Of course it is not to be supposed that the Verification Principle is itself invulnerable to criticism. It has been very severely criticized, and its application has in fact been considerably modified in the course of the past twenty-five years by those who adhere to it. Especially since 1950 there has been a noticeably growing doubt about the notion that all religious, theological and metaphysical problems are only linguistic problems in disguise. Nevertheless, the enormous attention to linguistic analysis that has characterized philosophical discussions in the past few decades could not fail to make religious thinkers turn their attention increasingly to problems about the nature of religious language.

Uniqueness of Religious Commitment Disguised by Religious Language

The religious commitment is unique, and all religious discourse has therefore a unique point of reference. But we have seen that the language used by religion is in itself often quite ordinary, so that it disguises the uniqueness. This reflection has an important consequence: while, on the one hand, all religious utterances may be expected to be incomprehensible without the "clue," nevertheless, on the other hand, religious utterances may be expected to be classifiable into types that should correspond, to a great extent, at any rate, to what is to be found in other sorts of language.

Symbolism

Symbolism is an extremely difficult and controversial subject in modern philosophy; so much so that it is better that we should not get involved at this point in controversial questions such as the relation between symbol and sign. We ought to note, however, that while a sign indicates, a symbol represents. Farmers will tell you that a certain kind of sky is a sign of rain; the hammer and sickle, on the other hand, constitute a symbol of the Soviet Union. It should be noted that most modern philosophers sub-classify signs and symbols, and it is even more important to observe that a sign may also be a symbol and a symbol may be a sign. For instance, the color of sky that is taken to be an indication of rain might be used as part of an emblem or heraldic device to represent, say, the idea of rain in contradistinction to the idea of a desert. The hammer and sickle, which have come to represent the Soviet Union or a political ideology that it purports to uphold, could also act as a sign: if you parachuted into unknown territory and began seeing the Soviet emblem decorating public buildings you would have no hesitation in taking it as a sign that you had descended upon the other side of the Iron Curtain.

Etymology of "Symbol"

The word "symbol" should be understood in terms of its etymology. In Greek, a *symbolon* was a tally; that is, it was each of two pieces of an object that two contracting parties broke between them as a token of their contract. Each party kept his piece in order to have proof of the identity of the person presenting the other piece. The one piece had to fit into the other. A symbol is therefore to be presumed to resemble what it represents, but the resemblance may not be apparent at first sight. Indeed, it usually is not apparent unless you have a considerable knowledge of the "setting." For instance, if you did not already have enough acquaintance with the Bolshevik Revolution or did not otherwise happen to know the hammer and sickle as the emblem adopted by the Soviet Union, the bare appearance of the emblem would not in itself make you recognize it to be something that "stands for" Russia. Likewise, if you were entirely ignorant of the origins of Christianity, the cross would not immediately suggest to you this religion rather than another. Once you know of the Crucifixion, however, and of the interpretation that Christians give to that event in history, the appositeness of the cross as symbolizing the Christian religion rather than Hinduism or Judaism or Islam would be very obvious indeed. Islam's emblem, the crescent moon, has likewise nothing in it to communicate to you its connection with Islam. For the connection to be obvious you must know a little about Moslem history. Once you know something about the "setting" of Christianity and Islam, however, you have only to see a book entitled *The Cross and the Crescent* to recognize it as one that has something to do with these two religions, probably with their impact upon each other.

Creeds as Symbols

There is a special, technical use of the word "symbol" in Christian theology that should be noted at this point, not only for its intrinsic importance, but because of its relevance to the whole question of religious language. The historic Christian Creeds (for example, the so-called "Apostles' Creed") are called symbols, and the study of them is known to theologians as a special field, Symbolics. Such a Creed is properly called a symbol of belief, for it is an attempt to express in language a faith-situation. The whole Creed hangs together as one expression; nevertheless it contains a number of expressions within it, traditionally called, in the case of the Apostles' Creed, the Twelve Articles. Suppose you take one of these articles by itself. Take the sixth: "He ascended into heaven, and sitteth at the right hand of God, the Father Almighty." Remember that in Greek, the original language in which the Creed was written, the word for heaven is simply the word for the sky. You might very well read the words, therefore, as if you were dealing with language such as: "He walked up Fifth Avenue and stood at the left of the Frick Museum." This would be nonsense. If you read the other eleven articles of the Creed along with this one, you ought to see that it is at any rate unlikely that you are dealing with that kind of language. You would actually be dealing with several kinds of language within the one document; but no awareness of this could by itself enable you to make sense of the whole. Not only would you have to interpret one article in the Creed in the light of the others; you would have to interpret the Creed itself in terms of a still larger frame of reference.

Facial Expression and Other Forms of Language

Even in the course of ordinary conversation we make use of various types of language. For instance, our facial expression is a form of language; so is our tone of voice. We sometimes pay to go to hear a distinguished speaker deliver a speech that we know we shall be able to read verbatim in the next morning's paper. We prefer, however, to go to hear him deliver it; moreover, we are hardly content with a seat in which we can hear him but cannot see him, for even this is important. Nor need it be mere curiosity: we may have seen the man dozens of times — every day, even. The point is that if we consider his speech to be really worth while, we account it worth our while to go to see and hear him deliver it, for we know that he will be communicating more than is communicated in the words themselves. Indeed, it would be a reproach to him if we were able to say that we might as well have stayed at home and read the speech in the next day's paper. Besides tone of voice and facial expression, a man will also use — especially if he is a Latin by race — a great many gestures, which form a language by themselves, helping the other languages he uses. Much of all this we could get on TV; but so informative are the various languages other than speech, and so delicate the communication, that we generally suppose it is preferable to see and hear him in the flesh than on a screen. If we really wanted to study his speech with very great care, the best plan would be to see and hear the speaker in person, then see it on TV, and finally read it in the paper.

We express ourselves in innumerable other ways besides these: a garden, for instance, may express what the owner cannot, for one reason or another, put into words. Flowers and plants may in fact be used in highly symbolic ways, as for instance in the medieval Lady Garden, now revived, which conveys much religious meaning to those who "know the language." Our great-grandparents used in their amorous communications, a "Language of Flowers" that was capable of expressing quite intricate emotions and of describing complex situations connected with them. We express ourselves in ritual and ceremonial: by a bow, a nod, a formal salute, or a wink, I express a particular response to a particular situation. It is to be noted that such observances have no significance in themselves: they acquire it from the circumstances. One of the writer's students, a Japanese girl, bowed at the beginning of practically every sentence, hers and mine. Wondering whether she were perhaps finding it necessary to do my bows for me vicariously, in addition to her own, I tried to contribute a few here and there myself. This seemed to work fairly well in a way. But when the next student, an American, came up for interview, I forgot to change and went on with the bows till this student's astonished eye caught mine. It was almost as if I had been talking Japanese and had gone on talking it with the American. The bows were a sort of gesture-language: my feeble attempts at it were all right in their place, but with the American student they were of course entirely out of place. Such languages are very restricted in scope and content: what can be done with them is limited compared with what can be done with speech. But we shall see that it is partly for this very reason that they usefully contribute to the complicated fabric of language systems that are found necessary in religion. Religion, being multidimensional, needs a multidimensional language.

Symbolism and the Mass

The Roman Mass may be taken as an example of numerous types of religious language being used concomitantly, like "parts" in polyphonous music. Throughout the Mass, the celebrating priest is using various gestures. For instance, he will frequently "make the sign of the cross"; he will at certain words place his left hand under his breast; sometimes he will join his hands together; sometimes he will extend them. Three degrees of bowing are used: one a slight nod of the head, another a somewhat deeper inclination of the head and shoulders, and yet another a deep bow. There are also various ways of directing the eyes: sometimes they should be directed to the Cross, sometimes "to heaven." At a certain point he will wash the tips of his forefingers and thumbs. At the elevation of the Host an acolyte or server will slightly lift the end of the priest's chasuble to symbolize the union of priest and people in the sacrificial act. A careful celebrant will see that the Host is raised in a straight line over the white cloth or "corporal," and as he replaces the chalice after the consecration he will see that both his hands are placed flat on the corporal before he genuflects. This he must do so that his right knee touches the ground. When he makes three crosses with the Host over the mouth of the chalice he will take care to see that his hands do not pass the chalice rim. He will move from the "south" side of the sanctuary to the "north" side to read the Gospel, so symbolizing the direction in which the Gospel was first spread, from Jerusalem northwards to the Mediterranean lands and beyond. But all this time he will be using words too. Some of these will be intended to be audible; others will be meant to be inaudible, being said in a very low voice, while others again will be said only under his breath, secretly.

If it is a High Mass, the choir will be singing the *Sanctus* while the priest is already saying to himself the entirely different words of the prayer beginning *Te igitur*. The Book will be "incensed" three times before the deacon sings the words of the Gospel from it, while two candle-bearers stand by. If it is Palm Sunday, a special "tone" will be used in singing the story of the Passion. All this elaborate and complicated ritual expresses and symbolizes ideas. It does not do so in the same manner as does, say, the Creed, which also forms part of the Mass. But it is not only a case of a language of gesture and a language of words. The sequence of the prayers is itself symbolic, and there is an elaborate symbolism in every article of dress worn by the clergy. The wax tapers, originally utilitarian, have acquired intricate symbolic meaning. The taper, being consumed while spreading its light, is held to symbolize the sacrificial death that brought light to the world. The white wax produced by the bee symbolizes the human nativity of the Logos (Christ) made flesh in the womb of the Virgin Mother. The medieval writer Hugh of St. Victor provides the following symbolical interpretation of the taper: "Just as wax is formed from the juice of spotless flowers in the virginal body of the bee, and this, made into a taper, surrounds the wick, and from the union of these two the light is produced, so in like manner the Body of the Lord, taken from the spotless Virgin Mother and surrounding His glorious soul, when united to His divine nature, sheds its light over all creation."

These are but a few instances to illustrate the complexity of the symbolism connected with the Roman Mass. Even if the worshiper's mind wanders from what is going on at the altar, his eye is met at every turn by iconographic representations throughout the building; his ear is greeted by music of a peculiar sort; even his nostrils are assailed by the smell of incense that symbolizes the rising of prayer from the hearts of the people to the Throne of God. Nor should it be supposed that the Reformed Church has no place for nonverbal symbolism, for though the Reformers protested against neglect of the symbolism of the Word, they insisted upon the importance of the Sacrament in the life of the worshiping Church. The one, they said, ought not to be separated from the other. The symbolism of a religion, becoming impoverished or decadent, may indeed require reform; but in religion no one can avoid the use of symbolism, nor should one wish that it were possible to do so. The more lively the religion the more complex its symbolism has to be, for it is thus that it secures what protection it can get against the ever-present danger of literalism, which is fatal to the life of any religion.

Use of Symbol Presupposes Knowledge of Clue

The complexity of religious symbolism is a safeguard against literalism, but this fact does nothing to make the symbols signify anything to those who do not have the clue. There is, indeed, no conceivable way in which a symbol could ever be of any use to anyone who does not already have some kind of experience of what it symbolizes, and in the case of religious symbolism the experience itself presupposes a commitment that is unique in its comprehensiveness and vivacity. The language of religion is akin to the language of love: it presupposes an interpretation of all experience in terms of the loved object to which the lover is so fundamentally dedicated that he is willing to risk everything upon his trust in the object of his love. It is true that one may be in love with a dream-object; but none more than a lover is aware of the distinction between the experience of being in love with a dream-object and the experience of being committed to another whose reality is as indubitable as the reality of one's own self-awareness. The Christian likewise knows that much religious symbolism symbolizes dream-objects ("man's quest for the divine"!); but it is impossible for him to confound such symbols with those which symbolize events that have made possible his encounter with The Other; e.g., the Cross (death of Christ) and the Empty Tomb (resurrection).

"Performative" Utterances

The language of lovers is itself, however, of various kinds, having various functions to perform. The absent lover repetitiously assures his beloved of his undying affection. His assurances are as genuine, as sincere, as human love can make them; they may nevertheless also have the other functions of reminding the lover of his commitment, and they may act also as a warning to himself against philandering and infidelity. A wife has sound reasons besides mere personal vanity for expecting frequent assurances of her husband's love, and for protesting against any tendency of his to plead that his assurance is unnecessary since he gave it only a few weeks ago. The love-language is also part of the wooing process itself, having therefore the function of a "performative" utterance. So part of the language of worship is an element in the worship itself. That is what is meant by preachers who say that the service of corporate worship in church is not merely a *reminder* of a "real experience" but is *part* of the encounter with Christ. On the other hand, another kind of religious symbolism is used in theological reflection, which is not intended to have any such "performative" function at all. Both the theologian and the metaphysician talk about religion, using metaphors and analogies; but the theologian is a special sort of metaphysician — one who takes into account and presupposes the actuality of a religious situation, so that he conceives his task in terms of the consideration of the implications and consequences of a special commitment. Theological symbolism differs in several important ways from the symbolism used in religious worship, for it has a different function to perform. Theology, like metaphysics, is concerned with relating symbolic forms to the Being that lies beyond them. The metaphysician faces so much difficulty in doing this that it is not surprising that many philosophers are disposed to deny the possibility of his ever doing it at all. The theologian seeks, however, only to give a coherent account of the very complex situations that arise from the unique commitment apart from which theology would have nothing to talk about. This self-limitation on the part of theology is its weakness and its strength: its weakness since it must present its results as, in some sense, a "closed system," and must therefore be unsatisfactory in the light of all lively religious experience itself, apart from which it has no conceivable interest to anyone at all; its strength because it points continually to the special attitude and the unique commitment that are the indispensable clue to an understanding of its symbolic forms. When the religious worshiper cries, "O Thou who art infinitely exalted above our loftiest thoughts yet art nearer to us than life itself," the theologian recognizes the situation symbolized in the worshiper's prayer; but it is the business of the theologian, as such, to treat the situation discursively, analyzing the worshiper's utterance in such a way as to discern and draw forth the intellectual consequences of what is revealed in it. The kinds of symbolism suitable for such an enterprise are likely to be very dissimilar to those kinds that are suited to worship; as dissimilar as are mathematical symbols to the symbols of poetry. Nevertheless, both the symbols of the theologian and those of the worshiper have a common reference point. Apart from this reference point neither could have any meaning, and so no proposition or other linguistic utterance containing them could make sense.

Religious Commitment and Theological Prattle

A final note is necessary here. From the fact that a man seems to have great facility in *handling* theological terms it is not to be concluded that he necessarily has "the clue." He may, for a variety of reasons, have a psychological aptitude for theology *as a game*. Similarly, a person much given to religious devotion, or a person who endlessly "talks religion," need not by any means be one who has made the authentic encounter. A smart child can often learn to prattle extensively on the subject of love stories he has read. His prattling will usually evoke only a tolerant smile from his adult friends; still, it is possible that he might write an essay on the subject that would carry some measure of conviction with those who did not know the author and assumed that he must be a mature man who knew what he was talking about. Boy violinists, adding a highly developed mimetic gift to an innate genius for music, have sometimes played the violin as if they had the full range of adult emotions. Such phenomena have, of course, a psychological interest; but they do not at all affect our central contention that no forms of religious symbolism can have any significance apart from the commitment that is their reference point.

DISCUSSION ON CHAPTER 43

1. A map of the world symbolically represents the world. A distortion may be deliberately introduced, as in Mercator's Projection. Consider the principles involved with reference to their application to religious contexts.

2. Discuss, in view of the nature of religious symbolism, the use of the Verification Principle adopted by modern philosophers.

3. Discuss the notion of "polyphony" in religious symbolism.

44

Theological Language

Peculiarity of Theological Language

That theology should require a special sort of language with a peculiar logical structure need not surprise us. Every field of human inquiry or discussion has to find a language suited to its particular needs. The language of chemists would be of no use to psychologists, whose language would be likewise quite unsuited to the needs of the chemists. The languages used by chemists and musicians are so neat and crisp and tidy that political and legal theorists, groaning over the lengthy disquisitions they have to read, may cast an envious glance now and then at the work of those who seem to have a much easier way of saying things; but of course they know that it is the peculiarity of their own subject matter that makes it impossible for them to devise means of expression that would compare in brevity with chemical formulas or in accuracy with musical scores. Every subject matter has its own peculiarities and the problems of language are much greater in certain fields than they are in others.

Special Difficulties in Theological Language

The discussion of theology is attended by very difficult language problems. It is not only that it cannot compete in brevity or conciseness with chemistry or mathematics; it demands a structure so unusual that its very oddity must often be disguised under *apparently* ordinary linguistic patterns in such a way that the casual observer fails to detect the curious hidden structure. The casual observer, reading in a book on Christian theology the words, "In one God there are three Persons," may easily conclude that the Christian answer to the question, "Is God personal?" should be "God is tri-personal." It would not be particularly difficult to show the source of his confusion here: you would only have to explain that the word "person," being derived from the Latin word *persona* (the mask that an actor wore for a particular role) which was used in an attempt to translate a technical term in Greek philosophy, has at most only the vaguest connection with the modern notion of personality that is implied in the question, "Is God personal?" It would be more difficult to explain how it can be held that God is eternal while it is also held that one Person in Him "proceeds" from the other two. How can there be "procession" in that which is eternal?

Illustration of the Difficulties

In order to consider how one might go about explaining the significance of saying that God is eternal and that there is nevertheless "procession" in Him, we may begin by looking at the origins of Christian thought. How did anyone ever find it necessary to engage in discussions involving such extremely difficult linguistic problems? We may recall the circumstances as follows. The men who were attracted to Jesus, who heard Him preach, saw Him carry His Cross to Calvary, and believed that He, having died and being risen from the dead, walked and talked and dined with them before He "was parted from them," [1] recognized Him to be unique. Their attitude toward Him and their interpretation of their relationship to Him reflected this belief in His uniqueness. In their preaching they tried to express that uniqueness, using the terms that came to mind in their particular circumstances, notably the circumstance that they themselves were naturally most familiar with the language of their ancestral Jewish faith, but also the circumstance that there were sometimes Gentiles in their audience. In their endeavor to express the uniqueness of Him whom they proclaimed, they would say at one moment that He was the most perfect man in the whole human race, and the next moment they would be heard to declare that He was God. As the torrent of their eloquence poured forth you might have found one of them shouting that God had glorified His servant Jesus; then a minute later the same preacher would be calling Jesus "the Prince of life," that is, seeming to attribute to Him the authorship of life itself. If you had been in such an audience, hearing such a preacher for the first time, you might well have scratched your head and said, as in effect many of the hearers did say: "But wait a minute — which is it to be, God or man? We're really very interested to hear about this Jesus, and we want to learn your point of view on the subject. But surely there's a confusion somewhere: are you saying Jesus is God, or are you saying Jesus is man? He must be one or the other; no one can be both. Make up your mind and then perhaps we'll be able to follow you. At least we'll know where we stand." Then the preacher might say, "He is the Son of God." But how can God have a son? And even if God had a son, would not the son be another god? Was the preacher saying there were two gods?

Some members of the audience would see in their own way what

[1] Luke 24:51.

the preacher was trying to say. They "caught on." Others would not, and would conclude that the preacher was talking nonsense, because what he was saying would not fit the logical structure to which they were accustomed. Those who "caught on," the converts, believed they saw the point; but they had no language in which they could express it. The best they could do seemed to others to be a mere talking in riddles, and they had to admit themselves that it did *sound* like gibberish. Only very gradually were they able, with the help of those of their number who were good at that sort of thing, to devise better ways of expressing the unique situation they knew and wanted to describe. At first they experimented with various devices. Yes, Christ was the Son of God, they said; but He was not "a son" in the ordinary sense, for God was not "a father" in the ordinary sense. Christ, they suggested, was the "eternal Son" of God. He was not created by God; He is eternally generated by God. That took care of one misunderstanding; but it immediately posed another problem. Christ, they now seemed to be saying, was not a son in the ordinary sense, for He is eternal; nevertheless, He is generated, and is not that to say that He is begotten? Is it not in the nature of begetting that it should take place in time? At any rate, even if we waive this point, surely there can be no question but that a son must always come after his father? As Arius put it, surely there must have been a time when the Son did not exist? No, came the reply, not *this* Son; this Son is the "Only Son," not merely in the sense of being "an only child," but in the sense of being "the Unique Son" (*monogenēs, filius unicus, filius unigenitus*), and so you must not expect Him to stand in the same relation to His Father *in all respects* as a human son stands to his father.

Theological Language and Historical Context

To talk like this is to invite the question: "All right then, just tell me: in what respect is it that the relation between this Unique Son and His Unique Father is analogous to the relation between me and my father?" The questioner may be quite willing to accept the notion that the analogy is not to be pressed too far; but he insists that if there is to be any point at all in calling Christ the Son of God there must be some respect in which the human son-father relationship resembles or exhibits the Christ-God relationship. The difficulty is, however, that no one could really detect the resemblance without first knowing Christ. The use of the son-father analogy has by this time, however, created several types of misunderstanding, and so other devices are tried as correctives. Christ, it is said, is of the same "essence" as God. But how can Christ, who is also said to be a human being, be of the same "essence" as God? Is it not that He is such a very exceptional man that His "essence" may be said to *resemble* God's "essence"? Not at all, comes the reply: the whole point is that Christ has really two *natures*, a divine nature and a human nature. Two separate natures in one Being, Christ? No, the two natures are not separated; they are united. But how? And if they are united, then the woman who was empirically, physiologically, the mother of Jesus, must have been a woman who bore God in her womb. True: she was called, therefore, *Theotokos*, the God-bearer. Then she may be acclaimed the Mother of God? On the face of it, the statement that Mary is the Mother of God is absurd. If there is any doubt in your mind of this, you have only to reflect that it implies that Mary's mother, Anna,[2] is God's grandmother. But the very absurdity of the implication is a pointer to a peculiarity in the structure of the phrase "Mother of God." No one ever wanted to claim that the relation between Mary and God was a parent-child relationship such as that of Anna and Mary. Biologically, a child depends for its very existence upon its parents, and of course God could not depend for His existence on Mary or anyone else. Nevertheless, if Christ was God and man, as the Christians held, and if He was indeed physiologically conceived in the womb of Mary and was born of her as every child is born of his mother, then it could be said that Mary, being His mother, could be called the Mother of God. The word "mother" acquires, however, a peculiar meaning — one that it does not possess in ordinary discourse — because of the unique situation. Much importance was attached by many to the use of the phrase because it *drew attention* to the unique situation to which Christian faith testified, namely, that "God was in Christ." [3] Far from being a biological statement, it was an additional safeguard against neglecting the peculiarity of the situation, against falling into any position that might lead to the conclusion: "God was *not* in Christ."

These are only a few examples from the history of the development of Christian theology in the first few centuries of our era. They are intended to show, in a general way, how theological discourse arises, and what is the nature of theological propositions. Examples might well be taken, of course, from other sources. But the ones we have chosen indicate the characteristic situation that gives rise to theological reflection, and they illustrate the peculiarity of theological propositions, showing that their function is different from that of all other types of utterance. They plainly differ from empirical propositions such as, "There is a zebra in the zoo." They are not merely poetical utterances, such as

[2] According to an early tradition. Her name is not mentioned in the Bible.
[3] II Cor. 5:19.

> The frost-fires kindle, and soon
> Over that sea of frozen foam
> Floats the white moon.[4]

Nor are they of the same character as metaphysical propositions, which purport to make assertions about "being," "reality," and the like. As an example of metaphysical language we might take the following: "In dread there is no annihilation of the whole of what-is in itself; but equally we cannot negate what-is-in-totality in order to reach Nothing." [5] The technical terms used here have been devised in order to make statements about "first principles" — statements that have no empirical reference at all. Some propositions purporting to be theological may be really metaphysical ones in disguise, and no doubt genuine theological propositions raise questions that may be of interest to metaphysicians; but theological language expresses a concern or commitment that would be as out of place in metaphyics as it would be in chemistry or poetry. The language of Christian theology, moreover, is, as we have seen, meaningful only in its peculiar historical context. For instance, to talk as Christians do of the uniqueness of the Incarnation of God in Christ would have no meaning in the context of a religious tradition in which it was accounted quite common for deity and humanity to be conjoined — in Hinduism, for example, where *avatars* of deity are supposed to be not infrequent occurrences in the course of history. The Christian doctrine of the Incarnation acquires its peculiar significance only in the historical context of a tradition in which, as in Judaism, God is accounted so far removed from man that the last thing to be expected is that He should "become man." And yet, for the Christian, this act of God in becoming man is seen as the full, perfect and sufficient revelation of God to man, so that it creates that unique situation apart from which the many problems discussed in Christian theology cannot meaningfully be raised at all.

DISCUSSION ON CHAPTER 44

1. Discuss the proposition that religious discourse requires the life of an historic religious community as its frame of reference.

2. "If only there were fewer dogmas it would be easier to accept what the theologians say." Discuss.

3. The Nicene Creed affirms that Jesus Christ
   (a) descended from heaven,

---

[4] Walter de la Mare, *Winter.*
[5] M. Heidegger, *Existence and Being* (Chicago: Henry Regnery Co., 1949), "What is Metaphysics?" p. 368.

(b) was incarnate by the Holy Ghost, born of the Virgin Mary,

(c) suffered under Pontius Pilate,

(d) sitteth at the right hand of God the Father Almighty,

(e) shall come to judge the quick [6] and the dead.

Consider the various kinds of language used. For example, would it make any difference to the truth or falsity of (a) if it were conceded that there is no locality that may be called "heaven," or if it were affirmed that there is such a locality but that it is so situated that the expression "descended" is unsuitable? Would it affect the truth or falsity of (c) if it could be shown that contrary to what has been commonly supposed, Pontius Pilate was on vacation at the time of Christ's trial and his place taken by a deputy?

[6] I.e., the living.

EPILOGUE:

PERSONAL REFLECTIONS

Intellectual Integrity of the Religious Philosopher

The religious philosopher, in his singlemindedness and fidelity to the pursuit of truth for its own sake, is in the same case as any other philosopher. Far from taking sides, all genuine philosophers are on the alert for prejudice which, lurking at the back of their minds, might vitiate the impartiality, and consequently the success, of their enterprise. Their constant vigilance in this ought to be a background to all their thinking; as much so, to say the least, as that of a clever detective in a murder case in taking account of possible motives among his suspects. The religious philosopher is no exception; indeed his scent for prejudice is likely to be peculiarly sharp, for he usually has more experience than other men in encountering and detecting it.

It is true that, unless he is to be a Perpetual Sophomore, he must and will develop views of his own. But these views, though they may, and indeed must, be evident in his presentation, ought not to obtrude themselves in a *personal* way. He ought to be from first to last untainted by even the slightest suspicion of partisanship. It is not that he ought to lack convictions. On the contrary, he cannot be a very profound thinker, or even a very lively one, if he has insufficiently developed these. But they must be *intellectual* convictions. There ought to be in them no hint of confession of faith masquerading as mental activity. The religious philosopher's convictions are legitimate only to the extent that they are the outcome of the exercise of his métier.

The Religious Philosopher and the Theologian

In all this the religious philosopher is strikingly distinguished from the theologian. His relationship to the theologian is, however, unique. Since he is the only person in the world who is and must be willing to take the theologian seriously *at an intellectual level*, the latter ought

315

surely to pay him the respect that is due in return for intellectual sympathy, though in fact he not infrequently neglects this duty, to the detriment of his own moral and intellectual respectability. But the religious philosopher as such ought not to be a theologian *in his working hours*. Or, if he does wish to engage in the interesting but dangerous enterprise of leading a double life, he must be careful to remember that he *is* leading a double life: he is to beware of confusing his roles. As a theologian he is committed to the acceptance of certain postulates which may even be set forth in propositional form. As a religious philosopher he must practice a rigorous intellectual self-denial that precludes any procedure of that kind.

How the Religious Philosopher May Profit From Personal Commitment

There is, however, a more subtle element in the religious philosopher's situation. Though he is to have no intellectual commitment, he may have a personal commitment (for example, to theism or atheism), and although his intellectual activity in the exercise of his métier as a religious philosopher must be *independent* of all such personal commitment, it may be very profitably *informed* by this. Indeed, the character of the personal experience or encounter that is the ground of such personal commitment is not only singularly informative to the religious philosopher who has enjoyed it; it is in the nature of the case the most relevant and reliable information he can possibly bring to his field of investigation.

To say this is not to say anything novel or surprising to anyone familiar with the history of philosophy, even at the most rudimentary level. The principle we owe to Descartes, that thinking must begin with the self, has, since the seventeenth century, affected in one way or another, and for good or ill, the whole methodology of western thought. If religious questions are to be considered at an intellectual level, where am I to get information and other pabulum for profitably discussing them? I may read books about the history of religion; better still, I may observe, for example, in mosques and churches and temples, what religion appears to be, dramatizing myself as far as possible into the mood of the worshipers so as to become in some sense a Moslem in the mosque, a Jew in the synagogue, a Greek Orthodox Christian at the Solemn Liturgy, and a Quaker at a Quaker meeting. Growing learned in the history of religion, I may choose to conclude, with Max Müller, that "he who knows but one religion knows no religion," or with Adolf Harnack, who, speaking of Christianity, said that "he who knows this religion knows all religions." [1]

---

[1] "Wer eine Religion kennt, kennt keine," said Müller, to which Harnack replied: "Wer diese Religion kennt, kennt alle."

But unless I am singularly ungifted in philosophical criticism I cannot but reflect that I should in any case be better off with a definite personal commitment of my own, since I could study this at much closer range than anything else that might conceivably be available to me.

On the assumption — a necessary one — that I am scrupulously conscientious in my devotion to my philosophic task, there is an element of doubt when I am studying *your* commitment that is not present when I am studying my own. To be sure, in both cases there is a psychological question of an extremely obvious and elementary sort, namely, "Is the experience the result of subjective factors only and wholly explicable in terms of these?" But when the subject of my study is *not* myself I have to answer *also* the vital question, "Have I really understood what the experience *is?* Have I not, rather, misinterpreted its very nature?"

In examining my own experience I have at any rate the advantage of certainty in regard to the *manner* in which it presents itself to me. For example, if it presents itself to me as anything other than self-engendered; if I am even more certain that it is of the nature of an invitation by a Presence other than myself than I am sure that the man who has just walked into the room is really addressing me; then I cannot be satisfied with any slick explanation of it as either an instance of the power or range of complexity of my emotions on the one hand or, on the other, as falling under the category of aesthetic experience such as my narcissistic enjoyment of a poem or symphony or fresco might be. I recognize that I might be mistaken at some point in my interpretation of my own experience; but if I pretend to any kind of human knowledge at all I am bound also to make a distinction: this "religious" experience or encounter, whatever it is, is not at any rate to be identified with aesthetic experience, to which I am much accustomed, or with the emotional states which, under many guises, constitute a familiar element in my total awareness. To put the matter in sexual terms such as have come to play so large a part in the discourse of psychologists, we may say that it will be as difficult for you to persuade me that my "religious" experience is of the same character as my artistic experience, as it would be for you to convince a happily married couple that there is no difference between sexual intercourse and masturbation. They might, if they happened to be professional philosophers, consider the question by way of academic exercise; but you would not really expect this to affect their personal assurance on the subject. The personal assurance that forces a man to call his "religious experience" an "encounter" so as to distinguish it from the more narcissistic elements in his total awareness is no less unassailable. This does not mean that he cannot err in his interpretation. It certainly does not mean that his interpretation must be correct in every detail. It does mean, however, that the distinction his experience teaches him to make is strikingly relevant to any philosophical inquiry on the subject of religion.

The Relevance of Personal Commitment to Religious Philosophy

It is not mere curiosity that prompts people to ask, when they read a book about religious philosophy: "But what are the author's *personal* convictions? His intellectual *position* is not difficult to detect in the course of my reading of his book. But I should like to know what it means to him. Is he engaged in an academic pursuit? Is he playing an intellectual game? Or does his subject mean far more to him than this?"

Plainly such questions would never be asked of, say, a geologist. For all the geologist is likely to care *personally*, the moon might just as well be made of blue cheese. Scientists, it is true, may sometimes have a deep personal concern with their work beyond that of discovery. The case of Madame Curie springs at once to mind, and in our own day the work of atomic physicists has often been accompanied by personal soul-searching arising out of the peculiar implications of progress in this realm of scientific advance. But although the personal interest of a scientist in the implications of his inquiries and discoveries may provoke press interviews resulting in newspaper articles of passing interest to the general public, it really does not matter to anyone whether a scientist is, in his private attitude toward his work, a deeply sensitive humanitarian or a cold fish who does not even bother to reflect whether he may or may not be helping to destroy mankind. You do not ask, when you hire an accountant, whether he is a man that will rejoice with you when your balance sheet shows a profit and weep when he announces your bankruptcy. You want a good accountant who will, by doing his job properly, give you the required facts. Even in having your portrait painted, it would not deter you if you heard it said of the artist you had in mind, "Funny thing — he hates people and only paints portraits for a living; yet he is the best portrait painter in America." You would probably say, quite rightly, "I don't care whether he hates me or not — let him go ahead, so long as I can afford his fee." You might be curious about his misanthropy; but you would not let it interfere with your judgment of his professional capabilities.

Very different is the case of the religious philosopher. His personal commitment is not an accidental concomitant of his work. It is of the greatest relevance to it, for it is the indispensable special laboratory providing him with the most conclusive type of evidence available in his field. It is for this reason that some account will now be given of the author's personal concern with the problems discussed in this book, together with a statement of his personal attitude and commitment.

Autobiographical Background

I have never been able to find much natural sympathy with those who say that, having been brought up in a "religious" environment, they accepted it till they went to college, where, having decided they had had "enough of church," they "became skeptics," and that was that. My own skepticism began at a very much earlier age and was exceedingly fierce. It still is, though it has a thinner time nowadays, having found more than a match in my faith.

My early preoccupation with such questions was due in some measure, perhaps, to my European upbringing. Children in Europe are expected not only to behave but even to think as adults at a much earlier age than is common in America. In my day this was even more strikingly so. But there were in my case domestic circumstances and personal idiosyncracies that aggravated the situation. It happens that I am one of those persons whose recollections of childhood are vivid and go back to an extremely early age. Many of these recollections are connected with my maternal grandmother who, having been born in Scotland in 1828, was in her eighties when I was born there in 1909. (She had been almost fifty when her last child was born, and both my parents, whose only child I was, were past forty when I first remember them.) My parents' attitude toward religion was anything other than fanatical: it was, rather, one of deep reverence before an inscrutable mystery. Family worship in the evening was frequent, though there was no inflexible rule about it. In any case it was brief, consisting of a short chapter or passage from the Bible (always read in a tone of quiet reverence) and a prayer. The passage was read either by my father or my mother, or, when I was old enough to read, I might be asked to take my turn if the passage were accounted easy enough for me. The prayer was invariably offered by my father, for in our Scottish Presbyterian tradition it would have been considered indecent for a woman to offer prayer when a man, or even a boy over the age of fourteen, was available for the purpose. The father was the priest of the family. As for a woman offering prayer in the presence of a clergyman, the possibility had not even occurred to me till I was seven, when a female representative of some "fancy sect" called on us and, notwithstanding the presence of my uncle — a clergyman of very venerable appearance, with a clerical collar and huge black beard — had the effrontery to invite us to our knees in prayer to be offered by her. Even when my uncle had complied, I firmly maintained a sitting posture, regarding the whole proceeding as thoroughly blasphemous. Not even my uncle's subsequent explanation that she did not know any better, or his kindly injunction to me to exhibit a spirit of charity toward the ignorant and arrogant, had much effect upon me. I felt that he ought not to have permitted the outrage. My father would no sooner have presumed to offer prayer in the presence of my uncle than a male worshiper in St. Peter's Basilica would presume to ascend the papal throne and bestow the pontifical benediction.

Nevertheless, it was to my grandmother that I owed the most systematic religious instruction I ever received as a small child. In retrospect I admire her very much. At the time I loved her. I liked to visit her, and in the course of those visits, when we were alone, much of the time was devoted to religious instruction which she imparted with great dramatic power, for she was a very gifted and well-read woman. I have the most clear recollections of such instruction. from her at a time when I was certainly no more than two and a half years old. She got me to stand on a stool while she sat down and taught me to repeat verses, principally from the Lord's Prayer and the Twenty-third Psalm. These would be sometimes in English, which she enunciated with great clarity and exceptional beauty of diction, and sometimes in her native Scottish Gaelic, which I did not understand but which I faithfully repeated and afterwards generally forgot, so that more and more she resorted to English as the medium of instruction. The prize for a fair performance was a small glass of cream; excellence was rewarded with honey, of which I was fond. After these preliminary exercises, she would place me in a high chair opposite her and very close, so that I could see her face. Then followed a discourse far above my capacity to understand. I could only make out certain frequently recurring words such as "God" and "Heaven." Yet I understood far more than I could possibly have followed in words. For I watched her face, whose wrinkles seemed infinite in number and no less infinite in fascination, because somehow or other they seemed to communicate to me what she was saying in words far beyond my understanding. Her facial expression constantly changed. From that picture book I got impressions which I pieced together with the few words I understood. Somehow or other she succeeded in communicating to me her own sense of the awful Majesty and Glory of God, of how He could twirl the earth, the sun, the moon and all the stars within the palm of His hand far more easily than she or I could twirl marbles. Her vivacious old face, yellow as parchment, darkened with awe while her deep violet eyes turned slowly upwards as she began to speak of God. Her small white hands extended in a magnificent gesture as she endeavored to convey to me something of the infinite power of Him who, I gathered, spread out oceans and raised up mountains with a surer hand than we could employ in spreading butter on a slice of bread. The awful reverence in her voice, the mighty strength in her firm lips, and above all the flashing brightness of her piercing violet eyes, all conveyed to me the impression of a Being so tremendous, so great, so powerful, that even my father, even the strongest man on earth, must bow down in terror before Him. Whether through words or expression she also conveyed to me the sense that this Being was of such dazzling whiteness and brightness that if we could see Him — which mercifully we could not — we should instantly fall down dead, like little moths before a bright light.

Then, as I listened and watched, spellbound and enthralled, though no doubt also scared, her whole countenance would change with a dramatic swiftness. It was not merely that she was now smiling; her whole face glowed with a soft radiance till every wrinkle seemed to be lighted up from behind and smiling. Her eyes, gently moist, looked at me with encompassing affection as she told me that the most wonderful part of the story was yet to come, for He whose Presence was such as to strike terror in the heart of the strongest of men had Himself a heart as infinitely stupendous as the rest of Him. So it was, she explained, that He had chosen to become a little child smaller than even I then was, just so that He might help us, just so that He might make us able to be better than we are and so one day go to Heaven, a place very much more beautiful and exciting than earth.

Well can I remember how, on one such occasion, I was distracted for a moment by the sound of a mouse scratching behind the skirting board. I did not like mice.

"It's only a little mouse," she said. Then she added quietly, in her most magnificent manner, something like this: "How would you like to turn yourself into a little mouse and crawl behind the wall into the dark hole the mice live in, so that you might help them to grow into something more beautiful? You wouldn't. Neither would I. But the heart of our God who made us is greater than ours, and that is what He did for us when he became Jesus our Saviour. It was far more horrible for Him to become one of us than it would be for you or me to become a mouse. For we are only a little better than mice. But He is good and holy; He is perfect; He is Lord of all, King of all. . . ."

It was impressive. She told me of how cruel men had crucified Jesus, and of how He, being both God and Man, had risen in great glory and showed Himself to His apostles. She told me of how Thomas had at first doubted. Thomas was my father's name, so perhaps I listened with a sort of proprietary interest at that point. At any rate, the general impression I had was of being in the presence of realities far more vivid than those of ordinary life and so in many ways more interesting. It was certainly effective Christian instruction. Whether despite or because of the eighty years between us, she and I "clicked." The barriers of communication were surmounted, and by the time I was three I understood the meaning of orthodox Christianity as well as it need be understood by anyone not a theologian.

Though my grandmother lived well into her nineties, I rarely saw her after I was five, for she moved about that time to another town. When I was seven my father died. Sometime before then I had gone to Sunday school, an experience that so appalled and bored me that after two or three attendances I begged not to have to submit to it any more. I can remember nothing about it except that it was singularly dreary. Either on account of the preoccupation at home with my father's illness, or because Sunday school was felt to be unnecessary for my spiritual well-being, I was, to my immense relief, dispensed from having to endure further doses of it.

I Become an Atheist

Though I did not attend Sunday school, I went with unfailing regularity to church. During my father's illness I sometimes even went alone. By the age of eight I had become, however, very impatient of the whole business. It was, of course, impossible for me to express to myself with any precision, at the time, the nature of my changed attitude. The homiletic efforts of the minister, whose sermons were as dry as dehumidified dust, and who looked, at any rate to my hypercritical childish eye, for all the world like Humpty Dumpty (he was a short man with a disproportionately large head as unhirsute as an egg), had done nothing to stay the tide of my rising interior rebellion. The visits of a well-meaning elder with shaggy eyebrows and a monotonous discourse that revealed, to me, only a peculiarly striking emptiness, were unfortunate. His voice seemed to be admirably adapted to express his absence of religious insight: I recall having likened it to the growling of my own stomach when it was empty. He was probably a good stockbroker, and as far as I can now judge he was no doubt a man of notable moral integrity; but his success in having evaded the Pentecostal flame was spectacular. I conceived a peculiar distaste for him: soon he had become my principal allergy. Fortunately he called only four times a year, and as it was possible to prognosticate his visits to some extent, I was sometimes able to avoid them. Unfortunately, on the other hand, for my then flagging faith, these visits were closely associated with celebrations of the Holy Eucharist, so that any affection I might have acquired for that central act of Christian worship was undermined in advance. I had already, in any case, however, a definite grudge connected with the Sacrament: it seemed to be the privilege of the grown-up, many of whom appeared to me to be very much more interested in golf or some fancy way of cooking salmon than they were in the Mysteries of the Altar to which they alluded with much sanctimonious humbug. I felt an acute self-awareness; a sense also of the injustice of the situation. Egocentrically, I rebelled against it. Henceforth I sought to avoid churchgoing as far as possible. My efforts were not, however, entirely successful.

My disappointment with the elder, abundantly reinforced with parallel experiences, started in me a whole train of thought about God and the Church. At first my rebellion was of an anti-ecclesiastical rather than an atheistic kind. I was precociously addicted to literary creation, having begun to write short stories (of a sort) when I was seven. Within a year or so after that, my mother and other relatives were beginning to note with some disquiet an unmistakable tendency in my stories that was unfavorable to the Scottish Presbyterian tradition. The villain, who, in the first flowering of my literary efforts, had been generally an ogre or other such mythical and therefore socially innocuous personage, now too often turned out to be (sometimes with diabolical unexpectedness) a Presbyterian elder. Emboldened by the mirth of some of my readers, I even tried my hand at placing my villains within the ranks of the Holy Ministry. These artistic frolics were, however, but the prelude to a more serious interior revolt.

I cannot recall exactly how it began; but sometime at least a month or so before my ninth birthday I had developed an intense hostility toward all ideas connected with the Deity. I approached the whole subject of my own skepticism with some timidity. I was at first a little afraid of my own rebellion. But I realized that I could not go on forever without taking a stand. I felt in any case a coward for not having taken it before. Though still a little troubled by doubt, I felt increasingly disposed to regard the whole matter of religion as detrimental to life, a poison that was the chief source of the evil in the world. I determined to take a stand at last. I had more than once heard it said that God could strike down anyone who rebelled against Him. I decided to conduct a simple laboratory test. There was a narrow lane in our neighborhood which was rather secluded. I selected it as being, for various reasons, suited to my experiment. Going forth, ball in hand (to disguise, no doubt, my fell theological purpose), I proceeded to the site of the Great Experiment. Using a phrase I had heard in the Bible, I enunciated carefully the test words: "There is no God." I spoke them in a low whisper, lest anyone should overhear me, for like most atheists I did not have in any marked degree the courage of my lack of convictions. My heart seemed to put in an extra beat, as I uttered the words, for I was, I think, still a little afraid the thunderbolt might descend. However, after I had accorded the Deity a suitable interval for reply, and had then decided He had been given sufficient time, I proceeded to the formal conclusion that my case was now established.

Somehow, I was still haunted by doubt. The feeling grew uneasily within me that perhaps I had not done enough. I decided to rest at nothing short of perfection. Of all Persons in the Trinity, the most mysterious, it seemed to me, was the Holy Ghost. There was a curious notion in my mind that the Holy Ghost was supposed to be even holier than the other two Persons of the Trinity. (Theologians will be quick to observe that this was an error on my part: I can but plead the tenderness of my years at the time.) Lest the Holy Ghost should have been overlooked through a technical slip of mine, I determined to be more specific. Off I went once again to the cursing-place, where I formally uttered my solemn declaration of disbelief in the Third Person of the Trinity. Still no thunderbolt: indeed, the sun, which had been hiding behind a cloud, came forth just at that point with uncannily benign radiance. However, this time I did feel more settled in mind. The word "God" had become meaningless: at any rate, I had succeeded in locking up the meaning somewhere in my mind and throwing away the key of that particular mental closet. For at least three and a half years after that episode I did my best to maintain an interior attitude of hostility toward all religious concepts. I did not usually say much about it, partly because I did not see any point in distressing my mother and other relatives, partly because I feared (with excellent reason) that they were not disposed to take my juvenile atheism with the seriousness that I felt it deserved. I decided to postpone my formal pronouncements on the subject till they would carry more weight.

These years were unhappy. It was not only that I was prematurely developing what I would now call the atheist personality; my atheism was not entirely undisturbed. Formally, I persevered in my private hostility and in my unbelief. But as the range of my school subjects was extended, I was visited by occasional misgivings. These were certainly not engendered by any religious indoctrination at school. When I was twelve I even engineered a remarkable means of avoiding the brief so-called "Bible Study period" (innocuous though this would in fact have been to my unbelief, for it was conducted by a master who regarded it as a very unsatisfactory supplement to our studies in English literature), by volunteering to take Greek in addition to the program of Latin and French that was accounted proper to my age. So I "sat in" with much older boys and tried my hand at following what they were doing in elementary Greek. It was a heavy load: too heavy perhaps; but I felt a kind of grim satisfaction in the thought that I was doing something for my atheism. On the other hand, involvement in so many new subjects brought curious questionings. For the first time I had become aware of the reality of cultures other than my own. I felt them beckoning me. Hitherto I had thought of study as *my* act of finding out information — for example, rules of grammar, arithmetical "truths," and so forth; now it seemed I was in the presence of a whole universe of alarming richness and complexity that seemed to be alive and seeking out *me*. Everything, from chemistry to French, seemed to be unfolding itself, revealing itself, to me, and I felt I ought to be responding with greater alacrity than I was able to summon.

With all this came a strange sense of being less important than I had thought myself — less important in one way, yet in another way more important. For I was being shown all sorts of values (of course I could not then have put it that way) of whose existence I had hitherto been entirely ignorant. Gradually my orientation changed, so that I now felt myself continually in the presence of Something (I certainly would not then have called it Someone) extremely interesting that was acting upon me and revealing to me wonder upon wonder. I was much impressed by the reflection that it had been there all the time: it was I who had formerly been blind to it.

In terms of the account of conceptions of God that has been given in this book, that stage in my development might perhaps be called the crossroads between polytheism and pantheism. I had always had in earlier boyhood a predilection for folklore and "wonder" tales, and having now long discarded these as too childish for me I took a casual interest in books on theosophy that I had found in the library of my uncle's country manse at which I spent much of the summer vacation for several successive years about that time. I discovered also, however, in that library, at the age of twelve, Latin service books. The fact that they were in Latin prompted me to try my hand at making what I could of them. I overlooked the fact that they were technically against my atheistic principles. They opened yet another new world. Now a voracious reader, I was introduced by someone, before I was thirteen, to Dante, in Cary's translation. I read all the *Inferno* and several cantos of the *Purgatorio* and *Paradiso* with such intense delight that I can still recite long passages from memory. The fact that I could not then understand a tenth of the allusions, far from discouraging me or diminishing my pleasure, accentuated this: I felt, rather, in the presence of riches so immense and so provocative that it seemed as though they must keep indefinitely beckoning me. It was not the universe that was expanding; it was, rather, my capacity that was expanding, though not swiftly enough for my liking. But the overwhelming impression I was beginning to receive was of being in the presence of that which could reveal itself to me or withhold itself from me at will.

"But With Unhurrying Chase"

All this time I was also developing an increasing awareness of the enormous difference in the personalities of those around me. Some personalities seemed "dead," others full of a most mysterious quality that others lacked. This difference seemed to have nothing to do with age, sex, or any other "external" circumstance. In retrospect, my attitude toward this new awareness seems obscure: I had no means of explaining it to myself at the time; but it certainly troubled me. I do not think I consciously associated it with the early experiences that have been related: these had indeed been pushed as far as possible out of mind for they plainly did not fit my atheistical profession. The most troublesome aspect of my new awareness was that the mysterious quality that some people possessed, though it differed in degree from person to person, seemed curiously uniform in character. It was as if it came from the same source. Hardly less disconcerting was the inescapable fact that I found it both in people I happened to find congenial and in those for whom I had a personal aversion. Though the incidence was perhaps greater in the latter than in the former, it had to be admitted that my personal likes and dislikes had nothing to do with it. Reluctantly came the realization, however, that religion did seem to have something to do with it. Not that there was any ratio between the incidence of the mysterious quality and the decisiveness of religious affirmation. Far from it. But religion did seem to be *the arena in which mighty transactions were taking place.*

As interest in this discovery was aroused in my impressionable mind, not long after my thirteenth birthday, I found myself overwhelmed by the presence of the mysterious quality which was now, however, isolated from other people. It was as though I had tapped the Source. Yet I could not tap it at will. It seemed, rather, to be tapping me. Here came the real turning-point. I found it no longer possible to think of the mysterious quality as an "it": the quality, now wholly detached from the individual persons in whom I had once found it, came to me in a manner that was uncannily personal. I was forced to admit to myself that the only term I knew that fitted the case was one that fitted it perfectly — "God." The embarrassment of having to admit this to myself was mitigated, however, by the fact that I was able to persuade myself, with magnificent self-conceit, that my disbelief had been due to the fault of others who had entirely misrepresented God to me. (How ingenious is the human mind! I was very careful not to let any unwanted recollection of the excellent early instruction I had received from my grandmother come into the picture.) From God, whose Presence I now felt too keenly to deny, I could obtain no explicit guidance on any specific subject. My endeavors to secure such guidance met, it seemed to me, with passive rebuffs. God did not speak. My awareness of Him consisted in an awareness from time to time of my being in the presence of One whose holiness was so absolute and yet so personal that I could only wait upon His demands. Unfortunately, it seemed to me, He did not choose to communicate them to me in any detail. I think I probably expected something more in the nature of a clap of thunder and a voice from the clouds, as many people, older than I then was, have expected. At any rate, I neither saw any visions nor heard any voices. I was disappointed in this, and I think my disappointment had much to do with the great attraction that Roman Catholicism exerted over me in later adolescence. I could no longer deny the Presence of God: the reality of it was no less vivid than my self-awareness. But I was still able to perform a very convenient trick upon myself: I could indulge in the pretense that my conscience had nothing to do with that Presence. I carefully avoided the possibility that God might communicate His demands to me in my own moral consciousness. This consciousness, I argued to myself — very plausibly, of course — was far too undependable as a basis for action. In the course of this particular evasion of the divine impact, however, I learned a great deal, for my interest in Roman Catholicism led me, however prematurely, to do much reading in the history of Christian theology. My principal difficulty was, of course, that my regular studies left me too little time to pursue such reading as much as I should have wished. Still, I did not do too badly: it happened that I was sixteen before I ever had the opportunity of meeting a Roman Catholic priest, and by that time I had read so much in St. Thomas that the priest, being a simple old Irishman who had preserved a healthy boyish interest in football, looked upon my questions as those of an emissary of the Devil.

The very slow process of my later religious development and my long struggle between faith and doubt would take too long to tell here. Nor would it throw much light on the special subject in hand. I pass therefore to a relatively mature phase of my pilgrimage to exhibit the realities of the situation as I now see it.

The Edge Over Doubt

Though my theistic convictions now seem to me much firmer and more secure than they were when I first regarded myself as committed to them, my doubts and questionings have grown in proportion. I have never found it difficult, in principle, to be a skeptic, and in the presence of those who seem able to talk as glibly about religion as one talks about breakfast, I have found it not only easy but inevitable. In what may be called, in a pejorative sense, a "seminary climate," the vivacity of my skepticism knows no bounds. As soon as I am involved in the whirligig of slick theological chatter, my first reaction (and often my last) is to rebel by every means at my disposal. It does not matter whether the theology is of the more temperate kind that has some historical anchorage or whether I am dealing with those who have led a more sheltered life: in either case my skepticism is unfailingly evoked. I confess, however, that the pastime of satirizing theological slickness is open to the same moral objection as bullfighting: however you look at it, it is a cruel sport, for you are up against a ferocious, blind force. You *ought* to be able to make it destroy itself just because you are not quite so stupid as your adversary, and this is not, therefore, a very courageous engagement on your part. Yet you know very well that a little carelessness on your side means that the theological bull is sure to gore you to death, for you can hardly expect him to be of two minds about you, since he is never of two minds about anything. It seems to me that one might die in a better cause.

On the other hand, fifteen minutes with even a stuttering, let alone a loquacious, positivist is enough to make me want to get up and sing "Onward, Christian Soldiers." Conversation with positivists and atheists is, indeed, the most effective doubt-killer I know. It is certainly far more effective, in my experience, than either the most roaring revival meeting or the most carefully planned ten-day monastic retreat, both of which I have had occasion to sample. Whenever I find my faith to be in danger of flagging, I have no difficulty in discovering how to revitalize it. All I have to do is to hunt up an atheist acquaintance and ask him to be kind enough to deliver an attack on theism. If he should care to include a specific attack on the Christian faith, so much the better. In the intense egocentricity of the atheistic personality I unfailingly discover the most telling argument for theism. When your faith is enfeebled, there is no use, it seems to me, in trying to rehearse to yourself the arguments that have convinced you in the past: you might almost as well, when you are hungry, think of some delicious repast you have enjoyed. Nor is there usually much to be gained by trying to deepen your awareness of the spiritual blessings it has brought you: the best place to discover the value of water is not Niagara but the desert. It has often occurred to me, indeed, that a place should be found in the Christian liturgy for a prayer: "O Lord, we beseech Thee to surround us with atheists, that our faith may be continually nourished. . . ."

When a man affirms that the word "God" has no meaning, you are naturally ready to listen to what he has to say. You are willing to take him very seriously, since he is making an affirmation upon the most crucial topic that it is possible to discuss. But when you discover, as you are quickly bound to do, that what he has really thrown overboard is not, as it sounds, the meaningfulness of a word, but the meaningfulness of his entire life, you begin to interest yourself more acutely than before in what atheism implies. This will not automatically convince you of theism or even reinforce your adherence to the latter; but it will certainly do more for you than any textbook could ever do; more even than the presence of a theist whose faith seems to be, according to his own account of the situation, better rooted than yours.

Psychological Truisms

It has always seemed to me to be almost a truism to say that the psychological type of objection to any religious position is the most telling. It is bound to be the most telling, because it raises the question in what appears to be, after all, its most crucial form, namely, "Is my faith grounded in a metaphysical reality, or is it the expression of a subjective condition?" To point out that there is a relatively easy, psychological explanation of almost any religious experience I may care to describe is simply to draw attention to what everybody, however simpleminded, already knows: that if the experience is not the result of the divine impact, then it can very well be explained in psychological terms. From a logical point of view, this is not a very intricate proposition. The question that remains is, of course, whether I can really be satisfied that the psychological explanations are sufficient. Here I am obliged, surely, to remind myself that I have excellent "vested interests" in being able to be satisfied with them. Yet I am not.

Of course psychological considerations can go far toward explaining, if they do not indeed completely explain, the *form* in which even a genuinely religious experience is symbolized. I am sure that in my own case a different background would have resulted in a different symbolization. No doubt the fact that it was my grandmother and not my step-aunt or Mr. Bertrand Russell who happened to give me my earliest religious instruction, has irrevocably determined the *manner* in which my religious concepts have been formulated. To put the matter in popular religious terms: had the Lord imposed an Adventist environment upon me in childhood, it is very possible that my pilgrimage would have been even more stormy than it has been, and if I had been brought up in a devout Greek Orthodox home it is unlikely that I should have devoted so much of my attention in later years to belaboring Anglican friends who do not laugh vigorously enough at the antics of the sort of person who thinks religion a device for helping to build the kind of America that happens to be congenial to his political and sociological prejudices. Nor do I doubt that my choice of site for my early experiment on the Holy Ghost, and even the source of my inspiration for this indecent enterprise, can be to some considerable extent the object of psychological investigations whose results would be of great value to religious people if these were not forced by the brevity of human life to give their attention to more important matters.

Psychology can help to explain many things about religion. It can probably provide a better explanation than the historical one, already suggested in Chapter 6, on why we think of God as "up," and if we thought of him as "down" it could surely explain that too — at any rate when it is in the hands of that small minority of professional psychologists who do understand something of the nature of religion. Psychology can certainly explain why some people have no difficulty in appreciating worship that exhibits a modicum of historical perspective and liturgical sense — and can appreciate this to some extent even if they are not fortunate enough to enjoy the Christian faith — while others are content with services in which the Bidding is accomplished, to the extent that it is accomplished at all, by an interrogatory phrase attended by the rolling of a ministerial eye in holy epilepsy toward a heaven localized at 60° starboard of the nave. Psychology can help to explain, too, why it is possible for Quakers to be content to accept a solitary dogma without a single mitigating grain of salt, while Catholics are pleased to smother with that commodity more dogmas than they can number.

Psychology can do all that and much more. But nothing it can say about the father-substitute or the *id*, about libido or compensation, about Oedipus or Electra (or whatever is, in the case of hermaphrodites, the relevant complex), can conceivably shed any light upon the questions to which religious people most urgently desire an answer. The psychologists have done yeoman service to religion — a service that has received too little recognition — in capsizing those intellectuals who had never learned to discriminate between feeling and faith. There are many deeply religious people who wish only that the success of the psychologists in that laudable enterprise had been more extensive.

Far from my being satisfied with attempts to "account for" religion in psychological terms, the only circumstance that prevents my greeting such attempts with the hilarity that I was once able to bestow upon them is the much more elementary psychological fact that one really cannot go on laughing forever at the same joke. The human psyche is not so constructed. If you have ever had faith genuine enough to have caused you to grapple with even a prick of doubt, you know that anybody who is really satisfied with the characteristic psychological explanations of religion *ought to* be satisfied with them, because they admirably account for his condition. The problem with which you are still confronted is that they certainly do not appear to constitute an adequate explanation of *your* condition. They relate, no doubt, to elements in or concomitants of your condition; they do not explain the one element that most requires explanation. Indeed, in stating your dissatisfaction with the psychologists' remarks on the subject, anything you say, however polite in intention, is bound to sound to you (though happily it need not so sound to your more protected critics) a most impolitely extreme form of understatement.

The Mystery of Evil at Close Quarters

Intellectually, my skepticism has probably received its chief nourishment from a consideration of the mystery of evil. But that skepticism has been over and over again severely shaken by observations, particularly in the course of my pastoral experience, that have forced upon my attention an even more puzzling mystery. It is this: the mystery of evil appears horrific in inverse ratio to the extent to which it is removed from abstract reflection. For example, it was once my duty to visit and bring Christian consolation to an admirable young married couple who had two robust, lively and intelligent children, and whose third child, just born, was a baby girl without arms or legs and predicted to live. I trembled as I approached the home that had been visited by so great an affliction. In face of such a visitation of misfortune, anything I might say, it seemed to me, must sound glib beyond endurance. What purpose could there be, the parents would be sure to ask, in such a life? My comment would have to be that we could not see the purpose, but that, confident that God does reign, we might trust Him and believe that what seemed to us a tragedy was part of a purpose greater than we could understand. But how would this sound to them in their sorrow? To my astonishment, however, the parents, despite their distress, had already accepted their tribulation with profound resignation and were planning the future education of the afflicted child. Their faith in God was not shaken; on the contrary, it seemed to have been mysteriously strengthened. What they wanted from me was not, as I had feared, a "satisfactory" answer to the question, "How could a benevolent and all-powerful God permit this?" They wanted from me, rather, an assurance that the hand of God was not lifted against them in anger. They did not question that God was reigning; they wanted to be sure that *they* were right with God.

That it is less upsetting to one's faith to encounter real trouble in

life than to read about it in an armchair is a commonplace in pastoral
experience. Every pastor, surely, knows what it is to visit an afflicted
parishioner in order to bring Christian healing to the scene of grief,
and to find that the grief has already so healed the sufferer that it is
the latter who really brings spiritual refreshment to the pastor. Of
course, for every case of real trouble there are scores in which the
trouble is largely imaginary or self-induced. In dealing with the latter
the Christian pastor, if he is equipped for his task, can bring immense
consolation to his flock. But in the presence of those who would appear to the outside observer to stand most in need of consoling, the
pastor finds that not only has his work been done for him better than
he could ever hope to do it; it is he who has become the beneficiary
in the pastoral relationship. He who went out steeling his courage for
encounter with the mystery of evil finds himself in the presence of
the mystery of God. The limbless child, if she survives, will probably
find much less difficulty in believing in God than I do.

Moral Evolution

Never since I can remember have I been unimpressed by the enormous differences in quality between one human being and another.
While, as every novelist knows, every hero has his faults and every
villain his redeeming features, it is still remarkable how much people
differ. The contrast between the dullness, baseness, and meanness, of
many men and women on the one hand, and on the other the courage
and imagination and generosity of many others has always struck me
more forcibly than has any notion of my special kinship with my fellow humans. From my earliest childhood I formed the habit of
choosing "unlikely" companions, and to this day I find I have more
fellow-feeling with certain Japanese than I have with some of my own
relatives. So the homilies of the internationalists have always seemed
to me to be beside the point. I do not mean to say I have no racial
feeling: this is indeed a fairly strong element in my make-up; but it
evaporates immediately in face of my much stronger awareness of the
disparity among individuals. All these considerations, however, far
from inclining me toward dogmas about the sacrosanct solidarity of
the human race, dispose me, rather, to see it as an area of combat, a
"moment" in an evolutionary process in which a power, ever being
unfolded to me as holy, works incessantly in the creation of values
whose splendor is beyond my imaginings. While I do not feel myself
to be wholly devoid of imaginative power, I am quite incapable of
conceiving the end of a process that is so peculiarly fascinating. Nor
do I feel that, even if I could catch a glimmer of it, I could ever be
able to put this into human terms. In my Christian faith, however,
I believe that there is no necessity for anything of the sort, since all

that I need has been provided for me in the revelation of God in Christ. This revelation is of such a peculiar character that it convinces me of its completeness and perfection as the revelation of the nature of God to beings who, like myself, are within the area of combat that is humanity. No revelation could take place *in vacuo*: it must always be a revelation of x to y. Therefore I cannot say, for instance, that if Mars be inhabited, Christ is the full and final revelation of God to the Martians. For all I know there may be billions of other areas of combat in the universe. I can speak only of the one I know, the human area, of whose potentialities and limitations I have had sufficient experience to enable me to conclude whether, as a "divine work of art," the revelation of God in Christ is or is not perfect for the purpose for which, according to orthodox Christian testimony, it has been designed.

Science and Religion

Among what are commonly accounted "challenges to religious faith," the one that least impresses me is that which is usually called "science." Indeed, the supposed "tension" between "science" and "religion" seems to me to be the rankest of red herrings ever drawn across the path of truth. There is no such tension except to the extent that scientists are unscientific and religious people irreligious. This is, unfortunately, a considerable extent; but it is due largely to defects or limitations in our educational systems.

"Science," as the term is understood today, is in one sense a comparative newcomer to the scene of human accomplishment and discovery; but in another sense it is as old as human thought itself. In its earlier days — before the time of Socrates, for instance — science was just as much mixed up with superstition as ever was religion. Neither scientists nor religious people today are immune from these darker forces. Scientists are likely to have, as they do have, as many superstitions about religion as religious people have about science. Moreover, such are the defects in contemporary education that a man might nowadays attain high international standing as a biologist or chemist though he knows no more about the elements of religious thought than medieval popes knew about the quantum theory. True, the modern leader of scientific thought has one advantage over his counterpart in religion: the former, in order to attain popular acclaim, must be a good scientist, while the latter is frequently able to bamboozle vast audiences into perfervid applause though his ignorance of religion is no less painfully spectacular than his ignorance of science — and, indeed, of everything else except his professional technique as an "operator." But the modern scientist can be just as successful in displaying the vastness of his ignorance about religion as can be the modern theologian in exhibiting his misunderstanding of science.

Happily, there are many distinguished scientists who do know quite a lot about religious thought, as there are also philosophers and theologians who know a good deal about science, its methods, its aims, and its limitations. For obvious reasons, it is just these who are most reticent in making pronouncements outside their own field. The more a non-historian knows about history, the quieter he is likely to be in the presence of a distinguished professional historian. So the general public is less likely to hear about religion from scientists who know something about religion than they are to hear about it from the larger class of scientists who are simpleminded. Many indeed are the brash talks upon religious topics that I have heard, sometimes in high academic circles, from scientists whose ignorance of religion was such as to make them oblivious of the fact that the excruciation of their audience was due not to the possession by the latter of some religious "dogma" that made them insensitive to the truth, but simply to the fact that the audience was bored almost beyond human endurance. They were as bored as would be a modern congress of scientists condemned to listen to a lecture by a hairy Old Testament prophet on the futility of physics.

For my own part, I can certainly say that, my skeptical tendencies notwithstanding, I have never been able to see anything in scientific discovery that I could construe as even remotely detrimental to my religious faith. On the contrary, almost everything of importance the scientists bring to light tends, rather, to confirm or strengthen this. The moral topsy-turvyness of the world, the triumph of flagrant injustice, the enthronement in the counsels of men of the more unimaginative forms of human stupidity — all these can deal formidable blows to the faith I enjoy. When I hear, for example, as I did recently, of a will in which a lady left a large sum of money for the purpose of setting up a fund to ensure that her Pekinese dog should never have to eat any but the only cut of sirloin to which he was not allergic, and left the residue of her estate to the Presbyterian Board of Foreign Missions, my first reaction is vigorous. It is to doubt the existence of a God who apparently tolerates the spread of a pleasant delusion that it is consonant with belief in the divine justice to suppose that hell consists of nothing worse than everlasting roasting in fire and brimstone, while at the same time He foists upon the presumably innocent canine co-beneficiary of the Foreign Mission Board a mistress far below him in wisdom. But from the realm of scientific discovery no such tormenting doubts ever come into my consciousness. The wonders it has yielded, not least in recent years, fill me, rather, with awe and a sense of the infinite glory and majesty of God far stronger than any that is ever induced in me by the average or even above-average sermon.

This is not to say that what modern scientific discovery discloses to me fails to affect my conception of God. It affects it almost continuously. But it seems always to enrich it, never to impoverish it. My conception of God does not deteriorate into that of, say, the average anthropologist; it acquires instead a fresh robustness, a new vivacity, an overwhelming depth. So long as I can keep scientists off the subject of God in those cases in which they are not competent to treat it, I can listen to them with greater spiritual profit and enlightenment than I could possibly hope to get from a pilgrimage to the Holy Land. Among many other things, what I learn from them is especially effective in inspiring in me a sense of my own unworthiness to play even the humble role I do play in the process of the divine creation. With that sense of sin comes likewise the sense of having been "chosen" that is expressed in the theological doctrine of election. The awareness of my failure to make sufficient use of the abundant opportunities provided for me by God within the limits of the way He has prescribed for me, is accentuated by almost everything the scientists tell me. I am increasingly aware of having been walking, so to speak, over gold mines I was too stupid or lazy to discover.

Great scientists themselves are generally the least arrogant of men. Nor is this surprising, because for every experimental success a scientist can expect to achieve, he must face countless antecedent failures. The contrast between the humility of good scientists and good religious thinkers on the one hand, and the astounding arrogance of their brash and immature counterparts on the other, leaves me more deeply impressed than ever of the truth of my conviction that science and religion are engaged in a joint enterprise.

Am I a Better Man?

You might very well say to me: "All right. I like what you say; but now tell me, what has all this religion done for you? Has it made you a better man?" To this there are various conventional retorts commonly used to evade the point. I might, for instance, parry your question with another: "What do you mean by 'a better man'?" Or I might remark that the question you ask has not the same kind of importance for a Christian that it has for one who thinks of God chiefly as President-Emeritus (lately deceased) of a Mutual Self-Improvement Society.

Your question merits, however, a less flippant answer. For it is commonly recognized that religions are intimately associated with ethical behavior. Not least is this true of Christianity, since a criterion is provided by Jesus for the discernment of genuine from bogus claims:

"Beware of false prophets. . . . Ye shall know them by their fruits. Do men gather grapes of thorns, or figs of thistles? Even so, every good tree bringeth forth good fruit; but a corrupt tree bringeth forth evil fruit. . . . Wherefore by their fruits ye shall know them." [2]

Yet your question, though proper, is embarrassing. It is embarrassing because it compels me to disclose facts about myself that it would please me to withhold. Judged by conventional standards, my behavior is not only far from perfect; sometimes it is strikingly defective. But this is not what makes your question embarrassing. The real reason for the embarrassment is that you cannot understand the progress I have made, because you have no idea what a horror I was before I came under the influence of Christ. I was so self-centered that by all the rules I should have developed into an insufferable monster. Instead, I became, by comparison with what might have been expected, deeply interested in people and ready to "give" myself for them; eager, even, to sacrifice myself as a channel of Christ's love and power. If you had known me before, you would have to admit that the impossible had been achieved; that is, unless you were a Christian, for in this case you would know that such transformations are a commonplace in the Christian life. A blind man whose sight is restored does not lose confidence in his doctor when he is informed by the latter that he has astigmatism and will have to wear glasses. One is reminded of the stuttering missionary who, taunted that Christ surely had not brought him the expected "peace of mind," replied: "But before I knew Him I was d-d-deaf and d-d-dumb."

In my experience, life in Christ has made me "a better man" at such a radical level that the significance of the change in me cannot be appreciated by any superficial observation. The cure of a deep-seated cancer does not necessarily remove a wart from your chin. You may not *look* healthier than you looked with the cancer; but you *are* healthier.

Religion and Art

Long before I had reached that stage in my academic career in which I could undertake graduate studies at Oxford, I had already fully determined upon the subject of my doctoral dissertation: *Aesthetic Experience in Religion.*[3] The connection between art and religion had, no less than the contrast between them, for long intensely interested me; so much so that for a time I could think of almost nothing else. What at first puzzled me was the notion that any truly religious person could disparage beauty. I need not, of course, have troubled myself much on that point, since truly religious people never do; but I had accepted at face value the affirmation of

[2] Matt. 7:15–20.
[3] London: Macmillan & Co., Ltd., 1947.

several acquaintances who talked as though they were committed Christians and who nevertheless affected to look upon all manifestations of beauty, in art, culture or elsewhere, as being irrelevant to religion at the best and at the worst a danger to it. To me, beauty was then, as now, one of the great means of revelation. This is, of course, by no means an unusual view. It is not, however, universal. In the Latin Church, for example, it is the peculiar heritage of the Benedictine tradition and is not shared by many of the less ancient orders and congregations within the Roman Communion.

The passionate addiction to ugliness that is characteristic of much contemporary civilization is as difficult for me to understand now as it was then. How anyone can pretend to be indifferent to whether an object is made out of beautiful substances — such as marble and gold — or the latest plastic "substitute," on the pretext that it does not matter so long as the object "performs its function," is not easy for me to understand. In fact, of course, the plastic "substitute" does not perform its function by any means, even so far as I am concerned, for it is presumably part of its function not to nauseate me, and its success here cannot be said to be complete. Far from being satisfied with plastics for the construction of any object that cannot conveniently be hidden from my eye under normal conditions, like the ballcock of a lavatory cistern, I have never been able to admire them. Much less do I admire the minds of the commercially-interested propagandists who assure me that the "substitute" is no longer to be regarded as a "substitute" and, being now accounted better than that which it has been designed to imitate, is, of course, to be priced accordingly. What is chiefly attested by the success of such propaganda is the sad fact that the beauty of mahogany and porcelain must have been appreciated by far fewer people than was indicated in the sanguine estimates of yesterday's "cultivated" humanists.

That the veneer of taste affected by irreligious people should so easily collapse need not, however, much surprise us. Divorced from religion, no appreciation of art is essentially deeper than that of the crowds who go milling around bogus Chinatowns in search of an exotic-looking amulet or god of mercy. At this level of appreciation people are obviously liable to be taken in by the practical jokes of some modern artists. Indeed, but for the mercifully blatant crudity of much commercially-available contemporary religious art, they would be as likely as not to come home with the Sacred Heart as a companion piece for Confucius and place them on the mantleshelf on either side of a Buddha. I have never so far seen that particular ensemble, though it would by no means surprise me, for I have more than once heard its liturgical counterpart acclaimed as the ideal, not to say the most sophisticated, American college chapel service.

To find art belittled, slighted, or misunderstood among those who appear to be more serious-minded in their religion is discouraging. The aesthetic expression of any religion whose ideas are worth expressing must be magnificent, overcoming the limitations of poverty, frailty and human need. The riches of a lively faith are spread out in its liturgy. If your faith is lively, your liturgy should make a Pontifical High Mass at Rome, with an archbishop of the Mozarabic Rite assisting and a Uniate patriarch for the singing of the Gospel in Greek, look bald and colorless by comparison. Not always is this achieved, though it is impressive to many to behold the use God can make of even the smallest lacuna in the massive tapestry of ugliness raised against Him in so many forms of worship. It is remarkable that there is apparently no form of worship so ugly that God cannot find a way through it. Still, I have never seen why so much ingenuity should go into the labor of testing Him out on the point.

It has always seemed to me to go without saying that objects of beauty must entail sacrifice on the part of those who make them. The old Chinese proverb, "If you have two loaves, sell one and buy a lily," expresses this notion well enough. In the sacrifice it entails, the quest for beauty has much in common with religious pursuits. On the other hand, however, art can be a peculiarly selfish occupation. For it can, and frequently does, deliberately exclude all interest in the world beyond the artist, consecrating itself, in fact, to the service of a narcissistic religion whose principal aim is to enable the artist to live within the not very extensive confines of himself. Fundamentally, art, as a human activity, is no more than the expression of what the artist has it in him to express. If, being a cesspool, he expresses this well, he ought to be hailed as a good artist, though he may also have to be reported to the police. From the point of view of a religious faith, the interest and importance of art do not, of course, lie here. The relevance of art to religion lies, rather, in the marvelously pliable efficiency of art as an instrument of revelation. But when it is with its accustomed efficiency revealing only the moral bankruptcy of a gifted artist, it is playing a role that is irrelevant to religion. Artistic activity, therefore, though it can be an indispensable part in the revelation to man of that which is the object of religion, is also conspicuously capable of being used in the interests of egocentricity, in man's everlasting quest for armor against the onslaught of God's love. It is well known in legend that a guise of dazzling beauty is included in Satan's wardrobe.

Which is Me?

Above all, I am impressed by the puzzling complexity of human beings as soon as they become involved in the conflict. I share with many the awareness that

Within my earthly temple there's a crowd:
There's one of us who's humble, one who's proud;
There's one who's broken-hearted for his sins,
And one who, unrepentant, sits and grins;
There's one who loves his neighbour as himself,
And one who cares for naught but fame and pelf.
From much corroding care I should be free,
If once I could determine which is me.

To some it may come as a surprise to learn of the "three faces of Eve." In the course of encounter with God, the situation can never look so simple. I do not know "which is me"; but thanks to the faith in me that is ever ahead of the doubt that runs with it neck and neck, I know "where I am going." My resistance is not yet spent. But I am sure I shall win in the end, for I know He will.

BIBLIOGRAPHY

It will be seen at a glance that this bibliography is not to be used without discrimination. Its main purpose is to provide instructors with a convenient check-list of books from which to make their own recommendations.

The needs of students vary from group to group and from individual to individual. One type of student requires a challenge to his faith, another a challenge to his skepticism; many will have to learn, through reading, that their dogmatism is more arbitrary than they may have supposed. Hence the range of books listed must be, as it is, very wide. Not only are extremes of viewpoint represented; the variation in scope and treatment is considerable. Moreover, some books not strictly in the field of religious philosophy are included on account of their usefulness for background reading.

The instructor, whether he is obliged to deal with students in groups or is in the more fortunate position of being able to guide them individually, will judge the needs of his students and discriminate accordingly. What is one man's meat is another's dessert. A student may be challenged by the wit of a Chesterton or the piety of a Weil who would choke on Kant or Temple. Some still need to read William James. One man may be roused to religious thought by Leuba or Ayer; another, requiring no such provocation, may do better with a Niebuhr. Some will find a revelation in Pascal or Kierkegaard; others only an exasperation. The instructor is the best judge of what, in the circumstances, will make the student sit back and think, and what will make him just sit back.

Works not available in English are excluded from the list. This is in deference to the spectacular success of our educational system in destroying the inclination and therefore the capacity of many students for foreign languages at an early age, long before they reach college. Translation is at the best, however, a crutch. Instructors will therefore recommend where possible the reading of foreign works in the language in which they were written. The advantage of this should be obvious. If it is not, the instructor may inculcate some appreciation of it by explaining to his students the force of an observation made long ago by Cornford, that a person ignorant of Greek, who read in

Jowett's translation of Plato's *Republic* (549 B) that the best
guardian of a man's "virtue" is "philosophy tempered with music,"
might suppose Plato to be recommending, in the interest of preserving
male chastity, the study of metaphysics punctuated by exercises on the
violin. It is to be hoped that instructors will also call attention to the
regrettable though perhaps not wholly infelicitous circumstance that
the most valuable parts of modern works of foreign origin are sometimes entirely omitted in translation; for example, the very important
appendices of Maritain's *Les Degrés du savoir*. Moreover, if the attention of intelligent students is drawn to the fact that *The Idea of the
Holy* has to do service for so neat a title as Otto's *Das Heilige* —
thereby misleading the unwary into a misunderstanding of the whole
book — they may be led to the healthy suspicion that in religious
philosophy the hurdles are formidable enough without their having
to be tackled on crutches.

Adam, Karl. *The Spirit of Catholicism,* Revised Edition. New York:
Doubleday (Image Books), 1954.

Agus, Jacob Bernard. *Modern Philosophies of Judaism.* New York:
Behrman, 1941.

Alexander, Samuel. *Space, Time and Deity* (2 vols.). London: Macmillan, 1920.

Allport, Gordon A. *The Individual and His Religion.* New York:
Macmillan, 1930.

Anselm, *Proslogium.* . . . La Salle: Open Court, 1910.

Aquinas, Thomas. *Basic Writings of Saint Thomas Aquinas.* New
York: Random House, 1945.

———. *Summa Theologica* (trans. Dominican Fathers). New York:
Benziger, 1947–48.

Arberry, Arthur John. *Reason and Revelation.* London: Macmillan,
1957.

Aristotle. *The Basic Works of Aristotle* (ed. R. McKeon). New York:
Random House, 1941.

Augustine. *The Basic Writings of Saint Augustine* (ed. W. J. Oates).
New York: Random House, 1948.

———. *Confessions and Enchiridion* (trans. Outler). Philadelphia:
Westminster Press, 1955.

———. *Later Works* (*The Trinity; The Spirit and the Letter*; etc.).
Philadelphia: Westminster Press, 1955.

———. *The Problem of Free Choice* (trans. Pontifex). Westminster,
Md.: Newman Press, 1955.

Ayer, A. J. *Language, Truth and Logic,* Revised Edition. Oxford:
Oxford University Press, 1947.

———. *The Problem of Knowledge.* London: Macmillan, 1956.

Baillie, James. *Reflections on Life and Religion*. London: Allen and Unwin, 1952.

Baillie, John. *And the Life Everlasting*. New York: Scribner, 1948.

———. *The Belief in Progress*. New York: Scribner, 1951.

———. *The Idea of Revelation in Recent Thought*. New York: Columbia University Press, 1956.

Balfour, A. J. *Theism and Humanism*. London: Hodder and Stoughton, 1915.

Becker, Carl Lotus. *The Heavenly City of the Eighteenth-century Philosophers*. New Haven: Yale University Press, 1932.

Bennett, Charles A. *The Dilemma of Religious Knowledge*. New Haven: Yale University Press, 1931.

Berdyaev, Nicolai Alexandrovitch. *Freedom and the Spirit*. London: Geoffrey Bles, 1935.

———. *Solitude and Society*. London: Geoffrey Bles, 1938.

———. *The Destiny of Man*. New York: Scribner, 1937.

———. *Truth and Revelation*. London: Geoffrey Bles, 1953.

Bergson, Henri. *The Two Sources of Morality and Religion*. New York: Doubleday (Anchor Books), 1954.

Bertocci, Peter Anthony. *Introduction to the Philosophy of Religion*. New York: Prentice-Hall, 1951.

———. *Religion as Creative Insecurity*. New York: Association Press, 1958.

Bethune-Baker, J. F. *An Introduction to the Early History of Christian Doctrine*, Ninth Edition. London: Methuen, 1951.

Bevan, Edwyn. *Symbolism and Belief*. Boston: Beacon Press, 1957.

Boethius. *The Consolation of Philosophy*. New York: Modern Library, 1943.

Bonaventure. *The Mind's Road to God* (trans. G. Boas). New York: Liberal Arts Press, 1953.

Boodin, John Elof. *God and Creation*. New York: Macmillan, 1934.

Bookstaber, Philip David. *The Idea of Development of the Soul in Medieval Jewish Philosophy*. Philadelphia: Jacobs, 1950.

Bosanquet, Bernard. *What Religion Is*. London: Macmillan, 1920.

Bosley, Harold A. *The Quest for Religious Certainty*. Chicago: Willett Clark, 1939.

Bowman, Archibald Allan. *A Sacramental Universe*. Princeton: Princeton University Press, 1939.

———. *Studies in the Philosophy of Religion* (2 vols.). London: Macmillan, 1938.

Bradley, Andrew Cecil. *Ideals of Religion*. London: Macmillan, 1940.

Braithwaite, R. B. *An Empiricist's View of the Nature of Religious Experience*. Cambridge: Cambridge University Press, 1955.

Brandt, Richard B. *The Philosophy of Schleiermacher*. New York: Harper, 1941.

Brightman, Edgar Sheffield. *A Philosophy of Religion.* New York: Prentice-Hall, 1940.

——. *Nature and Values.* New York: Abingdon-Cokesbury, 1945.

——. *Personality and Religion.* New York: Abingdon, 1934.

Bronstein, Daniel J. *Approaches to the Philosophy of Religion.* New York: Prentice-Hall, 1954.

Brown, James. *Subject and Object in Modern Theology.* London: S. C. M. Press, 1955.

Bruner, Emil. *Revelation and Reason* (trans. O. Wyon). London: Lutterworth, 1947.

Buber, Martin. *Eclipse of God.* New York: Harper, 1952.

——. *I and Thou* (trans. R .G. Smith). Edinburgh: Clark, 1937.

——. *The Writings of Martin Buber* (selected by W. Herberg). New York: Meridian Books, 1956.

Buckham, John Wright. *The Inner World.* New York: Harper, 1941.

Bultmann, Rudolf. *Essays Philosophical and Theological* (trans. Greig). New York: Macmillan, 1955.

Burnaby, John. *Christian Words and Christian Meanings.* London: Hodder and Stoughton, 1955.

Burtt, Edwin A. *The Metaphysical Foundations of Modern Science,* Revised Edition. New York: Harcourt Brace, 1932.

——. *Types of Religious Philosophy,* Revised Edition. New York: Harper, 1951.

Bury, John. *The Idea of Progress.* New York: Macmillan, 1932.

Caird, John. *Introduction to the Philosophy of Religion.* Glasgow: Maclehose, 1894.

Caldecott, Alfred. *The Philosophy of Religion in England and America.* New York: Macmillan, 1891.

Calhoun, Robert Lowry. *God and the Common Life.* New York: Scribner, 1935.

——. *What is Man?* New York: Association Press, 1939.

Calvin, John. *Institutes* (2 vols.; trans. Warfield). Philadelphia: Westminster Press, n.d.

——. *On God and Man* (ed. Strothmann). New York: Ungar, 1956.

——. *On the Christian Faith* (selections from Calvin, ed. J. T. McNeill). New York: Liberal Arts Press, 1958.

Carrel, Alexis. *Man, the Unknown.* New York: Harper, 1935.

Casserley, Julian Victor Langmead. *The Christian in Philosophy.* London: Faber and Faber, 1949.

Cassirer, Ernst. *Language and Myth.* New York: Harper, 1946.

——. *The Philosophy of Symbolic Forms* (2 vols.; trans. Manheim). New Haven: Yale University Press, 1953–55.

Chandler, Arthur. *Christian Religious Experience*. London: Longmans, 1929.

Chesterton, Gilbert Keith. *Orthodoxy*. New York: John Lane, 1909.

Claudel, Paul. *The Satin Slipper* (trans. J. O'Connor). London: Sheed and Ward, 1931.

Coe, George Albert. *The Religion of a Mature Mind*. Chicago: Revell, 1902.

Collingwood, R. G. *Speculum Mentis*. Oxford: Oxford University Press, 1924.

———. *The Idea of History*. New York: Oxford University Press, 1936.

———. *The Idea of Nature*. Oxford: Oxford University Press, 1945.

Collins, James. *The Mind of Kierkegaard*. Chicago: Regnery, 1953.

Copleston, F. C. *Aquinas*. London: Pelican Books, 1955.

Cotton, James Harry. *Christian Knowledge of God*. New York: Macmillan, 1951.

Coulson, C. A. *Science and Christian Belief*. Oxford: Oxford University Press, 1955.

Creel, H. G. *Confucius, the Man and the Myth*. New York: Day, 1949.

Cullmann, Oscar. *Immortality of the Soul or Resurrection of the Dead*. London: Epworth Press, 1958.

Curtis, S. J. *A Short History of Western Philosophy in the Middle Ages*. London: Macdonald, 1950.

Daniélou, Jean. *Origen* (trans. W. Mitchell). New York: Sheed and Ward, 1955.

D'Arcy, Martin C. *St. Thomas Aquinas*. Westminster, Md.: Newman Press, 1953.

———. *The Mind and Heart of Love*, Second Revised Edition. London: Faber and Faber, 1954.

———. *The Nature of Belief*. London: Sheed and Ward, 1931.

Dawson, Christopher. *Progress and Religion*. London: Sheed and Ward, 1929.

De Burgh, William George. *From Morality to Religion*. London: Macdonald, 1938.

———. *Towards a Religious Philosophy*. London: Macdonald, 1937.

De Pauley, William Cecil. *The Candle of the Lord: Studies in the Cambridge Platonists*. New York: Macmillan, 1937.

Descartes, René. *A Discourse on Method* and *Meditations*. New York: Dutton (Everyman's Library), 1927.

De Wolf, L. Harold. *The Religious Revolt Against Reason*. New York: Harper, 1949.

Dixon, William Macneile. *The Human Situation.* New York: Longmans, Green, 1937.

Ducasse, Curt John. *A Philosophical Scrutiny of Religion.* New York: Ronald Press, 1953.

Dunham, James Henry. *The Religion of Philosophers.* Philadelphia: University of Pennsylvania Press, 1947.

Durkheim, Emile. *The Elementary Forms of the Religious Life.* New York: Macmillan, 1915.

Edwards, David Miall. *Christianity and Philosophy.* Edinburgh: Clark, 1932.

——. *The Philosophy of Religion.* Hodder and Stoughton, 1924.

Edwards, Jonathan. *The Philosophy of Jonathan Edwards* (ed. H. G. Townsend). Eugene: Oregon University Press, 1955.

Emmet, Dorothy Mary. *Philosophy and Faith.* London: S. C. M. Press, 1936.

——. *The Nature of Metaphysical Thinking.* London: Macmillan, 1949.

England, F. E. *Kant's Conception of God.* London: Allen and Unwin, 1929.

Fairbairn, A. M. *The Philosophy of the Christian Religion.* New York: Macmillan, 1903.

Farmer, Herbert Henry. *Revelation and Religion.* New York: Harper, 1954.

——. *The World and God.* London: Nisbet, 1935.

Farrer, Austin Marsden. *Finite and Infinite.* London: Dacre Press, 1943.

——. *The Freedom of the Will.* London: Dacre Press, 1958.

——. *The Glass of Vision.* London: Dacre Press, 1948.

Fechner, Gustav Theodor. *Religion of a Scientist.* New York: Pantheon Books, 1946.

Ferm, Vergilius Ture Anselm. *First Chapters in Religious Philosophy.* New York: Round Table Press, 1937.

Ferrater Mora, José. *Man at the Crossroads* (trans. Trask). Boston: Beacon Press, 1957.

Ferré, Nels F. S. *Evil and the Christian Faith.* New York: Harper, 1947.

——. *Faith and Reason.* New York: Harper, 1946.

Feuerbach, Ludwig Andreas. *The Essence of Christianity* (ed. and abridged, Waring and Strothmann). New York: Ungar, 1957.

Flew, Anthony G. N., and MacIntyre, Alasdair (eds.). *New Essays in Philosophical Theology.* New York: Macmillan, 1955.

Frank, Erich. *Philosophical Understanding and Religious Truth.* New York: Oxford University Press, 1945.

Fraser, Alexander Campbell. *Philosophy of Theism* (2 vols.). Edinburgh: Blackwood, 1895–96.

Freemantle, Ann. *The Age of Belief*. New York: Mentor Books, 1954.

Freud, Sigmund. *Moses and Monotheism* (trans. K. Jones). New York: Knopf, 1939.

——. *The Future of an Illusion* (trans. Robson-Scott). New York: Doubleday (Anchor Books), 1951

Friedman, Maurice S. *Martin Buber: the Life of Dialogue*. London: Routledge, 1955.

Fromm, Erich. *Man for Himself*. New York: Rinehart, 1947.

——. *Psychoanalysis and Religion*. New Haven: Yale University Press, 1950.

——. *The Forgotten Language*. New York: Rinehart, 1951.

Galloway, George. *The Philosophy of Religion*. New York: Scribner, 1922.

Gardner, Helen. *The Limits of Literary Criticism: Reflections on the Interpretation of Poetry and Scripture*. Oxford: Oxford University Press, 1956.

Garnett, Arthur Campbell. *A Realistic Philosophy of Religion*. New York: Harper, 1942.

——. *Religion and the Moral Life*. New York: Ronald Press, 1955.

Garvie, Alfred Ernest. *The Christian Belief in God*. New York: Harper, 1933.

Gilson, Etienne. *Being and Some Philosophers*. Toronto: Pontifical Institute, 1949.

——. *Christianity and Philosophy*. New York: Sheed and Ward, 1939.

——. *Dogmatism and Tolerance*. New Brunswick: Rutgers University Press, 1952.

——. *God and Philosophy*. New Haven: Yale University Press, 1941.

——. *History of Christian Philosophy in the Middle Ages*. New York: Random House, 1955.

——. *The Philosophy of St. Thomas Aquinas*. Cambridge: Heffer, 1929.

——. *The Spirit of Medieval Philosophy* (trans. Downes). New York: Scribner, 1940.

Goldman, Solomon. *The Jew and the Universe*. New York: Harper, 1936.

Harkness, Georgia Elma. *The Recovery of Ideals*. New York: Scribner, 1937.

Harris, C. R. S. *Duns Scotus* (2 vols.). Oxford: Oxford University Press, 1927.

Hartshore, Charles. *Beyond Humanism.* Chicago: Willet Clark, 1937.

Hatch, Edwin. *The Influence of Greek Ideas on Christianity.* New York: Harper, 1957.

Hazelton, Roger. *On Proving God.* New York: Harper, 1952.

Heard, Gerald. *Is God in History?* New York: Harper, 1950.

Hegel, George Wilhelm Friedrich. *Early Theological Writings* (trans. T. M. Knox and R. Kroner). Chicago: University of Chicago Press, 1948.

———. *Lectures on the Philosophy of Religion* (trans. E. B. Speirs and J. B. Sanderson). London: Kegan Paul, 1895.

Heim, Karl. *Christian Faith and Natural Science.* New York: Harper, 1957.

Hepburn, Ronald W. *Christianity and Paradox.* London: Watts, 1958.

Herberg, Will. *Protestant, Catholic and Jew.* New York: Doubleday, 1955.

Heschel, Abraham. *Man is not Alone.* New York: Farrar, Straus, 1951.

Hick, John. *Faith and Knowledge.* Ithaca: Cornell University Press, 1957.

Hicks, G. Dawes. *The Philosophical Basis of Theism.* London: Allen and Unwin, 1937.

Hocking, W. E. *The Meaning of God in Human Experience.* New Haven: Yale University Press, 1912.

———. *The Meaning of Immortality in Human Experience.* New York: Harper, 1957.

Hodgson, Leonard. *For Faith and Freedom.* London: Scribner, 1957.

Höffding, Harald. *The Philosophy of Religion.* London: Macmillan, 1914.

Horton, Walter Marshall. *A Psychological Approach to Theology.* New York: Harper, 1931.

———. *Theism and the Scientific Spirit.* New York: Harper, 1933.

Houf, Horace T. *What Religion Is and Does,* Revised Edition. New York: Harper, 1945.

Hügel, Friedrich von. *Essays and Addresses on the Philosophy of Religion* (2 vols.). New York: Dutton, 1924–26.

———. *The Reality of God.* New York: Dutton, 1931.

Hume, David. *Dialogues Concerning Natural Religion,* Second Edition with Supplement. New York: Social Science Publishers, 1948.

Husik, Isaac. *A History of Medieval Jewish Philosophy.* Philadelphia: Jewish Publications Society, 1940.

——. *Philosophical Essays* (eds. Milton C. Nahm and Leo Strauss). Oxford: Blackwell, 1952.

Hutchison, John A. *Faith, Reason and Existence.* New York: Oxford University Press, 1956.

Huxley, Aldous. *The Perennial Philosophy.* New York: Harper, 1945.

Huxley, Julian. *Religion without Revelation,* Revised Edition. London: Max Parish, 1957.

——. *Scientific Humanism.* Hollywood: 1954.

Inge, William Ralph. *Christian Mysticism.* New York: Noonday Press, 1956.

——. *The Platonic Tradition in English Religious Thought.* New York: Longmans, Green, 1926.

James, E. O. *The Concept of Deity.* London: Hutchinson's University Library, 1950.

James, William. *The Varieties of Religious Experience.* New York: Modern Library, 1936.

——. *The Will to Believe.* New York: Dover Publications, 1956.

Johnson, Howard Albert. *The Deity in Time: an Introduction to Kierkegaard.* Washington, D.C.: Washington Cathedral, College of Preachers, n.d. (pamphlet).

Jones, Rufus Matthew. *Fundamental Ends of Life.* New York: Macmillan, 1924.

——. *Pathways to the Reality of God.* New York: Macmillan, 1931.

——. *New Studies in Mystical Religion.* London: Macmillan, 1927.

——. *Studies in Mystical Religion.* London: Macmillan, 1909.

Jung, Carl Gustav. *Answer to Job.* London: Routledge, 1954.

——. *Psychology and Religion.* New Haven: Yale University Press, 1938.

——. *The Undiscovered Self.* Boston: Little, Brown, 1957.

Kant, Immanuel. *Religion within the Limits of Reason Alone.* La Salle: Open Court, 1934.

Kaufmann, Walter Arnold. *Critique of Religion and Philosophy.* New York: Harper, 1958.

Kelly, J. N. D. *Early Christian Creeds.* London: Longmans, Green, 1950.

——. *Early Christian Doctrines.* London: Black, 1958.

Kepler, Thomas S. (ed.). *Contemporary Religious Thought.* New York: Abingdon-Cokesbury, 1941.

Kierkegaard, Søren Aaby. *Attack upon Christendom* (trans. Lowry). Princeton: Princeton University Press, 1944.

——. *Fear and Trembling* and *The Sickness unto Death.* New York: Doubleday (Anchor Books), 1954.

——. *Philosophical Fragments* (trans. Swenson). Princeton: Princeton University Press, 1936.

——. *See also* Johnson, Howard Albert.

Kimpel, Ben. *Language and Reality.* New York: Philosophical Library, 1957.

——. *Religious Faith, Language and Knowledge.* New York: Philosophical Library, 1952.

——. *The Symbols of Religious Faith.* New York: Philosophical Library, 1954.

Knudson, Albert C. *The Doctrine of God.* New York: Abingdon Press, 1930.

Kroner, Richard. *The Religious Function of Imagination.* New Haven: Yale University Press, 1941.

Krutch, Joseph Wood. *The Measure of Man.* Indianapolis: Bobbs-Merrill, 1953.

Lamont, Corliss. *Humanism as a Philosophy.* New York: Philosophical Library, 1949.

——. *The Illusion of Immortality.* New York: Putnam, 1935.

Lamont, Daniel. *Christ and the World of Thought.* Edinburgh: Clark, 1934.

Langer, Suzanne. *Philosophy in a New Key.* Cambridge: Harvard University Press, 1942.

Leff, Gordon. *Medieval Thought, St. Augustine to Ockham.* London: Penguin Books, 1958.

Leuba, James H. *The Belief in God and Immortality.* Chicago: Open Court, 1921.

——. *The Psychology of Religious Mysticism.* New York: Harcourt, Brace, 1925.

Lewis, Clive Staples. *Mere Christianity.* New York: Macmillan, 1956.

——. *The Problem of Pain.* New York: Macmillan, 1943.

——. *The Screwtape Letters.* New York: Macmillan, 1944.

Lewis, Hywel David. *Morals and Revelation.* London: Allen and Unwin, 1951.

Lin Yutang. *The Importance of Living.* New York: Day, 1937.

Lippmann, Walter. *A Preface to Morals.* New York: Macmillan, 1929.

Liu, Wu-Chi. *A Short History of Confucian Philosophy.* London: Penguin Books, 1955.

Lossky (Losskii), N. O. *History of Russian Philosophy.* New York: International Universities Press, 1951.

Lotze, Hermann (Rudolf Hermann). *Outline of a Philosophy of Religion* (ed. Conybeare). London: Sonnenschein, 1892.

Lovejoy, Arthur O. *The Great Chain of Being.* Cambridge: Harvard University Press, 1957.

Luther, Martin. *On the Bondage of the Will* (trans. Packer and Johnston). London: James Clarke, 1957.

Macfie, Ronald C. *Science Rediscovers God.* New York: Scribner, 1930.

MacGregor, Geddes. *Aesthetic Experience in Religion.* London: Macmillan, 1947.

———. *Christian Doubt.* London: Longmans, Green, 1954.

———. *Corpus Christi.* Philadelphia: Westminster Press, 1959.

Macintosh, Douglas Clyde (ed.). *Religious Realism.* New York: Macmillan, 1931.

———. *The Problem of Religious Knowledge.* New York: Harper, 1940.

MacIver, R. M. (ed.). *Great Moral Dilemmas.* New York: Harper, 1956.

Mackintosh, Hugh Ross. *Types of Modern Theology: Schleiermacher to Barth.* London: Nisbet, 1937.

Macmurray, John. *Idealism against Religion.* London: Lindsay Press, 1944.

———. *Reason and Emotion.* London: Faber and Faber, 1935.

Macquarrie, John. *An Existentialist Theology.* New York: Macmillan, 1955.

Maimonides, Moses. *The Guide of the Perplexed* (ed. J. Guttmann; trans. Chaim Rabin). London: East and West Library, 1952.

Maritain, Jacques. *An Essay in Christian Philosophy.* New York: Philosophical Library, 1955.

———. *St. Thomas and the Problem of Evil.* Milwaukee: Marquette University Press, 1942.

———. *The Degrees of Knowledge.* New York: Scribner, 1938.

Marsh, John. *The Fullness of Time.* New York: Harper, 1952.

Martineau, James. *A Study of Religion,* Revised Edition. Oxford: Oxford University Press, 1900.

Mascall, E. L. *Christian Theology and Natural Science.* New York: Ronald Press, 1956.

———. *Existence and Analogy.* New York: Longmans, Green, 1949.

———. *He Who Is.* New York: Longmans, Green, 1948.

———. *Words and Images.* London: Longmans, Green, 1957.

Matthews, W. R. *God in Christian Thought and Experience.* London: Nisbet, 1930.

———. *Studies in Christian Philosophy.* London: Macmillan, 1928.

Mercier, Louis J. A. *The Challenge of Humanism.* New York: Oxford University Press, 1933.

Mesnard, Jean. *Pascal, His Life and Works.* New York: Philosophical Library, 1952.

Mitchell, Basil (ed.). *Faith and Logic.* Boston: Beacon Press, 1957.

Monsma, John Clover (ed.). *The Evidence of God in an Expanding Universe*. New York: Putnam, 1958.

Moore, Edward Caldwell. *The Nature of Religion*. New York: Macmillan, 1936.

More, Paul Elmer. *The Religion of Plato*. Princeton: Princeton University Press, 1921.

Morgan, C. L. *Emergent Evolution*. London: Williams and Norgate, 1923.

Müller, Max. *Theosophy*. London: Longmans, Green, 1903.

Mure, G. R. G. *Aristotle*. New York: Oxford University Press, 1932.

Nevius, Warren Nelson. *Religion as Experience and Truth*. Philadelphia: Westminster Press, 1941.

Newman, John Henry. *An Essay in Aid of a Grammar of Assent*. London: Longmans, Green, 1895.

Nicholson, John A. *Philosophy of Religion*. New York: Ronald Press, 1950.

Niebuhr, Helmut Richard. *The Meaning of Revelation*. New York: Macmillan, 1942.

Niebuhr, Reinhold. *Does Civilization Need Religion?* New York: Macmillan, 1927.

———. *Faith and History*. New York: Scribner, 1949.

———. *The Nature and Destiny of Man* (2 vols.: Vol. 1, *Human Nature*; Vol. 2, *Human Destiny*). New York: Scribner, 1941–43.

Noss, John B. *Man's Religions*, Revised Edition. New York: Macmillan, 1956.

Oman, John. *The Natural and the Supernatural*. Cambridge: Cambridge University Press, 1931.

Onians, Richard Broxton. *The Origins of European Thought*. Cambridge: Cambridge University Press, 1954.

Otto, Rudolf. *The Idea of the Holy*, Second Edition (trans. Harvey). Oxford: Oxford University Press, 1950.

———. *The Philosophy of Religion* (trans. Dicker). London: Williams and Norgate, 1931.

Oxford University Socratic Club. *Contemporary Philosophy and Christian Faith*. New York: Philosophical Library, 1952.

Pascal, Blaise. *Great Shorter Works of Pascal* (trans. Caillet and Blankenagel). Philadelphia: Westminster Press, 1948.

———. *The Provincial Letters* (trans. T. McCrie) and *Pensées* (trans. W. F. Trotter). Chicago: Encyclopaedia Britannica, 1955.

Paterson, William Paterson. *The Nature of Religion*. New York: Doran, 1926.

Paton, Herbert James. *The Modern Predicament*. New York: Macmillan, 1955.

Péguy, Charles. *A Vision of Prayer* (trans. A. and J. Green). New York: Pantheon Books, 1943.

Peirce, Charles Santiago Sanders. *Values in a Universe of Chance*. Stanford: Stanford University Press, 1958.

Pfeiderer, Otto. *The Philosophy of Religion on the Basis of Its History* (trans. Stewart and Menzies). London: Williams and Norgate, 1886–88.

Planck, Max. *Scientific Autobiography*. New York: Philosophical Library, 1949.

Plato. *The Dialogues of Plato* (trans. B. Jowett; 2 vols.). New York: Random House, 1937.

Plotinus. *The Philosophy of Plotinus* (selections, ed. Katz). New York: Appleton-Century-Crofts, 1950.

Pollard, William G. *Chance and Providence*. New York: Scribner, 1958.

Pratt, James Bissett. *Adventures in Philosophy and Religion*. New York: Macmillan, 1931.

Pringle-Pattison. *See* Seth.

Pünger, G. C. B. *History of the Christian Philosophy of Religion from the Reformation to Kant*. Edinburgh: Clark, 1887.

Radhakrishnan, S. *A Source Book in Indian Philosophy*. Princeton: Princeton University Press, 1957.

———. *Contemporary Indian Philosophy*, Second Edition. London: Allen and Unwin, 1952.

———. *Eastern Religions and Western Thought*. Oxford: Oxford University Press, 1942.

———. *Religion and Society*. London: Allen and Unwin, 1947.

Radin, Paul. *Primitive Man as Philosopher*. New York: Appleton, 1927.

Randall, John Herman, Jr. *The Making of the Modern Mind*, Revised Edition. Boston: Houghton Mifflin, 1940.

Reik, Theodor. *Dogma and Compulsion* (trans. Miall). New York: International Universities Press, 1951.

Ritchie, Arthur David. *Civilization, Science and Religion*. London: Penguin Books, 1945.

———. *Essays in Philosophy*. London: Longmans, Green, 1948.

———. *Studies in the History and Methods of the Sciences*. Edinburgh: Edinburgh University Press (Nelson), 1958.

Robertson, John Mackinnon. *A History of Freethought in the Nineteenth Century*. New York: Putnam, 1930.

Ross, W. D. *Aristotle*. London: Methuen, 1923.

Royce, Josiah. *Studies of Good and Evil.* New York: Appleton, 1906.

———. *The Conception of God.* Berkeley: Philosophical Union of the University of California, 1895.

Russell, Bertrand. *Mysticism and Logic.* London: Longmans, Green, 1918.

———. *Why I am not a Christian.* New York: Simon and Schuster, 1957.

Russell, Henry Norris. *Fate and Freedom.* New Haven: Yale University Press, 1927.

Ryle, Gilbert (ed.). *The Revolution in Philosophy.* London: Macmillan, 1957.

Sabatier, Auguste. *Outlines of a Philosophy of Religion,* Third Edition. London: Hodder and Stoughton, 1906.

Santayana, George. *Scepticism and Animal Faith.* New York: Dover Publications, 1955.

Sarachek, Joseph. *Faith and Reason: the Conflict over the Rationalism of Maimonides.* Williamsport, Pa.: Bayard Press, 1935.

Sayers, Dorothy L. *The Mind of the Maker.* New York: Harcourt, Brace, 1941.

Schleiermacher, Friedrich. *On Religion* (trans. Oman; abridged Waring). New York: Ungar, 1955.

Schweitzer, Albert. *The Philosophy of Civilization.* New York: Macmillan, 1958.

Sellers, R. V. *The Council of Chalcedon.* London: S.P.C.K., 1953.

Seth Pringle-Pattison, Andrew. *Studies in the Philosophy of Religion.* Oxford: Oxford University Press, 1930.

———. *The Idea of God.* Oxford: Oxford University Press, 1920.

Sheldon, Wilmon Henry. *God and Polarity.* New Haven: Yale University Press, 1954.

Smethurst, Arthur F. *Modern Science and Christian Beliefs.* New York: Abington Press, 1959.

Smuts, Jan. *Holism and Evolution.* New York: Macmillan, 1926.

Solovyov, Vladimir. *A Solovyov Anthology* (arranged S. L. Frank; trans. N. Duddington). New York: Scribner, 1950.

Sorley, W. R. *Moral Values and the Idea of God.* Cambridge: Cambridge University Press, 1919.

Spinoza, Benedict de. *Tractatus theologicus-politicus* (trans. Elwes). London: Routledge, 1895.

Stace, Walter Terence. *Religion and the Modern Mind.* Philadelphia: Lippincott, 1952.

Steere, Douglas V. *On Beginning from Within.* New York: Harper, 1943.

Streeter, Burnett Hillman. *The Buddha and the Christ*. London: Macmillan, 1932.

Suzuki, D. T. *Zen Buddhism* (ed. W. Barrett). New York: Doubleday (Anchor Books), 1956.

Taylor, A. E. *Does God Exist?* New York: Macmillan, 1947.

———. *Plato*, Sixth Edition. London: Methuen, 1949.

———. *The Faith of a Moralist* (2 vols.). London: Macmillan, 1930.

Temple, William. *Christianity in Thought and Practice*. New York: Morehouse, 1936.

———. *Mens Creatrix*. London: Macmillan, 1923.

———. *Nature, Man and God*. London: Macmillan, 1951.

Tennant, F. R. *Philosophical Theology* (2 vols.). Cambridge: Cambridge University Press, 1928–30.

Thomas, John Heywood. *Subjectivity and Paradox*. Oxford: Blackwell, 1957.

Thomas Aquinas. *See* Aquinas, Thomas.

Thompson, Samuel Martin. *A Modern Philosophy of Religion*. Chicago: Regnery, 1955.

Tillich, Paul Johannes. *Dynamics of Faith*. New York: Harper, 1956.

———. *Systematic Theology* (2 vols.). Chicago: University of Chicago Press, 1951–57.

———. *The Courage to Be*. New Haven: Yale University Press, 1952.

———. *The Interpretation of History*. New York: Scribner, 1936.

Trueblood, David Elton. *Philosophy of Religion*. New York: Harper, 1957.

———. *The Logic of Belief*. New York: Harper, 1942.

———. *The Trustworthiness of Religious Experience*. London: Allen and Unwin, 1939.

Tsanoff, Radoslav Andrea. *Religious Crossroads*. New York: Dutton, 1942.

———. *The Nature of Evil*. New York: Macmillan, 1931.

———. *The Problem of Immortality*. New York: Macmillan, 1924.

Turner, H. E. W. *The Pattern of Christian Truth* (A Study in the Relations between Orthodoxy and Heresy in the Early Church). London: Mowbray, 1954.

Turner, John Evan. *The Revelation of Deity*. New York: Macmillan, 1931.

Unamuno y Jugo, Miguel de. *The Tragic Sense of Life*. London: Macmillan, 1921.

Underhill, Evelyn. *Mysticism*. New York: Noonday Press, 1955.

———. *Worship*. New York: Harper, 1936.

Urban, Wilbur Marshall. *Humanism and Deity*. London: Allen and Unwin, 1951.

Vann, Gerald. *Morals Makyth Man*. London: Longmans, Green, 1938.

Ward, James. *Naturalism and Agnosticism*. London: Black, 1915.

Watkin, Edward Ingram. *The Bow in the Clouds*. New York: Macmillan, 1932.

———. *Theism, Agnosticism, and Atheism*. London: Unicorn Press, 1936.

Watson, John. *The Philosophical Basis of Religion*. Glasgow: Maclehose, 1907.

Webb, Clement Charles Julian. *Divine Personality and Human Life*. London: Allen and Unwin, 1921.

———. *God and Personality*. New York: Macmillan, 1918.

———. *Kant's Philosophy of Religion*. Oxford: Oxford University Press, 1926.

———. *Pascal's Philosophy of Religion*. Oxford: Oxford University Press, 1929.

———. *Problems in the Relations of God and Man*. London: Nisbet, 1911.

———. *Religion and Theism*. New York: Scribner, 1934.

———. *Studies in the History of Natural Theology*. Oxford: Oxford University Press, 1915.

Weil, Simone. *Intimations of Christianity among the Ancient Greeks*. (ed. and trans. E. C. Geissbuhler). London: Routledge, 1957.

———. *Letter to a Priest*. New York: Putnam, 1954.

Weiss, Paul. *Man's Freedom*. New Haven: Yale University Press, 1950.

———. *Reality*. Princeton: Princeton University Press, 1938.

White, Victor. *God and the Unconscious*. Chicago: Regnery, 1953.

Whitehead, Alfred North. *Process and Reality*. New York: Macmillan, 1929.

———. *Religion in the Making*. New York: Macmillan, 1926.

———. *Science and the Modern World*. New York: Macmillan, 1926.

Wieman, Henry Nelson. *American Philosophies of Religion*. Chicago: Willett Clark, 1936.

Wild, John. *Introduction to Realistic Philosophy*. New York: Harper, 1948.

———. *The Challenge of Existentialism*. Bloomington: Indiana University Press, 1955.

Williams, Charles. *He Came Down from Heaven*. London: Faber and Faber, 1940.

Wobbermin, George. *The Nature of Religion* (trans. T. Menzel and D. S. Robinson). New York: Crowell, 1953.

Wolfson, Harry A. *The Philosophy of the Church Fathers*. Cambridge: Harvard University Press, 1956.

Wright, William K. *Student's Philosophy of Religion.* New York: Macmillan, 1958.

Zimmer, Heinrich. *Philosophies of India.* New York: Pantheon Books, 1951.

Zuurdeeg, Willem F. *An Analytical Philosophy of Religion.* New York: Abingdon Press, 1958.

INDEX

The index does not cover the discussion questions appended to each chapter, or the personal reflections presented in the Epilogue.